A CENTURY *of* SPARTAN BASKETBALL

magic moments

BY JACK EBLING *and* JOHN FARINA

Library of Congress Cataloging-in-Publication Data

Ebling, Jack.
Magic moments : a century of Spartan basketball / by Jack Ebling and
John Farina.
p.   cm.
ISBN 1-886947-41-4
1. Michigan State University-Basketball-History.   2. Michigan
State Spartans (Basketball team)-History.   I. Farina, John, 1958-
.II. Title.
GV885.43.M53E35   1998
796.323'63'0977427-dc21   98-34924
CIP

Sleeping Bear Press
121 South Main
P.O. Box 20
Chelsea, MI 48118
www.sleepingbearpress.com

Printed and bound in the United States.

10 9 8 7 6 5 4 3 2 1

*To 100 years of "Magic Moments"—
and to another century of Spartan basketball memories.*

Acknowledgments

A complete list of thank yous would take well into the 21st century.

But special appreciation goes to everyone whose contribution has made Spartan basketball what it is today—from the players to the coaches to the diehard fans.

From MAC to MSC to MSU, the names have changed. The spirit has remained the same.

Thanks to all 503 letterwinners, from Matthew Aitch to Jon Zulauf, alphabetically, and from Ray Tower to Lorenzo Guess, chronologically.

Thanks to all 16 head coaches, from Charles Bemies to Tom Izzo, and to their unsung staffs.

And thanks to you.

From a personal standpoint, thanks to Sleeping Bear Press for its enthusiasm, support, and attention to detail.

Thanks to the *Lansing State Journal* and Michigan State University, our employers, for their cooperation in this project.

Thanks to Ed Senyczko, a sports editor of the *State Journal*, and Bill Kreifeldt, a public relations director with the Detroit Pistons, for giving two young men their starts many years ago.

Thanks to George Alderton, Bob Hoerner, Steve Klein, Jeff Rivers, and Gerry Ahern of the Journal and Nick Kerbawy, Fred Stabley, Nick Vista, Ken Hoffman, and John Lewandowski of MSU.

Thanks to Kevin Fowler, Bill Mitchem, Lynn Foth, Bruce Fox, Brian Burd, Greg DeRuiter, Rod Sanford, Margie Garrison, David Olds, Chris Holmes, and all the photographers who have chronicled the story.

Thanks to Val Berryman of the MSU Museum, Lanita Brown, Walt Sorg, Duane Vernon, and especially Mike Pearson, who could have written this book, for their help and support.

And especially, thanks to our families—our parents, our spouses Robin Ebling and Laura Farina and young fans Zach and Ali Ebling—for making our work so much easier.

Jack Ebling and John Farina

Contents

MICHIGAN STATE 100 SEASONS BASKETBALL

1899 1999

Jenison could pack them in—until the fire marshals arrived.

Jenison and the Early Gyms

It wasn't the first home of Michigan State basketball—just the best, said Earvin Johnson.

In its day—and there were 49 great years in the eyes of former athlete, coach and administrator Doug Weaver—Frederick Cowles Jenison Gymnasium & Field House was a state-of-the-art facility.

It has been a venue for boxing, fencing, gymnastics, handball, swimming, track, volleyball and wrestling, plus plenty of indoor football workouts.

But there was nothing quite like college basketball—and some classic high school action, too—in what looked like a giant jogging barn on Kalamazoo Street.

"You can have your fancy arenas with their cushioned seats," wrote *Detroit News* columnist Joe Falls. "Give me drafty, musty, majestic Jenison, where I learned to love the game of basketball."

"I just loved the smell of that place," said Spartan forward Bill Curtis. "And that portable floor was just unmatched. Jenison Field House . . . there was nothing like it!"

It was the site of NCAA Tournament Mideast Region play in 1963, when Mississippi State defied a racist governor and came north to play an integrated team, eventual champ Loyola of Chicago, for the first time.

And if you close your eyes for a Magic Moment, you can still see Johnny Green soaring, Terry Furlow scoring and Scott Skiles roaring for the Spartans in an ivy-covered showplace.

Long before those stars' first dribbles, Michigan Agricultural College fielded a basketball team with no established coach in 1898.

The Aggies played in the Armory, near what's now the Music Building, until 1918, then moved to a gym in today's IM Circle complex.

On February 15, 1930, they celebrated the dedication of Demonstration Hall, south of the Red Cedar River, with a 27-26 win over Michigan.

If his players had wanted to douse Coach Ben Van Alstyne, they couldn't have done it, since the closest showers were still north of the river.

That changed 10 years later with a palace that cost a whopping $1,707,750, including a $315,000 gift from Jenison's estate upon his death in 1939.

The first flashlight photo from Demonstration Hall was taken at the Notre Dame–MSC game in 1930.

Just who was this philanthropic ex-student and loyal fan whose name will forever be linked with athletics?

Jenison was an engineering major at MAC from 1902-07 and a successful real estate agent and insurance salesman in downtown Lansing.

"He had no eyelashes and no hair but was a wonderful dresser and a very sedate man," said George Alderton, the *State Journal* sports editor who gave the Spartans their nickname in 1925. "He left everything to his alma mater for whatever the college wanted to do with it."

That decision was to finish a new field house, with help from federal funds, patterned after a building at Purdue.

And on January 6, 1940, Michigan State College beat Tennessee 29-20 in the first game in Jenison before 6,700 fans.

"It was a real thrill after playing in Dem Hall," said forward Marty Hutt, the model for a sandstone sculpture on the front of Jenison. "And with showers now, we didn't have to run from the gym before and after games."

A raised basketball court was never assembled over the dirt floor until the end of football season, making Jenison's versatility a curse for coaches.

When Jud Heathcote first saw the building in 1976, he told Athletic Director Joe Kearney, "Joe!...We had a better place than this at Montana!"—to which Kearney replied, "Well, I'd certainly hope so!"

Practice conflicts and recruiting concerns were a way of life, though the problems didn't seem as important when a packed house would shake the rafters.

"We'd get teams in there, with the crowd so close and the noise so loud, and it was more than a sixth man," said center Jay Vincent. "It was more like a seventh. When we'd get it going, we were almost unbeatable there."

A rubberized Tartan playing surface was installed in 1970, then replaced with another wood floor that was better on the legs in 1979.

But after 15,384 fans jammed Jenison for the 1948 Kentucky game, fire marshals lowered the capacity to 12,500, then to 6,500, then 9,995, and finally the familiar count of 10,004 before a move to Breslin Center in 1989.

"If I'd known it would be so tough winning in Jenison Field House, I'd have made a donation to the construction of the new arena myself," said Illinois coach Lou Henson after one thrashing.

In 48 seasons in Jenison, the Spartans won 383 basketball games and lost 189—a .670 success rate.

And when 125 players and coaches returned to say goodbye on March 11, 1989, most remembered the good times and dusted off incredible memories.

Portable bleachers weren't the most comfortable courtside seats in the conference.

One of the first telecasts from Jenison Field House was in 1957.

Jenison Field House

Jenison's best individual performances

1. 50—**Terry Furlow**, MSU vs. Iowa, 1-5-76 (**MSU, 105-88**)
2. 48—**Jerry Lucas**, Ohio State, 2-11-61 (**OSU, 83-68**)
3. 48—**Gary Bradds**, Ohio State, 1-27-64 (**MSU, 102-99**)
4. 46—**Robin Freeman**, Ohio State, 1-28-56 (**MSU, 94-91**)
5. 45—**Manny Newsome**, Western Michigan, 12-4-62 (**MSU, 101-100**)
6. 45—**Julius McCoy**, MSU vs. Notre Dame, 12-21-55 (**MSU, 84-78**)
7. 44—**Jimmy Rayl**, Indiana, 1-5-63 (**Indiana, 96-84**)
8. 43—**Scott Skiles**, MSU vs. Ohio State, 3-8-86 (**MSU, 91-81**)
9. 43—**David Robinson**, Navy, 11-29-86 (**Navy, 91-90 OT**)
10. 42—**Terry Furlow**, MSU vs. Ohio State, 1-10-76 (**MSU, 92-82**)

The Big Ten's top brother tandem, Jay (left) and Sam Vincent, compete at Lansing's Walsh Park.

The Players

The Top 25

Earvin Johnson

With a "Magic" smile and an MSU sweatshirt, Johnson signs his autobiography, "My Life."

As a senior at Lansing Everett, Johnson has the basketball world in the palm of his hand.

He has been described as a once-in-a-century player.

If that's half as accurate as one of his passes, why have so many teams gone more than 100 years with no one remotely resembling Earvin Johnson?

Michigan State was lucky enough to have his services for two incredible basketball seasons—and his heart for many years before and after.

"There was a lot of joy, growing up in Lansing," said Johnson, who grew and grew and grew. "And whatever happened, we always had Michigan State basketball."

Without his contributions to that program, there wouldn't have been a 1979 National Championship celebration in Jenison Field House.

And to this day, there might not be a Breslin Center.

One can argue that the three most important events in school history have been:

- The arrival of legendary president-to-be John Hannah as a transfer student from Michigan's law school in 1922.
- An invitation to join the Intercollegiate Conference of Faculty Representatives—better known as the Western Conference or the Big Ten—over strong objections from Ann Arbor in 1948.
- And the difficult decision by a 6-foot-8 point guard to become a Spartan rather than a top-ranked Wolverine in 1977.

To understand why that choice was made and to appreciate the man who made it, we have to start at 814 Middle Street, in a modest home for a family of nine.

Earvin Johnson, Sr. had two jobs only because he couldn't have three. That's the kind of work ethic the fourth of seven children saw and absorbed.

From his mother, Christine, he inherited a smile that could light an arena and a winning personality.

As a youth, he was "Junior" to his parents, "June Bug" to the neighborhood grown-ups and "E.J." or "E" to his friends, as he developed his game at Main Street School and pretended to be Wilt Chamberlain.

But by the time Johnson left Dwight Rich Junior High and was bussed cross-district to Everett High against his wishes, he was about due for another name—a description as perfect as any could be.

Johnson (32) and Jay Vincent (center) battle in Jenison, where they'll share Spartan glory.

In the seventh game of his sophomore season, the unbeaten Vikings ripped preseason conference favorite Jackson Parkside, with Johnson scoring 36 points, grabbing 18 rebounds and handing out 16 assists.

"Fred Stabley, Jr. of the *State Journal* said I needed a nickname," Johnson remembered. "He said, 'Dr. J' is taken. And so is 'Big E.' . . . How about if I call you Magic?' I said, 'Fine. . . . Whatever you like.' And I never expected to hear it again."

Instead, Stabley went back to the office on Lenawee Street and called his longtime pal, Tim Staudt, at WJIM television to bounce the idea off of him.

"Fred said, 'I want to name him 'Magic.' If you go along with it, maybe it'll stick,'" Staudt remembered. "In my infinite wisdom, I said, 'That is waaay too corny. It'll never work.'"

Roughly 24 years later, people left Magic Johnson Theatres and drove home in time to see "The Magic Hour" on Fox television. And Stabley, the sports information director at Central Michigan since 1982, deserves a lifetime supply of popcorn.

He must have munched his share watching Johnson's teams go 22-2, 24-2 and 27-1 for a career mark of 73-5 under George Fox's able direction.

Included were classic matchups with Eastern High and standout center Jay Vincent, a crosstown rival and later a trusted teammate.

And when he wasn't competing against older players, Johnson would be watching and learning from the pros on trips with former ABA guard Charles Tucker, who would soon become a busy agent.

"I didn't have a Dr. Tucker," Vincent said of a school psychologist with an office at Everett. "He'd been taking Magic around since seventh grade, staying on him and keeping him focused. I don't know about anybody else, but I have to give Dr. Tucker a lot of credit."

As recruiters discovered a revolutionary player with superstar charisma, a battle for Johnson's affection began, though it could have been over quickly.

"It was the spring of Magic's junior year," said then-MSU coach Gus Ganakas, who was about to be reassigned. "Charlie Tucker was jogging in Jenison. He said he'd talked to Mr. Johnson about Magic coming to Michigan State and there was absolutely no question about it. . . .You take a Magic Johnson—even I could've coached him! But I was one year away."

"The No. 1 reason I was going to Michigan State was to play for Gus Ganakas," Johnson said. "I used to come to every game—and had since I was 10 or 11. So the coaching change kind of threw me for a loop. I knew Gus and saw him as a friend."

He saw the Spartans' first-year leader, Jud Heathcote, as a screamer and a stranger. But in 1976-77, Johnson had much more contact with assistants Vernon Payne, a carryover from Ganakas' staff, and Bill Frieder, an omnipresent Michigan aide.

"Frieder had me," Johnson said. "He really did. But I went off to the Albert Schweitzer Games in Germany and came home to this sea of green-and-white. The problem was still not knowing about Jud."

He knew all about MSU's players, past and present, which could only help the Spartans stay in the hunt.

"I remember Ralph Simpson's pink El Dorado after he signed with the ABA," Johnson said. "It was 1970, and we said, 'Can we have a ride?' He took all the kids in the neighborhood for ice cream.

"I loved watching Mike Robinson shoot. Then, I got to know Terry Furlow. He was the original trash-talker. He'd tell you how many points he was going to score on you, then do it. I never beat him one-on-one until the year he died, my rookie year in the pros. If they'd had the 3-pointer back then, it'd have been over! But he never forgot me. I loved him so much."

He liked two players who would soon be college teammates, Gregory Kelser and Jay Vincent, almost as much. And the feeling was mutual.

"I first met Earvin at St. Cecilia's in Detroit a couple of years earlier," Kelser said. "It was 1975, and I was going into my freshman year at State. He had the same smile then. And I remember Terry talking about him all the time. Terry loved him."

Two Earvin Johnsons shake hands at decision time, as Everett coach George Fox looks on.

No-look passes and no-loss months are two of Johnson's favorite things.

play him at center," Heathcote said. "I told him I might be a hick from Montana, but I understood basketball. I said he would be a catalyst for our fast break and handle the ball the way he always had."

Still, some apprehension remained until Payne paid one last visit to Everett to speak on Heathcote's behalf.

"He said, 'Earvin, you should go to Michigan State,'" Johnson said. "I asked him, 'Why do you say that?' He told me, 'That man can coach! He's not really the guy you see. And if you come, they'll win.' I said, 'Are you sure, Coach?' And he said, 'Earvin, I'm telling you, this guy knows basketball! He's really a good guy.'"

Payne, a former Indiana guard, had never delivered a sweeter assist.

"I'd just been hired as head coach at Wayne State," Payne said. "I remember coming back to Everett, getting Magic out of class and taking him to the library. We talked about Michigan State University, about Lansing and about people and how important they are in all of our lives.

"I said, 'You can play basketball a lot of different places. But I think it's important for us to think about the impact we can have on people with our decisions.' We were there about an hour. When we got up, I asked him to sign with Michigan State. He said, 'I'll sign tomorrow. We'll have a press conference.' I said, 'No! I want you to sign today!' And he said, 'OK, Coach.'

"I remember telling Jud, 'We're going to get this kid. He believes in the community. He believes in the support those people have given him throughout his career.' He really made a decision for the people of Lansing. And I think that says a lot about Magic."

If Payne hadn't made one last pitch, the position of the basketball planets might have shifted forever.

"I always loved Michigan State," Johnson said. "That never changed. But if Vern hadn't come to Everett, I probably would've signed with Michigan that week. Vern didn't have to do that. But he spoke from the heart. And I'm so glad he did. Vern Payne was right."

There was still a press conference at Everett that Friday. Bob Gross of the *State Journal* knew ahead of time and had the first story in that afternoon's paper, just after the announcement. But otherwise, tight secrecy was maintained.

Just ask Johnson's close friend Kenny Turner, who used to accompany him to Ann Arbor for Michigan games on Saturday afternoons, then blast back for Spartan games at night.

On the trip to Crisler Arena to watch Everett in the Class A final, Turner told his brother to wait in a traffic jam on Main Street, then dashed into a sporting goods store to buy a maize-and-blue diehard's outfit—jacket, cap, T-shirt, and shorts.

So when Johnson opened his press conference and said, "Any questions?...I

"But the thing I'll always remember was a day he came to Jenison with his hand heavily bandaged. We used to play four-on-four up to four points. And he dominated everything with just his left hand. It might have been the greatest performance I've ever seen—better than anything he did at State. At game point, he took a 17-foot jumper with his left hand. The thing went in!"

The Wolverines got to know him nearly as well. And Johnson liked the idea of playing with center Phil Hubbard, a junior-to-be.

Plus, it didn't hurt that Johnny Orr's team had been the NCAA runner-up in 1976 and the top-rated team after the regular season the following year.

As the decision drew near, the speculation was split. And so was Johnson.

With a press conference scheduled at Everett on Friday, April 22, Heathcote began to panic when Johnson missed an appointment that Monday.

But a meeting Tuesday night answered some questions. And a parting gift to MSU from Payne the following day made all the difference.

"Michigan had convinced him that since he'd be our tallest player we'd

have decided to attend Michigan—State University," Turner screamed, "WHAT?" while reading meters for the Board of Water and Light and listening on a transistor radio.

"The poor lady in that house thought something was wrong and came running down the stairs right away," he said. "But I took all those clothes and threw them in the trash. I never even wore them once. And I've hated Michigan ever since. That stuff cost me a lot of money! . . . Maybe Earvin should reimburse me."

He probably saved Turner enough gas money to compensate him several times.

One of the greatest winners basketball or any other game has known definitely rescued the Spartans enough times en route to back-to-back Big Ten titles.

Perhaps the best measure of Johnson's greatness is that MSU was 12-15 before he arrived and after he left. It was 25-5 and 26-6 with him in the lineup.

"What a time!" Johnson said nearly two decades later. "I'll never forget any of those games—not one of them. I like to close my eyes and think back to those times. You can't move forward if you can't look back. That's why I'm so grounded. It's why I'm still Earvin.

"Those are the times that made me Magic. It's nothing other than the Ohio State game, the Notre Dame game, the Indiana State game. That's the Magic!"

It ended too soon for the Spartans and just in time to save the NBA, as Johnson and Indiana State's Larry Bird entered the league together and were forever linked in 1979.

"I still remember when he was thinking about going hardship," Heathcote said. "He didn't really want to. But the timing was right. He had a chance to play with the Lakers, a winning team. Winning was very, very important to Earvin and is to this day."

Still, there were doubters for a player with a unique style of play—a talent who could have left after his freshman year but couldn't stomach the thought of losing when there was business to finish at MSU.

"He is a mediocre passer and ballhandler," wrote Bill Gleason in the *Chicago Sun-Times*. "He is a poor shooter and a poor defensive player. To hear the 'Golly! Gee!' analysts tell it, Johnson is 'another Oscar Robertson.' He isn't. Robertson could do everything. To compare Johnson with the 'Big O' is laughable. Johnson, right now, is not nearly the player Quinn Buckner was in his sophomore year at Indiana."

And Joe Falls of *The Detroit News* wrote: "He is not superstar material for the NBA. Maybe he can grow into it. But he isn't there yet, and some NBA scouts wonder if he will ever get there. In effect, he has only one shot. That's a soft one-hander when he works his way through the middle. And it's hard to see how that would be enough in the pros. Do you think those big boys in the NBA will let him float through the lane and get off such a shot? They'll slam the ball back in his face."

Heathcote must have laughed at that for days—when he wasn't crying.

"There were negative articles being written—that he wasn't good enough, couldn't run and couldn't jump," Heathcote said. "I said, 'E, only two people know how good you really are—you and me. You'll start on any team that drafts you. So let's not talk about basketball.' "

When he talked about the future and the opportunities with Kareem Abdul-Jabbar at center, the decision was made after Johnson drove a hard

Johnson directs traffic against Michigan's Tom Staton (23) in a 1979 Spartan romp.

bargain with Laker owner Jack Kent Cooke and agreed to a five-year deal worth $500,000—not even the NBA minimum today.

"When he got back, Earvin told me he was leaving," Kelser said. "By then, he was a different Magic. He'd seen the weather, the money, the big houses and the Mercedes. He wasn't pressed for cash. And I really think he would've come back for one more year if the Lakers hadn't acquired the No. 1 pick a few years earlier in a trade with New Orleans for Gail Goodrich.

"But they say everything happens for a reason. I don't think the 'Magic' thing would have worked anywhere but L.A. It was meant to be."

In retrospect, Johnson wondered if the NBA title he celebrated as the Playoffs MVP his first year would have been replaced by a second straight NCAA crown.

"If I'd have come back for my junior year, we'd have been right back there at the Final Four," he said. "Louisville won it that year. And they wouldn't have had a chance against us. We would've picked up Kevin Smith. Jay would've been healthy and happy. And with Mike Brkovich, Ron Charles, Terry Donnelly, a more seasoned Rob Gonzalez and some of the other recruits we lost, we'd have been rolling.

"If it'd been any other team in the NBA, I would've stayed. I'd rather have won another NCAA title than struggled in the pros. . . . But it didn't turn out too bad."

No one could have envisioned exactly how good. By 1992, he had five NBA championships, three MVP awards and the gold medal he couldn't have won in 1980 because of the U.S. Olympic boycott.

On loan from the Lakers, Johnson appreciates Jud Heathcote's sense of humor.

One of the NBA's five best players of all time leaves Piston guard Vinnie Johnson speechless.

Host Linda Ellerbee and kids ages 8-14 quiz Johnson in a Nickelodeon special on HIV and its effects.

"One thing Earvin could do like a Larry Bird and later a Michael Jordan was to make people play better than they are," Heathcote said. "That's an unbelievable intangible. And I've seen Earvin do that time after time after time."

"Will there ever be another Magic?" asked NBC broadcaster Dick Enberg. "That's a tough question. You hope there would be because of what he did for his university, his teammates and the world of college basketball. His smile would light up a gym and reflect the boyishness within the man."

That glow was replaced with a steely commitment on November 7, 1991, when Johnson retired from the NBA and told the world he was HIV-positive. Perhaps nothing he did before or will do after will mean as much as his efforts for AIDS education and research.

"Some people win overnight," said his coach with the Lakers, Pat Riley. "Earvin won overnight. But I think he has shown a greater prize can be earned from a stubborn commitment and defiant refusal to give in. He's going to give it the fight of his life to conquer this. And if there is a person in this world with the faith and the spirit to champion this cause, it's him."

"I'm the model and the experiment," Johnson said of an aggressive approach to medication, diet, and exercise. "And I don't mind being that. I couldn't be any happier than I am now. The doctors say, 'Whatever you're doing, keep doing it!'"

He's doing more than 10 men in perfect health could do. But then, he always did.

Johnson lends a different type of assist at the Final Four in Salt Lake City.

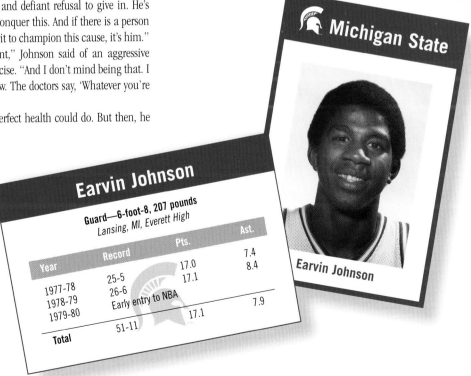

Michigan State

Earvin Johnson

Earvin Johnson

Guard—6-foot-8, 207 pounds
Lansing, MI, Everett High

Year	Record	Pts.	Ast.
1977-78	25-5	17.0	7.4
1978-79	26-6	17.1	8.4
1979-80	Early entry to NBA		
Total	51-11	17.1	7.9

Johnny Green

Green and his teammates get a lift after beating Indiana in a 1957 Big Ten showdown.

He never asked to have his number retired. All he ever wanted was a uniform to wear.

And no one in Michigan State history has worn a jersey and a pair of basketball shorts with more joy than John Green.

They called him "Jumpin' Johnny"—"Long John," "Pogo" and "Rubber Legs," too.

They also could have called him the second-best rebounder the Big Ten has seen and the best player the Spartans never recruited.

No one did, except perhaps the coach of his Army base in Atsugi, Japan, in late 1954. Before that, his only basketball was at a local YMCA.

"You have to remember, I was really small," Green said. "I was under 6-feet when I graduated from high school. I didn't think I'd make the team, so I didn't even go out for basketball."

That was Dayton Dunbar's loss and a local bowling alley's gain, as Green spent many of his afternoons and evenings setting pins instead of picks.

After graduation, he worked for a construction company and at a junkyard for six months, then joined the service during the Korean Conflict.

There, after turning 20 years old, Green sprouted to a full 6-5 and proved to be a late bloomer in more ways than one.

"I just kept practicing and playing pickup games," he said. "One night, I was shooting baskets and met Tom Foster, the coach at the base. He asked if I'd like to come out for the team. And I said, 'Would I ever!'

"Dick Evans, the football coach, saw I could leap pretty well and asked me to dunk. I did it on the second try."

At the Jenison farewell in 1989, Green is flanked by 1970s guard Mike Robinson and 1950s forward Julius McCoy.

Evans had been at MSU during the glory years in football under Biggie Munn and wrote a letter of recommendation to new basketball coach Forddy Anderson. Green followed up with a visit to campus while on leave in October 1955.

"When I was a senior, John Green came up and asked me to introduce him to Forddy," said Spartan star Julius McCoy. "I only have one regret. I wish he'd been there one year earlier. I don't think anyone could've beaten us. All we needed was someone to get a rebound."

That Big Ten title had to wait a year, but only after Green took charge of every aspect of enrolling and becoming eligible a full year later.

"He told me to come back and see him when I got out of the service, so that's what I did," Green said. "I got my transcript, enrolled in school and walked up and said, 'Here I am.'"

That gift from heaven—the ultimate walk-on—wasn't appreciated by an angry coach on January 2, 1956.

"We'd just lost a close one at Illinois," Anderson remembered. "I was really mad when we got back and said, 'You're not going to your dorms! . . . Get dressed! We're going to practice!' I was ready to whip everybody.

"Then my assistant, Bob Stevens, said, 'There's a guy out here, a John Green, who wants to talk to you.' I said, 'Arrrgh, bring him in!' I couldn't remember him.

"I said, 'Well, you have to fill out a form to get into school.' He said, 'I've already done that.' I said, 'You have to register for classes.' He said, 'I've already done that.' I said, 'You have to get your books.' He said, 'I've already done that.' So I said, 'Okay, go up and work with the freshman team,' figuring that would be the end of it."

Wearing a purple-and-white shirt, red-and-blue trunks, long green stockings pulled over his knees and ragged, black canvas basketball shoes, Green took several shots in the upstairs Jenison gym and missed badly.

But when Stevens said, "Try to rebound the ball," Green soared above the rim and snatched every shot—"like a giant hawk snaring sparrows," as Hall of Fame Sports Information Director Fred Stabley often described it.

"I was a grad assistant, and so was Stan Albeck," said former manager Bob Watts. "Forddy said, 'Boys, take him upstairs and see what he has got.' The first thing he did was jump out of the gym. . . . Work him out, hell! How do you work out a machine!"

"Jumpin' Johnny" soars between two Hoosiers for another high-altitude rebound.

It's easy being Green when you float above the clouds.

There was a saying around campus, "Never, never, never interrupt varsity basketball practice unless Forddy's mother has died." She was as healthy as ever when Stevens rushed downstairs and risked another life—his own.

"We'd already started practice," Anderson said. "And I was really mad. Then, Bob came down and said, 'Have your guys shoot some free throws.' I said, 'WHAT FOR?' And he said, 'Just have them shoot free throws and follow me.'

"We went upstairs where they had three courts. One was separated by a net that hung from a big cable about two feet above the basket. I walked in and saw John jumping up and grabbing that cable. I said, 'Find out what this boy needs and get it to him, no matter what!'"

Green never minded that initial snub and said he'd have done the same thing in Anderson's position.

"Forddy didn't have any information on me—just that letter from Dick Evans," Green said. "He asked me to go downstairs and get dressed. And the next thing he knew, I was dunking the ball. I guess he was impressed."

With Green on the freshman team that winter and ineligible until January 1957, few knew what the Spartans could be. Anderson understood immediately.

"Forddy complained that Green couldn't play in the first eight games," said then-assistant Sports Information Director Nick Vista. "I said, 'Forddy, we can't be that bad! How good is Johnny, anyway?' He said, 'John Green is the difference between nothing and winning the Big Ten championship.' He told me that in December. And a month later, we started our surge."

"He was our secret weapon once he became eligible," Anderson said. "But when John came to us, he was the rawest raw material you'd ever seen. Most of his points his sophomore year came on tip-ins and putbacks."

A *Detroit News* preseason preview had talked about a "Greene," with three e's—perhaps one each for electrifying, enthusiastic and embryonic.

"I was a starter that season until John was cleared to play," said center Chuck Bencie. "We used to practice against each other. And once he started to pick things up, you knew he'd be a great one. I can still see those alley-oop passes from Jack Quiggle, the first play they ever ran for him."

"I really had no style of my own," Green said. "I was ready to be molded. If I'd see something from another player, I'd try to do it. Julius was left-handed, too, and I'm sure I picked up some things he did."

Green never scored like McCoy and had a career average of 16.9 points. But his rebounding and shot-blocking made him a constant factor.

"My first game was against Michigan and Ron Kramer," he said of a 3-for-12, nine-point, nine-rebound day. "He was an All-America football player. And he really did a number on me. Not long after that, we won 10 in a row."

In the NCAA Tournament, Green dominated against Notre Dame sophomore star Tom Hawkins and had 20 points and 27 rebounds. And in a huge upset at Kentucky, he was bailed out by Bencie.

"I'll never forget John fouling out with about 12 minutes left," said WKAR broadcaster Jim Adams. "He stood on the bench, waved his warmup jacket over his head and did everything he possibly could to keep Bencie going."

"You just didn't beat Kentucky at Kentucky," Green said. "Adolph Rupp's teams were dominant there. But long before they had any black players, he came up to me at a function and said, 'Gee, I wish I had you on my team!'"

The following week at the NCAA semifinals, North Carolina All-American Lenny Rosenbluth was just as complimentary after Green grabbed 19 rebounds and blocked eight shots in a triple-overtime loss.

"He's 6-foot-5 and jumps like he's 6-foot-10," said Rosenbluth, who was 11-for-42 from the field with seven shots blocked. "He had the quickest hands I've ever seen."

Playing in just 18 of 26 games in 1956-57, Green smashed the MSU rebound record, then upped that mark from 14.6 to 17.8 per game as a junior.

He also set a Big Ten standard with 53.8 percent field goal accuracy in his second season. And in a head-to-head matchup with Indiana center Archie Dees, Green outscored the league's MVP 24-13 and outrebounded him 23-14.

"I'd put him in a group with Jackie Jackson, the old Globetrotter, and maybe three other guys as a rebounder," McCoy said. "He jumped out of sight. I know Julius Erving well. And Julius wasn't in his league."

Green routinely touched the top of an NBA backboard at 12-foot-6 and once dunked a ball 10 times in 15 seconds.

"I remember an alumni game when Robin Roberts, the great baseball pitcher, went up as high as he could and was eye-level with Green's belt buckle," Vista said. "That's when Robin decided not to play any more basketball."

Though Green said he got more publicity than he deserved, often at the

Green and MSU Athletic Director Merritt Norvell display a retired number.

expense of players like Larry Hedden and Tom Rand, his 1959 first-team All-America and conference MVP awards were well deserved, if not a bit tardy.

"He's worth at least 50 points a game to us," Anderson said. "Combine his scoring and defensive play with a bunch of psychological intangibles and I'm sure he's worth more than half our point total in any game we play."

Only Ohio State's three-time All-America center Jerry Lucas has a higher rebounding average among Big Ten players, 17.2 to 16.4. And Green still ranks No. 2 on the Spartans' list with 1,036 rebounds in just two-and-a-half years.

He spent 14 seasons in the NBA with New York, Baltimore, San Diego, Philadelphia and Cincinnati/Kansas City. And he was oldest player in All-Star Game history when he made his fourth appearance at age 37.

"The guy was beautiful," said Royals coach and Hall of Fame guard Bob Cousy. "What can I say about him? He was remarkable, fantastic, incredible!"

"I went back to my 10th high school reunion," Green said. "They didn't even know me. They didn't know anybody 6-foot-5. I was John Green then, not Johnny."

After retiring at age 39, Green went into the restaurant business and had one of the most popular McDonald's franchises on Bay Parkway in Brooklyn, near La Guardia Airport.

He was a charter member of the MSU Hall of Fame and returned to see his jersey retired and raised to the Breslin rafters.

"I always knew the meaning of work," Green said. "In school, I was married. Then, Jeffrey and Johnny were born on Easter in 1957. I knew I had to be productive in order to support them."

"I often wonder, 'Where are those twin boys?'" Anderson added. "I think to myself, 'They should be jumpin' somewhere!'"

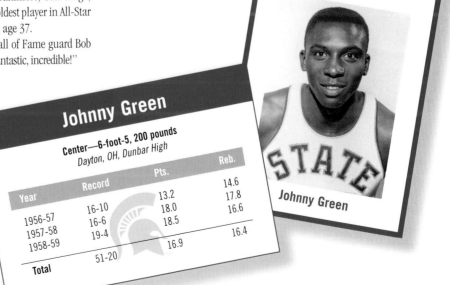

Michigan State

Johnny Green

Johnny Green

Center—6-foot-5, 200 pounds
Dayton, OH, Dunbar High

Year	Record	Pts.	Reb.
1956–57	16-10	13.2	14.6
1957–58	16-6	18.0	17.8
1958–59	19-4	18.5	16.6
Total	51-20	16.9	16.4

Gregory Kelser

Kelser's favorite neckwear is still a net from the Final Four in Salt Lake City.

Three players in Big Ten basketball history have scored more than 2,000 points and grabbed at least 1,000 rebounds.

Only one is under 6-foot-11 and has an honorary doctorate.

Gregory Kelser was "Special K" to Michigan State fans from 1975 to 1979—an All-America forward, a three-time team MVP, and a two-time captain.

Nearly two decades after winning a national title, he has won something every bit as precious—universal respect as a model Spartan.

Perhaps that explains why MSU President Peter McPherson picked Kelser to deliver the 1998 Spring Commencement address in Breslin Center, where his retired No. 32 hangs from the rafters.

"When the president asked if I'd serve as commencement speaker, I was taken aback," Kelser said. "I'd heard Bill Clinton was there a few years earlier. And I didn't know anything about the honorary degree. . . . What can you say? I was as honored to be associated with Michigan State that day as I've ever been."

The feeling has been mutual since Kelser's arrival on campus as a scrawny, 6-7 sleeper from Detroit Henry Ford High.

Born in Florida, he had grown up as far away as Okinawa, Japan, where he remembers watching the Notre Dame–MSU football "Game of the Century" in 1966 with a father who was a huge Spartan supporter.

But after moving to Detroit in 1972, Kelser quickly became a Michigan fan.

"All through high school, I cheered for the Wolverines," he admitted. "I even have pictures of me in a Michigan shirt. They were the team on top and were easy to cheer for. They were always in the hunt for the Rose Bowl."

They weren't in the hunt for Kelser, preferring more heralded players like Phil Hubbard from Cleveland and Alan Hardy from Detroit.

MSU wanted Hardy, too, but noticed Kelser in a Northwestern–Henry Ford struggle and nearly succeeded in signing both players.

Hardy was considering the Spartans, Michigan, and Minnesota, while Kelser had taken seven trips and pared his choices to MSU, which he had never visited, Minnesota, and Arizona State.

"Gus Ganakas never saw me play in high school," Kelser said of the Spartans' head coach. "But Vernon Payne, his assistant, did. And he followed the two of us to a tournament in Sharon, Pennsylvania, where Hardy pulled a fast one.

"We'd been keeping in touch and talking about schools that wanted us both. After we met with Vernon at our hotel, I said, 'Let's put this to rest right now. I like Michigan State.' Hardy said, 'I do, too.' And I said, 'Let's do it!'"

When Kelser called Payne that Saturday night and said, "We'll sign," Payne drove back to the players' hotel and worked out the logistics for separate Monday morning sessions in Detroit.

"He was at my house at 9 a.m." Kelser said. "My parents were really happy, as you can imagine. And right after I signed, Vernon left my house for Hardy's. An hour later, I got a call saying, 'Alan didn't sign.'

"I heard he got a call from Bobby Knight, asking him to visit Indiana. Three or four days later, he signed with Michigan. I would've signed with Michigan State anyway. But I didn't feel bad when Hardy hardly played as a freshman and sophomore.

"After our careers were over, he brought it up and apologized. He said he got caught up in the fact it was MICHIGAN. And there was a hint of remorse."

There was none for Kelser, especially when his team avenged considerable

frustration and led the Wolverines 46-16 at halftime their senior year.

But first came a post-signing visit to campus, a smooth adjustment as a student-athlete, an oh-so-close freshman season—Ganakas' last stand—and the arrival of dictatorial head coach Jud Heathcote.

"When I finally came to Michigan State, I got to know Terry Furlow," Kelser said of a volatile senior-to-be. "He'd had so much negative press for his role in the walkout the year before and for scuffles with other players. But he was the first guy who came to see me at the hotel. We always got along great. And no one ever worked harder."

Despite Furlow's offensive heroics, a last-game loss at home to Wisconsin cost MSU a share of third place and an NIT bid, sealing Ganakas' fate as a future administrator.

"That game was the biggest disappointment of my basketball career—even more than the Kentucky game that would keep us out of the Final Four two years later," Kelser said. "In '78, we knew we had a good team with almost everyone coming back. In '76, we were losing the heart and soul of our team."

That might not have been a terrible thing, given the total combustibility of a Furlow–Heathcote player–coach relationship.

"Could Terry have played for Jud? . . . I know I wouldn't have had to worry about being screamed at, and neither would anyone else," Kelser said. "They

"Special K" swoops to the hoop in an NCAA Semifinal blowout of the Quakers.

Kelser works for post position against Minnesota's Kevin McHale in 1979.

were two very clashing personalities. It's difficult to imagine them lasting for a year. But was Terry a jerk? No! He was a nice guy and an amazing talent. I never did beat him one-on-one."

One-on-one was out, and one way to do things—his way—was in the day Heathcote arrived from Montana with a steady stream of one-liners.

"My first year had been almost too easy," Kelser said. "Terry, Bob Chapman, Benny White and Edgar Wilson really took me in. Every freshman should have it that good.

"My second year was tougher, though I averaged nearly 22 points. Gus and Jud were like night-and-day. I always knew Gus was boss, as I did with every coach I ever had. But with Jud, there was never a doubt."

Kelser flourished under Heathcote's teaching and benefitted from the return of the dunk to the college game—a play that would become his trademark.

His first slam had come at age 15 and had cost him 25 pushups when an angry coach had asked for layups.

Under Heathcote, the alley-oop feed to Kelser from a gifted freshman guard would soon be a staple of MSU's offense and a pre-ESPN way to get recognized.

Earvin Johnson and Kelser were peanut butter-and-jelly as an open-court combination and might have invented more than just "Spartan Showtime."

"After Greg would score, we'd give ourselves a high-five," Johnson said. "Back then, nobody was doing it. One day, I just held my hand up, and Greg slapped it. Before long, everyone did it, even in the NBA."

The trick for Heathcote was to give his team more reasons to celebrate—a tough assignment in a 12-15 debut, bolstered by two wins from forfeits.

And to do that, even before Johnson arrived, a key ingredient was getting Kelser to approach his potential, especially as an offensive player.

"He could always rebound," Heathcote said. "And he could always run. But there was enough potential there that we knew he should be doing more than he was. What helped Gregory tremendously was that he was a great worker. He worked and worked and made himself into a very good player."

He was always a little finicky and was described by two-year Spartan roommate Ron Charles as "a real neat-freak who studied all the time."

Though Kelser would prove he knew how to have fun, his fastidious nature was a source of amusement from his first year in a spotless uniform.

"I can't remember the game, but Greg comes running to the bench," Payne said. "Coach Ganakas stands up and thinks he's injured. Instead, Greg tells a manager, 'Go to my locker, and get this other pair of shoes.' Greg Kelser got some dirt on his shoe and wanted to wear a new pair! We're trying to win the game, and this skinny kid wants new shoes! . . . We couldn't believe it.

"I really think Greg has a shoe fetish. You couldn't get in his locker with all the shoes he had. And when he put them on for a game, it'd take him a half hour to tie the laces. If they flopped in a different direction, he'd have to retie them. Then, if he didn't feel right in warmups and didn't think he'd have a good game, he'd change them. He'd go back and get a new pair."

A new pair of players from Lansing, Johnson and center Jay Vincent, helped Kelser's chances for a national championship more than any shoe ever could.

"I always thought Kelser was a very good player," said Knight, whose Hoosiers would lose five of seven matchups with MSU in Heathcote's first three seasons. "I really liked Kelser before. He did a lot of things as a freshman and sophomore. But when Johnson came, the enthusiasm he brought acted as a catalyst for the whole team."

That was especially true when the Spartans were home before 10,004 rabid rooters, with thousands more waiting for seats some nights.

"Jenison Field House was a wonderful place for our team," Kelser said. "I wouldn't have changed a thing. With the volume there and the support we had, it was my favorite place to play in the Big Ten."

Suddenly, MSU improved to 25-5 and 26-6, winning an outright conference title in 1978 and sharing the crown with Iowa and NIT-bound Purdue in 1979.

Kelser was at his best in the NCAA Tournament, averaging 21.7 points and 12.3 rebounds in three games as a junior and 25.4 points and 10.6 rebounds in five convincing wins as a senior.

"No man, no matter how outstanding he might be, is going to achieve great things without solid companionship," said NBC broadcaster Dick Enberg. "Greg Kelser was an All-American in his own right. But it took those of us in the media a little longer to understand just how superb an athlete he was. The Tournament probably did more for Kelser that way than for Magic Johnson."

It was that sensational stretch, highlighted by a 34-point, 13-rebound effort against Notre Dame in the Mideast Region final, that prompted NBC analyst Al McGuire to say Kelser would be a better pro than Johnson.

"I've never been a better player than Earvin," said Kelser, who missed just

A quick first step carries Kelser past Larry Bird in a famous Final Four matchup.

two practices and one game in four years. "Very few players have. But I was a good player before he got there and a very good player with him at the point. The thing I learned when Earvin was there was how to be a champion."

National supremacy was well within reach after the Spartans' 80-68 silencing of the Fighting Irish in Indianapolis.

"I got a lot of joy out of that one," Kelser said. "To make it to the Final Four and win on my dad's birthday, after losing to Kentucky that same day the year before, meant a lot to me. And I remember Jud coming up to me after the game and saying, 'You made yourself a few dollars today.'"

He left as the school's No. 1 scorer and rebounder and as an Academic All-American who returned his first two summers in the NBA to complete his bachelor's degree.

After catapulting to the fourth overall pick by Detroit in the first round, Kelser had an injury-plagued pro career but parlayed that into a successful career in broadcasting, including analysis on Big Ten games and the hosting of MSU coaches' shows.

"Greg Kelser has been a role model on and off the court," McPherson said. "In basketball, where you must have a consistent 'sense of where you are' on offense and defense, he had an uncanny ability to anticipate and react. He not only positioned himself but positioned others to be in the right place at the right time.

"More importantly, throughout his life, Greg has put himself in position to help others

off the court, in real-life situations where terms like 'assist' and 'rebound' have more profound meanings and implications."

When it comes to his alma mater, Dr. Kelser's office is always open.

Michigan State

Gregory Kelser

Forward—6-foot-7, 190 pounds
Detroit, MI, Henry Ford High

Year	Record	Pts.	Reb.
1975-76	14-13	11.7	9.5
1976-77	12-15	21.7	10.8
1977-78	25-5	17.7	9.1
1978-79	26-6	18.8	8.7
Total	77-39	17.5	9.5

Gregory Kelser

Scott Skiles

No one has ever played with more fire than No. 4, who celebrates a win over Georgetown.

They called him "Jud Jr."—and he was smart enough to take that as a compliment.

Scott Allen Skiles had the perfect initials. No one ever played basketball with more sass than a 6-foot-1 point guard with something to prove to the world.

"He's not very fast. . . . But he makes up for it by being slow," joked a staunch defender, Michigan State coach Jud Heathcote.

On the court, he was quick enough to leave as the program's first National Player of the Year and its all-time leader in points, assists, steals and free-throw percentage.

Off the court, he was a bit too fast for his own good.

But the story of the most controversial and most confident Spartan athlete in history began in Walkerton, Indiana, with a hoop and a Nerf ball in his playpen.

By the time he led the 28-1 Plymouth High Pilgrims to the Indiana all-comers state title in 1982, Skiles' athletic feats were legendary, and not because he hit home runs in four consecutive at bats.

He was by far the biggest contributor for the smallest school since storied Milan High in 1954 to experience the ultimate in Hoosier Hysteria, thanks largely to a record-tying, one-day total of 69 points.

In an afternoon semifinal against Indianapolis Cathedral, Skiles warmed up with 30. And in the final that evening against Gary Roosevelt, he had 39, including a 25-footer to tie at the buzzer and 14 points in two overtimes.

"If they needed 30 points, he got 30 points," Heathcote said. "If they needed a rebound, he got a rebound. If they needed a basket inside, he dumped the ball inside. He had great court awareness and great court presence."

Skiles received the Hertz No. 1 Award from O.J. Simpson in New York as his state's top athlete but was a reluctant No. 1 at least once.

"I remember a game when I wanted him to get the school scoring record," said Plymouth coach Jack Edison. "He had 52 or 53 with about 4 minutes left and kept coming down and passing. That cotton-picker just wouldn't shoot! He kept dropping the ball off for 3-footers. Finally, I had to call timeout to tell everyone to make sure Scott shot the ball."

Skiles grew up just south of South Bend and dreamed of playing for Purdue, the nearest Big Ten school. But a recruiting gaffe cost Boilermaker aide Jay Williams his job and helped Heathcote, a connoisseur of guard play.

"That story is worn out!" said Purdue coach Gene Keady, when asked about it for the umpteenth time. "An assistant of mine said he couldn't play and wrote a letter saying we weren't interested. Now, I don't want to hear that any more! You want us to recruit 15 guards and make them all mad?"

It wouldn't have mattered to Skiles, who would have beaten them all out.

"You just have to go on what kind of feeling you get," he said of MSU's better-late-than-never recruiting effort, after an unsolicited letter of recommendation to Heathcote. "It's just a guess. Every school puts its best face on when you visit. I just got a better feeling for State than anywhere else."

The feeling was mutual when he started almost immediately as a freshman and scored 35 in a 101–94 triple-overtime win against Ohio State, including a 3-pointer with 12 seconds left in regulation and 10 of his team's final 14.

The next hint of what was to come was a CBS Player of the Game performance—24 points on 11-for-13 shooting from the field—in a 56-55 win over Oregon State his sophomore year in Jenison Field House.

On the road, Skiles was a villain straight from the World Wrestling Federation. And that was long before any brushes with the law.

"My style of play lends itself to people not liking me," he said of a fist-pumping, chest-thumping arrogance. "That stuff happened all the time in high school, too, every place I played."

Skiles' popularity plunged at home—in Indiana and Michigan—when he was arrested on August 19, 1984, in Plymouth for marijuana and cocaine possession, then was pulled over for running a stop sign and charged with impaired driving on September 24 of that year in East Lansing.

After a solid junior season, he pled guilty to the marijuana misdemeanor and was sentenced to a one-year suspended prison sentence, a year's probation and 120 hours of community service.

And after a guilty plea for impaired driving, Skiles received another night in jail, $280 in fines and fees and a 90-day license suspension—a normal sentence with an unusual lecture from Ingham County District Judge Thomas Brennan, Jr., a Spartan supporter.

A coach in the making, Skiles shares his ideas with assistant Mike Deane and Jud Heathcote.

Skiles runs the fast break and blows by Hoosier center Uwe Blab in Jenison.

Invoking the memory of ex-Indiana star Landon Turner, who was paralyzed in an auto accident, Brennan said, "If you believe that can't happen to you, then I want you to think again. Last year, 25,000 people in this country thought that way—and this year, they're dead. We're not talking about a minor traffic offense. People like yourself must understand that this is a matter of life-and-death."

Brennan also read from a *Sports Illustrated* story about the positive transformation of once-troubled great Pete Maravich, Skiles' boyhood hero.

But after being coaxed out for a few beers just after midnight more than five months later, a clear violation of his Indiana probation, Skiles was spotted in his red Fiero and stopped as he began a short trip home.

If he had walked, hitched a ride or called a cab that night, things would have been so much simpler for everyone involved in two states.

Instead, Skiles was charged again on November 7, 1985, after a .11 percent breathalyzer reading—a judgment call an angry coach has never understood.

"He was caught in the wrong place at the wrong time," Heathcote said.

"There are something like 800 people stopped in East Lansing for driving under the influence and 200 more on campus. Out of those 1,000, Scott Skiles had more negative publicity than the other 999 put together."

For every person who agreed with the overzealous-police theory, someone else voiced just as strong and just as loud a view that Skiles had to go.

The only one who could make that determination was Heathcote, who stood by his player and saved a soon-to-be-sensational season by limiting an immediate suspension to five days and one exhibition game.

"If he'd have said, 'Redshirt for a year,' I'd have redshirted," Skiles said. "If he'd kicked me off the team and taken my scholarship, then that's what would've happened."

"I've got to admire Jud for sticking with him," said assistant coach Herb Williams. "That helped make Scott the person he is." Jud said, 'Who can take the heat better, me or him?'"

Both were burned up, as the "Mothers Against Scott Skiles" campaign in Mid-Michigan and a surprising number of empty seats in Jenison were almost as tough to take as some key-waving, sugar-shaking crowds on the road.

"A lot of it came from the media," Heathcote insisted. "They gave a distorted picture of Scott as the town drunk instead of a guy who had a couple of problems over a 15-month period."

"Obviously, I wish I'd never gotten in trouble," Skiles said. "But I learned I can withstand anything anyone is willing to dish out. No one has any idea what it's like to go into an arena where 16,000 people are booing every time you touch the ball. That alone would make a lot of people crumble."

On the court, he was almost unflappable, hitting "shut-up baskets" in almost every arena and making converts as the James Dean of college hoops.

"I brought the trouble on myself," Skiles said in 1986. "But I've always been able to play basketball. Even on the worst day of my life, I think I could turn the other stuff off at game time and play."

"He's the most remarkable athlete I've ever seen play this game," said Iowa coach George Raveling. "For him to take all that abuse and play as well as he has is remarkable."

So was the impact he had on teammates in a shocking 23-8 ride to the NCAA Tournament's Sweet 16 and arguably the best individual season in MSU history.

"He just blocks everything out and concentrates on the game," said senior forward and former roommate Larry Polec. "He's intimidating. He's like a military leader, yelling at everyone to straighten things out. But we're used to corporal leadership. You know, Jud isn't the most gentle of coaches."

"Scott might have been slow, but he was a great competitor," said junior guard Darryl Johnson. "He had a great basketball mind and made you want to play to his intensity. A lot of times we did that. And with Vernon Carr, I think the three of us were the best backcourt in the country."

Sports Information Director Nick Vista came up with idea and assistant SID Mike Pearson was the broker for the "Spartan Scott Market," a stock-market spinoff and press release that detailed Skiles' accomplishments.

He played the full 40 minutes 13 times as a senior, fouled seven defenders out of the game and finished second in the nation in scoring behind Terrance Bailey of Wagner at 27.4 points per game—29.1 in league play with the largest scoring-title margin in 16 years.

And that was without at least 115 points Vista determined he would have had if the 3-point shot had returned one year earlier.

The 1986 Big Ten MVP gets a hero's welcome the following winter with MSU A.D. Doug Weaver.

The two best MSU guards to play in one backcourt, Sam Vincent and Skiles, pull together.

"Scotty Skiles . . . I've never seen anyone like him," Williams said. "He couldn't even dunk. But what determination!"

"Skiles is as gutty and cocky as any kid I've seen," said ESPN and ABC analyst Dick Vitale, who had called for a longer suspension. "And he backs it up! He's a young Muhammad Ali. He said, 'Bring on the Wolverines with their great backcourt!' Sometimes, I think he'd say, 'Bring on Isiah Thomas!'"

After a season of silence off the court, Skiles' first comments about his legal problems were to the *Lansing State Journal* and the *Flint Journal* in late January, two weeks before a story by Ivan Maisel in *Sports Illustrated*.

But the day after a sweep of Michigan in Ann Arbor, Skiles was brought back to Plymouth to be sentenced on the probation violation—a media frenzy at the Marshall County Courthouse.

"There's a line between right and wrong," said Circuit Judge Michael Cook. "And if you walk close enough to that line, you can stumble and fall

on the wrong side, as you apparently have. Being on probation means you attempt to walk as far away from that line as you possibly can."

Skiles was sentenced to 30 days in jail and would later serve 15, with 15 removed for good behavior. There, a guard would answer his simple requests with the soon-to-be-famous line, "This ain't no hotel, boy!"

"It's wrong that people assume I have a drinking problem," Skiles said. "I get brochures and things in the mail every day on alcoholism. It's nice that people are concerned. But it's offensive that people think I'm an alcoholic. I'm not!"

Fans who once worshipped his skill and courage were clearly divided.

"Scott Skiles is basketball," said Patsy Feece of Plymouth, who had seen every one of the Pilgrims' games in 1981–82. "Nobody can take that away from him. And the people who cheered him on four years ago shouldn't even try."

"It's not like I'm the mother of Charles Manson," said Marilyn Skiles.

She was the mom of the Big Ten MVP and the National Player of the Year,

as selected by CBS analyst Billy Packer and *Basketball Times* editor and publisher Larry Donald.

But analyst Al McGuire offered a dissenting view on a visit to Lansing: "Unlike my buddy, 'Ol' Pastryhead' (Packer), I didn't know he was that good. I don't think he really deserved to be an All-American—second-team maybe but not first-team."

There was no question with those who had watched him every day.

"If I had to pick an All-America backcourt, I'd put Scott Skiles at one guard," said an admittedly biased Heathcote. "Then, I'd put Scott Skiles at the other guard."

"Scott Skiles is a player," wrote Corky Meinecke of *The Detroit News*, a critic of Heathcote's handling of the case. "Make that the NCAA's Player of the Year. Not Student of the Year or Citizen of the Year or Crime Fighter of the Year. And those who vote for such honors should remember that."

Those who finally got a chance to see him in post-season play were in awe. "The mark of a great player is not only how well he plays but how he affects others around him," said Georgetown coach John Thompson. "Skiles is contagious."

"I'm going to coach him in an all-star game in Hawaii," said Kansas coach Larry Brown. "I hope he doesn't yell at me."

"Whenever I watch Michigan State, I'm afraid to turn the channel," said North Carolina State's Jim Valvano. "I keep thinking Skiles is going to jump out of the set and say, 'WHAT THE HELL DO YOU THINK YOU'RE DOING?'"

His stats spoke volumes with 2,145 career points, passing Gregory Kelser,

645 assists, passing Earvin Johnson, and 175 steals, passing Sam Vincent.

"I identify with Scott a lot," said Athletic Director Doug Weaver, another feisty, undersized athlete from Northern Indiana. "The difference between Scott and me is Scott is a helluva player."

Despite a serious back problem, Skiles played for Milwaukee, Indiana, Orlando, Washington and Philadelphia, setting an NBA single-game assist mark with 30 and climbing to third in career free-throw accuracy.

"My knee is a wreck. My back is a wreck. My game is a wreck. And my hair is falling out," Skiles said late in his stay with the Pacers.

But then-Milwaukee coach Don Nelson always thought he was fine and said, "If Larry Bird were created 6 feet tall, he just might be Scott Skiles."

Some day, Skiles might be like a lot like Bird—the 1998 NBA Coach of the Year—in another way.

"Scott would make somebody a helluva coach some day," Heathcote said in 1986. "He knows so much about the game. I don't think anyone I ever coached, except maybe Earvin Johnson, understood the game any better."

By 1997, Skiles was an assistant with the Phoenix Suns. But two years earlier, he took charge in the Jud Heathcote All-Star Tribute Game the way he had in 1986.

With his team behind by a point and 2.0 seconds showing, Skiles took the playboard from Johnson and drew a play that should have worked for a win.

That's the way "The Ol' Coach"—Jud Sr.—would have wanted it.

Michigan State

Scott Skiles

Guard—6-foot-1, 190 pounds
Plymouth, IN, High

Year	Record	Pts.	Ast.
1982-83	17-13	12.5	4.8
1983-84	16-12	14.5	4.6
1984-85	19-10	17.7	5.8
1985-86	23-8	27.4	6.5
Total	75-43	18.2	5.5

Steve Smith

Smith slices through defenders and passes off for an easy basket.

After a gift of $2.5 million, Smith tours construction of the Clara Bell Smith Student-Athlete Academic Center.

t's such a common name for such an uncommon person.

But it's the name he was given by Clara and Donald Smith in 1969. And for a loving son, that makes it a gift to cherish.

Steve Smith's goal is always to give something back—to his schools, his teams, his fans, his friends, his God and his family.

His mother said it best in 1990—15 months before she died with Steve at her side: "I don't want basketball to be the center of his life. God should be. When I call him at school, he says, 'Yes, Mama, I'm reading my Bible.'"

In four years at Michigan State, he took time to carry the program to an outright Big Ten basketball title, the winningest record in school history and the first three in a string of 10 straight post-season appearances.

Smith was the conference MVP as a junior and left as a two-time All-American and MSU's top career scorer with 2,263 points.

When he left an unprecedented $2.5 million donation to the $7 million Clara Bell Smith Student-Athlete Academic Center, it was a shining example of generosity and a lasting tribute to his biggest supporter.

"This is a dream come true," he said in 1997. "This isn't a gift from an athlete. It's a gift from a son. I wanted to give something back to the university. And my mom was always more than a mom. She was my best friend."

She was someone who never imagined Smith would sign a seven-year, $50.4 million contract with the Atlanta Hawks in 1996.

"I didn't think he had the makings of an athlete at all," she said. "It never entered my mind. I thought he would go to a junior college somewhere and work on computers."

Smith credits Richard Hayner, a physical education teacher at Courville School on Detroit's East Side, for helping him learn sound basketball basics.

He was 5-foot-9, 140 pounds as a ninth-grader and had to leap off stacks of crates to dunk for the first time.

But as a cocky sophomore, Smith's career nearly came to an end when he got a "D" on a test, defied Pershing High coach Johnny Goston's order to run laps and threatened to transfer to Highland Park High.

"I'm not doing it, Coach," Smith said. "I'm not running laps for anyone. You keep your laps. I quit!"

That was fine with his mother, who had greater concerns, as Goston explained: "She said, 'I really don't care if you quit. You're not in school to play ball in the first place. You're there to go to school. Go ahead and quit. . . . But you can forget about transferring. You're staying at Pershing. Period.'"

The next day, Smith was back with a request for reinstatement.

And if he wasn't on his backyard court with the likes of would-be stars Derrick Coleman, Doug Smith, Anderson Hunt and Willie Burton, he was at Hawthorne Recreation Center, the Franklin Settlement gym or St. Cecilia's, developing his game and dogging opponents in true Detroit style.

Smith attacks the rim and energizes the crowd at Breslin with a dunk against Indiana.

Missouri, Detroit, Eastern Michigan and Arkansas–Little Rock.

"I had no desire to go to Michigan," he said. "And if I hadn't gone to Michigan State, I probably would've gone to Missouri with Doug. But with Jud being so honest and telling me he already had one guard coming in, I took that as a challenge. I said, 'No kid from Illinois can beat a kid from Detroit.'"

Continuing to grow to more than 6-6, Smith averaged 26 points, 12 rebounds and 10 assists as a senior for the Doughboys.

And when highly touted and equally confident Jesse Hall arrived from Venice, Illinois, it didn't take long to settle the issue of dominance.

"Right away, Steve and Jesse got into it," said Spartan assistant Herb Williams of the oil-and-water roommates. "When they played one-on-one, Steve beat him handily. Then, Jesse made the mistake of saying, 'You were just lucky today.' Steve said, 'You can try again tomorrow. You're from Southern Illinois. In Detroit, we take guys like you and spit them out for dinner!'"

Publicly, Heathcote praised both and said, "I like them a lot. Jesse might be a little more ready to play right now. But Steve has the potential to be a great one. He's a multi-dimensional player who can do a lot of things."

Privately, he pointed to Smith the first day of practice and told Athletic Director Doug Weaver, "See that kid? He's going to be our next great guard."

"That skinny kid down there?" Weaver said. "You're kidding me!"

Smith liked bowling, tennis, and golf and was built much like a 1-iron.

But in an era when other Big Ten hotshots had sports cars and sport utility vehicles, Smith drove a 1980 Buick LeSabre with a faulty ignition system and had to flip a switch manually to start it.

He started to gain attention on the floor as a freshman, when his 18 points and seven assists were crucial in an overtime win over Indiana.

And his free throws with no time left beat Ohio State by one in Columbus.

"My freshman year was very hard," Smith said. "Jud was always calling me a wimp. George Papadakos and I heard that nearly every day. Sometimes, I wanted to tell him off. But he knew what he was doing. I started lifting harder to prove something to him."

By Smith's sophomore year, Minnesota coach Clem Haskins said, "He's just an outstanding player. He's listed at 6-6. But he's really 6-9. And he plays like a 7-footer."

In a 34-point eruption at Villanova, Smith led the Spartans to the NIT semifinals in New York's Madison Square Garden with 11-for-15 accuracy from the field and 10-for-10 work at the line.

"We saw nine films on him," said Wildcat coach Rollie Massimino. "We knew what he could do. He just did what he had to do and made every shot."

That brief taste of team success turned sour that summer when Smith

Amazingly, he wasn't even a first-team all-league choice as a 6-2 junior.

But when Smith grew to 6-5 the following summer, he caught the eye of MSU's coaches, who were there to see center Erik Wilson of Henry Ford High.

"We must've seen him five or six times," said Spartan coach Jud Heathcote, who liked Smith immediately. "I said, 'Why aren't we recruiting this guy?' The amazing thing is that all the Michigan assistants were at the same games we were, looking at guys like Mark Macon and Doug Smith."

That summer, MSU's find was mugged and hit with what appeared to be a pipe, leaving a nasty, one-inch scar on the back of his head.

But when Smith committed to MSU, Wolverine coach Bill Frieder blasted his staff about losing sight of a player called "Earvin Gervin" by Goston and "Magic Johnson with a jump shot" by Northern High coach Harry Hairston.

Though Smith had home visits from nearly two dozen schools, including ex-Spartan assistant Don Monson's Oregon program, he chose MSU over

In an emotion-packed win over Michigan, Smith is fouled by Sean Higgins.

Smith savors a moment with always-emotional center Mike Peplowski.

returned home and was teased about the Spartans' improvement to 18-15.

"I always felt funny when my friends were in the NCAA Tournament," he said. "They'd ask me when they'd ever get to see me play. It got so bad I wouldn't even take my NIT jacket home."

Smith began to answer those questions his junior year, opening with 36 points, nine rebounds and seven assists against Auburn in the Great Alaska Shootout and leading his team to a 3-0 mark as the tournament MVP.

But when Smith broke a finger against Eastern Michigan, Heathcote said, "I shudder to think what this team will be like without him."

It would be better than anyone dreamed, winning three games with Smith in street clothes and two after his speedy return to climb to 14-2.

After three losses in the next five games, including a last-second defeat in Ann Arbor on a tough shot by guard Rumeal Robinson, a better-known No. 21, Smith and his teammates planned their revenge and rolled off 12 straight wins.

"That game against Michigan hurt more than any other game," he said. "And the game when we beat them in Breslin Center meant more to me than beating Purdue for the championship. When all the students came on the floor, it was hot—real hot."

Almost as hot as Smith had been in a 25-point second half, before he grabbed a huge, green "S" flag and waved it in circles over his head.

"I'm still dazzled and dizzy over over what he did," said Wolverine coach Steve Fisher, after Smith had 36 points and nine rebounds. "He was shooting over smaller guys like Rumeal and Michael Talley. Tonight, it wouldn't have mattered if Wilt Chamberlain was on him."

He was even better at Minnesota less than two days later, pouring in 39.

"I'll tell you what," Haskins said. "I'm going to recommend him HIGHLY to any NBA scout who asks about him coming out early."

MSU was nearly knocked out of the NCAA Tournament by Murray State in the opening round—something that has never happened to a No. 1 seed.

The Spartans did head home sooner than necessary, losing a Sweet 16 overtime struggle to Georgia Tech, when Smith missed a foul shot and Yellow Jacket guard Kenny Anderson got credit for a tying basket with :00 showing.

"When I went to the line, I thought it was over," Smith said. "That free throw haunted me for a while. While our new arena is being built in Atlanta, we've had to play a lot of games at Georgia Tech. Whenever I saw Bobby Cremins, he'd bring that up. But he knows we should've won."

Smith always thought his team should win and was a completely different character on and off the court.

"He was like Dr. Jekyll and Mr. Hyde," Heathcote said. "Off the floor, you couldn't get him to say two words. But on the floor, every opponent was an enemy to him. That's the way he grew up on the playgrounds of Detroit."

"He's the only guy I know who can strut while he's backpedaling," said backcourt partner Mark Montgomery. "He'll say to the guy guarding him, 'How do you want it? Dunk or jumper?'"

But as Mark Nixon wrote in the *Lansing State Journal*, "If they made a movie about Steve Smith's non-basketball life, 'It might be, 'Mr. Smith goes to deportment school.'"

"He has always been that way," his mother said. "I don't like players with big heads. I hate that!"

His senior year, MSU was the preseason No. 1 pick of *Basketball Times*, largely due to Smith's offensive brilliance.

"Even I couldn't screw him up!" said ABC and ESPN analyst and former coach Dick Vitale. "And I've been known to screw up a few people. Steve Smith is a Rolls-Royce performer."

"He's the best big guard in the country. Period," said NBA superscout Marty Blake. "Can you find me some others? My problem is there aren't enough Steve Smiths."

Especially for the Spartans, who slipped from 28-6 to a disappointing 19-11 in 1990–91.

But before a loss to defending national champ UNLV at The Palace, Smith got an unsolicited compliment from a playground pal.

"The thing about Steve that impresses me the most is he's a giver, not a taker," said Runnin' Rebel guard Anderson Hunt. "He's the kind of guy who likes to share what he has. He's not in it for himself. Whatever he had growing up, he shared with everyone."

Including his shorts. He would trade trunks quite often with massive center Mike Peplowski, as a baggy-pants predecessor of Michigan's Fab Five.

Smith never joined Earvin Johnson in MSU's triple-double club but was good enough to get more praise than Mother Theresa on his last tour of the league.

"There are 15,138 people whose lives are just a bit poorer this morning," wrote Gordon Trowbridge in the *State Journal* after Smith's last home game.

"The thing Steve had was an unbelievable desire to succeed," said Spartan

assistant Tom Crean. "He had a great growth spurt in high school, after being one of the shorter guys. And there was always a chip on his shoulder that way. But he never stopped being a fighter. For working on his game and studying film, he's the best I've ever been around."

"Steve is a helluva player," said Indiana coach Bob Knight. "I really like the kid and have since he was a freshman. He's a tremendous example. I've never seen anyone give a better message to young kids by staying in school."

After one more buzzer-beater against Wisconsin–Green Bay in NCAA play, he was ready for the NBA as the fifth overall pick by the Miami Heat.

"Without question, he'll be a great NBA player," Johnson said. "Don't think of him as the next Magic. Think of him as the first Steve Smith."

As the one and only.

"I'm just happy to say I played with him," Peplowski said. "There aren't many guys you can say, 'Believe everything good ever said about him.' Joe Dumars is that way, too. He'll treat you like a million bucks."

When Heathcote retired, one player—guess who—took a red-eye flight to be in Breslin Center for his coach's final home game.

And when MSU asked for $100,000, the Dream Teamer gave 25 times that amount and honored his mother's commitment to education.

"Without her . . . there would be no Steve Smith to make such a gift," he said. "I've had great coaches, but none greater than my mom. I've had great role models, but none greater than my mom. I've had great teammates and fans, but none greater than Clara Bell Smith."

"If anyone has ever made a greater contribution, I have yet to hear about it," said Hall of Famer Bob Lanier, director of the NBA's Team-Up Program for volunteerism. "I applaud him for seeing the circle instead of the dot."

For his contributions as a player and a person, Smith earned the J. Walter Kennedy Award for sportsmanship and was *Courtside* magazine's Man of the Year.

"In an age when show-me-the-money greed runs rampant through the sports world, Steve Smith defies the stereotype of the self-absorbed jock," the *Courtside* announcement said.

"Why not?" he said. "I'm fortunate enough to have it. And even if I go broke some day, it's only money."

Only from Smith.

Michigan State

Steve Smith

Guard—6-foot-7, 200 pounds
Detroit, MI, Pershing High

Year	Record	Pts.	Reb.
1987-88	10-18	10.7	4.0
1988-89	18-15	17.7	6.0
1989-90	28-6	20.2	7.0
1990-91	19-11	25.1	6.1
Total	75-50	18.5	6.1

Steve Smith

Shawn Respert

Respert's 3-pointers made "Fire & Ice" sizzle.

Respert moves to the basket against Michigan's Jalen Rose.

He came to Michigan State in 1990 as the fourth-rated prospect in a class of four recruits.

Five seasons and 2,531 points later, Shawn Respert left campus as the Spartans' all-time leading scorer and most decorated player.

As he bid the fans at Breslin Center farewell with a memorable kiss of the "S" at midcourt, his goals of becoming a star and making the program stronger had both been accomplished.

His nickname was "Rusty." And it couldn't have been more of a misnomer.

Long, arching jump shots terrorized opponents from coast to coast for four years and made him one of the most feared players in the country.

"I remember a saying: 'Pressure either makes diamonds or busts pipes,'" Respert said. "I think we always looked forward to making diamonds, no matter what the pressure was."

Three years after his departure to the pros, some still say he's the Big Ten's last great pure shooter—perhaps the last of this century.

Fame wasn't always Respert's companion. Growing up in Detroit, he played in the shadows of friends like Jalen Rose and Voshon Lenard.

And on balanced teams at Bishop Borgess High, he was known more for his defensive skills than for any offensive fireworks.

Respert was considering Rice, Detroit, and Tulsa, hardly the biggest names in the game, when Jud Heathcote saw something special.

"Jud came down quite a few times," Respert said, dispelling the myth that his coach never left Ingham County. "He'd been down to see Parish Hickman, who was a couple of years older. But when I got to be a senior, Jud actually came down to watch me practice and work out.

"I figured you only live once. The best thing I could do was to take the big risk. Plus, going to a big school would allow me to get a good education. I looked at it as a no-lose situation."

Respert salutes the fans at Breslin after being recognized as the Spartans' career scoring leader.

including a 22-point effort in an upset of No. 2-ranked Arkansas.

"I still tease Oliver Miller about that win," he said of the former Razorback center. "He said their coaches had scouted us and talked about everybody else—Stephens, Montgomery, Peplowski—but didn't know about this Respert guy."

Respert led the Spartans in scoring four straight years and was third-team All-Big Ten as a redshirt-freshman, then finished fourth in the league in points as a sophomore.

Determined to earn his place in the headlines and to help MSU bounce back from a 15-13 season, he practiced morning, noon, and night, rolling off imaginary screens, planting both feet and rising to bury a jumper in the face of an imaginary opponent.

Obsessive? Probably.

Successful? Definitely.

"Shawn was a gym rat, always working on his game," said forward Dwayne Stephens, who watched Respert develop for three years. "He would come in before practice and shoot, then stick around and work some more. That's what I try to tell younger players—that Shawn and Eric (Snow) weren't always great. They just worked a lot harder."

Respert put up his share of great numbers, averaging 24.3 points as a junior, second only to the 31.1 average of Purdue's Glenn Robinson.

And his 92 3-point field goals set an MSU record, as did his 58 treys in league play.

"One thing I liked about Jud was he looked at basketball as an art, not just a game," Respert said. "I think he relished taking an average player and developing him into a better one. I had the raw skills. And he refined them."

MSU's leading scorer in 29 of 32 games began to draw national notice, earning third-team All-America mention.

A Breslin-record 43-point performance, including a Big Ten-record-tying eight 3's, left Minnesota coach Clem Haskins scurrying for cover.

"I'm ready to get back to the hills after seeing Respert left, Respert right, and Respert middle," Haskins said. "It was his show tonight. And that's a record against any team I've ever coached."

Always fueling Respert's engine was the need to get better, regardless of what he did the previous game.

"If we had an early afternoon game, say at noon or 2 p.m., Shawn would come over to Breslin early and shoot for about 30 minutes," Joplin said. "Jud wasn't too crazy about him doing that. We would have to hide Shawn sometimes."

Three games later, there was another 40-point effort, this time against Indiana.

The secret was out. Respert was for real.

So real the one-time unknown was fielding questions about the possibility of declaring himself eligible for the NBA Draft, where he was projected as high as the 15th pick.

In his final game as a junior, an 85-74 loss to Duke in the second round of the NCAA Tournament, Respert took just one shot in a scoreless first half, then had 22 points in the final 16:50.

Afterward, he announced, "This is proof Shawn Respert isn't ready for the NBA. I didn't have the capability to take the game over like Grant Hill."

His comments were meant to keep people from pestering him with the inevitable question, "Are you staying or going?"

But Respert began to think the NBA, at one time a dream, was now firmly in his grasp.

After committing to MSU, Respert tore his anterior cruciate ligament in a Catholic League Playoff game and was redshirted the following season.

For one Spartan coach, it was a nightmare revisited.

"I was at the game when he got hurt," said then-assistant Tom Izzo. "My first thoughts were, 'Oh, no! . . . Here we go again, just like 'Pep' (center Mike Peplowski)."

Defying doctor's predictions of a one-year rehab, Respert was back practicing that fall and polishing his skills.

"When I rehabbed the knee and got up to school, I probably got in more trouble for playing than anything else," he said. "About 10 times Jud would call and say, 'I heard you were over at the IM. You've got to quit that stuff!' And that pounding kind of hurt me when the season came around."

Respert spent much of his time in intense one-on-one battles with All-America guard Steve Smith, who could melt an opponent with sizzling offense.

"Steve would try to intimidate you and was really good at doing that," said assistant Stan Joplin. "I told Shawn that for Steve to respect him, he'd have to give it back to him. If Steve started to get physical, he had to push back."

Respert's first big splash came as the MVP of the 1991 Maui Invitational,

The talk, and there was plenty of it, dealt with his potential and how he compared favorably to other pros.

Finally, in one of the most widely anticipated press conferences in MSU basketball history, Respert joined his parents, Henry and Diane, and Heathcote and announced his decision in a jammed Breslin press room:

"After thinking about a lot of things, what's best for me and my family, the best decision right now is to stay in school another year."

"It's not just the money," Henry added. "Dollars can buy a lot of things. But they can't buy values. And they can't buy that sheepskin when you walk across that stage."

With those words, the stage was set.

The MSU basketball program breathed a sigh of relief and geared up for a season-long farewell tour that nearly produced a Big Ten championship.

"I really didn't make my final decision until I met with Coach the morning before the press conference," Respert said. "Sometimes, when people are about to retire, they kind of take the year off as kick-back time instead of being as intense as when they started.

"He told me, whether I left or not, he thought we were going to have a good team. And he said he was looking forward to getting started and ending his career on the right note. Those were the magic words for me."

The "Fire & Ice" tandem of Respert and Snow helped the Spartans to an overall record of 22-6 and rankings as high as No. 7 in the nation.

And with a publicity campaign Respert encouraged, the pair became linked as arguably the best backcourt in MSU history.

"Eric and I complemented each other so well," Respert said. "What helped us wasn't just what we did on the floor. It was what we did off the court, too. We clicked. We pushed each other as students as well as athletes."

Their squeaky clean reputations weren't even tarnished by hijinks few outsiders saw.

"One day, we were in the locker room getting ready for practice," Respert remembered. "You know how Jud's pants were always sagging down? Well, one of the guys put on Mike Peplowski's pants and ranted and raved around the locker room, hitting himself in the head. It was hilarious—until Jud walked in and caught us. We had to run about 20 extra minutes that day.

"Then, in the spring, the black fraternities had a picnic. Eric and I ran into a couple of friends, and one of them asked me if I drank. I said I didn't. So this guy gave me something and said it was fruit punch. I didn't think anything about it, though Eric was giggling. I just remember drinking it for about five minutes. . . . And that's all I remember. They tell me I was doing backflips and talking trash to parked cars."

Respert had opponents talking to themselves in 1994–95, capturing first-team All-America honors and being chosen as National Player of the Year by *The Sporting News* and the National Association of Basketball Coaches.

And that was after he represented his country in the Goodwill Games, with teammates like Damon Stoudamire of Arizona, Michael Finley of Wisconsin, and Alan Henderson of Indiana.

"It was a good experience," Respert said. "But I hated Russia. I think I lost 10 pounds. I was living off crackers and peanut butter the whole trip."

He lived off Snow's precision passes as a senior and led the league in scoring, though a loss to Weber State in the first round of the NCAA Tournament was a crash landing.

"We just ran out of gas," Respert said. "There was nothing left. We stayed so focused all year, got to that point and couldn't give any more. I think we were exhausted."

Respert became the Big Ten's all-time leading scorer in conference games and moved into second place overall behind Indiana's Calbert Cheaney.

But the one game that summed up his career was a heroic effort at Michigan before a CBS television audience.

He left the floor with a badly sprained ankle with 1:26 left in the first half after scoring just three points.

The question seemed to be: "How many weeks will he miss?"

And even someone as hard-boiled as Heathcote thought Respert was through for the day.

Suddenly, who should appear in the second-half layup line but No. 24.

He scored 30 points in a fabulous last 20 minutes, as the Spartans rallied for a 73-71 win that was needed psychologically as much as in the standings.

"Good players play," Michigan coach Steve Fisher said succinctly.

For Respert, it was a vindication of sorts—a realization that through his efforts, the spotlight shifted.

"That was the breakout game where people had to talk about both Michigan State and Michigan," Respert said. "That was what the whole university needed. It always seemed Michigan found a way to pull the big games out. That was a big game for us and couldn't have come at a better time."

For Spartan basketball, neither could Respert.

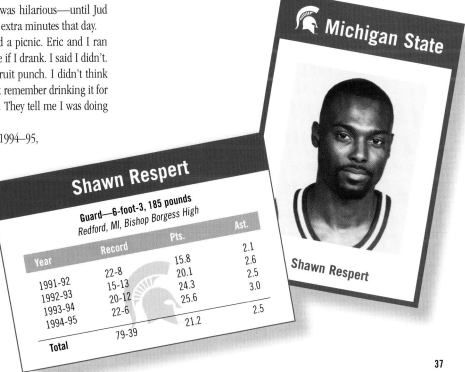

Michigan State

Shawn Respert

Guard—6-foot-3, 185 pounds
Redford, MI, Bishop Borgess High

Year	Record	Pts.	Ast.
1991-92	22-8	15.8	2.1
1992-93	15-13	20.1	2.6
1993-94	20-12	24.3	2.5
1994-95	22-6	25.6	3.0
Total	79-39	21.2	2.5

Chet Aubuchon

The original Michigan State basketball magician was nearly a full foot shorter and 70 pounds lighter than Earvin Johnson.

But Chet Aubuchon, "Houdini of the Hardwood," performed similar sleights-of-hand 40 years earlier in Demonstration Hall and Jenison Field House.

Seldom has a nickname been any more appropriate than for the Spartans' first All-American in the sport—an inspiration as a player and as a molder of young men for almost 30 years.

"When I first came to school as a student, the only guy I heard about was Chet Aubuchon," said ex-MSU coach Gus Ganakas. "All they talked about was his wizardry. Later, he became a very dear friend. He's the finest, most honest, most considerate person I've ever met."

Aubuchon came to campus from Gary, Indiana, in 1937 at the urging of Spartan Athletic Director Ralph Young, a native of nearby Crown Point, Indiana.

Since a Crown Point team had just won the Indiana AAU basketball championship in back-to-back years, Young invited its three stars—Aubuchon, Max Hindman and Bob Phillips—to visit MSU.

"The Gary Gang," as they'd soon become known, gave everyone a hint of things to come in an impromptu scrimmage against the Spartan varsity.

"Some guys were practicing in old Dem Hall," Aubuchon said. "They asked if we'd like to play them and had some extra uniforms handy. We thought it might be fun. And it was really fun. . . . We beat the socks off them."

Aubuchon couldn't remember the first time a sportswriter switched from "Li'l Aubie" to "Houdini" in a story.

But the headlines started early in his career and have continued for 60 years, through his 1998 induction into the Indiana Basketball Hall of Fame:

"Aubuchon Puts on Show in Victory; Soph Guard leads State Team in Neat Win," said *The State Journal* in December 1938.

"Aubuchon Shines in Rough-Tumble Fray; Gary Gang Clicks," screamed the *Detroit Free Press* in January 1940.

"Hardwood Houdini Proves Size Isn't Everything in Basketball," said a Newspaper Enterprise Association feature story in February 1940.

The New York Times, Chicago Tribune, Jersey City Journal, Omaha World-Herald, South Bend Tribune, Milwaukee Journal and *Tucson Times* all profiled Aubuchon's exploits.

And when MSC traveled to New York's Madison Square Garden for a game against Long Island, the game program featured a cartoon sketch and a glowing description:

"There isn't a trickier ballhandler and passer playing college basketball. He's almost a wizard when he gets his hands on that ball, and his ability to pass when off-balance and in unexpected directions is a crowd-pleaser. He has a very deceptive dribble, bouncing the ball high, and will frequently carry it the length of the floor through opposing players."

If that sounds like a larger point guard who'd lead the Spartans to an NCAA title, the tribute was meant for a 5-foot-9, 137-pounder with the peripheral vision of Johnson, Bob Cousy or Pete Maravich.

"I could always fake people out," Aubuchon said. "I'd practiced the footwork so many times. It was 'bing, bing, bing' and another basket."

When no teammate was open, No. 3 often showed why he led Ben Van Alstyne's ballclub in scoring in 1939-40.

Against Notre Dame, that included roughly a 75-footer—a shot, not a one-handed heave—that connected from the opposite foul line at the end of the first half.

"That was something I'd practiced for a long, long time," Aubuchon said. "And when I shot that baby, in she went. Even Coach got a little excited. He said, 'I don't know how you got it up there. I'm just glad you did.'"

With work-study aid, he also dug test holes for the Farm Lane Bridge, paced off the steps for Mary Mayo Hall with MSC President Robert Shaw, laid the cement for the first tennis courts and planted the trees near Ralph Young Field.

About the only job Aubuchon failed to complete was to persuade high school classmate Tom Harmon, a Heisman Trophy winner at Michigan, to join him in East Lansing.

But in the summer of 1940, before what was supposed to be his senior year, Aubuchon cut his finger in a campus electrical shop and developed a life-threatening infection.

"We're trying to save this boy's life," Van Alstyne said after massive blood tranfusions for lead poisoning. "We're not worrying about him playing basketball again."

Aubuchon spent nearly six months in three hospitals and was greeted at Lansing's Sparrow Hospital one morning by Michigan basketball captain Herb Brogan.

"He was one of first guys who came to see me," Aubuchon said. "I really appreciated that. He said, 'Hang in there. You're going to make it. Whatever you do, don't give up.'

"I told him, 'Hey, don't worry about that. I don't know what those words mean.'"

Aubuchon was determined to return, though most people figured his career was finished. And he did just that in 1941-42, serving as captain and lifting the Spartans to a 15-6 mark.

"Coach, I did my best," one frustrated opponent said. "But that guy seems to be traveling in two directions.'

After helping the College All-Stars beat the Harlem Globetrotters 63-39, Aubuchon traveled through the South Pacific for 27 months of active duty as a Naval officer.

After his release, he played with the Detroit Falcons in the first season of the National Basketball Association—six years after he was told he'd never play again.

Aubuchon returned to MSC in 1949 and served one season as an assistant basketball coach under Al Kircher.

SPARTAN ACE

CHET AUBUCHON

MICHIGAN STATE'S GREAT 140-POUND GUARD AND ALL-AMERICA CANDIDATE.

A MASTER DRIBBLER AND BALL HANDLER, AUBUCHON IS PROOF THAT THERE STILL IS A PLACE IN BASKETBALL FOR A LITTLE MAN....

(Excerpt from a program printed for a game between Michigan State and Long Island University at Madison Square Garden, January 27, 1940.)

CHESTER AUBUCHON: There isn't a trickier ball handler and passer playing college basketball. He's almost a wizard when he gets his hands on that ball, and his ability to pass when off balance and in unexpected directions is a crowd pleaser. Aubuchon has a very deceptive dribble, bouncing the ball high and frequently will carry it the length of the floor through opposing players. He is only 5 ft. 10 in. tall and weighs but 138 pounds. "O-Bee," his nickname, is not only an excellent feeder, but he scored 90 points on his own account. A dead pan. A fine softball pitcher in the summer months.

Then, he taught and coached in Owosso, where he met his wife, and worked in Holly before settling in Port Huron.

Aubuchon spent 22 years at Port Huron Junior College, which became St. Clair County Community College during his stints as basketball coach, athletic director and dean of men.

There, he earned one more nickname, "Port Huron's oldest teenager."

"He helped more students with grants, loans, the draft and other things than anyone else at the college," said former student government president Chris Cole. "And he never asked for anything, not even a free ticket to a college function."

Aubuchon was inducted into the Port Huron Sports Hall of Fame in 1964 and the MSU Hall in 1996 and received the key to the city of Port Huron.

"I don't know why they did that for me," said Aubuchon, age 81, by phone from his retirement home in Ruskin, Florida. "My wife doesn't know either. . . . She won't give me the key to the place we live in today."

Janet Aubuchon needs to keep her eye on that key. If her husband pretends it's a basketball and plays "Houdini" again, she'll never find it.

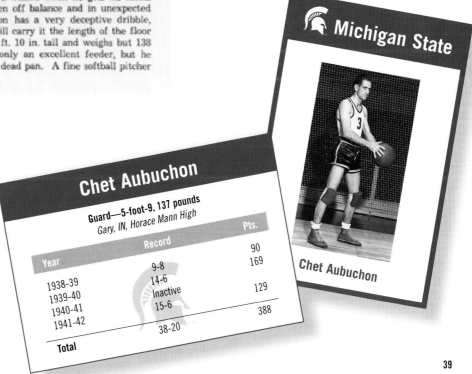

Michigan State

Chet Aubuchon

Chet Aubuchon

Guard—5-foot-9, 137 pounds
Gary, IN, Horace Mann High

Year	Record	Pts.
1938-39	9-8	90
1939-40	14-6	169
1940-41	Inactive	
1941-42	15-6	129
Total	38-20	388

Rickey Ayala & Al Ferrari

Always playing bigger than his height, Ayala skies for a hook shot.

The acrobatic Ferrari penetrates and hovers in the air for a jump shot.

a year ahead of me and thought I could play in college. I think he liked me because I always gave him the ball."

All Ferrari needed was for someone to give him a chance. And Newell did that, with Ayala's help.

"Our coach, Henry Goldman, wrote Pete a letter," Ayala said. "It said, 'You already have Rickey. You ought to take a look at Al.' So Pete said, 'Do you know an Al Ferrari?' I said, 'Sure, I played with him.' And I set up a meeting for lunch for the four of us at the Paramount Hotel.

"I had to come back by automobile and said, 'Why don't you come back with me, Al, and look at the campus?' When we got there, I took him right to Jenison. We wound up in a pickup game against Leif Carlson and Erik Furseth, a couple of real hatchet men.

"The funny thing was, Al's recollection of me was that I was a star. He kept feeding me the ball. Finally, I said, 'I'm going to give you the ball.' He said, 'Is it okay if I fight back?' After that, he tore them up."

"He and Al just killed them," said Newell, who couldn't believe what he was seeing. "Al was such an acrobatic player—almost like a Jordan in a sense, in terms of pure athleticism."

Still, Newell wasn't quite sure what to do with the 6-3 Ferrari—a sleek, high-speed model—as a sophomore.

"Pete had never seen me play in high school," Ferrari said. "And I was wild in those days. I wore a bandana and was real cocky. Let's just say I was a little unusual.

"But I really had no other option than Michigan State. And I think that coaches strike helped me in a way. Instead of just playing for my high school team, I played eight or nine hours a day in different leagues."

Coming off the bench, Ferrari scored 22 points in an 80-63 upset of top-ranked Kansas State in 1952, led the team with 16.0 points per game and

T hey wanted to be a part of it, from New York, N.Y.

And because of Rickey Ayala and Al Ferrari, Michigan State basketball was a lot more fun for everyone in the 1950s.

Both played at Brooklyn Technical High and appreciated each other's talents.

But neither would have made it to MSC if not for Ayala's persistence—first, in convincing new coach Pete Newell that he could be admitted; then, in persuading Ferrari to join him in East Lansing.

At barely 5-foot-6, few Spartans have made a bigger contribution than the program's first African-American player.

"Rickey wanted to come with me because he knew I played small guards," said Newell, whose San Francisco team with 5-9 Rene Herrerias ruled the 1949 NIT in Madison Square Garden.

"But when he showed me his transcript, I said, 'You couldn't get in a reformatory with this!' He said, 'If I get in, will you let me come out for basketball?' He didn't want a scholarship. And I said, 'If you can get in with this, you can do all the recruiting for me.'

"Sure enough, when school started, Rickey showed up. To this day, I don't know how he got in. I didn't know anyone in admissions who could've helped him."

Ayala knew Ferrari, whose senior season at Brooklyn Tech, an all-boys school with 6,600 students, had been cancelled by a city-wide coaches' strike.

"I only played one year of high school ball," Ferrari said. "But Rickey was

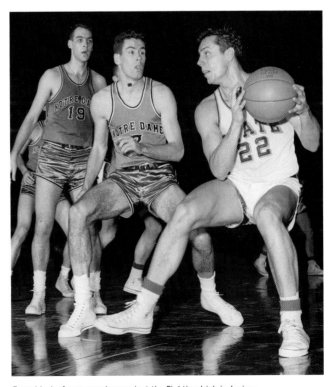

Ferrari looks for an opening against the Fighting Irish in Jenison.

Ayala, the school's first African-American player, prepares for a free throw.

Ayala was always into something. And Ferrari wasn't far behind.

"You never knew when Rickey was running a scam on somebody," Newell said. "He would get the Indiana guys and play them for money. I think Rickey financed his first two years of school with those two-on-two games. He was so damn smart—a coach on the court but smarter than most of us."

Newell was no dummy, either, and devised a strategy to let teams try to post Ayala, a great defender and the team's third-best rebounder. Once, Newell even told Ayala to let Minnesota score a basket. By the time the Golden Gophers learned it was a set-up, they had three players in new positions.

When Newell finally bribed and steered Ayala into a new major—hotel and restaurant management—Ayala had an unavoidable conflict with classes. That led to a failing grade in accounting, which wound up being his strong suit.

"They had this really ridiculous rule that you were ineligible if you flunked one class, regardless of your grade-point," said Ayala, who couldn't play winter term. "There was a misunderstanding. But it was my fault. And I regret it to this day. That team was the finest I ever played on."

It featured forward Julius McCoy and Ferrari, who was well on his way to a school-record 1,109 points, including 21 free throws in his final home game against Indiana, despite never being named first-team All-Big Ten.

"We called him 'Moose,'" Furseth said. "And when 'Moose' went to the hole, look out!"

When he went to various watering holes, Ferrari took a few young players with him.

"He was a street player and a tough guy who served me my first college beer," said guard Pat Wilson. "He'd throw down a few at a local pub, then go out the next night and score 30. He could really get up and down the court, even after some tough evenings. And his elbows were just vicious."

"Al was a player I inherited," said Forddy Anderson, his coach as a senior. "Talk about a plugger! He never stopped going. And he became one of the best racquetball players in the country, which didn't surprise me."

He also became a six-year NBA veteran with the St. Louis Hawks and the Chicago Zephyrs, before a 35-year career with Lincoln National Life.

Meanwhile, Ayala spent two years with the Harlem Globetrotters, then began a distinguished career that included 32 years as the CEO of two Detroit hospitals.

In 1997, Ayala was honored with MSU basketball's Distinguished Alumnus Award—and with an unofficial designation as the school's best unpaid recruiter.

earned the first of three straight Spartan MVP awards.

"I remember the *State Journal* saying, 'Come see No. 1 Kansas State. . . . Oh, by the way, Michigan State might show up, too,'" Ayala said. "We showed up, all right! When Kansas State called time, they were down 11-1. It was Al's finest performance. No one could've guarded him that night except Jesus."

Ferrari wasn't the only player Ayala tried to attract to the program, with Duquesne great Sihugo Green ready to transfer until Newell said no.

"Si and I were like brothers in New York," Ayala said. "He came to visit during Christmas break and fell in love with the place. I brought him to practice, and Pete said, 'Oh, my God, you know Sihugo Green?' I said, 'Pete, I can get him.' But the kind of guy he was, Pete said, 'I can't do that to Dudey Moore,' the Duquesne coach. My only concern was to win."

"I said, 'Rickey, you can't do that,'" Newell remembered. "He said, 'I know. . . . But he could really help us.'"

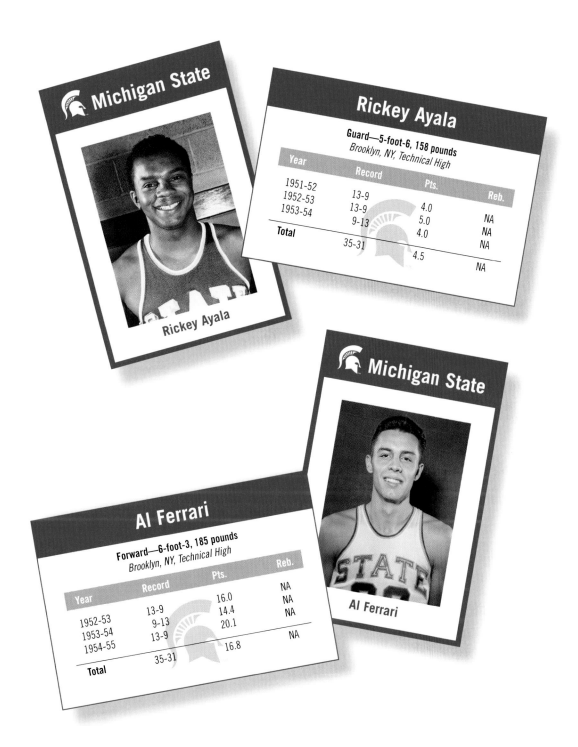

Michigan State

Rickey Ayala

Guard—5-foot-6, 158 pounds
Brooklyn, NY, Technical High

Year	Record	Pts.	Reb.
1951-52	13-9	4.0	NA
1952-53	13-9	5.0	NA
1953-54	9-13	4.0	NA
Total	35-31	4.5	NA

Rickey Ayala

Al Ferrari

Forward—6-foot-3, 185 pounds
Brooklyn, NY, Technical High

Year	Record	Pts.	Reb.
1952-53	13-9	16.0	NA
1953-54	9-13	14.4	NA
1954-55	13-9	20.1	NA
Total	35-31	16.8	NA

Michigan State

Al Ferrari

Julius McCoy

"Hooks" maneuvers inside and unleashes his offensive arsenal.

They called him "Hooks" because of his hands, not for one of the countless shots in an incredible offensive repertoire.

But several people could have given Julius McCoy another appropriate nickname—"The One Who Got Away."

The three-sport standout from Farrell, Pennsylvania, near Pittsburgh, got away from Penn State because of a coach's recruiting blunder.

He got away from so many defenders from 1953 to 1956 that he shattered almost every Michigan State game, season, and career scoring mark.

And to nearly everyone's loss, he got away from the NBA, instead becoming the all-time leading scorer of the Eastern Basketball Association.

"I just liked to make a good move and get the ball to the basket," McCoy said. "I never shot a lot of hooks. I was a forward, not a center. Most of my shots came from 17 feet or on drives to the basket."

He could have made those left-handed shots for the Nittany Lions, a Final Four team in 1954, if Spartan football assistant Duffy Daugherty hadn't been around.

McCoy, an All-State halfback, was so good the Pittsburgh Steelers tried to sign him after his senior year of high school.

But the Western Pennsylvania 100- and 220-yard dash champ loved basketball, too, and was one of the top offensive players in the nation in 1952.

"We won football and basketball championships, and I never knew which sport I wanted to play," McCoy said. "But Penn State said, 'We don't give a darn about basketball. We just want you for football.'"

Daugherty, who loved to recruit in his home state, took a different approach and convinced McCoy he cared about him as a person, not just a prospect.

"Duffy said, 'Whichever sport you choose, the most important thing to me is that you come to Michigan State,'" McCoy remembered. "At that very moment, I decided to do that."

When McCoy chose to play only basketball as a freshman and sophomore, no one could have been happier than Newell.

"Julius was an All-World basketball player in high school," Newell said. "He was the best kid I ever recruited, in terms of national reputation."

McCoy scored 18.6 points per game as a sophomore, the highest average in Newell's four seasons, and connected in every conceivable way, including a last-second free throw that beat Illinois.

"Julius possesses more natural ability as a scorer than any boy we've ever had," said assistant John Benington in 1953. "He has about as wide a variety of shots as you could ask for."

McCoy took off his glasses and tried contact lenses—and football—as a junior. But an ankle injury reduced his scoring average to 16.7 in the first season under Forddy Anderson.

"We could've been better the next two years if Pete hadn't left," McCoy said. "We all would've been better players. It wasn't that Forddy wasn't a good coach. But we wouldn't have had a such a huge transition."

The real McCoy returned with glasses as a senior and drew rave reviews, smashing Al Ferrari's school single-game scoring record of 35 points by double-digits.

"Seven Notre Dame firefighters tried in vain to put out the blaze but were forced back by the flames as McCoy poured 45 points through the hoop," wrote Lad Slingerlend of the *State Journal*.

In a memorable duel with Ohio State's Robin Freeman, McCoy was outscored 46-40 but had a steal and basket for the winning points—all that mattered to him.

"To win that game was the highlight of my career," McCoy said. "Robin was one of the greatest shooters ever to play the game. To match him that way and leave with a win was something I'll always be proud of."

McCoy also had 41 points in a victory over Michigan, one of five wins in his six games against the Wolverines.

"Michigan was always a grudge game," McCoy said. "We knew it would be a blood-and-guts, win-at-all-cost game. And we beat them five in a row."

Against players like the Wolverines' football-basketball star Ron Kramer, respect came slowly but was McCoy's to keep.

A man for all seasons, McCoy shows his form on the track.

Some still say McCoy's best sport would have been football.

"He's the real thing and his name is Julius," wrote George E. Van of the *Detroit Times*. "It's obvious he never had a rattle, or anything else, as a toy. He must have started with a basketball."

Whatever skills he started with, he kept under Anderson's leadership. For a coach who loved scoring, McCoy was almost an ideal player.

"I often said at clinics, 'Julius did everything wrong. He shot on the way down. He shot off-balance. And he had lousy fundamentals. . . . All he did was break every scoring record at Michigan State,'" Anderson said.

"I just let him go when he had the ball. I sure didn't spend any time teaching him how to shoot. He already knew how to score."

McCoy broke Ferrari's Spartan career mark by 268 points and finished with 1,377—still No. 11 on MSU's all-time list.

"Julius got all my shots when I left," Ferrari said. "He averaged almost 28 points a game. But he was a fabulous player."

He was a second- or third-team All-American on most respected lists in 1956, despite giving up several inches to many opponents at 6-foot-2.

"Height is no handicap," McCoy said. "If a person can play basketball, that's all that matters. The rest of it is a lot of bunk, as far as I'm concerned."

The Big Ten's No. 2 scorer played for Newell in the 1956 East–West All-Star Game in New York's Madison Square Garden.

And he had 17 points for the College All-Stars against the Harlem Globetrotters in Detroit's Olympia Stadium, as his team went a respectable 10-11.

McCoy was sought by the St. Louis Hawks but was drafted into the Army. When he re-entered civilian life in 1958, the Hawks had just won the NBA title and decided not to make any changes.

So McCoy signed with the EBA, now known as the CBA, and played 13 seasons, once scoring 27 free throws in a game.

He was the league's Rookie of the Year, a six-time All-Star and a member of the CBA's 50th-Anniversary All-Stars.

"One of the saddest things to me was that Julius never made it to the NBA," said Ferrari, who played six seasons in the pros. "He was so fast. And when he came to camp with the Hawks, I was really worried.

"But when he didn't make it with us, the Pistons wouldn't even give him a look. With only eight teams and 88 players in those days, it was tough to make it in the NBA."

Instead, McCoy has worked nearly 30 years for the Pennsylvania Department of Transportation—a grateful employer that has never let him get away.

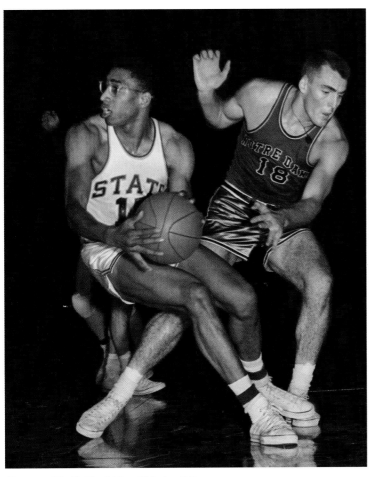

Glasses and the Fighting Irish couldn't stop McCoy.

Julius McCoy

Forward—6-foot-2, 190 pounds
Farrell, PA, High

Year	Record	Pts.	Reb.
1953-54	9-13	18.6	NA
1954-55	13-9	16.7	NA
1955-56	13-9	27.2	10.0
Total	35-31	20.9	NA

Michigan State

Julius McCoy

Horace Walker

Walker crashes the boards and pulls down another rebound against Minnesota.

With help from trainer Gayle Robinson, Walker recovers from an apparent injury.

A hands-on approach to life never hurts when those hands are as strong as our hearts and our minds.

And no one in the history of Michigan State basketball has been stronger in those areas than Horace Walker.

As a forward and center for the Spartans from 1957 to 1960, he was a rebounding python. As an alumnus, he has given back to his school and his conference with the gift of precious time. And as a lifelong learner, he has been a diligent student long after he quit being an athlete.

Walker's career began in Chester, Pennsylvania, not far from Philadelphia, and brought him to East Lansing in 1956. A part of him has never left.

"I left Pennsylvania because I wanted to establish my own identity," Walker said. "Julius McCoy had played at Michigan State. And I knew he was somewhat of a legend. But he was from the opposite side of the state."

Walker was on the opposite side of the spectrum from most Spartan athletes. On an early sports information questionnaire, he listed his hobbies as art, music, and sports writing.

"I painted quite a bit in high school," said the 6-foot-3, 210-pounder. "It was hard to do at Michigan State. But I picked that up again later on.

"And I didn't follow up on the sports writing. I was the sports editor in high school. But when I got to college, I thought I could conquer the world. I saw coaches and writers weren't making a dime. . . . And I think that's still true for one of those groups."

Walker walks above the basket to snare a loose ball in Jenison.

Sharp guy, that Walker. And he was worth writing about from his first days of practice, when he embarrassed MSU coach Forddy Anderson.

"When the freshmen would arrive each year, I'd take them upstairs in Jenison for demonstrations," Anderson said. "When Horace was guarding me on a drive, I took a quick first step and went right around him. I thought to myself, 'Geez, this guy needs to work on his footwork!' When I went around him for another layup, he swatted that ball into the 10th row."

The basketball skills came easy. But after playing the first eight games as a sophomore, he was sidelined by a natural science course. In the days when one failing grade meant ineligibility, he threw up an academic airball.

"Those were different times academically," Walker said. "We didn't have copying machines in the library. All our notes were on 3x5 cards."

He had plenty of time to take those notes as the Spartans went 9-5 without him in the winter of 1958 to finish 16-6. By the time practice began that fall, Walker was on his way to excellence in the classroom and on the court.

"Coming off the bench, Horace nearly tied John Green in rebounding, which was unbelievable," Anderson said. "He and John just decided who'd get each rebound. It was nice to know the opposition was only going to get one shot."

"Playing with Johnny Green was a lot of fun," he said of a 19-4 season and the school's first outright Big Ten title. "I've never seen anyone with as much desire to excel. To be a great rebounder, you have to want to be a rebounder. We used to tell the guards, 'Just shoot and we'll get it!'"

Walker averaged 13.3 points and 13.5 rebounds as a junior—a tease of what was to come the next year with Green in the NBA and every ball suddenly available.

Though the Spartans dropped their last five games and fell to 10-11, Walker had one of the finest individual seasons in school history with 22.6 points and 17.7 rebounds per game, plus 79.8 percent accuracy at the line.

"Pound-for-pound and inch-for-inch, Walker was just as good a ballplayer as Green," said Anderson, who called Walker "the best player I ever coached" in 1960. "And as fabulous as John was, I'm not sure Horace wasn't a better rebounder."

He set a Big Ten mark with 18.3 rebounds per game in league play—a record 39 years later. And 28 rebounds against Iowa's Don Nelson, one of his five 20-20 performances, is still the MSU standard and the league's sixth-highest total.

"When he went for the ball, no one ever took it away from him," Anderson said. "He had a great nose for the ball. He wasn't big. But he had perfect timing and the strongest hands of anyone I've seen.

"We used to warm up with pushups. And Horace would do pushups with his fingertips, not his hands. Then, one-by-one, he'd go from four to three to two and finally do 10 pushups with just his thumbs!"

Walker said he couldn't recall those thumbs-only exercises but would often use two fingers to make calisthenics more of a challenge.

The toughest test for an undersized center was a matchup with Indiana's 6-11 Walt Bellamy. But Walker made that a mismatch with an amazing effort—29 points and 26 rebounds.

"I've never seen anyone work harder for position," said Spartan assistant coach Bruce Fossum, later the school's longtime men's golf coach. "Once, when Bellamy went up, Horace stuffed him and pinned the ball on the board. You could just see Bellamy's hands peel off the ball."

"He was the toughest I faced," Walker said. "He had tremendous size. But he didn't know how to use it yet. I think he learned that the day I graduated."

In a 31-point win over Michigan, the biggest MSU blowout in the series, Walker sent a message of his own with 24 points and 24 rebounds.

"Every Michigan game was intense," he said. "We were still the little-sister institution and had to prove ourselves to people in Ann Arbor. Plus, they were notorious for having three or four football guys on the roster."

Walker had 30 points and 20 rebounds against Illinois, 24 and 23 against Minnesota and 27 and 16 in a near-stunner of NCAA champ-to-be Ohio State.

"They had the great Jerry Lucas, John Havlicek and a substitute by the name of Bobby Knight," Anderson said. "We had a one-point lead in Jenison. And Lucas scored the winning basket in the closing seconds."

After earning All-America honors and a tryout invitation for the 1960 U.S. Olympic team, Walker was the 17th overall pick and the third-round choice of the St. Louis Hawks.

During a contract dispute, he played for the Denver Truckers, then signed with Chicago of the NBA in 1961–62.

He ended his career with the Grand Rapids Tackers while completing his

master's degree at MSU and working on a doctorate at Wayne State.

Walker also earned a Program Management Development degree from Harvard after 12 hours of class seven days a week for 28 consecutive weeks.

"I always put a bigger hurdle in front of myself than the one I just cleared," he said. "I think that prof I had as a sophomore at Michigan State would be proud of me now. . . . I still have that natural science book."

After 21 years as an executive with Crocker and Wells Fargo banks, Walker walked away but continued to represent several NFL players.

He has worked on four continents and served on countless commissions, including the MSU Development Council and the Big Ten Advisory Committee.

"I get back at least three times a year," Walker said. "That place has a special meaning to me because of people I met in a great melting pot. Looking at records is like looking at a junior high yearbook. Who cares? . . . But people and relationships, that's what it was all about."

Michigan State

Horace Walker

Horace Walker

Forward/Center—6-foot-3, 210 pounds
Chester, PA, High

Year	Record	Pts.	Reb.
		3.8	4.4
1957-58	16-6	13.3	13.5
1958-59	19-4	22.6	17.7
1959-60	10-11		13.8
Total	45-21	15.6	

Ralph Simpson

Simpson and Ron Gutkowski (24) go after a loose ball.

His sophomore year was a good career for many college basketball players.

It was also the only varsity season for Michigan State star Ralph Simpson.

The 6-foot-5 guard from Detroit Pershing was the nation's No. 1-ranked high school player as a senior—something not even Earvin Johnson can claim.

In 1969–70, he averaged 29.0 points and 10.3 rebounds per game, was a unanimous All-Big Ten selection and gave every indication he would become the greatest Spartan ever.

But "a poor man's Oscar Robertson" was the first of eight children. And when an impoverished family called, Simpson signed a controversial contract with the Denver Rockets under the ABA's hardship rule.

The greatest hardship might have been the hole it left in the MSU program, as he went on to star in Denver for six years and to play four more years for four NBA teams after the pro leagues' merger.

"When you watched Ralph, you knew right away," remembered Spartan coach Gus Ganakas. "It wasn't like watching Terry Furlow or even Mike Robinson in high school. Ralph was mature."

He was also ineligible as a sophomore, as Ralph, Sr., a former Globetrotter, had his son moved to play for Will Robinson at Pershing.

As a junior on a team with basketball man-child Spencer Haywood, Michigan football stars Glen Doughty and Paul Seal and Tiger baseball player Marvin Lane, Simpson stole the show with a record 43 points in the 1967 Michigan Class A title game against Flint Central in Jenison Field House.

While working as a bellhop that summer at Kutscher's Country Club in the Catskill Mountains, he was spotted by legendary coach Joe Lapchick and whisked away for a three-week basketball tour of Europe.

After Simpson hit 12 of 14 shots and scored 26 points in the Dapper Dan Classic for seniors in Pittsburgh, he was the top prospect on so many lists it was Christmas in April for a neighborhood mail carrier.

Simpson blocks Dave Hart's layup, while Gutkowski shields Wolverine star Rudy Tomjanovich and Jim Gibbons (41) awaits a loose ball.

Simpson's pro basketball career included a stay with the Pistons.

"I don't know how many schools contacted me," Simpson said. "Some say it was as many as 300, But I wanted to play at home so my family could see me. It boiled down to Michigan State and Michigan. I just liked Mr. Benington."

John Benington was easy to like, though Simpson's coach had other ideas.

"His dad opted for Michigan State over my protests," said Robinson, who had sought the Spartan job when Benington was hired. "Michigan got on him later and never did catch up. Either school was all right, I guess. But I was more friendly with the Michigan coach, Dave Strack."

Simpson's father was a friend of ex-MSC guard Rickey Ayala, who had a hand in the Spartans' recruiting effort but never turned it into a fist.

"His father asked me, 'If he was your son, where would you send him?' " Ayala remembered. "I said, 'I'd send him to Harvard. There are more important things than basketball.' When I told John that, he said, 'Are you nuts? When I'm through with him, he'll never have to work another day in his life!'

"A finer young man than Ralph, you couldn't hope to meet. But John insisted we weren't going to bend any rules or do anything shady. He said, 'Rick, if we get the kid, great. If not, we'll all live through it.'"

Benington didn't live long enough to coach his greatest catch, dying of a massive heart attack before Simpson's sophomore year.

First-year assistant coach Matthew Aitch wasn't sure he would survive long, either, during a recruiting visit that took longer than expected.

"Ralph's mom had a barbecue joint in a real bad area," Aitch said. "Whenever I'd stop, I'd always make sure I could see my car out the window. One day, the only parking spot was where I could just see the back half of it. I was in the place about 45 minutes, and someone stole my battery."

Simpson signed with MSU to jump-start a sputtering program, then declined an invitation to be the only high school player at the 1968 U.S. Olympic Trials and perhaps co-star with Haywood in Mexico City.

In three games for an unbeaten Spartan freshman team, he had 46 points against Notre Dame, 42 against Michigan and 33 against Western Michigan. Even his pickup games drew 3,000 people.

As a sophomore, he saw the Broncos again and scored 42 on 19-for-25 shooting, while grabbing 16 rebounds. He made two all-tournament teams in December. And after just 11 games, "Super Ralph" was described as the best offensive player in MSU history.

"Even then, he was a lot like Oscar," said Robinson, a collegiate scout for the Detroit Pistons. "He had the same type of temperament and talent. Ralph could do just about anything."

"He had agility, strength and range on his shot," Ganakas said of the

195-pounder. "Developing our team around him was really a no-brainer."

Opposing coaches shared that sentiment and lined up with gushing tributes.

"He's a much better player than Cazzie Russell was as a sophomore," said Strack, who had just been replaced by Johnny Orr in Ann Arbor.

"I'd take him over Purdue's Rick Mount," said Minnesota's Bill Fitch.

The problems began when the Spartans lost two more games in one tournament than Simpson did in two years at Pershing—and when Ralph's father decided he should be an unpaid assistant.

"We lost a couple of games at the foul line, just the way we said we could," Ganakas said. "When I mentioned that again and asked the team, 'Where are more games lost than anywhere else?' Ralph got up and said, 'Right here at Michigan State, Coach.'

"Then, we were playing at Indiana, and I felt this tap on my shoulder during the game. It was Ralph's dad. He said, 'Gus! Gus! I want to talk to Ralph!' I said, 'Get outta here!' But it was a long walk to the locker room there. And I heard he cornered Ralph at halftime."

Ralph, Sr. was critical and domineering. His son was just the opposite and once complained, "How come my father gets to sit up there in the radio booth when no other parent does?"

Ganakas arranged a meeting with Ralph, Sr. in Brighton and said, "Ralph loves you. He seeks love from you. He doesn't need another coach. I'm the coach. And he can't have two of them."

From that day on, the wheels started turning to reunite Haywood, a hardship case after one great year at Detroit, with Simpson in the ABA. The emergence of junior guard Rudy Benjamin as a solid scorer at MSU didn't help.

When Ganakas heard the rumor at the 1970 Final Four that his star might be leaving, he called Simpson in and was told not to worry.

But in April, Ralph, Sr. had a heart attack and couldn't make child-support payments to his ex-wife and seven children 16-and-under. With no food in the house, there was only one thing to do.

While running Benington's old basketball camp at Crystal Mountain, Ganakas got the devastating news of Simpson's three-year, $1 million deal, with roughly $700,000 in deferred money.

Typically, Ganakas responded in a humanistic way few coaches could.

"Certainly, we'll miss him next year," he said. "But I don't hold anything against Ralph. How could he pass up the opportunity? . . . What the pros ought to do is sign all the players they think can help them. College basketball can stand on its own."

The NCAA wasn't as sure and asked for a boycott of the ABA. The league declared the contract invalid, meaning he couldn't play as a pro or a collegian, then relented after Simpson sued for $3 million.

Six months later, his mother was still receiving Aid to Dependent Children from the government. Simpson had a pink Cadillac he didn't even like. And Ralph, Sr. had a gold El Dorado.

"His father was a pivotal person in that situation," Robinson said. "Gus didn't really know the father. But he was a ne'er-do-well financially. The money meant more than anything else. I didn't think he was ready to leave. And I still don't! I tried to get him to stay. It almost wrecked a long relationship. But his daddy pushed him out the door."

Simpson averaged 20.4 points in six seasons in the ABA, then spent time with Detroit, Denver again, Philadelphia and New Jersey, never scoring the 100 points in a game Robinson once predicted.

After retiring, he had several brushes with the law in Colorado over personal and professional matters, including a failed marriage, a dog-racing venture and a credit counseling business that led to a sentence of 10 years probation.

Ganakas only knew the Simpson who nearly led the Big Ten in scoring—and the one who wrote him a long letter of apology four months after leaving.

Michigan State

Ralph Simpson

Ralph Simpson

Guard—6-foot-5, 198 pounds
Detroit, MI, Pershing High

Year	Record	Pts.	Reb.
1969-70	9-15	29.0	10.3
1970-71	Hardship with ABA		
Total	9-15	29.0	10.3

Mike Robinson

Robinson drives inside against the Hoosiers.

He was too small to be a big-time scorer, much less to lead the Big Ten in scoring twice.

But when the big kids told him "Beat it!" on the basketball court at Spain Junior High in Detroit, Mike Robinson found another hoop and beat the best defenders in the world—imaginary men.

By the time he grew—well, sort of—to all of 5-foot-11, 150 pounds, the Detroit Northeastern High senior was the second leading scorer in the city in 1970 behind another decent shooter, George Gervin.

Two years later, he was Michigan State's first conference scoring champion, the first of six winners in 10 years.

Two years after that, Robinson was MSU's top career scorer by 340 points and the winner of a Naismith Award as the nation's best player under 6-feet.

His work ethic hadn't changed. And the people who wouldn't let him play were nowhere in sight.

"I've known Mike since he was 12 years old," said Northeastern coach Robert Smith, the father of Spartan guard Kevin Smith. "He'd come to rec games with mud on his feet and a ball he used to play with outside in the snow.

"When the games were over for the night, Mike would try to con me into letting him have the key. Most times, I just ended up putting him out. And I hated to do it. He looked like a hurt little puppy."

When the "Big Dog," Glenn Robinson of Purdue, led the league in scoring in 1993, it had been 21 years since a first-year player had the highest point total. . . . There must be something about that name.

But before "Mike Rob" hit his first feathery jumper in Jenison Field House, he studied another guard who would score in bunches, 6-foot-3 Dave Bing of the Detroit Pistons.

"I saw he wasn't as tall as the guys who were guarding him a lot of times," Robinson said. "But he could still score over them. He gave me hope. I knew if I could perfect my shot, I could score over anyone."

When he was in junior high, he first caught the eye of MSU coach Gus Ganakas at a clinic in Detroit. And the Spartans never lost track of him.

Yet, Ganakas still wasn't sure what he had until well into Robinson's freshman season, when he averaged more than 34 points and was called for goaltending twice.

There was little doubt when Robinson had 25, 29, 20 and 32 points in his first four varsity games or when he ripped Michigan for 37 in a 96-92 triumph his sophomore year, when swingman Pat Miller added a career-high 26.

"He was so quiet and unassuming," said center Bill Kilgore. "But he loved the game as much as anyone. And he had the greatest jumper I've ever seen. He'd put it in one hand and drop the other one down. I still teach that shot today."

His hands weren't big enough to palm the ball. And Robinson said he would push off occasionally with his free hand, though it was never detected.

"I'd never seen a shot like that," said point guard Gary Ganakas. "They didn't have the 3-point line. But Mike could launch from anywhere. He was rock-hard, lightning quick and could really jump. He'd come out to 20 feet, hit a few, then backdoor you."

Robinson was fearless inside, could catch any pass and could have been an Anthony Carter–type wide receiver if he had switched sports.

But he wasn't a perfect player. As a shooting guard at every level, he never became a great ballhandler. And he was never selfish enough to satisfy his coach.

Always looking to score, Robinson is ready to pounce.

Robinson, the year's top player under 6-foot, meets UCLA legend John Wooden.

"He didn't shoot enough in the games," Ganakas said. "We kept telling him he should be shooting it 25 to 30 times a game."

Ganakas' son remembered a different attitude one day after practice.

"He told me, 'Let's play Around the World. I'll shoot first!'" Gary said. "He started in the corner and worked his way around. He missed a shot, chanced it and made it, then kept going all the way back. I never even got to shoot! He just had me there to rebound! When he made the last one, he ran in the locker room, laughing."

The 5-foot-5 Ganakas, half of the smallest backcourt in the country, helped Robinson win back-to-back scoring crowns in 1972–73 with well-timed passes. And with a different point guard in 1974, his production slipped.

But perhaps there were other reasons that kept him from becoming just the fifth three-time scoring champ in Big Ten history, joining John Schommer of Chicago from 1907-09, Don Schlundt of Indiana from 1953–55, Terry Dischinger of Purdue from 1960–62 and Rick Mount of the Boilermakers from 1968–70.

"One of the diseases of disappointment is jealousy," said Robinson after three straight 13-11 seasons. "Maybe I've been the victim of some of that. I've never felt the success of the season depended on winning the scoring championship.

"It was brought up in one of the early-season meetings that we couldn't win the Big Ten if I won the scoring crown. I don't know how that assertion was drawn. Being captain, I didn't want to cause dissension. But look at Michigan and Campy Russell."

Those who looked at Robinson saw a model of how an All-American, a three-time All-Big Ten pick and a three-year team MVP should carry himself.

"He loved to shoot the ball and did that as well as anyone," said guard Benny White. "But Mike fit right in with the crowd. He never considered himself a star. In terms of hype, he definitely wasn't."

A request for information by the World University Games selection committee asked about Dave Robinson, not Mike. And the *State Journal's* Fred Stabley, Jr. wrote, "Who is Mike Robinson? . . . Outside of the Midwest and the Big Ten, that's a very good question."

Bob Knight learned who Robinson was in his first season as the coach at Indiana, when a 36-point outburst beat the Hoosiers.

"Robinson is capable of getting 40 points in any game," said Michigan's

Johnny Orr, after No. 31 had done just that for a career-high at Northwestern. "He's that good. All you can do is hold down the number of shots he takes. That's the only defense against him."

"I was on campus two months and thought Mike Robinson never missed a shot," said guard Bob Champman. "He was one of the most phenomenal shooters in Michigan State history. He'd shoot and the ball would walk back to him, as if it were on a string. His rotation was that good."

He had a layup with :08 left in a 67-66 win at Minnesota and a three-point play on a putback with :04 showing in a 73-70 win over Northwestern in 1974.

But Robinson's shining moment came on February 2nd that year when he swished a 20-footer at the buzzer to beat Purdue on regional television.

"When people ask, 'Who was the best player you coached?' they figure I'm going to say, 'Ralph Simpson,'" Ganakas said of a 1970 All-American and 10-year pro. "But I only had Ralph one year. I had Mike three years and enjoyed that very, very much."

He was the MVP of the Kodak Classic and the Senior Bowl Tournament and scored 30 or more points 15 times before returning to campus to earn a master's degree and play in the Jenison farewell game in 1989.

"I think Jud Heathcote called me Methuselah," Robinson, then 37, said of a Biblical figure who lived 969 years. "I'm not sure about that. But I'm sure I want to give this a shot."

He always gave it his best one. And that shot was usually good, except in terms of the NBA.

In training camp with the Cleveland Cavaliers, Robinson earned a second look with a 40-point scrimmage against the veterans. But the Cavs couldn't keep two 5-11 guards and chose Foots Walker at the final cut.

The word was he was just too small. . . . Hadn't we heard that somewhere before?

Michigan State

Mike Robinson

Mike Robinson

Guard—5-foot-11, 150 pounds
Detroit, MI, Northeastern High

Year	Record	Pts.	Reb.
1971-72	13-11	24.7	3.0
1972-73	13-11	25.3	4.2
1973-74	13-11	22.4	2.9
Total	39-33	24.2	3.4

Terry Furlow

It's Furlow's world, as Iowa would soon discover in an MSU-record 50-point outburst.

Furlow slices down the lane and splits the Fighting Illini.

He wanted the ball. He wanted it all.

And when Terry "The Trigger" Furlow was right, there was nobody better.

The 6-foot-5 forward from Flint Northern High still holds the Big Ten record for points in a conference season with 588, a 32.7 average.

He was a two-time league scoring champ, a two-time All-Big Ten choice and an All-American his senior year.

But when fans think of Furlow, the magic and tragic number is 25. It was the jersey he wore and the range he had with a picturesque jump shot. It was also his age when he died in a car wreck on May 23, 1980.

"When people say my name, I want goodness to be associated with it," Furlow said. "I want them to say, 'He was a very good athlete. He was a nice gentleman. I liked him off the court as well as on the court.'"

Friends like Bob Chapman and Earvin Johnson liked him immensely. Foes, including those at MSU, saw a disturbing side.

"Terry and I go back to high school," Chapman said. "He hosted me on my recruiting visit and was a very, very dear friend. If Terry liked you, you knew it. If he didn't, you knew that, too. He spoke his mind. And you always knew where Terry was coming from."

He came from total obscurity. In a program that won Michigan Class A titles in 1971–72, Furlow was a candle with as much heat as light.

"Terry had some problems," said Flint Northern coach Bill Frieder. "We couldn't seem to get them straightened out. So we kept him down on the reserve team his junior year. He changed a great deal between his junior and senior seasons, worked hard, set goals and became a tremendous asset."

Though Michigan-bound Wayman Britt got most of the attention and was a much better all-around player at that stage, Frieder would be the first to tell you Furlow had greater talent.

"We were recruiting Wayman quite hard," said MSU coach Gus Ganakas. "I couldn't even remember Terry. They had four guys who were all about the same size. Finally, I ran into him in the hall one day, and he introduced himself. I didn't figure he'd qualify academically.

Furlow rips a rebound away from Purdue's Michael White.

"Then, I got a call from Frieder. He asked if we had an interest in Terry and said he'd qualified. I said we'd take him and sent him a tender. We never even made a home visit. I didn't see him again until he enrolled in school and ran into me on the stairs in Jenison."

If Furlow didn't hit the ground running as a freshman, he learned enough to know he could dominate games and most social situations.

"He was our entertainment on the road that year," said 1972–73 captain Bill Kilgore. "He'd do this Johnny Cash imitation you couldn't believe. As a player, he was developing a great jump shot. But he had an attitude some people wouldn't condone."

The star of those teams was guard Mike Robinson. But Furlow thought he was a better shooter and nearly proved it by making 10 of his first 13 shots against Notre Dame, which had just ended UCLA's 88-game win streak.

Furlow's fingers cooled at the worst possible time—on an airball that gave the Fighting Irish just enough time to win at the buzzer.

"When I came here, I only knew one thing," he said. "I was going to try my best to be the best basketball player ever to come out of Michigan State. When I leave, I want people to say I was the best ever to play here. And I think people will."

That confidence made Furlow the great scorer he became and a lightning rod for criticism, both deserved and unjustified.

"His junior year, he wanted to win the Big Ten scoring title," said guard Benny White. "That was his mission. And that's what he did. Terry didn't think anybody could shoot better than he could."

"He used to call me 'Schoolboy,'" Chapman remembered. "We'd be on the road, and he'd say, 'Don't worry, Schoolboy. . . . I'm going to turn those boos into oohs!' And in most cases, he did. He made a lot more of those shots than he missed."

He never seemed to miss a chance for negative headlines. In roughly a year, there was the walkout and suspension before the Indiana game, a conference inquiry over a sucker punch to Illinois' Rick Schmidt, an assault on student trainer Don Kaverman and a scuffle with teammate Pete Davis.

Yet, there was an endearing side that made him popular with the media and a team captain. Ganakas still loves him. And so does a player who was "Little Fella," not "Magic," when he first saw Furlow work.

"Terry Furlow was the best Spartan nobody knew," Johnson said. "We'd play for two hours. Then, he'd say, 'C'mon, Little Fella! and would shoot 300 jumpers. After that, he'd play me one-on-one and beat me 15-0 every day.

"He'd say, 'That's all right. Sooner or later, you're going to score.' And sure enough, I scored three or four months later. But he'd protect me. I'd come to Jenison in ninth grade, and he'd say, 'No, no, Little Fella has got to play!' He came to my games in high school and made all the other players come, too."

If he made Ganakas' hair gray sooner than it would have been, a Furlow believer has forgiven him.

"A lot of people badmouth Terry," Ganakas said. "But he was dedicated to being the best player he could be. In those days, you never worried about drugs. And he never seemed to have any trouble with alcohol, just with his temper."

Certainly not with defenders. In a win over Michigan as a junior, he was 11-for-13 from the field and 11-for-11 at the line in outscoring Britt 33-6.

"I just made up my mind no one was going to score on me today, not Britt or anyone else," Furlow said. "He's an extremely good player. He's one of the guys who helped me win a state title as a senior in high school. But I was determined not to let him do anything on offense or defense today."

As a senior, after rejecting an offer from Memphis of the ABA, he set the MSU and Jenison marks with 50 points against Iowa on a Monday, had 48 three nights later at Northwestern and hit Ohio State for 42 more that Saturday.

His 18-for-29, 14-for-15 work against the Hawkeyes is still on the mind of their coach at the time, Lute Olson.

"That was one of the most awesome displays of shooting I've ever seen," Olson said. "Whatever he threw up went in. After he hit 50, he came to the bench and shook my hand. Some people thought he was rubbing it in. But that wasn't it."

Furlow had a poster of Muhammad Ali in his locker. And Jack Berry of the *The Detroit News* wrote, "There was Furlow, floating like a butterfly, stinging like a bee, stinging like no Spartan shooter in history."

He definitely impressed NBA scout Jerry Krause, who could open a jewelry shop with his rings as general manager of the Chicago Bulls.

"He's a great college player, and I can envision him being even better as a pro because he won't be counted on to do everything," Krause said.

It didn't turn out that way. Furlow was a first-round draft pick of Philadelphia and a roommate of Julius Erving. But he soon wound up in Cleveland, Atlanta, and Utah.

He loved Atlanta and made it his home, but died in Linndale, Ohio, near Cleveland, when his car left I-71 at 3:10 a.m. and hit a utility pole. There were three open beer cans nearby and Valium and cocaine in his bloodstream.

"I was shocked," White said. "If you knew Terry, he loved himself and loved his body. He was always looking in the mirror. But he also loved people. He was around the wrong ones. And once you're in that lane, it's hard to jump back. That's why I think he took his own life."

"Because of what happened, people have never given Terry his due respect," Johnson said. "He was the Big Ten's leading scorer when the league was as tough as it has ever been, when two teams played for the national title. And he wore that letterman's jacket with as much pride as anyone has. He loved being a Spartan. . . . I wish we would honor him. He deserves that."

Terry Furlow

Forward—6-foot-5, 190 pounds
Flint, MI, Northern High

Year	Record	Pts.	Reb.
1972-73	13-11	5.7	3.4
1973-74	13-11	14.1	7.1
1974-75	17-9	20.4	6.8
1975-76	14-13	29.4	7.7
Total	57-44	17.8	6.3

Michigan State

Terry Furlow

Jay Vincent

Vincent poses matchup problems for every team, not just the Hoosiers.

Before he was ever "Big Daddy," he was a big brother. But he was just as big a pain for opponents in high school, college, and professional basketball over a span of 21 seasons.

Though Jay Fletcher Vincent's name will always be linked with Earvin Johnson's, his accomplishments should stand on their own—and stand much taller than he was.

At a shade under 6-foot-8 and roughly 240 pounds, all he did at Michigan State was start at center on back-to-back Big Ten championship teams, lead the league in scoring twice, edge Indiana's Isiah Thomas for the conference coaches' MVP award and leave as the school's No. 2 all-time scorer.

Yet, it's not quite fair to say he left. He was just away on a business trip—for 14 years.

After three seasons at Lansing Eastern High and four at MSU, Vincent spent a decade in the NBA and four years in Italy, then came home for good.

"I can't leave this place," said the Mason resident and Mid-Michigan businessman. "It's a nice place to raise a family. And for me, it's where everything started."

Vincent began competing against Johnson in third grade in a cross-city rivalry that spread to Walter French and Dwight Rich junior highs, then to Eastern and Lansing Everett.

"Sometimes I wish one of us hadn't grown up here," Johnson said. "Then, Jay would've gotten the credit he deserved. Growing up, we were good friends—as we are now. But I played against Jay a lot more than I wanted to."

"I used to say, 'Jay, it's better for Magic to be here,'" Vincent said. "He could have 30 points and 12 assists, while I'd have 40 points and 12 rebounds. Somehow, he'd always get the headlines. But that made me tougher."

So did his coach at Eastern, the legendary Paul Cook.

"Coach Cook was my first ear-yanker," Vincent said. "He'd say, 'Jay! Jay! . . . You can't do that!' I'd never had a coach who yelled. I said, 'It's just a game. I'll quit!' But all the skills and fundamentals I developed, I owe to him and my junior high coach, Clyde Ethington."

Cook's teams ranked with the best in the state but never made it out of their Class A district, losing three straight years to Everett in games that could have been quarterfinals or better.

"That was a shame," Johnson said. "Their teams were good enough to win the state title a lot of other years, no question."

The Quakers did beat the Vikings in a regular-season classic in a packed Jenison Field House.

But Johnson had his pick of colleges. Vincent wasn't even the No. 2 prospect in the state, trailing Birmingham Brother Rice guard Kevin Smith, who would join him in East Lansing after a transfer from Detroit.

"I considered Michigan and visited Minnesota," Vincent said. "I liked Minnesota. But it was a long way from home. It was five hours by air from home vs. five minutes. I thought Michigan would take me if Magic came. If not, I wouldn't have been surprised if they never called again."

While Johnson was playing in the Albert Schweitzer Games in Germany, Vincent made a commitment and showed he was his own man.

"Everyone thought I'd just follow Magic to Michigan State," he said. "I wanted my own identity. We'd talked about going to the same school many times. But I thought I better decide before Magic did."

Spartan coach Jud Heathcote didn't know what he was getting until a summer all-star game at Everett High, when Johnson and Vincent were invincible.

"Jay did things so easily," Heathcote said. "The end result was usually greater than what you saw. You'd watch him in a game, pick up the stat sheet, see he had 25 points and 10 rebounds and go, 'Wow! How'd he do that?'"

"No one noticed until our Michigan AAU team went to Boca Raton, Florida, and put on a show they'll never forget," Johnson said. "*Sports Illustrated* did a piece on us. And against people like Albert King and Kelly Tripucka, Jay averaged in the high 20s. No one could stop either one of us."

In his first game as a Spartan, Johnson struggled mightily against Central Michigan, only to have Vincent come off the bench and score 25 points.

"I never did anything flashy," Vincent said. "I might have dunked five times in my whole career. On a team with a flashy passer and a flashy dunker, I'd score my 20, and no one would notice. My baskets counted. But I was a

When Vincent commits to MSU, few see how important that day will be.

Soft hands and surprising grace let Vincent rule underneath.

lineman, and they were the running backs."

"Jay never got the respect he deserved," said Gregory Kelser, the dunker Vincent mentioned. "Once against Illinois, he really got hot. And Eddie Johnson hollered at his teammates, 'Would somebody guard that fat pig!' . . . It was the funniest thing I've ever heard."

Vincent was easy to take lightly anywhere but at a mandatory weigh-in.

"Jud always complained about my weight," he said. "To this day, when someone mentions a scale, I want to pick it up and throw it at him. But I didn't understand the importance of conditioning until my second or third year in the pros. I'd have been a much better player at 225."

Vincent might have needed more weight to whip centers like Syracuse's Roosevelt Bouie, Ohio State's Herb Williams, and Purdue's Joe Barry Carroll.

And in the 1978 Far West Classic, he felt right at home against Washington State's Stuart House, a top recruiting target when Heathcote arrived in 1976.

"Jay had the softest hands of anyone I ever coached—just great, great hands," Heathcote said. "As a junior and senior, people saw how good he could be—the second-best player ever from Lansing."

First came the greatest personal disappointment of Vincent's career—a national championship run while he was sidelined or severely restricted by a stress fracture in his foot.

"I thought that would be the one time I could showcase my talent," he said. "I wanted to let everyone know we were more than just Magic and Greg. It was very depressing and took me a long time to get over that."

Vincent hobbled through his junior season at 75 percent effectiveness and still led the league in scoring, earning an invitation to the Olympic Trials.

As a senior, with electrodes implanted in his foot to help fuse the bone, he was dubbed "The Bionic Ballplayer" by team orthopedist Herb Ross.

Vincent supplied another tag: "Back-to-back scoring king."

"People said, 'Don't be selfish,'" he remembered. "But Adrian Dantley said, 'Show me a player who's not selfish, and I'll show you a player who's not successful.' You have to be a little selfish to make it."

Vincent's production wasn't the problem. A lack of help made all the difference his last two years, as the Spartans slipped in the standings.

Even as the UPI conference MVP, he had to settle for second-team all-conference in the AP vote of the writers.

Vincent lasted until the 24th selection in the 1981 NBA Draft—the first choice of the second round by the Dallas Mavericks.

In a sensational rookie year, Vincent had 40 points against New York at the end of three quarters. And playing longer than anyone imagined, he averaged 15 points per game with six teams from 1981 to 1991.

"Jay Vincent is a velvet bull," said Seattle scout Dave Harshman, an MSU assistant in the championship years. "He's sneaky-strong and sneaky-quick."

There was nothing sneaky about his move to Italy, where he played another four years as a featured scorer.

"If you won, they'd give you the world," Vincent said. "If you lost, they'd run you over with their cars."

After owning record stores and more than 100 rental houses in Mid-Michigan, he started a successful home-inspection business, House Masters.

Perhaps that means an avid Putt-Putt player and a bowler who once had a 188 average can improve those skills.

"Bowling—that's one place not even Magic can touch me!" Vincent said. The other category where it's not even close is in being underappreciated.

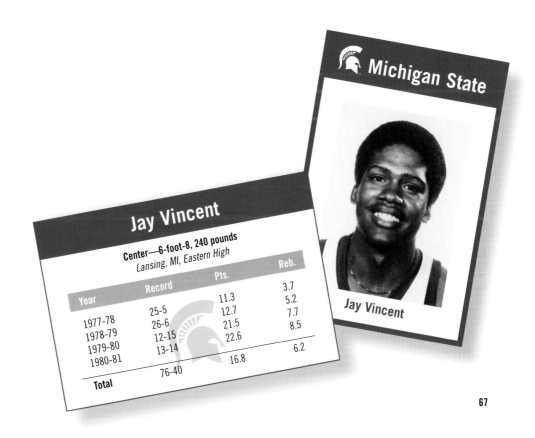

Michigan State

Jay Vincent

Center—6-foot-8, 240 pounds
Lansing, MI, Eastern High

Year	Record	Pts.	Reb.
1977-78	25-5	11.3	3.7
1978-79	26-6	12.7	5.2
1979-80	12-15	21.5	7.7
1980-81	13-14	22.6	8.5
Total	76-40	16.8	6.2

Jay Vincent

Sam Vincent

An explosive burst carries Vincent past Illinois' Anthony Welch.

Two great one-on-one players, Vincent and Michigan's Gary Grant, battle in Ann Arbor.

The Senior Night salute was for a three-time team MVP—and for an MVM, a Most Valuable Mom.

But Sam Vincent didn't mind sharing one of the longest, loudest ovations in Michigan State basketball history.

Despite his Big Ten scoring title and two more crowns for brother Jay, the most productive Vincent had to be Ella, who was largely responsible for 3,765 Spartan points from 1977 to 1985.

For eight straight seasons, her sons ranked among MSU's top three scorers, averaging 16.8 points and pacing their teams five times in a six-year span.

And that didn't begin to count the shots made inside the Vincent home.

"They'd put brown grocery sacks in the doorway and use anything they could get for a ball," Ella said. "I'd get mad. But I always knew where they were. And thank the Lord, I'd rather have them into something like that."

Her five sons—Johnny, Jesse, Joe, Jay and James, who became Sam by age 10 for his alleged resemblance to a cartoon character—spent more time on a neighborhood playground court in Lansing than anywhere else.

"I'll never forget my first dunk," Sam said. "I was in seventh grade. And we were playing outside at Walsh Park. My hand wasn't big enough. But I saw my friend, Craig Fields, could do it. I knew I was bigger than him."

"Sir Slam" inherited Jay's numbers—44 at home and 45 on the road—at Eastern High and led the Quakers to the 1980 Class A state title as a sky-walking 6-foot-2 forward.

The Vincents led Paul Cook's teams to a 124-21 record from 1974–77 and 1978–81 and set 19 individual scoring records, including Sam's 61-point masterpiece against Waverly High his senior year.

Shortly thereafter, he became a *Parade* All-American and the first recipient of Michigan's Mr. Basketball Award from the *Detroit Free Press*—by a 587-573 vote over Flint Central guard and Michigan signee Eric Turner.

But despite the pleas from Michigan's coaches to join Turner in a dream backcourt, Sam followed Jay a few miles east and became a Spartan.

"I was close to going to Michigan—very close," said a would-be theater education major who wasn't acting when he seemed to be torn. "Bill Frieder is a super person and a super recruiter. But I'm basically a homebody. And Jay thought I should go to MSU."

"I thought he might go somewhere else," Ella said. "Johnny went to Michigan and almost had Sam convinced. Coach Frieder came to our house at 6 a.m. to sign him that day. I couldn't tell him Sam wasn't signing."

When he finally agreed to trade in his Eastern blue-and-gold for the green-and-white, after MSU students had wooed him with banners, it was another gift from the Mid-Michigan area to Jud Heathcote's up-and-down program.

"To have Magic Johnson and the Vincent brothers hail from Lansing is something we can all be proud of," said Gus Ganakas, the Spartans' head coach for seven seasons and a broadcaster during Sam's career. "How many

Vincent salutes the crowd before his final Spartan home game, alongside his mother, Ella.

communities have three players like those three?"

If they had all played together, it would have been unfair to opponents.

"It would've been nice to play with Sammy a year," Jay said. "I'll admit I pushed him to Michigan State. And he had a great career there. But I still believe his teams should've done a little more with Kevin and Scott."

Kevin Smith and Kevin Willis, who didn't quite make the century's 25 best performers, and Scott Skiles, who did, were just a few of his teammates.

"When I came to Michigan State, a lot was made about us not getting along," Skiles said. "That was false. We always got along."

On the court, however, there was confusion about conflicting roles in the backcourt their first two seasons together.

"Sam was our leader," said disciple Darryl Johnson. "He wasn't a true point guard. But he had a hanging jumper than was impossible to stop. And going against him in practice for two years made me so much better."

With Johnson a freshman, Skiles a sophomore, Sam and Ken Johnson sophomores and Willis and Ben Tower seniors, the 1983–84 Spartans were picked eighth in the nation in *Sports Illustrated's* preseason preview.

But the most talented team of Heathcote's 19-year tenure lost seven straight games while Sam was sidelined with an ankle injury, then went 8-3 after his return.

"It was just the way the Lord wanted it," he said. "My injury was a positive in the long run. It helped me mature and gave me an opportunity to get my degree. I was thinking about turning pro. And almost everyone, except a Magic, needs a fourth year. I know I did."

That final season was Sam's time to shine and become a first-team All-American, as chosen by *The Sporting News.*

He would slip and slide, dip and glide and drive past stunned defenders—a sleek, expensive sports car just waiting for an open road.

"As far as I'm concerned, he's the best player in the Big Ten," Skiles said of an award that would go to Michigan junior Roy Tarpley in 1985. "No doubt, he's the best guard. I've never played with a guy as talented as Sam. I want him to win the Big Ten scoring title."

That he did with 23.7 points per game—23.0 for all 29 contests.

Sam's crowning moment was a 39-point gem in an 81-72 win at Purdue, when he had 25 in the second half and eight straight in overtime.

"It's a shame more people couldn't have seen the Purdue game," Heathcote said. "That individual performance was unbelievable."

"I've said ever since I came into this league that Sam Vincent is the best offensive guard in the Big Ten," said Purdue's Steve Reid. "And he's been exactly that the last three years."

As a repeat all-conference pick, Sam left as MSU's No. 3 all-time scorer.

"He's the best player in the Big Ten and one of the best guards I've seen in this league," said Indiana coach Bob Knight, after a 31-point eruption in a 68-58 Spartan win in Bloomington. "The thing I really like about him is he understands the flow of the game."

"You have to ask yourself, 'Who's better at the guards?'" Heathcote added. "Steve Alford at Indiana? He went 3-for-14 the other night. Bruce Douglas at Illinois? He has struggled all season. If you want to make a case for the Michigan guys, they haven't had nearly the stats Sam has. I think he should be a unanimous All-Big Ten pick, a shoo-in."

His final game was a 32-point effort in an NCAA Tournament first-round loss to Alabama–Birmingham, a 70-68 game that kept him from ever reaching 20 wins with the Spartans, though his No. 11 could easily be retired.

"As it turned out, those were four of the best years of my life," Sam said. "It was frustrating at first, not winning, because I've always thought of myself as a winner. And it took some time to adjust to Coach Heathcote—about three years, in fact. Now, I realize all that screaming is for your own benefit. If you can play for him, you'll have a good start in life."

His pro career started as a first-round pick of the Boston Celtics and provided him with a World Championship ring in 1986.

But after stints in Seattle, Chicago, Orlando, and Milwaukee, his career was cut short by an Achilles tendon tear.

He can always remember scoring 27 points in the first half of a game against Detroit in the 1988 NBA Playoffs, the Bulls' only win in that series.

And Sam is the only player to have been an NBA teammate of Larry Bird and Michael Jordan and one of Magic's men in pickup games in Jenison Field House.

He ran the Back to Basics Basketball Camp in Lansing and the AAU Youth Excel Program, then became a part-owner, general manager, and head coach of the Cape Town Kings in South Africa.

But Sam never had more fun than winning a televised game of HORSE from Jay with a 40-foot jumper or beating him in a trash-talking game of Putt-Putt.

Just putting a ball in a hole—those Vincent boys were at it again.

Michigan State

Sam Vincent

Sam Vincent

Guard—6-foot-2, 180 pounds
Lansing, MI, Eastern High

Year	Record	Pts.	Ast.
1981-82	12-16	11.7	2.0
1982-83	17-13	16.6	2.2
1983-84	16-12	15.6	3.0
1984-85	19-10	23.0	4.0
Total	64-51	16.8	2.8

Antonio Smith & Mateen Cleaves

MacKenzie Greer, 8, wears the shirt he designed to salute MSU's Flint foursome.

Cleaves runs the show as a passer, scorer and defender.

t's a nice combination—blue-collar guys in green jerseys.

Especially when they hail from a close-knit community like Flint, Michigan, where "work" has never been a four-letter word. Or when Antonio Smith, Morris Peterson, Mateen Cleaves, and Charlie Bell— "The Flintstones"—account for 56.1 percent of Michigan State's points, 49.1 percent of its rebounds and 70.6 percent of its assists, as in 1997–98.

"We joke around that it's a Flint thing," said Cleaves, the Big Ten's MVP and a first-team All-American as a sophomore. "But we're not really caught up in that. What it is now is a Michigan State thing. We're all here for the same reason—to win a championship."

It started with Phillip H. Wessels in 1905. Ever since, his city has sent more basketball lettermen to MSU than areas six times its size.

So what is it about Flint that makes it such a fertile area for athletes—and for Spartan coaches in all sports?

"In the neighborhoods we came from, you had to play sports or there was nothing else to do," Cleaves said. "Then, following guys like Glen Rice and Jeff Grayer and Andre Rison, we were brought up on basketball. Plus, there are so many gyms and playgrounds open."

"Flint has always been a working-class town," said WKAR radio's Earle Robinson, whose numbers at Southwestern High were surpassed by Bell—in his first game. "It's the only city with its own international games. It has very

good coaching. And it takes its sports very seriously. It's more important to win the city championship there than a state championship."

That's reflected in some one-word descriptions of the typical Flint player—Smith: "Warrior," Peterson: "Worker," and Cleaves: "Fearless."

Guard Anthony Mull, who grew up with all three, said, "If I told 'Tonio, Pete and Mateen that running through a brick wall would make their games better, they'd be running through every brick wall on campus."

But why have so many athletes from what was once "The Auto City" shown up to shine in East Lansing?

"It's one of those things where one success story leads to another," said Hall of Fame sportscaster Bob Reynolds, who began at WFDF radio and helped recruit football great Don Coleman for Biggie Munn. "They say, 'What the heck, I can do that, too!' And it means something in Flint to have played where their friends and family can all see them."

"There has definitely been an affinity for Michigan State," Robinson added. "Starting with Coleman and Leroy Bolden, it has reached out to the black athlete from Flint. And that's all it took. Flint guys will work for the rest. Look at the incredible work ethics Terry Furlow and Rison had."

Cleaves' father, Herb, was well aware of the city's relationship with MSU athletics and made that point early and often to an outstanding point guard.

"That had a lot to do with my decision in recruiting," said a two-time Class A All-State pick from Northern High. "For a lot of years, guys have come here from Flint and gotten a fair deal. You can see them now in the NBA and the NFL. So when people say Flint has been good to Michigan State, I say Michigan State has been good to Flint."

An excellent defender, Smith keeps Michigan's Robert Traylor on the perimeter.

The latest wave of mutual affection began in 1995, when Smith from Northern, then Peterson from Northwestern, signed with the Spartans. Cleaves followed in 1996, with Bell arriving the next year.

"I just liked Michigan State better," said Smith, who picked MSU over Minnesota, as did Peterson. "I never seriously considered Michigan. That name has never left me shell-shocked, the way it does some people."

In Smith's case, the primary influence was his mother, Debora, who raised four children, including football stars Fernando and Robaire and daughter Zaire, while working as a line operator at an auto supply factory.

"Antonio's mom is the enforcer," said Cleaves, who has known the Smiths since he was 9 years old. "When she'd come home, if I'd done something wrong over there, I'd hide under the bed. When she says 'No', it's 'No!'"

"She's like a friend, really," said Smith, the Big Ten's leading rebounder in 1997. "The sacrifices she has made for us mean so much to me. But she's a very disciplined person. The best advice she ever gave me was, 'Be polite to everyone. Give everyone respect.'"

Smith moves past the Buckeyes' Otis Winston and drives to the basket.

Smith got that message for keeps after the usual adolescent testing.

"I remember when he was in 11th grade and wasn't listening," his mother said. "He said he was tired of me telling him what to do. I straightened that out right away, believe me."

Today, when Smith sees fit to talk, even E.F. Hutton would listen.

As the Spartans' first sophomore co-captain since some guy named Johnson 19 years earlier, he was a rock and a rudder for Tom Izzo's program.

"We have four guys from Flint on this team," said senior co-captain Steve Polonowski. "But there's one definite leader. It only takes one grab from Tone. . . . Whatever you were doing, you're not doing it any more."

At close to 6-foot-8 and 250 pounds, Smith has a near-perfect physique and a nose for the basketball than can be almost Rodmanesque in its tenacity.

Shooting can still be a problem. But Smith is probably the team's top all-around defender. And with 697 rebounds, he could challenge Gregory Kelser's career record of 1,092 with a sensational senior season.

"Antonio has his rough edges," said MSU coach Tom Izzo, who made Smith his first recruit. "But he's more intelligent than anyone ever gives him credit for being. And he's such a great competitor."

As a senior at Northern, he led his team to a Class A title with a pair of wins in Breslin Center. The following year, with Cleaves and Robaire back, the favored Vikings never came close.

With Cleaves bothered by a variety of health concerns, Northern couldn't hope to repeat its back-to-back titles of 1971–72, even with a player who had embarrassed heralded Mike Bibby months before at the Nike Camp.

After considering Michigan and Cincinnati, Cleaves picked the Spartans, too. But first, he was a passenger in a near-catastrophic rollover accident at 5 a.m. on a recruiting visit to Ann Arbor and Detroit—the trigger for an investigation that eventually cost Wolverine coach Steve Fisher his job.

A resulting back problem and an inability to move comfortably for nearly a year spoiled what should have been a better season for Cleaves and MSU.

Still, only six true freshmen have ever scored more points in their debuts with the Spartans. And after shedding nearly 30 pounds and dedicating himself as few players have, Cleaves became an impact performer.

He had terrific second halves in wins against Illinois and Northwestern. But after playing a major role in an emotion-packed win over Michigan, he made some poor postgame decisions and was arrested on alcohol-related charges.

Though they were eventually reduced to one civil infraction punishable by fine, Cleaves' was suspended for the first half of the Wisconsin game and suffered a damaged reputation.

"That was the maddest I've ever been at him," said his mother, Fran. "But it's a real challenge at that age to be a role model. What I wish people would know is what a good kid he is and how much he does for people."

Smith goes up for a rebound against Illinois Jarrod Gee (32) and Brian Johnson.

Cleaves, an elementary education major, has an effervescent personality and can deliver a powerful message about right and wrong, as he did five days after his incident to a spellbound seventh-grade basketball team.

"He's capable of being an Academic All-American, too," said his mother and No. 1 fan. "He just gets a little lazy sometimes. But I can't tell you how glad I am he chose Michigan State, with all the people who care."

"The only problem is she's getting a little crazy with this basketball thing," Cleaves said. "She had four sons play football and basketball. And she didn't know anything about either of them. Suddenly, I come to the bench and she's standing up, pointing to her head to say, 'Play smarter!'"

If he does that and has the season he's capable of producing, Izzo's first marquee recruit can do more than lead the league in steals and assists again.

He can be the best player in the country and the leader of an NCAA championship team—like another fair MSU point guard.

But the way Earvin Johnson worked on his game and competed, perhaps we were all misled. Are we sure he wasn't originally from Flint?

Cleaves jumps for joy in a 1998 win over Princeton which meant a trip to the Sweet 16.

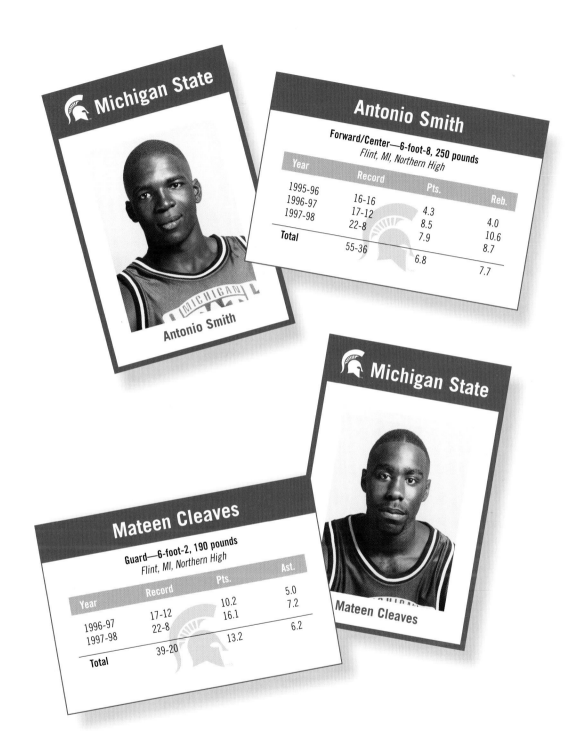

Michigan State

Antonio Smith

Antonio Smith

Forward/Center—6-foot-8, 250 pounds
Flint, MI, Northern High

Year	Record	Pts.	Reb.
1995-96	16-16	4.3	4.0
1996-97	17-12	8.5	10.6
1997-98	22-8	7.9	8.7
Total	55-36	6.8	7.7

Michigan State

Mateen Cleaves

Mateen Cleaves

Guard—6-foot-2, 190 pounds
Flint, MI, Northern High

Year	Record	Pts.	Ast.
1996-97	17-12	10.2	5.0
1997-98	22-8	16.1	7.2
Total	39-20	13.2	6.2

Jack Quiggle

Quiggle launches a jumper over Ohio State's Frank Howard.

There's nothing quite like high school basketball in hoops-crazed Indiana. And Jack Quiggle was the king of Hoosier Hysteria in 1953. As a junior center, he led South Bend Central to the most cherished of all state championships.

Four years later, he was a hero again as a junior guard at Michigan State—and a villain in Indiana after helping the Spartans beat the Hoosiers to earn a share of the Big Ten title and an NCAA Tournament bid.

But before he was named a first-team All-American by the Helms Foundation, Quiggle stumbled on January 23, 1957, then recovered in heroic fashion.

"After our fourth straight loss, I told the players I'd better not hear about anyone breaking training rules," said MSU coach Forddy Anderson. "At about 11 that night, some do-gooder, an alumni friend of ours, called and said Jack was at a party. Now, I was stuck and had to confront him."

"He got caught with some beer bottles," said center Chuck Bencie, Quiggle's roommate as a freshman and sophomore. "Forddy had to suspend him for a game. And I know that really bothered Jack."

It bothered Anderson, too, His team was 4-7 and looked nothing like the team that would come within one point of a spot in the NCAA final.

"The team wanted me to keep him on the roster," Anderson said. "But he wouldn't go to Minnesota, which put us in a real tough spot."

Since the Spartans were 0-8 in Williams Arena, a 72-59 upset was even more shocking without the team's best player.

"We went up there without Jack and played one of the greatest games we've ever played," Anderson said of a win that triggered a 10-game streak. "Larry Hedden had 25 points. And when we got back, Jack was waiting at the airport. I never had another problem with him."

Quiggle wrote the following letter that appeared in the *State Journal*:

"I want to take this opportunity to apologize to the student body, basketball team and coaching staff at Michigan State for my breaking training rules last week.

"I hope my experience will serve as a worthwhile lesson to athletes in the future. My one hope is to play the best basketball I know how and to be of help to our fine team."

He did just that the rest of the year, coming off the bench to score 21 points in a 19-point win over unbeaten Ohio State.

"Sinner Becomes Saint for Spartans," one headline screamed after Quiggle was carried off the court by his teammates.

"Jack Quiggle, a 19-year old junior from South Bend, came out of the penance pen to lead Michigan State to a startling upset," wrote *Detroit Times* Sports Editor Edgar Hayes.

Quiggle hit a 25-foot set shot with eight seconds left to beat Purdue 68-66 in West Lafayette, then had 26 in a win at Illinois.

But he was at his best against Indiana in a game his team had to have. MSU led 36-33 with 17:17 to play. When Quiggle scored 18 of his game-high 23 points in the next 9:57, the cushion grew to 64-41.

Quiggle beats two Purdue players to a loose ball as Julius McCoy looks on.

In the NCAA Tournament, he had 22 against Notre Dame and 20 against North Carolina, not counting a 40-footer just after the horn that would have won it.

And he was just as effective as a passer, often finding Green with lob passes from out-of-bounds for spectacular tip-ins and dunks.

"We complemented each other very well," Green said. "Without the ball, a guy inside can do nothing. Jack was as good a passer as there was."

"John was one of the first real jumpers, and Jack had super instincts as a lead guard," said forward Max Gonzenbach. "They had the first alley-oop dunk in the history of Jenison. People had never seen anything like it."

Injuries spoiled a shot with the Detroit Pistons. After a basketball tour of Latin America, Quiggle coached high school ball, then went into sales.

He died of cancer in California in 1989, shortly after the last game in Jenison.

Michigan State

Jack Quiggle

Guard—6-foot-3, 190 pounds
South Bend, IN, Central High

Year	Record	Pts.	Reb.
1955-56	13-9	7.3	5.6
1956-57	16-10	15.3	5.6
1957-58	16-6	11.5	5.3
Total	45-25	11.6	5.5

Jack Quiggle

Pete Gent

Gent and a friend bask in the glow of Beaumont Tower.

H e wrote the book on switching sports after a college career has ended, then told the sordid tale of professional football as few others have.

But before George Davis Gent played five years as an NFL receiver or wrote "North Dallas Forty" and five other books, he spent a lot of time in Jenison Field House—first leading Bangor High to a Michigan Class C basketball title, then pacing Michigan State in points for three straight seasons.

Gent was the straightest of arrows at MSU from 1960-64, then a rebel who'd cause the Cowboys as much discomfort as he suffered with three knee operations, serious back and rib injuries, a broken leg and a dislocated ankle, a broken thumb, dislocations of every finger and 12 broken noses.

"I was just on my way to Tampa for the second International Conference on Ethics in Sports—which may well be an oxymoron," he said. "College athletics is the same way. The players can get treated like rental cars. But I have to say I love Michigan State and am proud to have gone there."

He left with MSU's second-highest season and career point totals and with huge games—22 points in a win over Kansas as a junior and 34 vs. Bowling Green, 33 vs. Oklahoma, 31 vs. Notre Dame and 30 vs. Illinois as a senior.

"The last shot I took for Michigan State was a 30-foot jumper for a huge win at Ohio State," Gent said. "But I also remember having to guard Jerry Lucas, giving up five inches, and having John Havlicek guard me in '62."

"He was a little obnoxious at times," said teammate Stan Washington. "I remember he always had something to say and usually put his foot in his mouth. He was a funny guy, a real character."

His coaches remember the good things, despite two years of tough sledding.

"Pete Gent was a beautiful player and one of the first great white jumpers," said MSU coach Forddy Anderson. "He'd jump a foot higher than the defender when he shot. And he was a helluva passer. But I had no idea he was such a good writer. When I saw his book, I was really impressed."

"I recruited Pete at Bangor," said Spartan assistant Bruce Fossum of a player Michigan eyed for basketball and football. "Duffy Daugherty helped us some. But Pete had a great pair of hands and was a brilliant guy. I don't know what happened later. I just know I can't say enough good things about him."

Gent left with a 3.3 grade-point as an Honors College advertising major and received the Conference Medal of Honor from the Athletic Council.

But before he could take a job with Foote, Cone, and Belding in Chicago, assistant football coach Dan Peterson put Gent's name—and every Wolverine's—on a form letter the Cowboys had sent in search of possible defensive backs.

When Dallas scouting director Gil Brandt followed up with a phone call and Gent ran three 4.6 40's after not working out for a month, Brandt flew in with a choice of free-agent deals for a Baltimore Bullets' NBA draft pick.

"I plan on making the team," Gent said, accepting the smaller bonus of $500 and the larger salary of $11,000. "I'll have $500 more when I do."

When he returned to work on a master's degree after a so-so rookie season, Gent wasn't sure he liked pro football. Law school at SMU was another option.

From basketball to football to best-selling author.

"That's when I talked to John Hannah," Gent said of MSU's greatest president. "He said, 'You don't want to do that! You should be right back here.' . . . Sometimes I think, 'What if I'd done that?'"

Life in the fast lane, with a business deep in debt and plenty of drug use in Dallas, New York, California, and Mexico, made Gent see things differently.

Then came *North Dallas Forty*—the book and film exposé with Nick Nolte as Dallas receiver Phillip Elliot, a thinly veiled version of Gent.

"It's the finest piece of literature from the fun-and-games subculture," wrote *Detroit News* columnist Jerry Green of a critically acclaimed work.

After *Texas Celebrity Turkey Trot*, *The Franchise* and *The Conquering Heroes*, he moved back to Michigan and wrote *The Last Magic Summer*, a moving true story of a father and son—of a team and a dream.

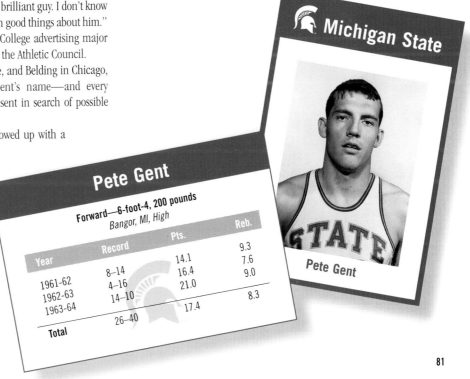

Michigan State

Pete Gent

Pete Gent

Forward—6-foot-4, 200 pounds
Bangor, MI, High

Year	Record	Pts.	Reb.
1961-62	8–14	14.1	9.3
1962-63	4–16	16.4	7.6
1963-64	14–10	21.0	9.0
Total	26–40	17.4	8.3

Stan Washington

Washington nearly hits his head on the rim against the Wildcats.

f Johnny Green wasn't Michigan State's No. 1 skywalker, another No. 24 could leap and change lightbulbs in the rafters at Jenison Field House.

At 6-foot-3 and 170 well-packed pounds, Stan Washington had springs in his legs and steel in his heart to intimidate rivals.

He had 34 points in a win over Wisconsin and outscored NCAA scoring leader Dave Schellhase 31-30 in a rout of Purdue in 1966. But he saved the best for last—23 points on 11-for-14 shooting from the field in an upset of Michigan.

"Stan was the smoothest sonuvabuck you've ever seen," said Forddy Anderson, his coach as a sophomore and junior. "He could jump almost

as high as John Green, grab that ball and jam it through the hoop."

Washington earned the nickname "Champ" at Detroit Northwestern High, which had just produced baseball players Willie Horton and Alex Johnson, track star Henry Carr, and football player Matt Snorton.

"There was a lot of city pride," said Washington, who used to dedicate free throws to family members and neighborhood friends. "More than anything, that's probably what motivated me in the early '60s. It was still hard for blacks to get into Big Ten schools."

When MSU decided it wanted Washington, it sent in the heavy artillery.

"I'd always loved Johnny Green, one of the first players I remember seeing," he said. "But until my senior year of high school, I didn't think

Washington leaps between Michigan's Cazzie Russell (33) and Oliver Darden.

"If we'd had one more guy, we would've won the Big Ten my senior year," Gent said. "Rebounding is timing, not size. And even as a sophomore, Stan had the kind of elevation that let him change his mind in the air. He'd give me a signal, take off from the corner and make some incredible dunks."

He averaged more than 10 rebounds per game each season and was fearless enough to challenge Ohio State's Dick Ricketts on Senior Night in Columbus, when he took a swing and nailed Curtis instead.

"They even had the governor there to honor their team," said then-assistant sports information director Nick Vista. "They needed a win to stay ahead of Michigan. And when Stan went at it, the fans booed unmercifully.

"But the Spartans pulled it out at the end and gave the Buckeyes their first home loss in 35 games. It was a very subdued ceremony. And Forddy, who'd just been tossed in the shower, came back to courtside for a radio interview."

Though MSU plunged the following season, Washington was the MVP with 21.3 points per game and set an MSU mark with 85.1 percent free throw accuracy.

He was a smart player and an All-Big Ten choice. Washington wouldn't just block shots. He'd rove and intercept them, with one snare against Archie Clark of Minnesota sparking a 20-point win in a surprising senior year.

That athleticism led to an offer to play defensive back for the NFL's St. Louis Cardinals. Instead, a fourth-round pick of the Los Angeles Lakers opted for pro basketball and almost made it with L.A., Detroit, and Indiana.

After three seasons in the minor leagues, Washington has worked for the Michigan Department of Corrections since 1972 and been assistant deputy warden in the Jackson cellblocks for more than 20 years.

Perhaps justice was done when his son, Saddi, starred at WMU and just earned his first shot at pro basketball. He wore No. 24, too.

I'd go to college. I couldn't believe Michigan State would recruit me.

"Earl Morrall of the Lions, Norm Masters of the Packers, and Horace Walker came and took me out to dinner. Western Michigan had been recruiting me, too. But when they sent those three to see me, wow, it was over."

"I saw him first down in Detroit," said assistant coach Bruce Fossum. "I said, 'Forddy, you've got to come see this guy! We've got to have him!' For a guy his size, he was lightning. He had something like a 40-inch vertical leap and could touch the top of the backboard."

Washington teamed with versatile Pete Gent as a sophomore, with forwards Bill Curtis and Marcus Sanders as a junior and with Curtis and center Matthew Aitch as a senior on teams that could always score.

"Stan was my roommate and never thought I was tough enough," Curtis said. "He used to try to toughen me up and pick on me. All we needed my first two years was a tough guy inside. If only Bubba Smith had come out..."

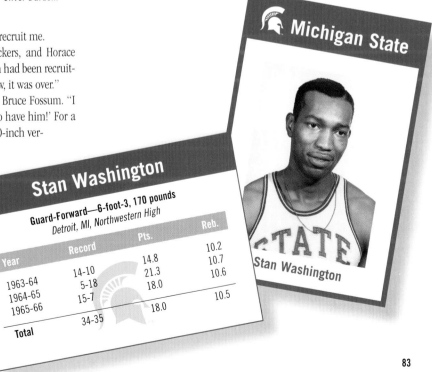

Stan Washington

Guard-Forward—6-foot-3, 170 pounds
Detroit, MI, Northwestern High

Year	Record	Pts.	Reb.
1963-64	14-10	14.8	10.2
1964-65	5-18	21.3	10.7
1965-66	15-7	18.0	10.6
Total	34-35	18.0	10.5

Michigan State

Stan Washington

Lee Lafayette

Lafayette wheels to the basket against the Wildcats.

He could have been a UCLA Bruin and a three-time national champion.

Instead, Lee Lafayette was a bear of a player for Michigan State in the late 1960s.

"The Tree," as the greatest player in Grand Rapids basketball history was known, had more than 60 major scholarship offers in 1965.

He met a young center named Lew Alcindor at a recruiting banquet at Michigan and nearly joined him in California in John Wooden's program.

He also considered the Wolverines and the Purdue Boilermakers—a perfect fit for a guy named Lafayette.

But a recruiting effort that started with Forddy Anderson's staff paid dividends when new coach John Benington signed his first great player at MSU.

Benington had asked Spartan captain Bill Curtis, another South High star, about the chances of landing Lafayette. When Curtis said, "Don't worry. I've got him," Benington said, "You'd better! Your scholarship depends on it."

So did the Spartans' chances for the conference co-title they won in 1967 and for respectabilty the next two years.

84

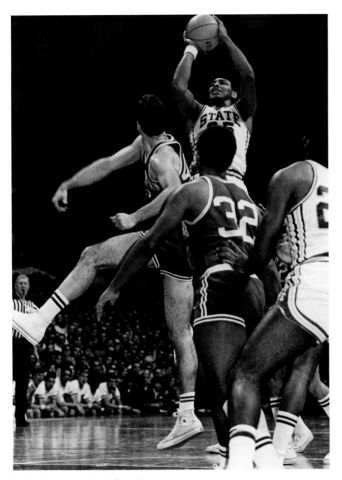

Lafayette goes over the defense to score.

against Iowa, then caught fire and led his team to victory, Benington said, "I told Lee the game was close enough. He could open up any time he wanted."

"He was a real jokester," Lafayette said. "But he sure ran me enough."

When Lafayette reported for his senior season at center at close to 230 pounds, he earned a new nickname from Benington—"Porky."

"We were eating before a game at Northwestern, and I wanted this piece of chocolate cake," Lafayette said. "He thought it would slow me down and said I'd have to pay for it myself. That's what I did and went out and scored 33 points. Before the next game, his wife baked me a chocolate cake."

That was when Michigan standout Rudy Tomjanovich, with a 27-point scoring average, came to East Lansing. Lafayette outscored him 14-5 and outrebounded him 16-8.

"Lee is the best defensive center in the Big Ten," Benington said. "He has the best concept of defense on our club and one of the best I've seen."

After leading his team in scoring and rebounding as a junior and center, the two-time Spartan MVP was named All-Big Ten and was a fourth-round pick of the San Francisco Warriors.

He signed with the ABA's Pittsburgh Pipers, was the last player cut and moved on to Europe, where he played three and a half seasons. After a year with the Grand Rapids Tackers, he completed his degree.

After he'd had his fill of basketball, Lafayette began a successful career in youth development and family and child services.

He was one of the few who could have his cake and eat it, too.

"It really didn't bother me to watch UCLA win all those titles," Lafayette said. "I only wish Michigan State had gone further. But I made my choice. And I have no regrets."

If he had gone to UCLA or most other schools, he would have been a forward or perhaps even a shooting guard. But at MSU, the 6-foot-6, 220-pounder wound up at center, staring up at players a lot shorter than Alcindor.

Lafayette had a sensational start as a sophomore forward with 20, 23, 15, 20, and 19 points in his first five games.

"Lee was my roommate," said center Matthew Aitch. "He'd been a high school All-American and was probably the best talent we had. We used a deliberate system and didn't look to score that much. But given a chance, Lee was just an offensive machine."

He certainly wasn't a hunter or a fisherman, as Aitch discovered when he nearly got shot by Lafayette on one excursion.

But when it came to shooting the basketball and playing at both ends of the court, few players were better than No. 35.

After Lafayette missed eight straight shots

Lee Lafayette
Forward/Center—6-foot-6, 220 pounds
Grand Rapids, MI, South High

Michigan State

Lee Lafayette

Year	Record	Pts.	Reb.
1966-67	16-7	14.8	9.7
1967-68	12-12	16.8	10.5
1968-69	11-12	18.7	10.3
Total	39-31	16.8	10.2

Bill Kilgore

Kilgore shows why he's the master of the hook shot.

Michigan State hasn't had many 7-footers—three, to be exact: Sten Feldreich, Kevin Willis and George Papadakos.

But in Bill Kilgore, the Spartans had a 6-7 center who played as big as anyone in the Big Ten.

Only one MSU basketball player, the great Johnny Green, had more rebounds in a span of three seasons than Kilgore's 814 from 1970 to 1973.

The River Rouge, Michigan, native is still No. 4 on the school's career rebounding list and No. 1 in a lot of ways with coaches and teammates.

"He's one of the most unselfish individuals I've ever encountered," said Gus Ganakas, who took over as head coach just as Kilgore came to campus. "I'd have liked to have five more just like him."

That might have made it difficult to score from the perimeter. Then again, it's hard to lose if you get every rebound.

"Killer," a three-time team MVP, got more than his share, despite giving up inches and pounds to every center in Jenison—and to one assistant coach.

"He was a lot smaller than me," said massive 6-10 Bob "Bevo" Nordmann. "But Bill had the heart of a lion with the tremendous abuse his body took. He gave up two, three, four or even five inches night after night. It's just too bad we didn't have a big center to go with him."

It was up to Kilgore to stop 7-footers like Luke Witte of Ohio State and Kevin Kunnert of Iowa, plus 6-8 to 6-11 loads like Ken Brady of Michigan, Jim Brewer and Ron Behagen of Minnesota and George McGinnis, Joby Wright, and Steve Downing of Indiana.

Coach Gus Ganakas says goodbye to a three-time team MVP.

"He was never appreciated enough," said 5-5 point guard Gary Ganakas. "We had such a small team in '72 with Mike Robinson at 5-11, Pat Miller at 6-2 and Ron Gutkowski a slim 6-6. But the most undersized guy was Kilgore, not me. I didn't have to go there and outrebound 7-footers."

"I just had to work harder," Kilgore said. "Shooters, we had. But someone had to go get the ball. And you can be the biggest guy or the greatest jumper in the world. Rebounding is all hard work and conditioning."

Size didn't matter to a player who starred for a Class B state champion in 1969 in Jenison Field House, then considered MSU, Michigan, and Dayton.

"John Benington was one of the main reasons I came to State," Kilgore said of a coach who died of a massive heart attack in Jenison in September 1969. "He was a straightforward guy. But I was sold by the campus, too."

He didn't have to sell Ganakas, who made Kilgore an immediate starter and could have had a nice team in 1970–71 if Ralph Simpson had stayed in school instead of signing with the ABA.

"If we'd have had Ralph, we definitely would've been a title contender," Ganakas said. "I wouldn't have thought that before the season. But Kilgore made that much difference."

In an 82-70 win at Ohio State, the only Big Ten loss for the Buckeyes that season, Kilgore outscored Witte 21-16 and outrebounded him 16-8.

Stranger yet, the Spartans had to wear OSU's red road uniforms that Saturday since their green game gear was swiped, then recovered later on a tackle by All-America safety and part-time basketball player Brad Van Pelt.

But Kilgore's favorite game was a 91-85 win at Kentucky over Adolph Rupp's last team, much to some bigoted fans' dismay.

"They still weren't big on integration," Kilgore said. "And we endured some terrible name-calling that really got our adrenaline going. They used the big N-word and said, '_____, go home!' We said, 'That's where we're going! We don't want to stay here. And we're taking this victory with us.'"

"I remember Adolph Rupp telling Coach Ganakas that we didn't really deserve to win, that his boys just had a bad game," said swingman Pat Miller. "And I remember him referring to Kilgore and Mike Robinson as 'colored boys.' The next year, he left. And Kentucky started recruiting black athletes."

They would've had to search the entire commonwealth to find one with as much class as Kilgore.

"We nicknamed him 'Captain Smooth,'" said guard Benny White. "He was so smooth the way he played with the finger rolls and hooks. Every big-time center we played, he dominated. Plus, he was like a big brother. He taught me the most important thing was to get a degree."

With a major in labor and industrial relations, Kilgore worked for Fruehauf for 20 years before starting R.K. Enterprises, a human resources consulting firm in Belleville, Michigan.

That's short for Ryann and Kristen, his basketball-playing daughters.

"I've been their coach up until high school, and I expect at least one state championship, if not two," he said. "They're in the 6-foot range as a sophomore and freshman. I know Michigan State is looking at them already."

It would be great to have another Kilgore on campus—especially if she doesn't have to guard a 7-footer.

Michigan State

Bill Kilgore

Center—6-foot-7, 220 pounds
River Rouge, MI, High

Year	Record	Pts.	Reb.
1970-71	10-14	14.2	12.8
1971-72	13-11	14.8	11.1
1972-73	13-11	16.7	9.9
Total	36-36	15.3	11.3

Bill Kilgore

Lindsay Hairston

Hairston plays above the basket against the Hawkeyes.

Broken legs, broken hearts—but never a broken backboard.

Nor, from all indications, a broken spirit.

At Michigan State, he was "Windex" for the way he cleaned the glass.

And in a season with the Detroit Pistons and more than 22 years playing and coaching in France, there have been times when Lindsay Hairston has shined.

But there was always a question, always a doubt, always a might-have-been.

"Lindsay is a hard guy to describe," said close friend and ex-Spartan teammate Benny White. "He seemed selfish at times. But if you knew him, you saw he cared for his team, his university, and especially his family."

At just 6-foot-7, 186 pounds, with a splay-legged shooting style, Hairston looked more like a pipecleaner than one of the league's premier players.

Somehow, he battled much taller and wider players in the pivot, led the conference in rebounding twice and was first-team All-Big Ten in 1974–75.

"His legs were so badly bowed as a child, the doctors were afraid he wouldn't be able to walk unless they were straightened out," said Spartan coach Gus Ganakas.

Hairston hollers, while Gus Ganakas maps his next move.

"People always insist on comparing us," Hairston said. "I guess it's always going to happen. But that doesn't mean I have to like it."

In his first game at MSU, he scored 45 points and fueled the Hairston–Russell fires until their freshman meeting became a can't-miss event.

After averaging 29.9 points that season, Hairston joined center Bill Kilgore and guard Mike Robinson in what should have been a deadly three-pronged attack. But an adjustment to forward proved difficult. And Hairston was a much better player at center after Kilgore left.

One problem was the NCAA's no-dunk rule, which hurt No. 45 as much as anyone. He had a habit of fumbling the ball underneath. And he dunked a couple anyway, at the price of technical fouls.

"If I could've dunked in college, we might've won 23 games," Hairston said. "It's just a whole different game. A big guy has a chance to block your shot in close. When you can take it to the hoop, there's no way to stop it."

As a junior and senior, there were few ways to stop an explosive leaper with extremely long arms—the Spartans' MVP as a senior on a team that featured Big Ten scoring king Terry Furlow.

"Michigan State finally got on the basketball map this year," Hairston said at the team banquet. "People know that we exist. When we go places, I don't hear people mistaking us for Michigan any more. The good record (17-9), beating Notre Dame and maybe the walkout have started people talking."

Many blamed Hairston for that insurrection. But his coach never did. Ganakas just wished the Detroit Pistons' third-round pick had grown.

"Lindsay could always jump," he said. "The only problem was he never got any bigger or stronger. Campy grew. Lindsay didn't."

He actually lost two inches and 14 pounds from his recruiting dimensions.

"It wasn't because he didn't eat," White said. "His mother was one of the best cooks around. She'd make sure we all ate well and had something to bring back."

While living in East Lansing or France, Hairston had an appetite for turnaround jumpers, soaring rebounds, and blocked shots— his just desserts.

Thus, both legs were surgically broken, then reset extremely well.

At Detroit Kettering High, Hairston was an All-America center and a recruiting target of roughly 300 schools. He narrowed that list to four—MSU, Michigan, New Mexico, and Louisville—then signed with Ganakas' program.

"Some offered a car and things like that," Hairston said. "But you don't really know if they mean it or not. Mr. Ganakas was honest with me and told me what to expect. I respected that."

The Spartan coaches thought they had a better shot at Pontiac Central star Campy Russell, who wound up at Michigan and led all Big Ten scorers in 1974.

Before, during, and after recruiting, Hairston and Russell were always compared— a bit unfairly, with different positions and responsibilities.

Michigan State

Lindsay Hairston

Lindsay Hairston

Forward/Center—6-foot-7, 186 pounds
Detroit, MI, Kettering High

Year	Record	Pts.	Reb.
1972-73	13-11	11.5	7.9
1973-74	13-11	16.5	13.6
1974-75	17-9	19.3	11.5
Total	43-31	15.8	11.0

Darryl Johnson

Johnson dribbles past Ron Kellogg of Kansas in the 1986 Sweet 16.

"Shadows" refers to more than the Michigan State alma mater.

It's a one-word description for the basketball career of Darryl Johnson.

The 6-foot-2, 170-pound guard never got the credit he deserved at Flint Central High or MSU. Instead, he had to settle for points and victories.

From 1981 to 1983, "D.J." became the first player since the early 1950s to play on three Michigan Class A state championship teams. And in his first three seasons with the Spartans, his teams averaged more than 19 wins.

After starring as a senior, he played in virtually every professional league—including the NBA as a 30-year-old rookie—before his current stint in Europe.

Yet, he was often lost in the shadow of other standouts—teammates Eric Turner and Marty Embry and opponent Antoine Joubert in high school and backcourt predecessors and partners Sam Vincent and Scott Skiles in college.

Johnson dunks and nearly catches his tongue against Eastern Michigan.

When Johnson signed with the Spartans over Detroit and Eastern Michigan, that decision rated just five paragraphs in the *Lansing State Journal*.

Yet, in his first conference game, he hit a 13-foot jumper with seven seconds left to beat Iowa.

Western Michigan coach Vernon Payne, who was responsible for signing another guard named Johnson six years earlier, said, "You know Michigan State must be a good team when it can afford to have Darryl Johnson on the bench."

A broken foot in the off-season and a bad back spoiled his sophomore year.

But Johnson's solid season as a junior was no surprise to the Big Ten MVP.

"He's been a great shooter ever since he has been here," Skiles said. "I play with D.J. every day. Nothing he does surprises me. When he throws up a jumper, it goes right in the middle."

After Skiles scored 40 points in a 91-79 triumph over Michigan in Jenison, it was Johnson's turn for revenge.

"Antoine will be checking me," Johnson said of the teams' second matchup in 1986. "And I don't mind that at all. I always like to go against Michigan. I like to prove I wasn't the only guard in the state that year."

He was the best guard on the court in the rematch, contributing 26 points and eight assists in the Spartans' 74-59 win in Ann Arbor.

Johnson had just been named the Big Ten Player of the Week after hitting 24 of 30 shots from the field—13-for-18 accuracy in a 30-point effort against Iowa and 11-for-12 work in another win over Minnesota.

And Lynn Henning of *The Detroit News* offered a recipe for instant offense: "Preheat basketball court to 75 degrees. Remove one Darryl Johnson from the bench, mix with teammates and pour ball into his hands. Let him shake and bake until the ball rises and steams through the net. Serves one basketball team."

As a senior, Johnson shot 91.0 percent at the line, still an MSU record, and scored 42 points against BYU. He even made *Basketball Times*' All-Rodney team for dangerous Dangerfields.

When the Spartans failed to win, Johnson was ripped for not being Skiles.

Finally, the spotlight was his. And he didn't have a "D.J." to help him.

"I don't like to whoop and holler," he said with a smile that seldom disappeared. "I just go out and take care of business."

As a Flint Central senior, Johnson had 30 points on 11-for-17 shooting from the field and 8-for-8 work at the line in an 84-80 win over Detroit Southwestern. In contrast, Joubert set a Class A championship record with 47 points—but needed 40 field goal attempts and ice packs for his arm.

The day before, in Jenison Field House, Johnson had weaved and hit a 14-foot bank shot with :07 left in a semifinal win over Detroit Kettering.

But when Flint Central's Stan Gooch argued on behalf of his star and said, "I think Darryl is the finest all-around player in the state," few listened.

Though he shot 55 percent from the field and 64 percent in the state tournament, he was hardly noticed by Michigan or eight other Big Ten schools.

Michigan State

Darryl Johnson

Darryl Johnson

Guard—6-foot-2, 170 pounds
Flint, MI, Central High

Year	Record	Pts.	Ast.
1983-84	16-12	6.0	1.2
1984-85	19-10	5.3	1.3
1985-86	23-8	16.6	4.0
1986-87	11-17	22.1	4.0
Total	69-47	12.9	2.7

Matt Steigenga, Mark Montgomery & Mike Peplowski

Steigenga takes the ball to the basket and muscles in for the score.

The top three high school basketball players in the state of Michigan in 1988 all said yes to Michigan State, which had just gone 11-17 and 10-18.

Ten seasons after that leap of faith, the Spartans have played in 10 straight post-season tournaments and won 91 more games than they've lost.

If we can't say soaring forward Matt Steigenga, cerebral point guard Mark Montgomery and spirited center Mike Peplowski were All-Americans, we can't deny they were all-important with their combined contributions.

With forward-center Parish Hickman and guard-forward Jon Zulauf, they were "The Oft-Forgotten Five"—an all-in-state incoming class.

When Montgomery and Peplowski gave verbal commitments to assistant coach Tom Izzo on October 10, 1987, less than an hour after a 17-11 football win over Michigan, it sent an unmistakable message.

And when Steigenga agreed to join them, Jud Heathcote had the makings of a championship team, with guard Steve Smith and Kirk Manns and forward Ken Redfield already on campus.

"Mark and I had talked about where we were going," Peplowski said. "I said, 'I'm damn sure not going to Michigan!' So after that football game, I said, 'Why are we bullshitting around? Let's drop a bombshell. . . . Let's commit right now!'"

"That was the game when Michigan threw seven interceptions," Montgomery remembered. "We all ran out on the field and celebrated. It felt like we were part of everything already. The environment seemed perfect. And that's when we told Tom we were coming."

Izzo's initial reaction was to wait for the punchline to a cruel joke. But recruiter's euphoria followed—for at least one coach.

"When we told Jud the same thing, he said, 'That's great,' and walked away," Peplowski said. "He must've been thinking, 'Now, I can chew their asses!' But it was the best decision I ever made."

For Steigenga, a high school All-American who first dunked in seventh grade, the choice of MSU over North Carolina wasn't as simple.

"Jud was different from any coach I'd met," he said. "I knew he wouldn't coddle me. But when I went to a practice at Chapel Hill, I saw Dean Smith rip into his players. I thought, 'He's not much different from Jud.'"

By the time they left campus, Steigenga and Montgomery were part of 10 more victories than any Spartan basketball lettermen.

Steigenga started a school-record 123 games, despite a stress fracture in his foot, and left as MSU's No. 11 all-time scorer. Montgomery played in 126 games, another career high, and was once No. 2 in steals and assists.

"I thought Matt was a great player," said forward Dwayne Stephens. "He could've been better if there hadn't been so much pressure on him. Everyone said he didn't have fire and was a pretty boy. But Matt was a tough kid. And Mark was a coach on the floor."

"Matt was the best pure athlete I've ever seen," Peplowski said. "That includes Michael Jordan or anyone else. If they had a 'Superstars' competition, Matt would win. He could throw a football almost 100 yards. He barefoot waterskied on his first attempt. He's a great tennis player. And he has taken more money from me on the golf course than I care to remember."

Everyone remembers Peplowski, who had seven surgical procedures on his knee and a need to experience life to the fullest, whatever the consequences.

Peplowski helped rescue teammate Bobby Hurley of Sacramento after a traffic accident. Besides the Kings, he played for Detroit, Milwaukee, Washington, and Golden State, and spent time in the CBA and Spain.

Today, he's a bank executive and a budding broadcaster.

Montgomery, who played in Germany, Sweden, and Lithuania, is an assistant coach at Central Michigan and a likely candidate to return to the Spartans.

And Steigenga, who spent a year in Spain, three years in Japan, and three stints in the CBA, had a short stay with the Chicago Bulls.

But all three will be remembered for being bullish on MSU when recruiting had been a bear of a time.

Montgomery dares his man to drive and prepares for a steal.

"We roomed together as freshmen," Montgomery said of an "Odd Couple" arrangement. "I knew he had a lot of heart and would fight through whatever injuries he had. If he had to go through a wall, I felt sorry for the wall."

Peplowski loved motorcycles. And his motor was always running. But he's remembered as an all-time favorite interview and the school's No. 3 rebounder.

"If I start telling 'Pep' stories, even the ones fit to print, that means I was present," Steigenga said. "There's guilt-by-association, you know.

"He loved to get up and sing 'Heartbreak Hotel' with this local band. And when he lived on the sixth floor of Wonders Hall, he bought a bass and an amp. He'd take the screen out and sit in the window with his legs hanging out, playing so loud you couldn't believe it.

"But he loved to hunt and fish and had a compound bow. He thought he was Ted Nugent or something. Once, he shot an arrow down the hallway and put a hole in the firedoor. I guess someone saw him. So I said, 'Bring the bow down to my room.' Now, I'm an accessory!"

Peplowski squeezes the air from another rebound.

Steigenga shows his athleticism with a trapeze dunk.

Matt Steigenga

Forward—6-foot-7, 220 pounds
Grand Rapids, MI, South Christian High

Year	Record	Pts.	Reb.
		8.7	4.5
1988-89	18-15	10.4	3.5
1989-90	28-6	12.6	4.9
1990-91	19-11	10.2	4.5
1991-92	22-8		4.3
Total	87-40	10.4	

Michigan State

Matt Steigenga

Michigan State

Mark Montgomery

Mark Montgomery

Guard—6-foot-2, 170 pounds
Southgate, MI, Aquinas High

Year	Record	Pts.	Ast.
1988-89	18-15		
1989-90	28-6	3.7	3.2
1990-91	19-11	3.6	2.9
1991-92	22-8	7.5	5.8
Total	87-40	7.0	6.3
		5.3	4.4

Michigan State

Mike Peplowski

Mike Peplowski

Center—6-foot-10, 270 pounds
Warren, MI, De LaSalle High

Year	Record	Pts.	Reb.
	Injury-redshirt season		5.8
1988-89	28-6	5.3	6.9
1989-90	19-11	7.7	8.6
1990-91	22-8	13.3	10.0
1991-92	15-13	14.5	
1992-93		10.2	7.8
Total	84-38		

Eric Snow

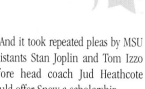

Snow finds a passing lane around the Wolverines' Dugan Fife.

And it took repeated pleas by MSU assistants Stan Joplin and Tom Izzo before head coach Jud Heathcote would offer Snow a scholarship.

"The first time I saw him was in summer camps in 1990," Izzo said of a true student-athlete with a 3.7 g.p.a. at McKinley. "I said, 'All I know is, every game he plays, his team wins.' And that's the way he played for us."

Moving all the way out to point guard, as extreme as any conversion could be, it was rough sledding for Snow as a freshman and almost as treacherous a trip as a much-maligned sophomore who couldn't connect from the foul line.

"We may have lost a couple of games that year because Eric missed free throws," Heathcote said. "But we won some games because of him, too. And he may have been a better defender as a sophomore than he was as a senior."

By then, Snow was recognized as the Big Ten Defensive Player of the Year.

He led the Spartans in steals and assists three times and shared team MVP honors in 1995 with shooting star and backcourt partner Shawn Respert.

"The 'Fire & Ice' theme was good for us and good for the school," Snow said. "It got national attention and helped sell tickets. I've actually met people who've said they decided to go to Michigan State because of me and Shawn—people as far away as Arizona."

It was almost that long a trek to the NBA for a player who shot 26.8 percent at the line as a sophomore, 44.9 as a junior and 60.8 as a senior.

But Herbert and Susie Snow didn't raise a quitter. And her "Pookie" spent more 8 a.m. sessions with Joplin than the coach's wife ever did.

"When they were leaving, Mark Montgomery and Dwayne Stephens told me, 'If you play defense, Coach will play you,'" Snow said. "I thought, 'If that's all I have to do . . . ' I'd never really done it before. And when I went home, my high school coach said, 'What's this stuff about you playing defense?'"

f he said, "Meet you after practice," you had to ask, "Which one?"

But after all his early-morning workouts, it all worked out for Eric Snow.

No one in Michigan State basketball history silenced more doubters than the not-so-little brother of Spartan linebacking great Percy Snow.

As a 6-foot-3 power forward and a shameless scorer at Canton McKinley High, Snow was rejected by nearby Ohio State, the school of his athletic dreams.

The rumors about his passing were just as unbelievable to folks in Ohio.

But Snow led the league in assists twice and set a Big Ten record as a senior with 141 setups in conference play.

He finished No. 5 on the all-time assist list with 599, behind Illinois' Bruce Douglas, Michigan's Gary Grant, Purdue's Bruce Parkinson, and MSU's Scott Skiles—all of whom had many more starts.

When left alone at the top of the key or when he could take the ball to the basket on some of the fastest fast breaks Breslin Center has seen, Snow was capable of scoring 18 points, as he did against Michigan.

He shot 51.4 percent from the field as a junior, including a 5-for-5, 15-point effort in an NCAA Tournament win over Seton Hall.

And Snow shot 52.0 percent as a senior, while averaging 10.8 points, the third-highest contribution on a 22-6 team.

But his strengths were still pressuring the ball and delivering perfect passes for a quick release from Respert, the Big Ten's No. 2 career scorer.

"I'll never forget winning at Michigan, when Shawn had 30 in the second half," Snow said. "We were behind. And Shawn had hurt his ankle. He said, 'Everyone will say Jimmy King locked me up. We've got to do something!' I said, 'I'm coming to you all the time. Just be ready.' . . . I guess he was."

Since Snow became a starter, the Spartans are 9-0 against a troubled OSU program through the 1998 season.

And with continued emphasis on a once-glaring weakness, his success at the foul line improved to 71.2 percent in his second season in the NBA.

"Of all the guys I've been around, Eric had the toughest situation," Izzo said. "The national abuse he took for his shooting was cruel."

"The thing with Eric is that he improved every year," Heathcote said. "Mark my words, he can be an impact player in the NBA. He'll never be a great shooter. But he'd be a great guy to have on your team in any league."

He has already played for Seattle and Philadelphia and has at least one move left in him when his playing days are done.

Snow met his wife, DeShawn, on campus as an MSU freshman. And the business major said he plans to come back and earn a master's degree.

"The saddest game for me was my last one at home—and we killed Wisconsin," he said. "My teammates in Philadelphia say, 'Man, you liked college that much?' But I didn't like Michigan State. I loved it."

Snow was the first person to call Izzo in Maui after his first Spartan head coaching win. And don't be surprised if those roles are reversed one day.

Snow hollers instructions past Purdue's Porter Roberts.

Michigan State

Eric Snow

Guard—6-foot-3, 190 pounds
Canton, OH, McKinley High

Year	Record	Pts.	Reb.
1991-92	22-8	1.1	0.9
1992-93	15-13	4.3	5.2
1993-94	20-12	6.8	6.7
1994-95	22-6	10.8	7.8
Total	79-39	5.9	5.3

Eric Snow

Jud Heathcote and protege Tom Izzo plead the Spartans' case.

The Coaches

A Magnificent Seven

Jud Heathcote

His fist is clenched. A Jud-thud to the forehead is sure to follow.

W hen George Melvin Heathcote leaves this earth, God had better be ready.

Otherwise, we're sure to hear, "Geez! Can't you get a little more help?"

For 19 seasons at Michigan State, the world's least-patient man helped a lot of young men become better basketball players and better people.

A few of them even understood that before they left Heathcote's program.

As a teacher of shooters, a defensive strategist, and a quick-witted speaker, there was no one better.

If Heathcote didn't win as many games or titles as some figured he should, he did more than any coach in school history—and, as always, did it his way. We should have known that the day he arrived as Gus Ganakas' successor in 1976, after impressing a selection committee that demanded a disciplinarian.

"It will be very apparent to everyone in the program and on the periphery that I am going to run the show," Heathcote said at his first MSU press conference. "I will coach the players. The players will not coach me.

"Everyone coaches a different way. Some get the job done in a very, very quiet way. I am not a quiet person. I try to develop a relationship where the players know a lot is demanded of them. If I can't develop that relationship, it is going to be very hard for any player to play for me.

"I am probably more of a negative coach than I should be. But it isn't, 'Roll it out there, guys, and let's see what we can do.' There is going to be a lot of direction. And if you call that discipline, our kids will be very, very, very disciplined."

New MSU Athletic Director Joe Kearney had wanted to hire Marv Harshman away from Washington but was told he should try to get Heathcote instead.

"I always felt Jud had a better understanding of people than anyone I knew," said Harshman of his seven-year assistant at Washington State. "He knew how they really felt about things and how to get the best out of them."

After interviews in Chicago with Don DeVoe of Virginia Tech, Lee Rose of North Carolina–Charlotte, Bill Hess of Ohio, and Darrel Hedric of Miami, plus a courtesy chat in East Lansing with Ganakas aide Dick Versace, the choice was an unknown comic from Missoula, Montana.

"I had a press conference when I was hired at Montana, too," Heathcote deadpanned. "The other guy and I got along very well.

"But you're lucky to have dynamic leadership from your new athletic director—Joe asked me to say that. I think you've hired a super football coach in . . . was it Darrell Royal or Darryl Rogers? . . . Darryl Rogers! Then, you've got me. And two out of three ain't bad.

"Do I feel confident? Yes. Do I feel apprehensive? Yes. Am I afraid? No. . . . But there is a clause in my contract that says I can be hung in effigy at any time—with a live body."

Heathcote was a perfect case in point for UCLA wizard John Wooden's line: "You have to have talent to win. But not everyone can win with talent."

When he had the players, no one was better at maximizing their abilities, earning National Coach of the Year acclaim.

But Heathcote was a much better scout than a salesman and paid a price for refusing to bend the rules or tell the standard recruiting lies.

His coaching style was like coarse sandpaper. And those who could endure that friction often became smoother on and off the court.

"Having played two years for Coach Ganakas, it was a very difficult adjustment for me," said guard Bob Chapman. "Coach Ganakas related to his players a lot better. Coach Heathcote had the Army mentality, where you beat someone down. And I didn't see a lot of building back up."

But many came to appreciate his brutal honesty and demand for perfection.

"I love Jud Heathcote," said Edgar Wilson, whose No. 33 was retired—after some guy named Johnson wore it. "I played for him, then worked for him. He was good to me and good for the program."

"The thing I understood was that he was the coach and I was the player," said inherited forward Gregory Kelser. "And that was the bottom line. If you

Heathcote lobbies for an over-the-back call.

With almost as many wins as gray hairs, Heathcote chats with friend Bob Knight of Indiana.

understood that and took what he was saying, without getting caught up in how he was saying it, you became a better player."

"Jud is someone special in the game of basketball," said guard Terry Donnelly, one of Heathcote's first Spartan signees. "When I got there, I didn't think I'd be around too long. But I learned a lot by being with him."

One of the first signs of his strategic brilliance came in 1977, when an outmanned team lost in overtime to No. 1-ranked Michigan in Ann Arbor.

The following season, MSU ruled the Big Ten with an explosive running game and nearly beat eventual champ Kentucky in the NCAA Tournament's Elite Eight.

But in 1978–79, the Spartans wouldn't be stopped, as Heathcote's matchup zone held stars in check and helped to produce a national title.

"Jud was brilliant that way, just brilliant," Kelser said. "The day before we faced Indiana State for the championship, Earvin Johnson played on the scout team and was better than Larry Bird ever was. That left no doubt about how we wanted to guard him—like handing off a baton to the next guy. And Bird had never seen anything like it."

Some of Heathcote's players had never heard anything like the high-decibel feedback they received at practice, including Johnson's favorite line, "Be a guard, not a garbage!"

"Coach Heathcote had his own way of doing things," said center Jay Vincent. "When he'd go on a rampage, I'd think, 'Why is he always yelling at me? Yell at Magic once in a while!' It took me four or five years of pro basketball before I saw what he was trying to do."

"The good things in my life since I left Michigan State, I attribute to what Jud taught me," said forward Ben Tower. "A lot of times, it was difficult to see what he was saying while you were playing for him. But when you got away for a while, you knew you really loved him."

"Jud was very tough on me," said guard Steve Smith, a Big Ten MVP and NBA star. "He used to say I'd never make it in the pros, trying to get me to work harder. Now, when I see him, I'll ask, 'Do you think I'll ever make it?' He'll say, 'You made it. . . . But you still have a lot of work to do.'"

"There were no surprises," said center Mike Peplowski. "If you screwed up, you knew what was coming. He punched me in the chest one time. But I learned a lot of survival skills and how to be mentally tough. As a bank officer now, I have millions of dollars in loans I oversee. It's a high-stress environment. But it's easy after playing for Jud."

Heathcote's sense of humor was nearly as strong as his sense of urgency.

"After the Far West Classic in 1978, he changed our flights to get home a few hours sooner," said manager Darwin Payton. "We wound up stuck in Denver for two days. Then, when we finally landed at Metro, it took a long time to get our luggage. So Jud hopped on the conveyor belt, rode back and started yelling at everyone. Before long, two security men ushered him out."

"We were in Tennessee for the NCAA Tournament in 1990 and weren't being waited on," said forward Dwayne Stephens. "Finally, Jud said, 'What the hell is going on? We've been sitting here a half-hour! . . . You'd better go get some help or we'll be here forever!'"

But some of the best Heathcote stories came from trusted assistant Mike Deane and alter-ego Scott Skiles, who added, "When people say I'm just like him, I hope they're talking about basketball and not looks."

"I'll never forget my first recruiting trip with Jud," Deane said. "He hated to go off campus. So we flew into Syracuse for the New York State Fair, didn't have perfect directions and parked too far away from the gate for his bowed legs and square knee. By then, he was all over me.

"When I went up to get two tickets, the guy at the gate said, 'You only need one.' Right away, Jud thought, 'Hmmm, even in your hometown, they know 'The Ol' Coach!' So when I walked in, Jud tried to walk in behind me. The guy said, 'Sir! . . . Over in the last gate. In New York, all our senior citizens get in free.' . . . And that was 14 years before he quit coaching!"

Skiles, assistant Stan Joplin and guard Eric Snow are still laughing.

"We had a walk-on named Paul Horton—a great guy about 6-9, who never played," Skiles said. "One game, we were ahead by about 30, and the students were chanting, 'We want Paul! . . . We want Paul!' When Jud got up and walked to the end of the bench, everyone cheered. But instead of putting him in, he said, 'Hey, Paul, they want you over there. . . . Why don't you go see what they want?'"

"One time, Jon Garavaglia swore in a game, and Jud jumped all over him during a timeout," Joplin remembered. "He said, 'Jon! Goddamn it! You can't be talking that blankety-blank! . . . My minister is right over there. And he doesn't want to hear that bullshit!'"

"He used to tell me I shot like some guy from a long time ago," Snow said. "It turned out to be a guy without any arms! . . . Jud was the best. He used to say, 'You hate me now. But you'll love me when I'm gone.' By my senior year, the other players thought I was his son. Everything he said turned out to be right on the nose."

Heathcote slammed a ball off his nostrils during a sideline tantrum at Illinois and was steamrolled in practice by center Mario Izzo.

But where others saw a wild character, 19-year secretary Lori Soderberg saw a boss with a huge vocabulary and a caring heart.

"People ask me if he stomps his feet and bangs his head in the office, the way he does on the court," she said. "He's nothing like that. But no one realizes the things he does for people, in and out of the program. I think he'd

Johnson and Heathcote hug after the 1989 reunion game, the last MSU basketball appearance in Jenison.

have been a great athletic director. . . . He'd be great now."

He certainly had enough experience dealing with disappointment and criticism, especially when he stood by Skiles amid legal problems his last two seasons.

"If I'd been coach, I'd have kicked the guy off the team, no questions asked," Skiles said in 1986. "I feel worse about what I put him through than anything else that happened. Coach isn't related to me and wasn't involved in any of the incidents. But he had to go right down with me."

"Skiles handled it extremely well, much better than 58-year-old coach Jud Heathcote, who complained loud and long about what he called 'media harassment,'" wrote Corky Meinecke in *The Detroit News*. "He was particularly paranoid in Dayton, site of the first round of the NCAA Tournament."

But Heathcote's definition of loyalty and sense of what was right and fair

was endorsed by Athletic Director Doug Weaver and President John DiBiaggio.

"I don't know Scott Skiles very well," DiBiaggio said. "But I know Doug Weaver. I've come to know Jud Heathcote. And damn it all, if they believe in Scott Skiles, so do I!"

"You have to understand, times were changing on college campuses with newspapers and police," said CBS and ESPN analyst Bill Raftery. "The days of a phone call and the coach coming down to get a player out of trouble were gone. The age of responsibility was dawning. But Jud stuck with him. And Scott straightened himself out."

Shortly before that, Heathcote suffered a mild heart attack in the summer of 1984 and brought Indiana's Bob Knight and Purdue's Gene Keady, natural rivals and intense competitors, together on a friend's behalf.

In his best Sinatra pose, a man who always did it his way says goodbye.

"Gene and Bob talked about what they should do," Heathcote said. "Finally, Gene said, 'I'm going to tell Jud if he ever needs a heart transplant, we'll send him yours. . . . I know it has never been used.'"

Another time, Knight called and said, "Jud, I've got to talk to you. You're the only friend I've got in this conference." As you'd expect, the answer was, "Bob, . . . don't jump to conclusions."

Heathcote nearly set age-group records in the high jump when his teams were denied wins over Kansas and Georgia Tech in the 1986 and 1990 Sweet 16's due to timing errors.

But nothing hurt him as much as allegations of booster impropriety by forward Parish Hickman and a move by the MSU administration to dictate when he would retire.

"I could not believe it! . . . I still can't believe it! . . . Not Jud Heathcote!" Johnson said. "We were in Jenison one day, playing four-on-four. And I said, 'Jud, I don't have any money. Can you buy me a soda?' He said, 'Sorry, 'E,' I can't do it. It's against the rules.'

"He's the straightest guy you'll ever find that way. Jud wouldn't even promise a guy he could start! And he lost people because of that, too."

An investigation upheld Heathcote's previously unquestioned integrity. But after getting Tom Izzo named as his eventual successor, he stayed around one season longer than his original plan in order to leave on his terms.

No one else at MSU could have been a friend of three combustible parties—feuding football coach George Perles, Board of Trustees chairman Joel Ferguson and A.D. Merrily Dean Baker.

And no one but Heathcote could have gotten away with the playful jab, "Joel has a lot of talent. He could've been anyone or anything he chose to be. . . . Why he chose to be himself, I'll never know."

That line and more of Heathcote's wit and wisdom were captured in his 1995 autobiography, "Jud: A Magical Journey."

But after a 22-6 farewell with parting gifts at every stop and a new Aurora for his retirement days in Spokane, Washington, nothing said more than the Jud Heathcote All-Star Tribute Game, with the return of his greatest players and a capacity crowd in Breslin Center.

"I'm going to be a coach when I'm done playing," Skiles said prophetically in June 1995. "I have several friends who are coaches. If I needed advice, I'd contact them. And Jud would be the first one I'd call."

"I just want to say that . . . I'm going to miss you," said a choked-up Johnson, speaking for all the players at center court. "You've done a lot for all of us. You've taken boys and made us men. . . . I just love you."

Izzo thanked Heathcote the best way he could—by proving his mentor's faith was well-placed with a Big Ten title and National Coach of the Year recognition in 1998.

"I can't tell you how much I owe him," said Izzo, with Heathcote on hand for the trophy presentation at the Final Four. "He hired me as a part-time assistant in 1983, then hired me back right away when I went to Tulsa in 1986. He put up with me for 12 years. But to Jud, there was always a right way and a wrong way. And the right way was the only way."

His legacy lives on.

Jud Heathcote

Head basketball coach

Year	Big Ten	Overall
1976-77	9-9	12-15
1977-78	15-3	25-5
1978-79	13-5	26-6
1979-80	6-12	12-15
1980-81	7-11	13-14
1981-82	7-11	12-16
1982-83	9-9	17-13
1983-84	9-9	16-12
1984-85	10-8	19-10
1985-86	12-6	23-8
1986-87	6-12	11-17
1987-88	5-13	10-18
1988-89	6-12	18-15
1989-90	15-3	28-6
1990-91	11-7	19-11
1991-92	11-7	22-8
1992-93	7-11	15-13
1993-94	10-8	20-12
1994-95	14-4	22-6
Total	182-160	340-220

Michigan State

Jud Heathcote

Ben Van Alstyne

Van Alstyne and his nucleus: Robin Roberts, Sam Fortino, Matt Mazza, Oliver White, and Don Waldron.

H is players and friends knew him as "Van." But he was also the original "Gentle Ben."

Ben Van Alstyne came to Michigan State in 1926—one year after it ceased being MAC—and stayed for 35 years.

As head basketball coach from 1926 to 1949, the longest tenure in school history, his teams won 231 games and lost 163, a .589 success rate.

As golf coach from 1932 to 1961, Van Alstyne's teams finished as high as fifth in the nation in 1944 and featured five Big Ten individual champs.

And as a positive influence on thousands of students as a friend and a professor of physical education, he was an uncrowned champion.

"What I remember most about 'Van,' as he was affectionately known, is

that he was a gentle man and a gentleman," said forward Bill Rapchak, the leading scorer on Van Alstyne's 22nd and final team.

"He was the sole reason I attended Michigan State. He taught me a lot about the game of basketball and about the game of life. My first year at State, I lost my father rather suddenly and needed someone to lean on. Besides being my coach, 'Van' was also my confidante. I respected him for it and always will."

Respect followed Van Alstyne wherever he went. He served on the ethics and membership committees of the basketball coaches association, was one of the first advisors for Wilson Sporting Goods and was named to the Helms Foundation Hall of Fame for basketball achievement in 1959.

Athletic Director Biggie Munn salutes Van Alstyne, a Helms Hall of Fame inductee.

The 1918 graduate of Colgate—and a basketball, football and baseball star there—began coaching in high school in Asheville, North Carolina. He then went to Ohio Wesleyan in 1921 and was 75-31, .708, in five seasons.

Van Alstyne worked wonders at MSC, inheriting a team that was 5-13. In his second, third, and fourth seasons, his program went 11-4, 11-5 and 12-4, respectively.

After 10- and 9-game win streaks in those years, Van Alstyne put it all together in 1930–31 with a 16-1 mark—still the best for any Spartan team with more than a six-game schedule.

The highlight of that era was a 27-26 win over Michigan on February 15, 1930, as more than 6,000 fans turned out for the dedication game in Demonstration Hall.

MSC was led by the Grove brothers, Don and Roger—two of Van Alstyne's all-time favorite players.

"Little (Don) Grove was a guy who played with his head, as well as his heart," Van Alstyne said. "He was a fierce competitor—every ounce of him. I'll pick him as my All-Everything player."

He was All-Unconscious in a game against the Wolverines that led to a rule change in college basketball to protect injured players.

After being knocked cold, Don Grove could only lie motionless as teammates and opponents leaped over and around him, with MSC unable to call a timeout since it didn't have the ball.

Usually, when the Spartans had possession, they kept it until they could get a good shot—35 percent or better in those days.

"Gentle Ben" with mid-1940s star Sam Fortino.

When a team averaged a point per minute in Van Alstyne's first MSC decade, it was considered an offensive juggernaut.

But one of the best examples of what his ball control system could do came in 1932 when the Spartans beat Michigan 14-13 in double-overtime.

"The place was a madhouse," Van Alstyne said of Dem Hall. "And the teams fought on as if the fate of the world hinged on the outcome."

His 1934–35 team beat Stanford, Marquette, Michigan, and Kentucky and finished 14-4, including a 10-game win streak.

By that time, Van Alstyne had succeeded "Sleepy Jim" Crowley as MSC's golf coach in the off-season and had rejected several other job offers.

Until 1938, he'd never had an athlete in either sport who could control a ball like guard Chet Aubuchon, MSC's first basketball All-American.

"I called him 'The Flying Dutchman,'" Aubuchon said. "He was very quiet and easy-going. But his wife (Madelon) used to sit in the front row and really get after the officials.

"I liked him very much. He never forced anything on his players and gave me a lot of freedom. He could see I had a little more experience than the other players and could get them to do what had to be done."

That adaptability was shown when the school didn't field a team in 1943-44 due to World War II, then resumed play with an all-new outfit that somehow managed a 10-7 record, including an incredible 66-50 upset of Kentucky.

"I remember when we called the *State Journal* with the score, whoever answered the phone told Nick Kerbawy, our publicity director, to call back when he was sober, then hung up," Rapchak said. "It was the 'Coca-Cola Upset of the Week.'"

The Spartans were so green at the start of that season Van Alstyne told them to wear jersey numbers around campus so they'd become more familiar with each other.

"It sounded like a queer idea," he said. "But the boys eventually became acquainted."

Van Alstyne had already met a young army reserve candidate named Robin Roberts and had asked him to return to campus to play basketball when the war ended.

"Our army team played a practice game against Michigan State," said Roberts, a baseball Hall of Famer after a fabulous pitching career for the Philadelphia Phillies. "Basketball was really my first love. In those days, I thought I might go into pro basketball."

With Sam Fortino and Roberts at forward and Rapchak at center, the program quickly became competitive again and had four wins over Big Nine teams—including Michigan and league champ Ohio State—the following year.

But the week before the 1947–48 season began, Van Alstyne suffered an appendicitis attack before practice and was rushed to St. Lawrence Hospital.

If it was all a motivational play, it worked perfectly, as assistant Al Kircher took over and delivered a 43-38 win over the Wolverines.

A month later, Van Alstyne and center Bob Brannum nearly led MSC past Kentucky again, falling 47-45 before the largest crowd in Jenison Field House history.

"Ben was about the nicest man I ever met," said Brannum, a Kentucky transfer. "Going from someone like Adolph Rupp to Ben was like night and day. Where Rupp was a mean guy with lots of ways to make you miserable, Ben would never say some of those things."

He said goodbye to Spartan basketball in 1949, after announcing his resignation early that season, left campus in 1961, and died in Southfield, Michigan, in 1972 at age 79.

"Ben was a good coach," Brannum said. "He won his share. He never had the record Rupp did. But he never had the same kind of players. He was just an honest man."

In Van Alstyne's bespectacled eyes, that was what mattered most.

Michigan State

Ben Van Alstyne

Head basketball, golf coach

Year	Record	Year	Record
1926-27	7-11	1938-39	9-8
1927-28	11-4	1939-40	14-6
1928-29	11-5	1940-41	11-6
1929-30	12-4	1941-42	15-6
1930-31	16-1	1942-43	2-14
1931-32	12-5	1943-44	No games—WWII
1932-33	10-7	1944-45	9-7
1933-34	12-5	1945-46	12-9
1934-35	14-4	1946-47	11-10
1935-36	8-9	1947-48	12-10
1936-37	5-12	1948-49	9-12
1937-38	9-8	**Total**	**231-163**

Ben Van Alstyne

Pete Newell

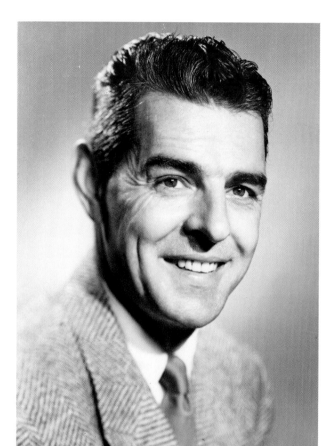

Newell gave MSC its first Big Ten win and a big boost in respectability.

More than 44 years after his last game in East Lansing, Pete Newell still has a basketball team—the greatest victory of all.

In four seasons at Michigan State College, Newell's players went 45-42. They also went to class and on to successful careers, if not necessarily to better things.

Every year, those alumni meet and share marvelous memories with the man who made everything possible, one of the great basketball minds of all time.

"We never won anything, but I think we turned the program around," said Newell, who inherited the remnants of a 4-18 team. "I take a lot of pride in these players. You don't have to have a lot of great wins to make it a great experience."

"We're cohesive because of that man," said reunion organizer Bob Watts, a manager who often drove opponents nuts. "He had a tremendous influence on millionaires, doctors, lawyers, and some coaches, too."

During a Thanksgiving morning practice in 1950, Newell realized his players had nowhere to go for dinner. He left assistant John Benington in charge and returned to announce a catered meal at his home.

"We met at the Union and walked down together," Watts said. "Pete had card tables set up with one cigarette and one glass of wine at each seat. He said, 'You can have the cigarette and have the wine. But that's the last you're going to have until March.'"

When G.I. Bill assistance ran out for Watts, Newell gave him a scholarship and had him stay in a secret penthouse in Shaw Hall.

"We used to send a manager down to sit on the visitors' bench in those days," Newell said. "Bob would root like hell for Michigan State. Once, Ozzie Cowles of Minnesota asked him, 'Are you always this obnoxious?' And Bob said, 'I try to be.'

"Bud Foster of Wisconsin said, 'Pete, I need a favor. Will you make sure you don't put that guy—I don't know who he is—on our bench? I'm afraid I'm going to kill him! Half the time, he's right in my face. I can't even see the game.' So I kept him off the Wisconsin bench—but never Minnesota's."

When forward Erik Furseth heaved a ball at Watts, who was refereeing a scrimmage, Newell blew his whistle and said, 'Forwards, I can get, Erik. Managers, I can't."

He got as much from the 1950–54 Spartans as anyone could have, after leaving San Francisco, the 1949 NIT champion.

"Our facilities at San Francisco were pre-War—World War I," Newell said. "We had hot and cold running water—hot one day and cold the next. We played in Kezar Pavilion, which sat 4,000, then moved to the Cow Palace, which wasn't built for basketball, as you'd assume.

"So when I walked into Jenison Field House, I couldn't believe what I saw—three practice courts, an arena with more than 10,000 seats, a locker room with more than one locker and hot and cold water the same day."

Newell was hired by Athletic Director Ralph Young on the recommendation of Bradley coach Forddy Anderson—a favor that was repaid in 1954.

"I must've been the seventh or eighth guy they offered the job to," Newell said. "We were just going into the Big Ten. And the only freshman coming in was Erik, who was on a football scholarship.

"I used to tell people, 'We only lost two games in four years at Michigan State.' But that was football. I was coaching basketball. So I used that 'we' a lot."

He used whatever tricks he could find on January 6, 1951, to produce a 67-62 upset at Northwestern in the Spartans' first Big Ten game.

"Pete said, 'Twenty years from now, when you tell people you played in this game, the one question they'll always ask is, 'Did you win?'" Furseth remembered. "With that, we ran through the walls. The funny thing is, that's the one question no one has ever asked me."

Newell's greatest win at MSC was a stunner over No. 1 ranked Kansas

Newell, second from left, is flanked by players Bob Carey, Ray Steffan, and John Moore in 1950.

State in the 1952 Holiday Tournament, one night after a loss to John Wooden and seventh-ranked UCLA before just 2,425 in Jenison.

A disgusted Newell had divorced himself from the team, figuring the Spartans would be blown away. But after Benington's pregame talk, MSC led a much taller team when Newell entered the locker room at halftime and found his giant-killers standing tall on their stools.

"Pete was a genius," said guard Rickey Ayala, MSC's first black player and a Newell favorite. "We used to play cards on the road. And I never saw him lose a game. If we could've executed his plans, we would never have lost."

Newell's reverse-action offense and emphasis on man-to-man defense required individual sacrifice and weren't for everyone. But a sharp sense of humor helped.

"We were watching Wisconsin hit every shot it took," said forward Al Ferrari. "Pete called time and said, 'Don't stand right under the basket. You'll have lumps on your head.' But what a great man and a tremendous coach."

After a third-place Big Ten finish in 1953, the loss of guards Ayala and Dick Wesling and forward Keith Stackhouse wrecked a team Newell thought would win the league.

"Pete was an innovator," said center Ray Steffen, who went on to coach 32 seasons at Kalamazoo College. "We had a four-corner offense before Dean Smith knew the shape of a basketball."

Newell, Smith, and Bob Knight are the only coaches with NIT, NCAA, and Olympic championships. And if you ever mention Newell to Knight, be prepared for a 10-minute tribute.

Born in Vancouver, British Columbia, and raised in Southern California, Newell starred at Loyola of Los Angeles, graduating in 1940 and playing a year of baseball in the Brooklyn Dodger chain.

When he'd had more than his fill of Michigan weather, Newell left MSC for Cal at age 38 and led the Bears to the 1959 national title.

"I wasn't surprised at all," said forward Julius McCoy. "Pete had the things

As a player and a loyal assistant, John Benington learned the game from Newell.

that made champions. And I can't say that about a lot of people. But Pete was that caliber of a person and still is."

After his team beat Cincinnati with Oscar Robertson and West Virginia with Jerry West in the Final Four, Newell coached those all-time greats and Ohio State star Jerry Lucas to the 1960 gold medal in Rome.

A general manager of the San Diego Rockets and Los Angeles Lakers and chief consultant for the Golden State Warriors, Newell was named to the Basketball Hall of Fame in 1979.

Long before that, Newell founded the Big Man Camp, which has helped nearly 100 NBA players with fundamentals they'd forgotten or never known.

"Pete Newell is kind of like the F. Lee Bailey of basketball," wrote *L.A. Times* columnist Jim Murray. "When your game comes under indictment, get Newell."

Adoring former Spartans try to do that every year, when everything old is Newell again.

"Pete's Boys"—(seated) Bill Bower, Bill Eckstrom and Bob Watts; (standing) Duane Peterson, Bob Armstrong, and Ray Steffen—at one of their annual reunions.

Michigan State

Pete Newell

Head basketball coach

Year	Big Ten	Overall
1950–51	5-9	10-11
1951–52	6-8	13-9
1952–53	11-7	13-9
1953–54	4-10	9-13
Total	26-34	45-42

Pete Newell

Forddy Anderson

Anderson goes over strategy with, clockwise from left, Bob Anderegg, Larry Hedden, Johnny Green, Jack Quiggle and Tom Rand in 1957.

If you wanted fast-paced fun, on or off the basketball court, there was only one man to coach your team.

Maybe you should give him a call in Oklahoma City. Forrest Aldea Anderson might be free as he turns 80 years old.

In 11 seasons at Michigan State, he nearly took teams to the summit twice, then endured a frightening freefall that finally cost him his job.

From 1955 to 1959, with stars like Julius McCoy, Jack Quiggle, Johnny Green, and Horace Walker, the Spartans were 46-24 in Big Ten play with a shared title and an outright championship.

Overall, they were 77-38 with the school's first trip to the NCAA semifinals in 1957 and a spot in the Mideast Region Final two years later.

For a variety of reasons, MSU plunged to 23-61 in the league and 48-86 in all games from 1959 to 1965.

But perhaps the best measure of Anderson's performance and lasting popularity was the reaction the day he was fired—April Fool's Day, 1965—by Athletic Director Biggie Munn, whose football coaching success in East Lansing will never be matched.

Though Anderson's final Spartan team was 1-13 and 5-18, fans were generally optimistic about the future of the program, to the point a dummy was hung in effigy near the Union Building with the message "Fire Biggie."

"The man was brilliant," said 1960s star Pete Gent. "I don't think anyone knew more basketball than Forddy. The frustrating thing was that only a few of us understood how brilliant he was. With his pressure offense, there was always motion. And it was all built on diagonals and triangles."

Anderson gets a triumphant ride after winning the school's first Big Ten title.

So is the system the Chicago Bulls have used to rule the NBA in the 1990s. But Anderson's version wasn't his only contribution to the game as we know it.

He was among the first to suggest the use of three officials, instead of two.

He urged the Big Ten to forsake its Saturday–Monday schedule and adopt a Wednesday–Saturday plan, as it did successfully nearly three decades later.

He pioneered the use of pregame music as a psychological tool.

And to get his players to pass the ball more, instead of slowing their attack by dribbling, he came up with a new piece of equipment.

"I want more speed," Anderson said before the 1956–57 season. "So a friend of mine made a mold of a basketball. And we had a ball made from plastic. You can do everything else—even shoot it. But it won't bounce."

Though his program later experimented with a 12-foot basket, nothing could have prepared his players for the heights they reached after beating Kentucky in the Mideast Region final in Lexington in Anderson's third season.

"You could feel the tension and nervousness," he said. "We just had a handful of students. Everyone else was rooting for Kentucky. At first, I thought the officials were, too.

"When John Green tipped one in near the end of the first half, Hagen Anderson took the basket away and called a fourth foul on John. The teams sat at the ends of the court, not on the side, in those days. And when they came down for the free throws, I was three feet away from Hagen.

"I said, 'Is there anything in the rulebook you haven't called tonight?' He turned around and said, 'I haven't called a technical foul yet.' I didn't say another word the whole second half."

The word that Munn should hire him in 1954 came from outgoing coach Pete Newell, who had received a similar referral from Anderson when A.D. Ralph Young looked for leadership four years earlier.

"Forddy was a hot coach at the time and a very good friend," Newell said. "When I left, I said, 'Biggie, I think I can get you the best damn coach around!' He said, 'Who's that?' He didn't care much about basketball."

"The first time, I was at Bradley and had just finished second in the NIT and the NCAA when John Hannah called," Anderson said of an athletics-appreciative president. "I turned the job down and recommended Pete. When Pete left, I couldn't say no and was happy to get a second chance."

The Gary, Indiana native and boyhood friend of Tom Harmon had starred at Stanford under Everett Dean, earning induction into the school's Hall of Fame.

As an enlistee and a chief petty officer, he went from player to coach when the legendary Tony Hinkle left Great Lakes Naval Training Station to take over at Bradley. And during a 32-5 stint at Great Lakes, Anderson was named Coach of the Year at age 25 by the Chicago Basketball Writers Association.

Art Gowens, Anderson and assistant Bob Stevens shout instructions in Jenison Field House.

He was 32-23 at Drake and 142-55 at Bradley before a 125-124 run at MSU.

"I was a tuba player in the high school band and formed a little orchestra," Anderson said. "So music has been a part of my life from day one. I've always believed there's a great correlation between music and athletics and tried to do something to bring the two together.

"The last 20 minutes before a game is the most ulcer-producing time for a coach. And when you go into a locker room and no one is talking, you know you're in trouble. So I decided to play slower tunes, then build up faster and faster. When I'd come in, they'd be banging on the walls, ready to go."

The players went along with Anderson's ploys, except when he told Green and Horace Walker to clean a messy garage and get everything off the floor.

"We nailed everything we could to the walls—even his galoshes," Walker said. "He said, 'I guess you guys pulled one over on the old man.' And I told him, 'Hey, you said not to leave anything on the floor!'"

Anderson got even with a scouting report that instructed Walker to ignore forward Joe Roberts when the Spartans nearly beat mighty Ohio State in 1960.

"The report said Joe couldn't shoot from outside," Walker said. "We called timeout when he hit three 20-footers in a row. When I got to the bench, I said, 'Who in the hell gave you that information?'

"But Forddy was really a mentor to me. He'd be like a sergeant and break you down, get rid of all your bad habits, then build you back up."

Defense wasn't his strong suit. But before a win over Detroit, he showed he cared about stopping opponents. When U-D coach Bob Calihan said he'd had a vision that MSU star Julius McCoy would foul out, Anderson said, 'You're quite a prophet. . . . Julius hasn't guarded his grandmother all year!'

But Anderson's specialty was crowd-pleasing offense. His 1963–64 team averaged 92.1 points, broke the 100-point barrier 10 times, and scored 118 against Oklahoma and ex-assistant Bob Stevens—all Spartan records.

Eventually, academic casualties, problems in recruiting, Michigan's rise and Anderson's love of nightlife were too much to overcome. If a doctor had told him to give up wine, women, or song, the story is he would have said, "I'll quit singing."

Forddy's way was almost always the right way in the late 1950s.

"He had a horrible drinking problem at the end," Gent said. "It was a time when everyone drank. And no one ever saw fit to deal with it.

"There was a side of him that was so brilliant and so charming. But I remember when Lonnie Sanders stole the ball and was 10 yards ahead of everyone for a go-ahead layup. Forddy jumped up and called a timeout we didn't have. I reached over, grabbed his collar and ripped the back of his coat in half."

After attending the Big Ten coaches meetings and zeroing in on a much better incoming class, Anderson was fired abruptly at age 46.

"Biggie called me over one day and said, 'You have to release a story,'" said then-assistant sports information director Nick Vista. "It was Forddy being fired. Their relationship had deteriorated. But when the announcement came, Dr. Hannah was away. And I don't think Biggie ever ran it past him."

Other stories say Munn was supposed to fire Anderson the day Hannah left for a trip to Nigeria, though that hardly seems like Hannah's style.

"I'm sorry Mr. Munn doesn't consider me adequate to continue the duties involving the basketball fortunes of Michigan State," Anderson said. "For this, I am deeply disappointed."

Amid speculation he might succeed Dave DeBusschere as the Pistons' coach, he soon became A.D. and basketball and golf coach at Hiram Scott College, a first-year school in Scottsbluff, Nebraska, with 528 students. His first team went 12-3. And he stayed six years before budget problems killed athletics.

After several sales-related jobs and coaching opportunities in Peru and Sweden, he became a scout under Newell at Golden State and for Boston.

His last great contribution? Convincing the Celts to draft an obscure, odd-looking kid before his final season. Larry Bird was Anderson's kind of player.

Forddy Anderson

Head basketball coach

Year	Big Ten	Overall
1954-55	8-6	13-9
1955-56	7-7	13-9
1956-57	10-4	16-10
1957-58	9-5	16-6
1958-59	12-2	19-4
1959-60	5-9	10-11
1960-61	3-11	7-17
1961-62	3-11	8-14
1962-63	3-11	4-16
1963-64	8-6	14-10
1964-65	1-13	5-18
Total	182-160	340-220

Michigan State

Forddy Anderson

COACH PROFILE

John Benington

Benington shouts instructions, as assistant Gus Ganakas looks on.

Benington models a coaching jacket, with help from faculty representative John Fuzak.

He had been "Old Dad" since he starred for an NIT champ at age 27.

Those who knew John Benington would say he never lived to be old enough.

In 10 seasons at Michigan State—as an assistant basketball coach from 1950 to 1956 and as head coach from 1965 to 1969—Benington made more friends and fewer enemies than anyone who spent a decade in Jenison Field House.

When he died of a massive heart attack in a coaches' locker room at age 47, he left behind more than a wife and nine children.

Benington left a void that few replacements could hope to fill.

"There wasn't a better-liked guy in the whole area than John Benington," said Athletic Director Biggie Munn, the man who hired him. "He cared about people and made his players men. As a result, his teams won games."

The Spartans won 10 of 14 conference games in each of his first two seasons as head coach—a nine-win improvement—and were 54-38 overall.

"John Benington is the only coach who could win a Big Ten game for each of his children and consider it progress," wrote Bob Pille in the *Detroit Free Press*.

"You know how it goes," Benington countered. "As soon as a kid is born, he starts crying because he doesn't have a baby brother."

With raccoon rings around his eyes and more jokes than hair, his specialty was disarming opponents with self-deprecation and stubborn defense.

When asked about his playing days under Pete Newell, Benington said, "I went to San Francisco before Bill Russell did. In fact, when Russell left, they retired my jersey."

When asked if he had decided who would cover Purdue sensation Rick Mount, he said, "Yes, I have. But I'm not telling you. I don't want that kid dropping out of school."

In the last photo taken of him before his death, Benington talks with Big Ten supervisor of football officials Herm Rohrig.

And when he landed at Ypsilanti's Willow Run Airport at 2 a.m. after a recruiting trip, he phoned sleeping Michigan coach Dave Strack and said, "C'mon over for a cup of coffee! I'm awake. You should be, too."

Benington never played a minute of high school basketball in Findlay, Ohio. He wanted to try out for the team but was told he was wasting his time. After 40 months of Army duty, he came to USF and went out for football.

"We heard about this real good athlete—about 6-foot-4, 215 pounds," Newell said. "But when he got there, he was about 6-4, 160. He'd been in the Battle of the Bulge and hadn't eaten for about a month. On a clear day, you could see through him.

"They didn't have any football shoes big enough to fit him. The day I went out there, they were practicing goal-line stands. John was playing fullback in a pair of brown suede shoes, just getting killed. After practice, I told him, 'You're no longer a football player.'"

He was always a basketball coach. And when Newell agreed to come to MSC in 1950 as soon as his baseball coaching was completed, he sent Benington to conduct spring basketball practice and relay daily reports.

"I was the captain of the first team John ever coached, the Michigan State freshmen," said guard Rickey Ayala. "He took me on scouting trips down to Michigan and made me look at the game in a way I never had. He was the love of my life."

When Newell left to coach at California in 1954, Benington was bypassed by Munn. But he stayed two more seasons as an assistant to Forddy Anderson before becoming head coach at Drake for two years and at St. Louis for seven,

where his most vocal critic was Billiken play-by-play man Harry Caray.

Benington took five St. Louis teams to the NIT, with centers Bob Ferry and Bob Nordmann among his standout players. There, he collaborated with Newell on *Basketball Methods*, a bible for coaches for nearly three decades.

When the job came open with the Spartans again, Benington's name soared to the front of a list with head coaches Bob Stevens of Oklahoma, Stan Albeck of Northern Michigan, Ray Skinner of Vanderbilt, Ray Meers of Tennessee, Lefty Driesell of Davidson, Jack Ramsay of St. Joseph's, Bob Cousy of Boston College, assistants Bruce Fossum of MSU and Jim Skala of Michigan and ex-East Lansing High leader Gus Ganakas.

But before he replaced Anderson on April 22, 1965, Benington interviewed at Notre Dame and was seen as the logical choice.

"We'd never really thought that much about coming back to East Lansing," said his widow, Barbara. "He was virtually assured he'd get the Notre Dame job. They never even bothered to call him. He heard they'd hired Johnny Dee on the car radio. John didn't get mad. He got even."

His teams beat the Fighting Irish the next four years by a total of 62 points. And Benington finished third in the National Coach of the Year voting in 1966 behind Kentucky's Adolph Rupp and Texas Western's Don Haskins.

He signed top Michigan high school players like forward Lee Lafayette from Grand Rapids and attracted center Matthew Aitch and others from Moberly Junior College in Missouri, coached by his good friend Cotton Fitzsimmons.

"I can't think of a single situation where he talked about people in a

negative way," Aitch said. "He's the only person I've ever met who could get something good out of every situation."

When Benington recruited swingman Pat Miller of Menominee, in Michigan's Upper Peninsula, he stayed in Miller's home overnight, wore Mr. Miller's T-shirt to bed and tried to shave the next morning with Miller's sister's razor—only to learn it didn't have a blade.

And while trying to land his top all-time recruit, Detroit Pershing guard Ralph Simpson, Benington gave us a look at why he was so admired inside and outside the coaching profession.

"Those were the days when prospects got kidnapped," said Ganakas, by then a Spartan assistant. "We had to mail his tender from Detroit and had an appointment to see his coach, Will Robinson. But we passed this broken-down jalopy with two black couples on the side of I-96 near Williamston.

"John always drove. And he put on the brakes. I said, 'What are you doing? We don't have time!' He said, 'You always have time for people.' We got out of the car and got them going again—to the racetrack! Two days later, we signed Ralph Simpson."

Benington never got to coach the nation's No. 1 prospect. On April 11, 1969, he suffered a serious heart attack after a paddleball game. After months of recovery, he eased back to work and was declared fit for the season.

He was an avid golfer and once shot 71 at Forest Akers West. But after an alumni golf outing, Benington passed up a chance to play the next day. He said he had work to do on campus and sent Ganakas to break the course record.

Late that afternoon, everyone in the MSU community suffered a broken heart. Apparently, Benington went downstairs and jogged, then collapsed on the floor near the shower, where his body was found.

"He was doing just great," Barbara Benington said. "Then, my daughter called me at work and said he hadn't come home. I was in a meeting at Sparrow Hospital. And I finally went looking for him. I saw his car in the parking lot and found him at about 8 o'clock."

Nordmann, who had become an assistant coach, had just joined her at Jenison, where the worst fears of Spartans everywhere were realized.

"It was quite a shock because I was one of the last people to see him alive," said 1966 captain Bill Curtis. "He seemed to be in great shape. I hadn't seen him since the first heart attack. And we talked about basketball for a long time in the locker room. He was really excited about his team."

Team Benington is still winning today, with four children in coaching.

The John Benington Memorial Fund, spearheaded by assistant football coach Henry Bullough, raised $23,673, not counting two $10,000 scholarships.

The National Association of Basketball Coaches magazine ran a two-page tribute with the simple message, "It's nice to be important. It's more important to be nice."

And 23 years later, a perpetual nomination was received for the MSU Athletics Hall of Fame from intramurals staffer and paddleball opponent Russ Rivet.

It listed Benington's current address as "Heaven."

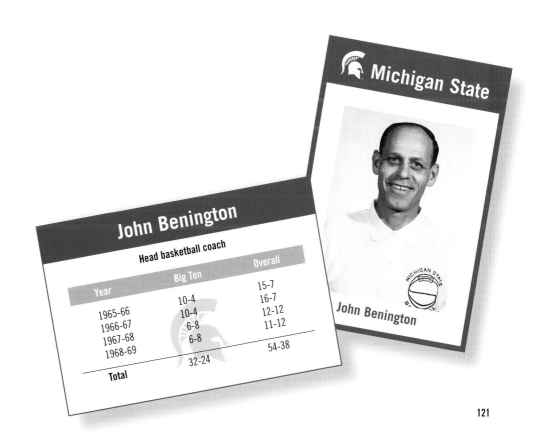

Michigan State

John Benington

John Benington

Head basketball coach

Year	Big Ten	Overall
		15-7
1965-66	10-4	16-7
1966-67	10-4	12-12
1967-68	6-8	11-12
1968-69	6-8	
Total	32-24	54-38

Gus Ganakas

Ganakas' last staff: from left, assistants Pat Miller, Vernon Payne and Dick Versace.

He is the only Michigan State basketball leader to beat Illinois, Iowa, Ohio State, and Purdue twice in the same year.

A few weeks later in 1976, after five straight winning records, including the second-highest victory total in the school's first 77 seasons, Gus Ganakas got a new title.

Former coach.

If he hadn't been fired and reassigned within the department, Ganakas would have been guaranteed the services of Lansing prep stars Earvin Johnson and Jay Vincent.

Sophomore Bob Chapman and freshman Gregory Kelser were already on campus.

And we can only guess whether Ganakas would have won an NCAA title with that group—or, as some wonder, whether he might have won two.

"Coach Ganakas didn't get the credit he deserved," said Chapman, his first coach's No. 1 booster. "There's no question in my mind we'd have won with Gus. I often say, 'Jud Heathcote should thank Gus every day that he got to sit in on Gus's championships.'"

What's irrefutable is that Ganakas has had a longer association with MSC and MSU athletics and a greater impact than any Greek except Sparty.

The Mount Morris, New York native came to campus in 1946, before Biggie Munn, Duffy Daugherty, and the return of green-and-white football uniforms.

Other than a few months as a teacher and coach in Olivet, Ganakas has never left East Lansing through rocky times and trips to the mountaintop.

"I wanted to go to school on the G.I. Bill, and my brother mentioned Michigan State College," he said. "I'd never heard of it. But I got a letter to come take an entrance exam in Jenison Field House. I had to ask where that was. I thought it was a house in the middle of a field."

He had served 25 months as a gung-ho Marine, including involvement in the Battle of Okinawa, and had just recovered from back surgery.

Ganakas played freshman and junior varsity baseball but didn't make the JV basketball team until his sophomore year. He was smart enough to know his future was as a coach, not an athlete—and to earn two degrees in four years.

"We lived in a trailer for $17 a month, then in barracks apartments," said Ganakas, who was married as a sophomore. "When John Hannah built housing for servicemen after the war, that was a key to Michigan State's growth. He wanted to build a university his football team could be proud of."

After a year as a volunteer coach with the MSC freshmen and his stop in Olivet, Ganakas taught math and coached basketball and football at East Lansing High, leading the Trojans to the 1958 Class B state basketball crown.

There, he became close with Spartan coach Pete Newell and assistant John Benington. But a year before Benington returned to succeed Forddy Anderson in 1965, Ganakas was hired as director of the Ralph Young Scholarship Fund.

"It was very traumatic that they opened the doors at East Lansing without me," a reluctant fund-raiser said. "I started to get withdrawal pains. But I could still walk to work—a few blocks south instead of north. And in those days, once you committed to a job, you took it.

"I played in so many outings, when they asked my daughter, Marcy, what her dad did for a living, she said, 'Oh, he plays golf for Michigan State!' I didn't even like golf then. I used to hope it rained."

He inquired about the basketball job when Anderson left and was asked about being a co-coach with assistant Bruce Fossum, as bizarre as that sounds. But Ganakas thought Northern Michigan's Stan Albeck was close to being hired when Benington was named.

In 1966, when Benington aide Sonny Means became the coach at Western Michigan, Ganakas was offered that job. When he was asked to think it over, he said, "Give me a couple of seconds. . . . OK!"

One month later, Eastern Michigan asked for permission to talk to him about its head coaching vacancy. Benington said, "Go." Ganakas said, "No." And EMU hired Jim Dutcher.

The following March, the Spartans earned a share of the Big Ten title. But since Indiana had gone one year longer without an NCAA Tournament appearance, MSU stayed home in the days of a single Big Ten representative.

In 1969, Ganakas' world changed when Benington suffered a heart attack in April and, after an apparent recovery, died in September.

Athletic Director Biggie Munn quickly promoted Ganakas to coach a team with sophomore sensation Ralph Simpson and just a 6-foot-6 center, Jim Gibbons. After a 3-6 start, Ganakas got lucky in his Big Ten debut at Indiana.

"We were down by one with seven seconds left and had to go the length of the court," he remembered with typical self-deprecation. "I told Ron Gutkowski to throw the ball in, figuring we'd get him out of the way. He did, and Ralph dribbled to the corner, took a long shot and missed. Who the hell do you think tipped it in? . . . Gutkowski! That's the kind of competitor he was.

Ganakas relays strategy to his backcourt.

Ganakas and assistant Bob Nordmann lobby for a call on the road.

"But late that year, I got a call at home from Biggie. We'd just lost by three to Purdue. And he said, 'Is the simpleton there?' My daughter turned around and said, 'Dad, it's for you.'"

Ganakas was never great with directions, once getting lost on a walk from the locker room to the bench on the road.

But he's best known for helping great scorers and for hurting his chances of keeping the job by allowing 10 players to walk out, then return the next day, in 1975.

"I always thought Coach Ganakas was very good technically and had a lot of compassion for his players," said swingman Pat Miller, later an assistant coach. "Sometimes that was misunderstood and taken advantage of."

Still, the most persistent criticism concerned the playing time of a 5-5 point guard—his son, Gary, who had 17 assists against Rochester in 1972, three more than Johnson's recognized school record.

"Those were very difficult times," said assistant coach Bob Nordmann. "Gus was such a nice guy. He'd give people tickets behind the bench. And they'd sit there and abuse him! The rest of his family was in tears.

"The thing is, Gus didn't want to play Gary. I had to push him into it. I said, 'He's the best guy we've got! If the goal is to win basketball games, Gary deserves to play.' If the team had won, it wouldn't have mattered."

Ganakas couldn't win with constant charges of nepotism and the need to play a locker-room lawyer who resented his father's resistence.

"I was very hateful of my dad," Gary said. "I had a lot of bad things to say about the coaching and told the other guys, 'He's an ass!' He tried to get me to transfer. But when Ralph left for the ABA and Tim Bograkos signed a baseball contract, somebody had to play.

"The first year, he'd play me on the road but not at home. He could've kicked a guy off the team once. But that would've meant I'd have had to start.

"Then, I'd get horrible phone calls, with people screaming obscenities. Once, I nearly went up in the stands. The ref gave me the ball on a throw-in, and I gave it right back to him. I turned around to go after a guy."

Today, many of Ganakas' players go to great lengths to praise him.

"I learned a lot from Gus," said center-turned-businessman Bill Kilgore. "I learned how to communicate with people and how to be open and honest."

"I wish I could go back and change a lot of things," said guard Benny White. "He was way ahead of his time in terms of the number of black players he had. And when I saw him lose his job. I felt really bad."

So did a son who had come to appreciate his father's predicament, even if he didn't agree with some decisions.

"The easiest thing to do would've been to kick those guys off the team after the walkout," Gary said. "He'd have been a hero. Instead, he did the humane thing and made the tough decision. I wouldn't have done that."

With no soap in the showers, long bus trips to games and ridiculous budget restrictions, Ganakas didn't know where to turn for help.

"I didn't even know who the trustees were," he said. "I never fraternized with anyone that way. I knew Biggie was my boss. That was it."

When a stroke ended that relationship, Ganakas was powerless to stop the purge that eventually cost him his job during a football inquiry.

But for more than 22 years, he has been part of the solution as an assistant A.D., a Spartan broadcaster, and an administrative aide to Tom Izzo.

"Gus was a friend and a father figure," Chapman said. "He taught me about basketball and more about life. When faced with adversity, do you sit and stew or pick yourself up and continue to fight? The true test of a man is how he responds to adversity. It's pretty clear how Gus has responded."

Michigan State

Gus Ganakas

Head basketball coach

Year	Big Ten	Overall
1969-70	5-9	9-15
1970-71	4-10	10-14
1971-72	6-8	13-11
1972-73	6-8	13-11
1973-74	8-6	13-11
1974-75	10-8	17-9
1975-76	10-8	14-13
Total	49-57	89-84

Gus Ganakas

Tom Izzo

A basketball coach with a football mindset assumes a baseball catcher's crouch on the sideline at Breslin.

The 1998 Big Ten Coach of the Year ballots had just been counted when a point guard's tribute said what no trophy could.

"That's my guy!" conference Player of the Year Mateen Cleaves said of demanding-yet-understanding Tom Izzo. "He's a father, a brother, and a friend all in one. If I'd had a vote, I wouldn't have just put a check by his name. I'd have been out campaigning and passing out flyers."

A jump shot away in Breslin Center, Izzo had just finished saying all the right things to a group of 11- and 12-year-olds.

"I think he's more than the Coach of the Year," said Okemos youth leader John Cawood. "He's the Coach of the Next Generation. He's a builder of people and a builder of confidence."

Later that month, Izzo was named the National Coach of the Year by the Associated Press and the United States Basketball Writers Association for leading Michigan State to a share of the league title and a berth in the NCAA Tournament's Sweet 16.

"Maybe this is an I-told-you-so," said his Spartan mentor, Jud Heathcote. "I was instrumental in Tom getting this job because he deserved it and I knew he would do a good job. He took a young team with a great point guard and overachieved all year."

It was no different than what Izzo has done his whole life, knocking down doors that were closed but not locked by outworking and outwilling opponents.

To appreciate the proudest of Yoopers, you should know his great-grandfather worked in the iron mines and was killed in one, his grandfather was a cobbler who worked to age 89, and his father finished high school in his late 30s, then was elected president of the Iron Mountain School Board.

"Don't ask me who can make it and who can't," Izzo said. "I'm one of those guys who believes in miracles. I tell our players that when people say we spend too much time dreaming, I want them to dream."

His dreams began in a town of 8,500. And when he dropped to the floor in tears after a missed free throw with :02 left in the 1972 Class B Regional Final, Izzo became even more of an inspiration than he already was.

Undersized and unrecruited, he went to Northern Michigan as the 25th man in a 25-man program, made his first career start against MSU and became a third-team Division II All-American.

There, he roomed with his workout buddy from high school and best friend to this day, quarterback Steve Mariucci, head coach of the San Francisco 49ers.

"We were just a couple of wallflowers who wanted to succeed," Mariucci said of an amazing pairing. "We had a bet to see who was going to be the head coach at Notre Dame first."

A better path for Izzo began with a head coaching job at Ishpeming High, which promptly won a league title, then with an assistant's position at NMU.

He took a $15,000 pay cut to become Heathcote's third assistant in 1983 and spent 12 seasons earning the trust it took to earn a final promotion.

"I always thought Tom would take over," said ex-Spartan aide Herb Williams. "He was loyal. He worked his tail off. And everyone liked him. But in 1986, he went to Tulsa for about a month before Mike Deane left for Siena. When Tom went in and told J.D. Barnett he wanted to go back to Michigan State, J.D. threw all his stuff out in the hall."

Izzo has never looked back and has been the key figure in recruiting players who've been in 10 straight post-season tournaments.

"He was so sincere about everything," said former point guard Mark Montgomery. "There were no lines of B.S. and no promises. And wherever we were that summer, he was there, too. He built great relationships."

Izzo built a great one with Chris Webber in a five-year recruitment, then saw the missing piece to MSU's national championship puzzle head to Ann Arbor, with help from Wolverine boosters.

The Spartans never had a chance at the best players money could buy and often had to answer questions about Heathcote's age and disposition.

But Izzo refused to recognize "isn't" and "can't" as anything but four-letter words, once showing up at assistant Brian Gregory's door after bedcheck with a VCR and more Michigan tapes the morning of a 67-64 triumph.

"I knew Tom would be an excellent coach," said ex-forward Dwayne Stephens. "There was never a doubt in my mind. When we won the Big Ten title in 1990, I realized how much went into college basketball. We didn't have nearly the talent of some of the other teams in the league. And when people couldn't talk to Jud, everything fell on Tom."

"I've been impressed from the first time he called and asked how I wanted him to handle recruiting," said former center Mike Peplowski. "I said not to call me. And he's the only one who did that. He didn't have to. We clicked right away. It never crossed my mind that he wouldn't be a great head coach. He cares too much for it to be any other way."

Izzo talks strategy with Jason Klein and gets his message across.

Izzo signals for one final shot—and one winning effort.

In his debut in 1995–96, without All-American Shawn Respert and all-time Izzo favorite Eric Snow in the backcourt, MSU battled a brutal schedule and went 9-9 in the Big Ten and 16-16 overall.

The following season, the Spartans were 9-9 and 17-12. And in a stunning breakthough in Izzo's third year, the program improved to 13-3 and 22-8—again trimming its losses by four.

"The players and assistants deserve the credit," he said, continuing to take the job more seriously than himself. "I actually think we did just as good a job the first year to be .500. The fact is, it takes players to win."

If there was a signature moment, it might have come in 1995, when Izzo pulled four players out of practice and arranged a mandatory 7 a.m. study session with disgruntled professor Charles Scarborough that drummed home the importance of academics.

Or it could have come after a loss at Northwestern in 1997, when Izzo solved the problem of slow starts with a 20-minute rebounding free-for-all just before a win over Penn State—a session that forced forward A.J. Granger to change a bloody uniform.

"That night was the turning point," said Tom Crean, Izzo's chief assistant

and former roommate. "It could all have come crashing down. But that was a genius move and typical of Tom. He knows what he wants and knows how to get it. He demands perfection. But the players can go to him."

Izzo's intensity in practice and before, during, and after games would shock those who can't believe he'd rather be a football coach.

"He'll never sit back on the bench with his legs crossed," Crean said before drawing two parallels to Heathcote. "But I don't think he'll take a basketball and slam it up his nose, either. I really don't care if he hits his head. I just hope he doesn't hit his assistants."

Izzo has hit it off with Earvin Johnson, who talks to him two or three times a year and has volunteered to help in any way possible.

"He's a really good guy who loves his team," Johnson said before a 1998 win over Michigan. "I never felt he was comfortable until this year. Now, it's his team and his style. He doesn't have to do what Jud did. And there hasn't

been a Spartan team—ours included—that plays defense and pressures the ball the way they do."

Despite a no-agent contract worth roughly $600,000 per year—or nearly 100 times what he earned when he came to East Lansing—Izzo is still the first one in the office most mornings.

A blue-collar workaholic is clearly much more at home in green. But he has relaxed just a bit, thanks largely to wife Lupe and daughter Raquel.

"I can cry in front of my players and laugh in front of them," Izzo said. "I'm not afraid to do either one. Whatever I am, I'm human."

Two years ago, he was ridiculed on sports talk shows as an assistant who should never have been promoted. Today, he's the "Wizard of Iz."

It's all the same guy—the one who did a grown man's work at age 14 and will do the work of any three men if that's what it takes to win.

Michigan State

Tom Izzo

Tom Izzo

Head basketball coach

Year	Big Ten	Overall
1995-96	9-9	16-16
1996-97	9-9	17-12
1997-98	13-3	22-8
Total	31-21	55-36

The kings of college basketball are greeted at the Capitol in Lansing after the Parade of Champions.

The Teams

A Big Ten (11)

1978–79

A long student tunnel to the court in Jenison ends with a breakthrough banner.

Only 31 schools have won national titles in 60 years of NCAA Tournaments.

If the 1978–79 Michigan State Spartans weren't the best of all those champions—and you could argue they might be—Jud Heathcote's players were certainly one of the most exciting teams to reach a Final Four.

MSU didn't just win. It smashed five tourney foes, including Mideast No. 1 seed Notre Dame and 33-0 finalist Indiana State, by a total of 104 points.

Earvin Johnson, a 6-foot-8 guard with eyes in his ears, played a different game than his befuddled, first-time opponents had ever seen.

And Gregory Kelser, a 6-7 forward who read his mail above the rim, was the ideal partner for an acrobatic, mid-air ballet.

"Johnson and Kelser . . . partners in destruction," said broadcaster Bill Flemming on "Spartan Magic," the NCAA's 1979 highlight video.

But they weren't alone in producing a second straight Big Ten crown at 13-5—the same record as Iowa and Purdue—and a 26-6 overall mark.

When healthy, Jay Vincent, a not-quite-6-8 center with soft hands and stunning grace, was a load for any taller defender.

Ron Charles, a 6-8 forward and center, went from starter to sub to starter again and was a model of efficiency, seldom missing.

Mike Brkovich, a 6-4 shooter, scored the season's four biggest points from the line just before the buzzer and on a dunk before the first eyeblink.

And Terry Donnelly, a 6-2 guard, provided stability and perfect shooting when MSU and ISU gave the game a boost that's still being felt.

"When you talk about 1979, you talk about Johnson, Vincent, and Kelser," said hoopaholic Dick Vitale. "But they had the perfect support players in Donnelly, Brkovich, and Charles. And they played so well as a team."

Much of that credit must go to Heathcote, who made the perfect mid-season moves for the Spartans to win 15 of their last 16.

Terry Donnelly drives against Cincinnati in the Pontiac Silverdome.

"I remember how big they were," said Indiana's Isiah Thomas, then a high school senior in Chicago. "When they went to their matchup zone, they were almost impossible to shoot over or rebound against. But they were also a fun team to watch."

That wouldn't have been nearly as enjoyable if Johnson had applied for the NBA Draft after his freshman year in 1978, as he briefly considered doing.

"The Kansas City Kings had the first pick and offered me $275,000," he said. "But I knew we were going to win it all the next year. Unless they'd offered me something incredible, I was going to stay in school."

With every key contributor except guard Bob Chapman back from a 25-5 team, it was easy to see why Johnson thought that way.

And after nearly beating eventual champ Kentucky the previous March, anything but a perfect post-season would have been a huge disappointment to players, coaches, and fans alike.

First, however, MSU had to make it that far—a greater achievement than anyone could have imagined when it felt the effects of a draining late summer tour of Brazil.

After a workman-like win over Central Michigan and an ugly scrum against Cal State Fullerton at home, the Spartans romped by 40 at Western Michigan.

But after a 70-69 loss at North Carolina, Heathcote's players struggled past Cincinnati in the first college basketball game in the Pontiac Silverdome.

A blowout of Heathcote's alma mater, Washington State, and solid decisions over Oregon State and Indiana gave 7-1 MSU the Far West Classic title.

And a 2-0 Big Ten start against Wisconsin and Minnesota in always-jammed Jenison Field House gave no clue of the near collapse to follow.

The Spartans lost back-to-back road games on improbable shots at the buzzer by forwards Eddie Johnson of Illinois and Arnette Hallman of Purdue.

After a 24-point whipping of the Hoosiers in the second of three triumphs over Bob Knight's club, MSU was fortunate to slip past Iowa in overtime.

"If we'd lost that game, we never would've been in the NCAA Tournament," Kelser said. "We were clearly better than Iowa, though we never could guard Ronnie Lester. And Brk's two free throws saved our season."

"The Golden Arm," as Brkovich was known, couldn't rescue the Spartans in Ann Arbor. A disputed foul against Johnson with no time left allowed Michigan guard Keith Smith to sink a free throw for a 49-48 victory.

Two days later, everything fell apart in an 83-65 humiliation at lowly Northwestern, leaving the 4-4 Spartans four games behind Ohio State.

"It was crazy," Kelser said. "Northwestern did everything right. And we couldn't do anything right. Two days wasn't enough time to regroup from the Michigan fiasco. And I could sense before the game we just didn't have it. I wanted to throw in the towel. As a result, we got killed."

Reports of MSU's death were premature, as Heathcote's decision to start Brkovich and bring Charles off the bench helped significantly. And the Spartans began to run again after an emotional gripe session.

"When we walked out of that meeting, there was a renaissance," Kelser said. "There was a much better feeling about ourselves and the coaching staff. Jud said he'd back off a little bit. And he did—for one game. Then, he went back to being his old self. But by then, we were winning."

Before that Monday afternoon therapy session, there was another outburst from Heathcote that helped, Vincent said.

"After we lost to Northwestern, Coach was really mad," he remembered.

Mike Brkovich dunks over Kansas All-American Darnell Valentine.

Matthews hit a prayer from midcourt in an 83-81 thriller.

As the Mideast's No. 2 seed in the NCAA, MSU opened in Murfreesboro, Tennessee, against Lamar, which had just stunned Detroit.

With Heathcote convincing his players they could be beaten and Lamar foolishly mocking him in warmups, the final was 95-64.

"Before the game, I wasn't quite sure who this Earvin Johnson kid was," loosey-goosey Lamar coach Billy Tubbs said 14 years later, after moving to Oklahoma. "My assistant said I ought to come out and watch him. I figured we'd run past them like everyone else. But they beat us so bad I never did see them going up and down the court."

That was the day backup guard Jaimie Huffman forever became "Shoes" for his struggle to re-lace and tie while play continued—and the afternoon NBC's Dick Enberg learned a lot more about Johnson and Kelser.

"We had 45 minutes before Notre Dame played Tennessee and asked if they'd come out and visit," Enberg said. "Instead, the network switched to another game and never got back to us. Earvin and Greg must've stood there for 25 minutes. Finally, I apologized. And they slapped me on the back and said, 'That's all right. . . . We'll catch you later!'

"That really reflected the kind of people they were and certainly endeared them to us. We in the press and in broadcasting were no different than anyone else. You had to be abnormal not to love Johnson and Kelser."

After dispensing with LSU 87-71 in Indianapolis, behind 18 points and 14 rebounds from "Bobo," as Charles was known, the Spartans finally had the chance they cherished in front of the NBC peacock and everyone else.

The Fighting Irish—an NCAA semifinalist the previous year—were on TV more than David Brinkley in those days and made MSU's blood boil.

"I remember Kelly Tripucka saying they'd win that day and get back to the Final Four," Kelser said. "We weren't going to let that happen."

An 80-68 thrashing started with Brkovich's dunk on a special play off the opening tip. But maybe it began even before that.

"When we got to the locker room, I turned on the music, as always,"

"He said some things I really can't say. Then, he said, 'We're going to win. You know why? . . . Because I said so! And I can whip anyone in here!' When he took off his coat, nobody stood up to challenge him."

His team stood tall in an overtime classic against OSU, as Johnson limped back to the court with a sprained ankle and sparked an 84-79 triumph.

"That was the game we absolutely had to win," Kelser said. "It's not like today, where they'll take six teams from a conference. The most that could go were two. Even sharing the title, Purdue had to settle for the NIT."

After surviving another scare from Northwestern, MSU clobbered Kansas 85-61 the following day in Jenison in a rare national TV appearance.

"After that, the show was on," Johnson said. "That's when it all kicked in. We started dunking on everyone and making fancy plays."

Consecutive road wins over the Hawkeyes, Buckeyes, and Hoosiers made the Spartans 9-4, 17-5 when the Wolverines came to town and left as corpses.

"We led 46-14," Johnson said of an 80-57 flogging. "Everyone kept hollering, 'Fourteen points! . . . Fourteen points!' That was our best game."

Payback wins over Purdue and Illinois and a victory at Minnesota locked up at least a share of the league crown and an NCAA berth.

But Wisconsin proved the Spartans could be beaten, when guard Wes

Johnson and Kelser face the media at a Final Four press conference.

Johnson shakes free for another easy basket in a Final Four romp against Penn.

match with East Region surprise Pennsylvania awaited.

"Just like we couldn't wait to play Notre Dame, we wanted to play North Carolina again, too," Kelser said. "They'd beaten us in Chapel Hill, in a game when we got zero calls. But we never got that chance. Penn took care of them."

The Quakers also reduced their chances of beating the Spartans to Powerball lottery odds by flapping their lips the day before the game.

"We wouldn't normally have been so high," Johnson said of a 101-67 domination. "But what did Penn do? They went on TV and said, 'They're not going to dunk on us!' I looked at Greg. He looked at me. And I said, 'OK, let's go!' If they'd kept their mouths shut, it probably would've been a 10-point game. Instead, they got us all jacked up."

Not very smart for an Ivy League school. And when the score was 50-17 at halftime, it didn't make for spell-binding television.

"I remember looking at the scoreboard and seeing it was something like 40-8," Enberg said. "I told Al McGuire, 'This is a disaster! I can't believe we have a whole second half to go!' I wondered if Pennsylvania would ever get into double-figures."

The Quakers actually got better looks at the basket than most MSU foes. And if they had taken off their blindfolds, it could have been a game.

NBC got the game of their dreams when the Sycamores and Larry Bird met

Jay Vincent and Kelser put the squeeze on Indiana State's Carl Nicks.

Johnson said. "Then, Jud came in to give us our last-minute instructions. I turned the music off. And he said, '"E," what are you doing? . . . I don't have anything to tell you that you don't already know. You know what to do.'"

If any Spartan players weren't sure, an often-volatile coach lowered his usual volume and summarized the game plan in a simple seven-word message.

"I didn't give a pregame speech that afternoon," Heathcote said. "All I did was write on the blackboard: 'LET'S GO OUT AND KICK SOME ASS.'"

"After that, they never had a chance," Johnson said. "We didn't want to beat them. We wanted to kill them. And we ran that team into the ground."

When it came to NBA talent, at least in sheer numbers, Notre Dame had a definite edge with Tripucka, Bill Laimbeer, Orlando Woolridge, Bill Hanzlik, Tracy Jackson, and Bruce Flowers.

"That was a very good team we had," said Irish coach Digger Phelps. "We had six pros. But we ran into the wrong outfit."

"That was Digger's best team," Enberg said. "And it was probably the National Championship game. If the Irish had been lucky, they'd have been sent to a different region."

Kelser was the best player in the nation that Sunday, scoring 34 points and grabbing 14 rebounds on St. Patrick's Day.

"I still think Notre Dame was the second-best club in the country that year," Heathcote said. "They had a whole NBA team, plus Rich Branning. But we knew we were better."

MSU's second Final Four trip took them to Salt Lake City where a mis-

Johnson snips the final strand of a priceless net in Salt Lake City.

MSU and "The Magic Man" in a matchup that helped change the game.

It glamorized the pass as never before and showed what can happen when 6-9 and 6-8 players care more about wins than points.

"Watching those two guys that night really excited me," said Dwayne Stephens, a Spartan forward 11 years later. "It made me want to go out and do the same things they did."

In an era with no 35-second clock and no 3-point shot, Bird and Johnson captivated the nation's fans in the first of many spectacular meetings.

But with Johnson impersonating Bird on the scout team in practice, MSU was able to master Heathcote's scheme of shadowing Bird with a matchup zone and win 75-64.

"We finally met our match," Bird said. "They just had a better team. They had a lot of guys who could run, jump, and shoot. On our team, if I wasn't hitting my shots, we were in for a battle and were probably going to lose."

Bird had to work for his 19 points but still moved into fifth place on the all-time NCAA scoring list behind Pete Maravich, Freeman Williams, Oscar Robertson, and Elvin Hayes.

Johnson was named the Final Four MVP with 24 points, while Kelser fought through foul trouble and nearly recorded a triple-double with 19 points, nine assists, and eight rebounds.

"Indiana State had Larry Bird but not the same supporting cast," Enberg said. "Michigan State had another great player in Kelser. And that's like having two great hitters in the middle of a lineup. You can pitch around one but not two.

"Most great teams have two or three brilliant players. They don't have one outstanding guy and four chemistry majors."

The chemistry and teamwork 20 seasons ago has never been surpassed in the Big Ten and has seldom been equaled.

"What I remember most that year is Earvin bringing the best out of a lot of other very good players," said George Fox, his high school coach at Lansing Everett. "The way he would move up the floor with the ball on the break and feed Kelser and Charles was just amazing."

"We were so versatile you couldn't stop us," Johnson said. "We caused so many matchup problems. And Jud was a master of breaking an opponent down. He would always design something to take the other team's star out of the game. Any team we played that wasn't in the Big Ten was in trouble."

Opponents in the 51st NCAA Tournament saw a depth-weakened MSU team, once Vincent suffered a foot injury against Lamar.

"Just think what we could've done if Jay had been healthy," Johnson said. "Man, we'd have been scary!"

The Spartans were frightening enough without him—and afraid of no one.

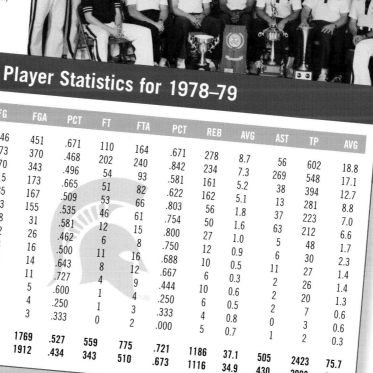

The 1978-79 Spartans: Front—Manager Randy Bishop, equipment manager Ed Belloli, assistants Fred Paulsen and Bill Berry, head coach Jud Heathcote, assistant Dave Harshman, trainer Clint Thompson and manager Darwin Payton. Back—Terry Donnelly, Greg Lloyd, Gerald Gilkie, Don Brkovich, Rick Kaye, Ron Charles, Earvin Johnson, Gregory Kelser, Jay Vincent, Rob Gonzalez, Mike Brkovich, Jaimie Huffman and Mike Longaker.

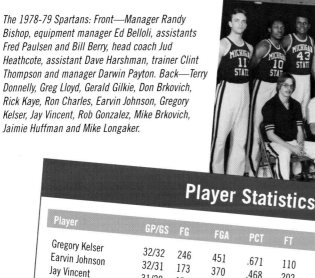

Player Statistics for 1978–79

Player	GP/GS	FG	FGA	PCT	FT	FTA	PCT	REB	AVG	AST	TP	AVG
Gregory Kelser	32/32	246	451	.671	110	164	.671	278	8.7	56	602	18.8
Earvin Johnson	32/31	173	370	.468	202	240	.842	234	7.3	269	548	17.1
Jay Vincent	31/28	170	343	.496	54	93	.581	161	5.2	38	394	12.7
Ron Charles	32/23	115	173	.665	51	82	.622	162	5.1	13	281	8.8
Mike Brkovich	32/15	85	167	.509	53	66	.803	56	1.8	37	223	7.0
Terry Donnelly	32/31	83	155	.535	46	61	.754	50	1.6	63	212	6.6
Rob Gonzalez	28/0	18	31	.581	12	15	.800	27	1.0	5	48	1.7
Gerald Busby	13/0	12	26	.462	6	8	.750	12	0.9	6	30	2.3
Greg Lloyd	19/0	8	16	.500	11	16	.688	10	0.5	11	27	1.4
Mike Longaker	19/0	9	14	.643	8	12	.667	6	0.3	2	26	1.4
Rick Kaye	16/0	8	11	.727	4	9	.444	10	0.6	2	20	1.3
Don Brkovich	11/0	3	5	.600	1	4	.250	6	0.5	2	7	0.6
Gerald Gilkie	5/0	1	4	.250	1	3	.333	4	0.8	0	3	0.6
Jaimie Huffman	7/0	1	3	.333	0	2	.000	5	0.7	1	2	0.3
MICHIGAN STATE	32/32	932	1769	.527	559	775	.721	1186	37.1	505	2423	75.7
OPPONENTS	32/32	830	1912	.434	343	510	.673	1116	34.9	430	2003	62.6

1956–57

Larry Hedden's long arm reaches in to break up a Wolverine's dribble.

Perhaps it was finishing 10-4 in the Big Ten and capturing the school's first conference title, a co-championship with Indiana.

Or maybe it was the way they battled in the NCAA Tournament, advancing to what's now the Final Four and stunning a college basketball giant.

Whatever it was, the 1956–57 season was more than a breakthrough for Forddy Anderson's Michigan State Spartans.

It was a wild climb that could have reached the top with a break or two.

No one would have expected that with the graduation of Julius McCoy, who averaged 27.2 points as a senior and left as the school's top career scorer.

But MSU was a better team with a more balanced attack than a one-man show, and wound up a deceptive 16-10 after a 4-7 start.

"We're a team without a star," Anderson said before the season. "We want to stress team play and develop every man as a potential scorer."

Despite that plan, the Spartans did little to dispel the preseason pes-

simism with a 4-3 December and a disastrous next three weeks.

MSU dropped a pair of one-point decisions at home—72-71 to Purdue and 70-69 to Michigan—ending a five-game series win streak.

An 86-76 nonconference loss at Notre Dame and a 70-51 whipping by 10th-ranked Ohio State in the new St. John Arena left the Spartans three games behind the league-leading Buckeyes.

But one problem vanished when sophomore center Johnny Green, who joined the team in January, became comfortable with Anderson and his teammates.

Another disappeared after a much-needed team meeting aired concerns of the coaches and players and turned a season around.

"There were problems with guys being late for practice and team functions," said sophomore Bob Anderegg, the team's sixth man. "It was all starting to add up.

"When we talked about it, everyone was candid. That opened the lines

Jack Quiggle drives for a score against the Wolverines.

of communication and helped us realize our potential. We had to change our ways and play together. And that's what we did. Right away, we got on a roll."

Much like the 1979 national champs after a mid-season soul-search, MSU went on a 10-game tear, matching the school's longest streak since 1934–35.

And the first win in that stretch came without junior guard Jack Quiggle, who broke team rules in Columbus and didn't make the trip to Minneapolis.

Without their top offensive player, the Spartans prevailed 72-59 behind 25 points from junior forward Larry Hedden and 15 from Green.

MSU's first victory in eight visits to Williams Arena was so decisive it was tough for Dick Gordon of the *Minneapolis Tribune* to believe.

"Neither the final score nor the fact State had been winless in Big Ten play can aptly describe the surprise package thrown at Ozzie Cowles' team in the most convincing home defeat in the maestro's nine-year regime," he wrote.

But the best aspect of the win occurred when the team returned to Lansing and was met by a contrite Quiggle.

"When we got back, Jack said he'd made a mistake and was sorry," Hedden said. "Everybody said, 'Let's go forward and forget about it.' And Forddy didn't use the suspension as a motivational tactic. He was more concerned that our play wasn't what it should be."

"What Jack did wasn't so bad," Anderson said. "We're glad to have him back. He's one of the best ever to play at State and will continue to be a great help the rest of the season."

Sophomore guard Tom Rand had to guard Quiggle every day in practice and noticed a meaningful change off the court.

"That was probably the best thing that ever happened to Jack—and to the rest of us, too," Rand said. "We pulled it together and won our first game without him. He realized that with him, we had three losses, and without him, we had our first win. So he came around and became more of a leader.

"Jack was a diamond in the rough—an other-side-of-the-tracks type kid. He had great instincts and was extremely talented. He wasn't the fastest guy. But pressure never registered in his mind."

Buoyed by the win at Minnesota, MSU removed the Buckeyes from the ranks of the unbeaten after six straight conference wins, 73-64 in Jenison Field House.

Quiggle, who sat out the first 10 minutes, had a team-high 21 points and grabbed nine rebounds, while Hedden added 17 points and Green 16 rebounds.

Anderson's idea of "Any man, any night'" began to take shape.

Senior forward George Ferguson had 20 points and senior guard Pat Wilson 15 at Illinois, ending a 21-game Fighting Illini win streak at Huff Gymnasium.

And Quiggle, who led his team with 15.3 points per game, hit a 25-footer with :08 left for a 68-66 win at Purdue.

"Jack just kept winning games for us," Anderson said. "And to win in West Lafayette is a real chore, believe me. After a layup, their student body would actually hold you. Meanwhile, they'd come up the floor five-on-four."

But the biggest shot was the shot-in-the-arm Green provided with his incredible leaping ability and 14.6 rebounds per game.

And since the Spartans had no one among the top 15 scorers in the Big Ten and just one player in the top 20, Ferguson and Hedden were huge contributors.

"George always was in the right place at the right time," Rand said of MSU's captain, a walk-on and a strong inspiration. "He was pure hustle and made baskets that nobody else could have made because of his desire."

Bench strength came from Anderegg, who would have been a starter on most teams; junior center Chuck Bencie, a starter before Green became eligible; and sophomore guard Dave Scott, the only Michigan native on the team.

"We had nine good players, which was a big advantage for us," said Ferguson, the best captain Anderson ever had. "I think that depth really pulled us through."

"Scott, Anderegg, and Bencie were instrumental, not only because they were ready to play but because of the competition they brought to every practice and scrimmage," said Hedden, an excellent perimeter shooter.

A 78-62 win at Wisconsin was MSU's ninth straight triumph. And when Indiana lost at Michigan, both teams were 9-3 when they met in Jenison.

Big Ten faculty representatives had just decided that, in case of a tie, the league's lone NCAA Tournament bid should go to the team that had been out of post-season play the longest.

Captain George Ferguson prepares to pass from the post against BYU.

Rough weather couldn't stop fans from waiting in line for hours when MSU met Indiana in a 1957 showdown.

Since MSU had never been to the NCAA and Indiana had gone in 1954, that meant the Spartans would go if they tied with the Hoosiers or tied for second place behind fading OSU, a program on Big Ten and NCAA probation.

Fan interest in the Indiana game was beyond belief, especially given the near-blizzard conditions in East Lansing.

With 1,000 general admission tickets for an 8 p.m. tipoff going on sale at 6:30 p.m., lines formed long before noon and stretched past Demonstration Hall and to Kellogg Center.

A turnaway crowd of 13,817 was well over the listed capacity of 12,500. And nearly 2,000 more stood outside to listen to the public address announcer.

Inside Jenison, MSU's fast break was too strong for the Hoosiers in the second half of a spectacular 76-61 win.

"What a game!" said Spartan superfan Duane Vernon. "People were in line for tickets at 8 a.m. Then, when the Red Cedar flooded, fans had to walk on planks to get there. But the place was bananas. And when Forddy pulled his starters one by one at the end, the crowd went crazy again and again."

Appropriately, the critical game was won with a collective effort.

Hedden gave give MSU a 35-31 halftime lead with 14 of his 22 points in the first 20 minutes. Quiggle exploded for 18 of his team-high 23 after the break. And Green dominated the boards, snatching 19 rebounds and adding 13 points.

As time expired, hundreds of fans stormed the court, hoisted Anderson and his players on their shoulders and gave them a triumphant exit.

"The time surrounding and following that game were great," Ferguson said. "The noise just reverberated around Jenison. It was one of the most exciting times ever on campus."

The excitement and fairy tale atmosphere continued in the NCAA Tournament. MSU, suddenly No. 11 in the nation, held on to top No. 17 Notre Dame 85-83 in a first-round game in Lexington, Kentucky, where it was easy being Green.

"People hadn't seen him much and weren't really sure what he could do," Anderson said. "John's forte was rebounding. And he had 27 against Notre Dame. But the 20 points was kind of a novelty."

That win set up a battle with No. 3 Kentucky on its home court—something that could never happen today—for a trip to the national semifinals.

Few gave MSU a chance at Memorial Coliseum. And at halftime, with the Spartans down 47-35 and Green having four fouls, a crowd of 12,500 figured it was watching Kentucky's 24th win of the season.

Instead, MSU played as well as any team could in the second half and won 80-68.

"They played like they were possessed," Anderson said.

Attacking the basket and hitting their outside shots, the Spartans tied the game at 54 before losing Green on a fifth foul with 12:18 to play.

That's when MSU beat Adolph Rupp's Wildcats at their own game, out-running a team that treated every game like the Kentucky Derby.

Bencie was outstanding, as the hosts managed just 21 second-half points and suffered only their fifth home loss in 14 years.

"Charlie always worked hard in practice," Hedden said. "When Johnny took over as the starting center, he never gave up and never complained or was bitter about it. When he had to come in and make a contribution, he was ready. He was that type of guy."

It was just that type of game—Spartan Basketball.

"That was Forddy's system," Hedden said. "Everybody got to contribute. But even with most of the tickets going to Kentucky, I remember a Michigan State flag being waved prominently."

With one second left, the school's first Big Ten title was well in hand.

Pat Wilson gets free but still has to deal with Hoosier big man Archie Dees.

"I remember walking into one of the taverns after we beat Kentucky, expecting their fans not to be too friendly," Ferguson said. "We were trying to be incognito, which was hard to do. Their fans recognized us and started to give us all sorts of compliments. I'd never seen that happen anywhere."

The following afternoon at Capitol City Airport, a crowd estimated as high as 10,000 jammed the runways to celebrate what Athletic Director Biggie Munn called the greatest comeback he had ever seen in sports.

"There were people all over the place," Rand said. "We couldn't land the first time, so we went back up. Some of the guys had hangovers. And going up again really didn't sit well. But when we did land, everybody got carried off on the fans' shoulders. It was really something to see and be a part of."

A 74-70 triple-overtime loss to No. 1 North Carolina in the national semifinals could have turned out differently if Quiggle hadn't injured his ankle in the opening minutes, if his buzzer-beating heave hadn't been ruled a fraction of a second too late or if Green had hit a simple free throw.

But nothing could take away from what MSU accomplished in a season when a projected also-ran refused to quit running.

The 1956-57 Spartans: Front—Jack Quiggle, Jim Stouffer, Harry Lux, George Ferguson, Pat Wilson, Dave Scott and Tom Rand. Back—Head Coach Forddy Anderson, Bob Anderegg, Tom Markovich, Johnny Green, Gary Siegmeier, Chuck Bencie, Larry Jennings, Larry Hedden, Joe Reading, assistant Bob Stevens and trainer Gayle Robinson.

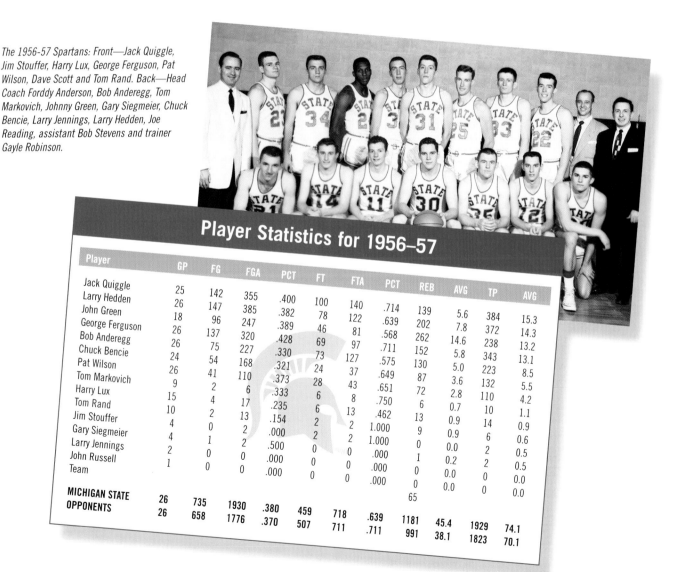

Player Statistics for 1956–57

Player	GP	FG	FGA	PCT	FT	FTA	PCT	REB	AVG	TP	AVG
Jack Quiggle	25	142	355	.400	100	140	.714	139	5.6	384	15.3
Larry Hedden	26	147	385	.382	78	122	.639	202	7.8	372	14.3
John Green	18	96	247	.389	46	81	.568	262	14.6	238	13.2
George Ferguson	26	137	320	.428	69	97	.711	152	5.8	343	13.1
Bob Anderegg	26	75	227	.330	73	127	.575	130	5.0	223	8.5
Chuck Bencie	24	54	168	.321	24	37	.649	87	3.6	132	5.5
Pat Wilson	26	41	110	.373	28	43	.651	72	2.8	110	4.2
Tom Markovich	9	2	6	.333	6	8	.750	6	0.7	10	1.1
Harry Lux	15	4	17	.235	6	13	.462	13	0.9	14	0.9
Tom Rand	10	2	13	.154	2	2	1.000	9	0.9	6	0.6
Jim Stouffer	4	0	2	.000	2	2	1.000	0	0.0	2	0.5
Gary Siegmeier	4	1	2	.500	0	0	.000	1	0.2	2	0.5
Larry Jennings	2	0	0	.000	0	0	.000	0	0.0	0	0.0
John Russell	1	0	0	.000	0	0	.000	0	0.0	0	0.0
Team								65			
MICHIGAN STATE	26	735	1930	.380	459	718	.639	1181	45.4	1929	74.1
OPPONENTS	26	658	1776	.370	507	711	.711	991	38.1	1823	70.1

1977–78

Kelser, Johnson, and Donnelly bask in the glory of another win.

t didn't all happen in one year—or even with one head coach.

But when the pieces were finally in place, the Michigan State Spartans were the equal of any team in college basketball in 1977–78.

They were runaway Big Ten champions at 15-3 and the school's first team to win 20 games, stopping a play or two short of the Final Four at 25-5.

Though Jud Heathcote's imprint was all over his second MSU team, a share of the credit also belonged to Gus Ganakas, who recruited co-captains Bob Chapman and Gregory Kelser and surely would have landed local sensations Earvin Johnson and Jay Vincent if he hadn't been reassigned.

"That wouldn't even have been a question," Johnson said.

"If Gus had still been here, none of us would've waited so long," Vincent said. "Everyone in Lansing wanted to play for Gus Ganakas. To us, he was a legend, with all the great scorers he had."

The transition from Ganakas to Heathcote was tough for everyone and

toughest for Chapman, who played two seasons for each coach.

"It was certainly two different styles," said Chapman, one of the best Spartans not to make our top 25 players. "I don't know if it was basketball philosophy as much as how they dealt with people. Both were sticklers for fundamentals. But Coach Ganakas related to his players a lot better. Coach Heathcote had the Army mentality, where you beat someone down."

Heathcote's teams beat 29 different opponents a total of 51 times in a two-year span. So his approach obviously worked on the court. And almost every player thinks more of his coach today than he did during windsprints.

"It was a very, very difficult adjustment for me," said Chapman, whose scoring average dropped from 19.6 points as a junior to 12.3 with a stronger team. "But Coach Heathcote and I were both competitors who wanted to win."

That was all but assured when Vincent signed his letter of intent with the Spartans and was guaranteed when Johnson decided to stay home.

"When Jay committed, I knew we'd have a good team," Kelser said.

Bob Chapman is the only player to have teamed with Mike Robinson, Terry Furlow, Gregory Kelser and Earvin Johnson.

"Getting 'Magic' was extra. But what we really needed was someone effective in the middle. And that someone was Jay."

"'Magic' is 'Magic,'" Vincent said. "He's the one who put us over the hump. But I think we would've had a very good team without him. A lot of people underestimated how good I'd be at the college level."

The most heralded incoming class in MSU history included guards Mike Brkovich from Windsor, Ontario, Len "Ice" Williams from Chicago, forward Rick Kaye from Detroit, and center Sten Feldreich from Sweden.

Feldreich, the program's first 7-footer, actually started the long-awaited season opener against Central Michigan and former Spartan Jeff Tropf.

But it was Vincent who came off the bench and saved the day with a 25-point debut in just 24 minutes, while Johnson was struggling with seven points and eight turnovers in a 68-61 win over the Chippewas.

"Did Jay ever get the respect he deserved? Heck no!" Kelser said. "We couldn't have won anything without Jay. Before he got here, we had Jim Coutre in the middle. You'd throw the ball in to 'Cout,' and anything could happen. You'd throw it in to Jay, and good things happened."

The toughest opponent for Vincent was often himself, with his weight always an issue and his confidence slow to catch up to his skills.

"'Magic' came back from a high school All-America game and said, 'Jay, those guys aren't as good as you,'" Vincent said. "That gave me a lot of confidence. But even my first two years at State, Coach didn't want me to take jump shots. He said I was a center. And I always thought I was a forward."

All that mattered against Rhode Island was that Chapman was in an MSU uniform. The 6-2 senior was 11-for-11 from the field and 8-for-9 at the line, scoring 30 points in 27 minutes of the season's first blowout.

"I looked up to Bob because he worked hard all the time," Kelser said of a player who was plagued by knee problems. "He was a source of inspiration for me. He was the one who really kept me going the year before."

With 23 points, Vincent was the only one who got going against Syracuse in the championship game of the Carrier Classic. The Spartans lost 75-67, as Heathcote and Orangemen assistant Rick Pitino were both hit with technicals.

After routing Wichita State, Western Michigan, and Middle Tennessee State at home, MSU made a statement with a 103-74 road demolition of Detroit. The Titans had John Long, Terry Tyler, Terry Duerod, and future Spartan Kevin Smith. But 36 points from Kelser and 22 from Chapman were more than enough.

Wins over Southern Methodist and New Hampshire by a combined 63 points gave MSU the title at the Old Dominion Classic in Norfolk, Virginia.

It also sent the Spartans into Big Ten play with an 8-1 mark, as they prepared to welcome defending champ Minnesota, with Player of the Year Mychal Thompson and Kevin McHale, to a raucous Jenison Field House.

Despite 27 points from Thompson and 17 from McHale, MSU rallied from a seven-point deficit with 4:07 left for a bizarre 87-83 triumph.

"I don't know how we could play Minnesota again and win," Heathcote said after the game. "I know it sounds funny, but when I look at the trees Minnesota has, I don't know how we won."

Especially when Kelser fouled out with 6:22 to play. But the Spartans prevailed with 31 points from Johnson—his career high by 11, to that stage—and a late technical on Golden Gopher William Harmon for bumping an official.

"The big fella's a player, isn't he?" Johnson said of Vincent, who held his own with 22 points against an All-American. "I guess you could say we're just a couple of fellas trying to let people know where Lansing is. . . . I think they're beginning to find out."

At least one coach already knew. Michigan's Johnny Orr, who nearly had Johnson's services, warned anyone who would listen.

"We were at the Big Ten Tipoff Luncheon, and John said, 'These guys think they know about Earvin. . . . They don't know anything about him! But they'll see!'" said Nick Vista, then MSU's assistant sports information director.

The Spartans whipped Wisconsin, with each starter scoring from 10 to 18 points, then waxed Illinois, which hadn't seen the suprisingly nimble Vincent.

"Jay must have had about 19 points at Assembly Hall," Kelser remembered. "Finally, Eddie Johnson yells at his teammates, 'Somebody guard that fat pig!' It was the funniest thing I've ever heard. But Jay could really shoot and pass. It was Jay and Earvin, not just Earvin, that made us champions."

They didn't look as fearsome in squeaking past Northwestern 67-63, as

Jay Vincent's soft touch means two points against the Hawkeyes.

Earvin Johnson's slight-of-hand electrifies the crowd in a win over Illinois.

Johnson committed 12 turnovers. But after wins in Jenison over Purdue and Iowa, the Spartans climbed to 7-0 in the league by rallying at Ohio State.

MSU's second loss was by five at Indiana—the only Hoosier success against the Spartans in five tries over a two-year span.

And there were serious concerns when MSU failed to score in the final 4:14 and lost 65-63 to Michigan in Jenison. Backup guard Mark Lozier blocked a Chapman breakaway, then swished a 25-footer at the buzzer for the win.

After victories over Indiana and at Iowa, the Spartans delivered a 73-62 payback to the Wolverines and freshman Mike McGee in Crisler Arena, where Johnson's last visit had produced a Class A crown for Everett High.

Just before tipoff, a group of Michigan students paraded with a huge sign: "Magic is an illusion. McGee is for real." And the wrong person noticed.

"Sure, I saw it," Johnson said after a 25-point effort. "When I see something like that, it just helps fire me up. But I don't have any grudge against Michigan—yet."

Orr, who had blown kisses to a hostile crowd in East Lansing, said the Detroit Pistons should draft Johnson immediately to fill the Silverdome. Then, he told MSU fans to enjoy their moment.

"Goodness, gracious!" Orr said. "Earvin plays guard, center, and even coaches a little—and he doesn't do a bad job. I tell you, it took them 30 years to get up there. And if he goes away, they're going right back down."

His math was a bit off, with the Spartans winning titles in 1957, 1959, and 1967 before Johnson's arrival and in 1990 and 1998 after his departure. But the point is well taken, with 12-win seasons sandwiching his stay.

"Earvin's attitude about winning was very infectious," Kelser said. "There aren't many players who make others play harder. Earvin did that. And all of us—Jay, 'Brk,' Ron Charles, Terry Donnelly and myself—were fortunate he came our way."

No one had a stronger bond than Kelser and Johnson, who had a sixth sense for the split-second timing of alley-oop passes and breathtaking dunks.

"As time passed, he developed more and more confidence in me," Kelser said. "If he threw the ball up, even if it wasn't a perfect pass, I'd get it and put it in. And I knew if I made a quick cut to the basket, the ball would be there. It was a very natural, instinctive-type thing."

That wasn't enough in a 99-80 pounding at Purdue. But MSU beat Ohio State, Northwestern, and Illinois before cutting down the nets at Wisconsin, where its first win in Madison in 15 years clinched the title.

"If you look back at the Big Ten that year, there were so many talented teams," Chapman said. "Minnesota had Mychal and McHale. Indiana had Kent Benson. Michigan, Purdue, Iowa, Ohio State . . .

"But I realized what we had as soon as everyone signed. There was no question we'd be a successful team. And the beauty was the way we jelled together. The team goal was more important than any individual accolades."

A second win over the Gophers in Minneapolis sent the 23-4 Spartans to the Mideast Region of the NCAA Tournament.

"Jud made us think he wasn't going to get on us that day, since the title was won," Kelser said. "That lasted about a minute. After that, you'd have thought we were playing to try to stay out of the cellar."

Johnson dunks over Kentucky's Jack Givens in the game MSU would love to have back.

In MSU's first post-season appearance in 19 years, it beat Providence 77-63 in Indianapolis and Western Kentucky 90-69 in Dayton, Ohio.

That set up a matchup with eventual NCAA champ Kentucky, with the winner advancing to the Final Four. MSU led 27-22 at the half but lost 52-49.

"I remember everyone saying how big they were and that we didn't have a chance," Charles said. "They had Rick Robey, Mike Philips, James Lee, and Jack Givens. But we still should've beaten them. They kept drawing fouls. And Kyle Macy kept hitting free throws."

"I still have nightmares about that game," Chapman said. "I joke to my friends, 'Why'd you have to bring that up? I was in counseling because of it.' But we were up most of the way. And I think Coach Heathcote learned something from it. When you have thoroughbreds, you don't pull back on the reins."

It didn't help that Johnson managed just six points—nothing like his 109 points as a sophomore in a five-game roll to the championship.

"We—especially myself—didn't understand what to do," he said. "When the game got tight and the referees started blowing their whistles, I didn't keep us together the way I should have. Instead, we fell into a trap of getting upset. And I had to learn a valuable lesson."

The Spartans learned they were as good as any team in the country and set out to prove that the following season.

"It was no surprise to me we got as far as we did," Chapman said. "I honestly felt we should've won it all that year. Unfortunately, that didn't happen. But whichever team had won that game was going all the way."

"It was probably just like the Notre Dame game the next year," Kelser said. "The winner in that region would win the national championship. And we should've beaten Kentucky, too. Instead, we slowed it down and played right into their hands when Earvin got in foul trouble."

The following weekend was tough for a team that believed it should be in St. Louis, instead of watching on television as Joe B. Hall's team celebrated.

"I think we would've beaten Arkansas and Duke in the Final Four," Kelser said. "They were too slow to stop us. I remember seeing the championship game and marveling at how Duke couldn't stop 'Goose' Givens."

That should have made him realize how MSU opponents felt all season.

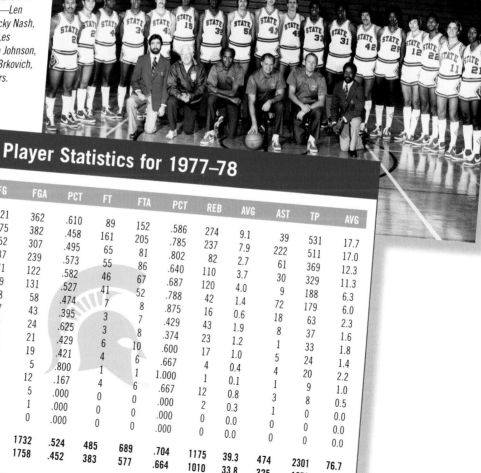

The 1977-78 Spartans: Front—Manager Dean Thedos, equipment manager Ed Belloli, assistant Bill Berry, head coach Jud Heathcote, assistant Don Monson and manager Darwin Payton. Back—Len Williams, Mike Longaker, Bob Chapman, Ricky Nash, Dan Riewald, Ron Charles, Gregory Kelser, Les DeYoung, Sten Feldreich, Jim Coutre, Earvin Johnson, Jay Vincent, Rick Kaye, Alfred Brown, Mike Brkovich, Nate Phillips, Terry Donnelly and Don Flowers.

Player Statistics for 1977–78

Player	GP/GS	FG	FGA	PCT	FT	FTA	PCT	REB	AVG	AST	TP	AVG
Gregory Kelser	30/30	221	362	.610	89	152	.586	274	9.1	39	531	17.7
Earvin Johnson	30/30	175	382	.458	161	205	.785	237	7.9	222	511	17.0
Bob Chapman	30/30	152	307	.495	65	81	.802	82	2.7	61	369	12.3
Jay Vincent	29/26	137	239	.573	55	86	.640	110	3.7	30	329	11.3
Ron Charles	30/3	71	122	.582	46	67	.687	120	4.0	9	188	6.3
Terry Donnelly	30/28	69	131	.527	41	52	.788	42	1.4	72	179	6.0
Mike Brkovich	27/0	28	58	.474	7	8	.875	16	0.6	18	63	2.3
Sten Feldreich	23/2	17	43	.395	3	7	.429	43	1.9	8	37	1.6
Jim Coutre	18/1	15	24	.625	3	8	.374	23	1.2	1	33	1.8
Alfred Brown	17/0	9	21	.429	6	10	.600	17	1.0	5	24	1.4
Len Williams	9/0	8	19	.421	4	6	.667	4	0.4	4	20	2.2
Don Flowers	9/0	4	5	.800	1	1	1.000	1	0.1	1	9	1.0
Dan Riewald	15/0	2	12	.167	4	6	.667	12	0.8	3	8	0.5
Nate Phillips	7/0	0	5	.000	0	0	.000	2	0.3	1	0	0.0
Mike Longaker	4/0	0	1	.000	0	0	.000	0	0.0	0	0	0.0
Rick Kaye	2/0	0	0	.000	0	0	.000	0	0.0	0	0	0.0
MICHIGAN STATE	30/30	908	1732	.524	485	689	.704	1175	39.3	474	2301	76.7
OPPONENTS	30/30	795	1758	.452	383	577	.664	1010	33.8	325	1973	65.8

1989—90

Fans storm the court and trigger a wild celebration after the title-clinching win over Purdue.

For some Michigan State Spartans, it was time to grow up. And for a team with all the pieces, a time to move up—all the way to the top of the Big Ten and the Sweet 16 of the NCAA Tournament.

With junior Steve Smith, seniors Kirk Manns and Ken Redfield, sophomores Matt Steigenga, Mark Montgomery, and Parish Hickman, redshirt freshman Mike Peplowski and freshman Dwayne Stephens, MSU earned its first league title since 1979 and won a school record 28 games in 1989–90.

The seeds were planted the previous year, when Jud Heathcote's youngest team reached the NIT semifinals in the last season in Jenison Field House.

"Getting to the NIT in New York definitely gave us confidence for the following year," Redfield said. "Our trainer, Tom Mackowiak, did a great job with our off-season conditioning. And everyone stayed on campus that summer."

That togetherness showed in the Great Alaska Shootout. The Spartans beat Auburn, Texas A&M, and Kansas State, as Smith was the MVP with 69 points, 26 rebounds, and 27 assists the weekend after Thanksgiving.

"There's always a team here that rises up and becomes a national contender," said Auburn coach Tommy Joe Eagles. "MSU could be that team."

The trip home left virtually no practice time before the Spartans faced Nebraska in the first regular-season game in Breslin Center.

But MSU delighted a sellout crowd and a worried Heathcote, building a 17-point lead in the first 11 minutes of an 80-69 triumph.

"We didn't want to be remembered as the guys who stunk up the new building," Manns said. "We really couldn't have asked for a better inaugural season."

Two more wins made MSU 6-0 and No. 25 in the nation as it headed to Illinois–Chicago, a program it had thrashed by 22 points the previous season.

In a complete turnaround, the Spartans played one of their worst games, turning the ball over 24 times in a 65-57 loss that wasn't that close.

"Hey, I still hear about that game," said Redfield, a Chicago native. "UIC guys remind me of it all the time. I actually lost to them twice in the four times we played them. But that game kind of pulled us together and

made us realize we weren't invincible."

Needing a leader on defense, assistant coach Tom Izzo finally found one in a forward who had nearly transferred to DePaul—twice.

"We knew we couldn't win if Steve was scoring 20 points, Kirk was shooting, and I was looking to score," said Redfield, who became the Big Ten Defensive Player of the Year. "We had to establish roles if we wanted to win. Looking back, I wouldn't change a thing."

A win over Eastern Michigan raised the Spartans' record to 9-2 but came at what appeared to be a steep price with Big Ten play a week away.

Smith, who was averaging a team-high 20.8 points, fractured the pinky on his left hand and missed the next three games. And Peplowski reinjured a surgically reconstructed knee, sidelining him for six more games.

Heathcote inserted Mark Montgomery and sophomore Parish Hickman into the lineup for the Oldsmobile Spartan Classic. And MSU responded by downing San Jose State and surviving a two-point chess match with Princeton.

"When Steve broke his finger, we all had to play—and I don't mean just show up, I mean PLAY!" Manns said. "We relied on Steve and would again when he came back. But when he was out, it gave the rest of us a chance to improve. Once he returned, we were all better and more confident."

The Spartans began conference play with a win at Wisconsin, with Manns scoring 20, Redfield 17 and Steigenga 13, including five critical free throws.

"Matt was kind of the wild card that year," Redfield said. "We never knew what we were going to get. But we knew we'd get something. The fact he was out there made him a threat and someone opponents had to respect."

A win at home over Iowa was keyed by Manns' 33-point outburst, including six 3-pointers, and Redfield's 16 points and eight assists.

At 5-1 in the Big Ten, MSU met defending national champ Michigan in Ann Arbor, anxious to end a four-game losing streak against the No. 7 Wolverines.

Instead, guard Rumeal Robinson, the hero of the 1989 NCAA Tournament, hit a running hook shot with :02 left to give Michigan a 65-63 win.

"Watching the reaction of their players to the win was interesting," Manns said. "They were dancing around. In my career, Michigan had beaten us pretty much like a drum. Based on their reaction, I'm thinking, 'We've arrived!' It showed we were getting where we wanted to be."

They weren't quite there yet, as seen the following Thursday when Minnesota became the first Big Ten visitor to win in Breslin, 79-74.

But at 5-3 and 16-5, the Spartans wouldn't lose in the next 50 days.

If one game turned the season around, it came in West Lafayette, Indiana, where MSU throttled No. 8 Purdue, 64-53—the Boilermakers' first league defeat and just the third win in Heathcote's 14 visits to Mackey Arena.

"When we got to Purdue, we were tired and sore because Minnesota had played such a physical game the night before," Manns said. "But Jud put us through a practice like it was Opening Day. I was even more beat up after that. I think he wanted to send us a message: 'You are better than this.'"

A win at Ohio State made Heathcote the school's all-time winningest coach with 233 triumphs, bettering Ben Van Alstyne's mark.

"If Jud was still coaching, I'd tell anyone who's playing for him just to listen," Redfield said. "He could be hard on you. But he was probably the best coach I've ever had. He knew his X's and O's better than anybody. His way of getting it to you was just different.

"One time, we were running in practice. And all of a sudden, he stops us and says to me, 'Why are you running this way? Run with your arms this way!' Now, I'm thinking to myself, 'I've been running the same way for 17 years.'"

Manns kept running and gunning, scorching Iowa at Carver-Hawkeye Arena with 30 points in an 87-80 win. Eight treys tied his Big Ten record and helped him take the conference scoring lead with a 20.8-point average.

Manns' evolution into one of the league's most feared scorers was a story in perseverance and maturity. After his sophomore year, an underachiever was ready to take his game elsewhere and met with Heathcote to tell him that.

"I was struggling because I was just fat and out of shape," Manns said. "It was all my fault. But I went into Jud's office and said maybe it would be better if I moved on and looked at other schools.

"He said to me, 'If that's what you think, then that's what you should do.' He didn't coddle me. He didn't tell me I was better than I was or try to get me to change my mind.

"I'm not sure what I expected when I went in there—maybe that he would try to keep me. But that wouldn't have been the best thing for me. A couple of days later, I thought, 'There is no way I'm running from this!' So I went back in and told him I'd like to stay if he'd still have me."

That summer, Manns went home and worked out every day. He left campus at 187 pounds and came back at 170—a different player physically and mentally.

His dedication paid off in 1989 when he exploded for 40 points against Purdue and 20 against Minnesota en route to Big Ten and *Sports Illustrated* Player of the Week honors.

Dwayne Stephens pushes the ball ahead on a fast break against Indiana.

Jud Heathcote and Steve Smith pass the 1990 Big Ten Championship trophy.

"That night against Purdue changed my life in a lot of ways," Manns said. "I got my confidence back and thought I was a player again. It all went back to the previous spring when Jud treated me the way he should have."

A sweep of Indiana set the stage for the rematch against Michigan. But it was a bittersweet win, as Manns, the league's No. 4 scorer, was diagnosed with a stress fracture in the right foot and was sidelined for three games.

As if the rivalry with the Wolverines didn't stir enough emotion, pre-game banter added fuel to a soon-to-be-raging fire.

"We beat them twice last year. We beat them this year. And we can go up there and beat them again," said Michigan forward Sean Higgins.

And much was made of a perceived snub by the Spartans during the player introductions in Ann Arbor.

"We don't mind," said Robinson, the Wolverines' leader. "It's no big deal to us. If they lose anyway, they're not going to want to shake our hands afterward. So they might as well get it over with."

That attitude had Redfield seeing red more often than than maize-and-blue.

"To me, the Michigan guys were prima donnas," he said. "My freshman year, I remember going to Crisler Arena and seeing guys driving 280-Z's. I also remember some guys wearing fur coats. And there we were in East Lansing, waiting to get our letterman jackets so we could be warm."

With MSU the underdog after Manns' injury, Smith put the Spartans on his back and carried them to a 78-70 win. He was 13-for-21 from the field in tying his career-high with 36 points.

Meanwhile, Redfield, Steigenga, and the Spartan Spirits student section held a distracted Robinson to 12 points and just two in the second half.

"We found out exactly how good Steve Smith is tonight," said Wolverine coach Steve Fisher. "He was just sensational. Every time we would cut into their lead, Smith would hit a big-time basket."

If Fisher thought Smith was sensational that Thursday night, he should have seen "Motor City Smitty" about 40 hours later.

Still floating in the clouds, he responded with 39 points, including the final basket with :29 left in a 75-73 overtime win at No. 17 Minnesota.

"We challenged all our kids to do more offensively—and I think the only

guy listening was Steve," Heathcote deadpanned. "Maybe I won't bring Steve back in the huddle when I talk about that again. In all seriousness, it was a team victory but a Steve Smith performance."

"We went into Williams Arena ready for war and wanting to repay them for beating us at Breslin," Stephens said. "But Kevin Lynch had a great look at a 3 with a few seconds left. That's one of those frozen moments—watching that shot go through the air and just missing."

The Big Ten title—or at least a share—was finally in reach. Despite Heathcote's fears, MSU led Northwestern all the way and used 23 points from Smith and 11 points and 12 rebounds from Peplowski in an 84-68 win.

One thing Heathcote got by himself was a spray of de-icer fluid, compliments of a Midway Airport employee.

"We're on the bus waiting for the guys to finish de-icing the plane," Stephens said. "So Jud decides he's tired of waiting and wants everybody on the plane. We're walking to the plane, and I'm right behind Jud and his wife, Bev, when the de-icer fluid hits Jud and splashes all over him.

"When we finally get seated, the stewardess asks what everyone wants to drink. And Jud says, 'I'll take an orange juice. . . . And while you're at it, why don't you throw it all over me.'"

Smith finds time for an autograph before the Spartan bus pulls away.

You could have thrown a blanket over MSU, 14-3, and Purdue, 13-4, heading into the final regular-season showdown. And it took Redfield's late deflection and a layup by Stephens to give the hosts a classic 72-70 triumph.

The Spartans entered the NCAA Tournament as the Southeast Region's No. 1 seed and played No. 16 Murray State in the opening round. In a battle of MSUs, the greatest upset in post-season history was barely averted.

Manns, who returned for the Purdue game but still wasn't 100 percent, came off the bench to post 21 points—the last two on an improbable, driving reverse layup with :43 left in overtime, as his team won 75-71.

"I was supposed to get the ball back to Steve," Manns said. "But Murray State took that away. I wasn't afraid to try to make a play. So I put the ball on the deck and got in the air. I never hung in the air very long anyway. I just flipped it up and in. It was a shot I had no business hitting."

MSU escaped a second time in Knoxville, Tennessee, beating UC–Santa Barbara 62-58, then ran out of luck and lost 81-80 in overtime to Georgia Tech in the Superdome in New Orleans.

When time expired, the Spartans had already enjoyed the time of their lives. And when it's time to pick the greatest teams in school history, they're in the Final Four.

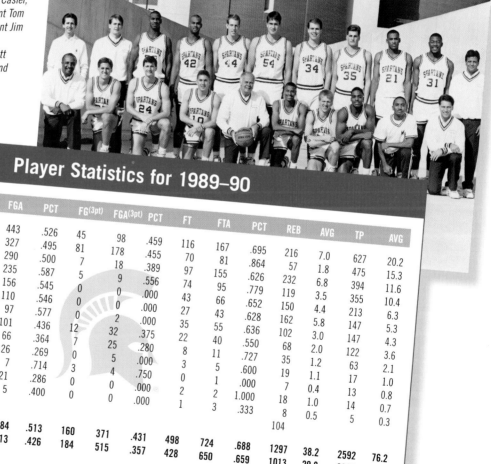

The 1989-90 Spartans: Front—Assistant Herb Williams, Jon Zulauf, Todd Wolfe, Kirk Manns, head coach Jud Heathcote, Mark Montgomery, Jeff Casler, Jesse Hall, manager Eric Spiller and assistant Tom Izzo. Back—Trainer Tom Mackowiak, assistant Jim Boylen, Ken Redfield, Parish Hickman, Matt Hofkamp, Mike Peplowski, David Mueller, Matt Steigenga, Steve Smith, Dwayne Stephens and assistant Tom Crean.

Player Statistics for 1989–90

Player	GP/GS	FG	FGA	PCT	FG(3pt)	FGA(3pt)	PCT	FT	FTA	PCT	REB	AVG	TP	AVG
Steve Smith	31/29	233	443	.526	45	98	.459	116	167	.695	216	7.0	627	20.2
Kirk Manns	31/24	162	327	.495	81	178	.455	70	81	.864	57	1.8	475	15.3
Ken Redfield	34/34	145	290	.500	7	18	.389	97	155	.626	232	6.8	394	11.6
Matt Steigenga	34/33	138	235	.587	5	9	.556	74	95	.779	119	3.5	355	10.4
Parish Hickman	34/12	85	156	.545	0	0	.000	43	66	.652	150	4.4	213	6.3
Mike Peplowski	28/23	60	110	.546	0	0	.000	27	43	.628	162	5.8	147	5.3
Dwayne Stephens	34/0	56	97	.577	0	0	.000	35	55	.636	102	3.0	147	4.3
Mark Montgomery	34/13	44	101	.436	12	32	.375	22	40	.550	68	2.0	122	3.6
Todd Wolfe	30/0	24	66	.364	7	25	.280	8	11	.727	35	1.2	63	2.1
Jesse Hall	17/0	7	26	.269	0	5	.000	3	5	.600	19	1.1	17	1.0
Jeff Casler	17/2	5	7	.714	3	4	.750	0	1	.000	7	0.4	13	0.8
Jon Zulauf	19/0	6	21	.286	0	0	.000	2	2	1.000	18	1.0	14	0.7
Dave Mueller	17/0	2	5	.400	0	0	.000	1	3	.333	8	0.5	5	0.3
Team											104			
MICHIGAN STATE	34/34	967	1884	.513	160	371	.431	498	724	.688	1297	38.2	2592	76.2
OPPONENTS	34/34	858	2013	.426	184	515	.357	428	650	.659	1013	29.8	2328	68.5

1997–98

Charlie Bell soars to grab another rebound against Minnesota.

t was a team that baffled the experts and beat the odds.

With a never-wavering belief in each other and a tenacious style that reflected its coach, Michigan State won its seventh Big Ten basketball title.

The 1997–98 Spartans tied Illinois at 13-3, reached the NCAA Tournament's Sweet 16 and were 10th in the final *USA TODAY*/ESPN poll with a 22-8 mark.

But it was the way Tom Izzo's players answered their doubters and conquered adversity that made them a group to remember.

"I said all along we had the kind of team people would come to like," Izzo said. "They're regular guys. But confidence is always the key to success. When you have it, you play a little better than you are."

The Spartans played well enough to please Izzo's mentor, Jud Heathcote—never an easy thing to do.

"People say, 'Ahhh, you'd have won the same way,'" said Heathcote, who retired as MSU's coach in 1995. "But I wouldn't have. I wouldn't have played as many guys as Tom has. And I wouldn't have had as many guys ready to play."

A starting lineup with two freshmen, a sophomore and two juniors, and a 10-deep playing group with just one senior was supposed to be a year away.

But the Spartans began to grow up in the late stages of 1996–97, when they advanced to the second round of the NIT and finished 17-12.

"Playing at Minnesota, they were No. 2 in the nation, had clinched the Big Ten and generally had everything going for them," said associate head coach Tom Crean. "We were only down by three with two minutes left. Even though we didn't win, we showed ourselves what could happen if we played hard.

"Another moment was after we got beat at Florida State in the NIT. The kids came back and got right in the gym and the weight room—working on their game as hard as ever after a long, grueling season. There was a hunger. And it just kind of snowballed from there."

Most preseason publications had MSU seventh or eighth in the conference and headed to the NIT for a third straight year, even with a healthier, slimmer Mateen Cleaves at point guard.

"When we saw the rankings, we were a little mad," said swingman Morris Peterson. "We just wanted to show everybody we could make some noise."

The Spartans' first screams came after the first exhibition. Senior guard Thomas Kelley, projected to be their leading scorer, was lost for the year with a broken bone in his foot.

That gave freshman Charlie Bell a better chance to contribute in the backcourt. All he did was start all 30 games.

MSU won three of its first four and beat Gonzaga 70-68 for the Coca-Cola Spartan Classic title, as forward Jason Klein hit an off-balance layup at the buzzer.

Even that excitement was tempered when Peterson, one of the team's most explosive players, fractured a bone in his right wrist.

Luckily, he shot left-handed. But he still missed the next three games.

The Spartans dropped two of those three, including a 56-54 snoozer at home against Temple, when several members of the media mocked a "Hoops on Fire" promotional campaign as "Ooops on Fire" and "Hoops on Ice."

The last laugh belonged to Mark Hollis, MSU's associate athletic director, who emerged as a prophet when Izzo's team began to sizzle.

First, however, there was one more stumble in Breslin Center. A 68-65 loss to Detroit left the Spartans at 4-3 and presented yet another problem when

Dribbling with "The Club" on his broken hand, Morris Peterson is still explosive.

swingman David Thomas suffered a knee injury.

The injury toll was mounting faster than trainer Tom Mackowiak could treat the players. And the critics were patting themselves on the back.

"It seemed the experts were right," Crean said. "The key period was Christmas break. We turned up the individual workouts, had double sessions and more film sessions. And the players really got better.

"The team knew the coaches weren't going to stand for being 4-3 and having all sorts of things said about the program. I think the players realized if they didn't bond together, it was going to be a long, long year. But if they did, good things could happen."

The first returns came before an ESPN audience—a 68-53 win over South Florida in Tampa. With New York Yankees owner George Steinbrenner in the stands, a basketball team with a football mentality dove for every loose ball and held the Bulls to .246 accuracy from the field.

The Spartans opened a lot more eyes with a convincing 74-57 win at Purdue, with 25 points from Cleaves and 15 rebounds from center Antonio Smith.

Bell and freshman forward Andre Hutson combined for 24 points in their first Big Ten game, as the stunned Boilermakers shot .346 from the field and were outrebounded 48-31.

"I think that game was our coming-out party," said Peterson, whose

"The Flintstones"—Charlie Bell, Antonio Smith, Morris Peterson, and Mateen Cleaves.

injury forced him to play defense and made him a force at both ends of the court. "We probably caught them with their backs turned. But we figured if we could beat the No. 1 team in the conference, who couldn't we beat?"

The victory fueled a 10-1 league start, the best in school history. And with Peterson and Thomas back, MSU attacked with depth and versatility. It was no longer just Cleaves and his caddies.

The Big Ten MVP still had his share of highlights, including a 24-point second half—with 17 in just 4:45—to beat Illinois 68-64, after his team had trailed by 16. He also had 32 of his career-high 34 points in the second half and the overtime of a 72-66 escape at Northwestern.

"I remember playing against Mateen in a 10-and-under league in Flint when I was 7 or 8," Peterson said. "We really didn't know each other. But I thought Mateen was really good, even at that age."

Smith, the oldest of the four "Flintstones," was the first recruit to commit to Izzo, after he became head coach. The strong-and-silent type led by example.

"Antonio was a big part of me getting better," said senior DuJuan Wiley, who blossomed in his second year as a junior college transfer and blocked 50 shots, the most since Ken Johnson in 1984–85. "I liked guarding Antonio. I could block his shot. And he could really defend me in the post. I think we made each other better.

"I would talk some trash to him, just to get him going. It would start at the beginning of practice. I'd say, 'Man, I've got your number today! You can't stop me!' I'd get Mateen to go over and say, ' 'Deuce' is going to bust you today!' Then, we'd really go at it. It'd be a war sometimes."

In a six-game stretch, the Spartans had five different leading scorers.

Peterson, nicknamed "The Club" for the soft cast he wore on his wrist, came off the bench to score 20 points in a 78-57 romp at Iowa.

Cleaves scored 25 in a win over Penn State. Bell had 17 against Indiana. Klein had a career-high 25 at Ohio State. And Smith had 17 in the rematch with the Hawkeyes.

At 11-2 in the Big Ten and 18-5 overall, MSU hosted 22nd-ranked Michigan and desperately wanted to end a five-game losing streak in the series.

"The teams that play smart against them are the ones that win," said visitor Earvin Johnson. "I met with the guys and told them, 'Look up there in the rafters. How many Big Ten champs are there? This is your opportunity!'"

After Johnson and Gregory Kelser stirred more emotions with pregame talks, the Spartans played their finest half of basketball in several seasons, racing to a 44-29 advantage.

and baseball caps that said 'Big Ten Champs' were passed around, and you saw some pretty excited guys."

The Spartans were met by a crowd of jubilant supporters at Capitol City Airport. And once back in Breslin, they were introduced to an overflow crowd at a monster truck show.

"That's the trouble with having a coach from the Upper Peninsula," Izzo said. "Most teams win a championship and get invited to the White House. We win and get invited to a monster truck show."

The regular season finale, a 99-96 overtime loss to Purdue, will be remembered for the pregame display of a title banner and a play that summed up MSU's season and never-quit attitude.

"I really struggled with that," Izzo said of the banner unveiling. "Minnesota did it last year before they played us. And I said the only way I'd go along with it this year was if Gene Keady said it was OK. Gene was great. He said, 'Your fans deserve that.'"

Trailing by two in the closing seconds, Klein launched a shot that was about to sail out of bounds. Instead, Hutson dove and flipped a no-look pass under the basket. And Peterson, who instinctively sprinted to the basket, grabbed the ball with :01 left and laid it in to force the overtime.

"Twenty years from now, it won't make any difference that you're co-champs," Keady said. "You're still the Big Ten champions. What matters is you got another one."

As the No. 1 seed in the first Big Ten Tournament, MSU learned a valuable lesson when it was stunned 76-73 by eighth-seeded Minnesota.

"That's what sports is about," said Cleaves, who struggled with 2-for-18 shooting and six turnovers. "Some games you never want to forget. Some you wish had never happened. . . . I learned a valuable lesson today."

The Spartans quickly regrouped as a No. 4 seed in the NCAA's East Region

The perfect form of Jason Klein produces another 3-pointer against Indiana.

The Wolverines battled back and crept within one with 4:55 left. But seven points by Klein in the last 2:05 gave MSU an 80-75 triumph.

The Spartans' euphoria ended when Cleaves and Hutson were arrested for alcohol-related charges. Izzo decided to bench both players for the first half of the game at Wisconsin, a potential title-clincher.

"The decisions didn't have anything to do with wins or losses," Crean said. "They had to do with the individual development of the people in the program and what was best for Michigan State basketball."

Freshman Doug Davis took Cleaves' starting spot, while Wiley replaced Hutson in the starting five. With Cleaves a cheerleader for the first 20 minutes, MSU trailed 26-20. But in the second half, the Spartans outscored the Badgers 36-21, holding Wisconsin to just two field goals.

"We were a little drained after that game," Klein said. "Then, the T-shirts

Izzo discusses what has to happen with Mateen Cleaves.

Freshman Andre Hutson slams against Wisconsin.

and nearly made good on a Final Four goal: "Send Antonio to San Antonio!"

MSU opened against 13th-seeded Eastern Michigan, with backcourt stars Earl Boykins and Derrick Dial, and won 83-71 in Hartford, Connecticut

The forgotten Bell had 22 points on his 19th birthday, while Cleaves had 20 and forced Boykins into 6-for-21 shooting.

"All the hype was about Earl Boykins and Mateen," Bell said. "Then, you had Dial, too. . . . No one was talking about me."

The Spartan staff worked round-the-clock to prepare for No. 8 Princeton and its vaunted back-door play. The players were fast-learners.

Izzo's team fought its way to a 63-56 win, as Cleaves led everyone with 27 points and nine rebounds. His 3-pointer with :35 left was one of the great clutch shots in school history.

"Fabulous, just fabulous!" said MSU President Peter McPherson. "I'm so incredibly proud of this team. Whatever happens, it never gives up."

"What I'll remember is how competitive they were," said ex-Spartan forward Ron Charles. "You picked them fifth. Most people said eighth. But when they laced them up, talent didn't mean as much as heart and character."

When MSU's season finally ended with a 73-58 loss to top-ranked North Carolina in Greensboro, the focus was all on the future.

"We want to get where Purdue is, in terms of consistency," Izzo said. "And in 25 years, we'd like to be North Carolina, in terms of tradition."

The next step is to try to post back-to-back titles for the first time in 20 years and just the second time in school history.

"I think they'll be a national factor next season," said CBS and ESPN analyst Bill Raftery. "They've shown they're a legitimate big-time program."

It's always better to show that in February and March—as the Spartans did—than to have people guess a team will be good in October.

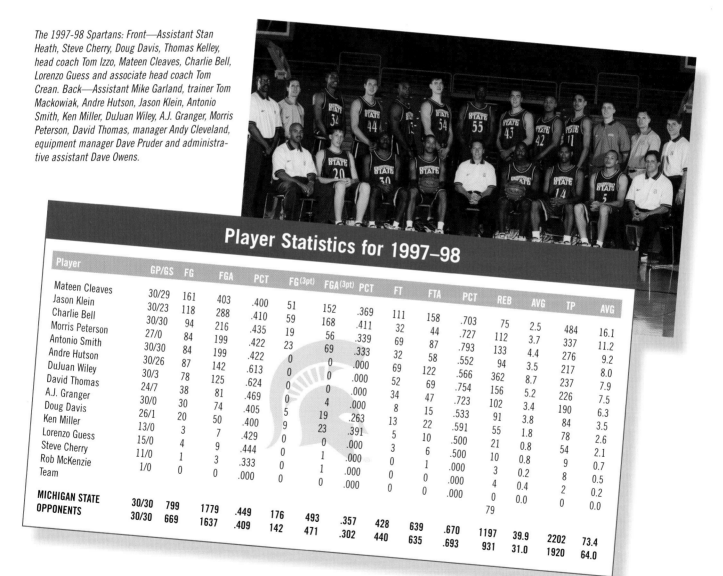

The 1997-98 Spartans: Front—Assistant Stan Heath, Steve Cherry, Doug Davis, Thomas Kelley, head coach Tom Izzo, Mateen Cleaves, Charlie Bell, Lorenzo Guess and associate head coach Tom Crean. Back—Assistant Mike Garland, trainer Tom Mackowiak, Andre Hutson, Jason Klein, Antonio Smith, Ken Miller, DuJuan Wiley, A.J. Granger, Morris Peterson, David Thomas, manager Andy Cleveland, equipment manager Dave Pruder and administrative assistant Dave Owens.

Player Statistics for 1997–98

Player	GP/GS	FG	FGA	PCT	FG(3pt)	FGA(3pt)	PCT	FT	FTA	PCT	REB	AVG	TP	AVG
Mateen Cleaves	30/29	161	403	.400	51	152	.369	111	158	.703	75	2.5	484	16.1
Jason Klein	30/23	118	288	.410	59	168	.411	32	44	.727	112	3.7	337	11.2
Charlie Bell	30/30	94	216	.435	19	56	.339	69	87	.793	133	4.4	276	9.2
Morris Peterson	27/0	84	199	.422	23	69	.333	32	58	.552	94	3.5	217	8.0
Antonio Smith	30/30	84	199	.422	0	0	.000	69	122	.566	362	8.7	237	7.9
Andre Hutson	30/26	87	142	.613	0	0	.000	52	69	.754	156	5.2	226	7.5
DuJuan Wiley	30/3	78	125	.624	0	0	.000	34	47	.723	102	3.4	190	6.3
David Thomas	24/7	38	81	.469	0	4	.000	8	15	.533	91	3.8	84	3.5
A.J. Granger	30/0	30	74	.405	5	19	.263	13	22	.591	55	1.8	78	2.6
Doug Davis	26/1	20	50	.400	9	23	.391	5	10	.500	21	0.8	54	2.1
Ken Miller	13/0	3	7	.429	0	0	.000	3	6	.500	10	0.8	9	0.7
Lorenzo Guess	15/0	4	9	.444	0	1	.000	0	1	.000	3	0.2	8	0.5
Steve Cherry	11/0	1	3	.333	0	1	.000	0	0	.000	4	0.4	2	0.2
Rob McKenzie	1/0	0	0	.000	0	0	.000	0	0	.000	0	0.0	0	0.0
Team											79			
MICHIGAN STATE	30/30	799	1779	.449	176	493	.357	428	639	.670	1197	39.9	2202	73.4
OPPONENTS	30/30	669	1637	.409	142	471	.302	440	635	.693	931	31.0	1920	64.0

1930–31

Roger Grove

Roger Grove—one of MSC's greatest all-around athletes.

The shorts didn't approach calf level.

The shoes were more like workboots.

And the basketball looked like a medicine ball.

But the 1930–31 Michigan State Spartans understood one thing that's still fashionable today.

Winning.

Ben Van Alstyne's best team did exactly that in compiling a 16-1 mark.

In an era with a jump ball after every basket, when outside shots were called "long toms," MSC's record .941 success for more than a six-game season has lasted a long time.

With America on the verge of a "New Deal," a new basketball power was springing up in the Midwest.

Dubbed "The Flying Dutchmen," the Spartans left some impressive foes in their wake in the early stages of Van Alstyne's career.

In 1929–30, MSC finished 12-4 with wins over Marquette, MIAA champ Kalamazoo, Carnegie Tech, and Michigan—all fine teams from that era.

With five seniors graduating, major holes were left by Donald Grove, a 5-foot-5, 120-pounder Van Alstyne would call the best player he ever coached, and center Fred DenHerder, known for his scoring at critical times.

Despite those losses, the Spartans still had senior forward Roger Grove, a strapping 6-foot-1, 185-pounder and one of the greatest all-around athletes ever to attend the school.

With guards Arthur Haga and Edward Scott, "The Three Aces" were co-captains and guiding forces of a team Van Alstyne loved to coach.

Grove was a star on the football and track teams, too. He played half-back and established himself as one of the nation's premier punters. Yet, he found time to break the school record in the pole vault in the spring.

The *State News* recognized Grove's athletic feats when a debate arose about whether an athlete could truly excel in both football and basketball.

A year earlier, he etched his name in school history with a "long-tom" from just shy of mid-court in the closing seconds of the dedication game in Demonstration Hall.

That shot brought a 27-26 win over Michigan in as dramatic a finish as Spartan fans have seen.

When Scott Grove said his father, Roger, used to practice precisely that play, it proved to be time well spent.

But the State cagers could win a game in any number of ways.

Want to see great defense?

The splendid skills of Haga and Scott led defensive stands that blanked Cincinnati in the second half of a 22-8 triumph and held Ohio Wesleyan to just one field goal in the final 20 minutes of a 25-17 victory.

Looking for a battle of wits and wills with Van Alstyne?

He successfully ordered a nine-minute second-half stall with a one-point lead over passive Marquette.

Finally, with Marquette forced to challenge in the waning moments, Grove pierced the defense and delivered a driving layup to seal the outcome.

The first clue about Van Alstyne's ability to adjust or innovate was a con-

Art Haga—a standout on the Spartans' best team of the first half-century.

tribution that remains a key part of today's game at all levels, not just with the Utah Jazz.

"Dad said the pick-and-roll originated with Van Alstyne," said Ted Grove. "According to him, it really confused a lot of opponents. They'd complain to the officials, looking for a foul to be called."

While employing a slow, deliberate style, State showed swashbuckling flamboyance—á la Douglas Fairbanks, Sr., the screen idol of the era—in venturing east and toppling Colgate, Van Alstyne's alma mater, on successive evenings, 41-31 and 50-30.

According to George Alderton, sports editor of the *State Journal*, the wins over the Maroons were significant for another reason.

"A Midwestern team which moves eastward usually finds the East somewhat hostile to dribbling tactics," Alderton wrote. "Traveling is called rather freely, with the result that it is well nigh impossible to move the ball except by passing."

Need another hero?

Try short but speedy Dee Pinneo, the starting forward opposite Grove and a 5-foot-6 John Stockton look-alike.

His late basket staved off an upset bid by Western Reserve and gave MSC a 25-24 victory.

Or how about center Randy Boeskoll, described as "elongated" at 6-4.

He quietly turned in solid performances on several occasions, including a rally for a 29-28 come-from-behind win over Brigham Young.

Boeskoll was an excellent jumper, important not only for rebounding but for controlling the center jump after each basket.

A 24-16 win over Loyola of Chicago in the final home game ensured a perfect 10-0 record at Dem Hall—State's first undefeated record at home since a 6-0 mark at the old Armory in 1910–11.

Perhaps it was fitting that a record-setting team became the first-ever MSC squad—and possibly the first from any school—to use air travel.

The Spartans flew from Grand Rapids to Milwaukee on two Kohler-operated planes to face Marquette.

MSC's 15th straight win, 24-21 in overtime, was keyed by Haga's 10 points.

"It's kind of ironic my dad was on that flight because he was scared to death of flying," said Dawn Eastman, the daughter of Roger Grove. "I think it stemmed from high school in Sturgis, when one of his close friends died in a plane crash.

"Through all the years, when he visited his three kids scattered all over the country, he always drove."

Van Alstyne's players drove, too, with the pick-and-roll.

But they knew how—and exactly when—to hit a game-winning shot from 40 feet.

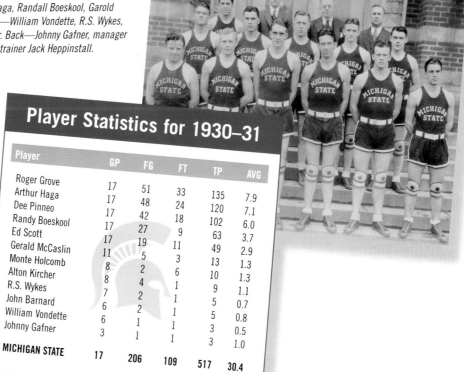

The 1930-31 Spartans: Front—Ed Scott, Art Haga, Randall Boeskool, Garold McCaslin, Roger Grove and Dee Pinneo. Middle—William Vondette, R.S. Wykes, John Barnard, Monte Holcomb and Alton Kircher. Back—Johnny Gafner, manager Robert Carruthers, coach Ben Van Alstyne and trainer Jack Heppinstall.

Player Statistics for 1930–31

Player	GP	FG	FT	TP	AVG
Roger Grove	17	51	33	135	7.9
Arthur Haga	17	48	24	120	7.1
Dee Pinneo	17	42	18	102	6.0
Randy Boeskool	17	27	9	63	3.7
Ed Scott	17	19	11	49	2.9
Gerald McCaslin	11	5	3	13	1.3
Monte Holcomb	8	2	6	10	1.3
Alton Kircher	8	4	1	9	1.1
R.S. Wykes	7	2	1	5	0.7
John Barnard	6	2	1	5	0.8
William Vondette	6	1	1	3	0.5
Johnny Gafner	3	1	1	3	1.0
MICHIGAN STATE	**17**	**206**	**109**	**517**	**30.4**

1958—59

From left, Johnny Green, Lance Olson, Bob Anderegg, Horace Walker, and Tom Rand get a grip as Forddy Anderson watches.

Forddy Anderson never believed bigger was better.

His 1958–59 Big Ten champs were so much better that size never mattered.

The best Michigan State basketball team before the Earvin Johnson era was undersized but never outfought, finishing 19-4.

A 12-2 conference mark brought the program's first outright title and its second crown in three seasons. That .857 success is still a school record.

And the Spartans' four-game edge over Purdue, Northwestern, and Michigan was the largest margin between first- and second-place teams since 1914.

"There wasn't much question in our minds that we were going to be a great team—not a good team, a great team!" said senior guard Tom Rand.

Johnny Green, MSU's tallest player at 6-foot-5, was on his way to All-

America status with 18.5 points and 16.6 rebounds per game.

Fellow senior Bob Anderegg led the Spartans with a 19.5-point average. And junior Horace Walker, also a 6-3 forward, added 13.5 rebounds per game.

An all-Green Bay, Wisconsin, backcourt of Rand, 6-2, and junior Lance Olson, 6-4, was capable of clutch baskets and suffocating defense.

And the bench included sophomores Dave Fahs, a 5-9 guard, and Art Gowens, a 6-2 forward.

"Johnny, Bob and I had played together since we were freshmen," Rand said. "Plus, I'd played with Horace and Lance my sophomore year. We had good chemistry and experience."

Despite a size disadvantage in almost every game, Anderson's team averaged a mind-boggling 63.7 rebounds in Big Ten play and 65.5 overall, a record that should stand forever.

"We were all well-built players," said Anderegg, a double-figure scorer in every game. "And Johnny and Horace were extraordinary leapers.

"Lance, Tom Rand, and myself were all pretty decent rebounders, too. And we averaged about 200 pounds. Still, most of the teams we played had 6-10 or 6-11 centers and forwards who were 6-8 and 6-9."

Anderegg was an outstanding high school athlete in football, basketball, and track. And those all-around skills made Anderson nervous.

"One day before practice, Bob, Lance, and Horace were messing around with the football," Anderson said. "Anderegg told Olson to go out for a pass. And Lance kept going and going. He finally yelled, 'Just throw it!'

"Bob threw that ball 100 yards in the air—and I mean 100 yards! I yelled to them, 'Pick up that football before anybody sees you. . . . And if anybody tells Duffy (Daugherty), I'll kill you!'"

The rebounding stats were staggering. And impressions were lasting, as seen by a 92-77 drubbing of Ohio State, including an 84-47 rebound advantage.

"They killed us on the boards," said an exasperated Buckeye coach Fred Taylor. "I've never seen such rebounding! Why, that Green went up and down twice before our kids could get their feet off the floor."

"We were good at positioning," Anderegg said. "And we also did well at tipping the ball, kind of like Dennis Rodman. If you couldn't grab it, you tried to tip it and keep it alive."

Bill Perigo, Michigan's coach, was in awe when MSU had a 23-rebound edge in a 103-91 win—then a school record for points.

"I've never seen a team with the spring and muscles MSU has on the boards," he said. "Green is absolutely amazing. And Walker isn't far behind."

Walker, an honorable mention All-Big Ten pick, was one year away from becoming Anderson's fourth and final Spartan All-American.

"I called him 'Poetry in Motion,'" Anderson said. "He did everything so easily."

If Walker was poetry, Olson was strong and steady in every way, especially in the classroom.

"Lance had a tremendous build," said Anderegg. "He had broad shoulders and was fast for his size. When he made his mind up to go to the bucket, you'd better get out of his way.

"He was also an exceptional student. If some of the guys had trouble with algebra or chemistry on the road, Lance would serve as a tutor and help out."

After winning its first four games with relative ease, MSU faced a serious challenge at the Dixie Classic in Raleigh, North Carolina.

After blasting Duke 82-57 and whipping No. 4 North Carolina 75-58, the Spartans lost 70-61 to No. 5 North Carolina State and just missed becoming the first non-ACC team to win the Classic in 10 tries.

"After we beat a good North Carolina team handily, I think we realized we were capable of beating anybody," Anderegg said. "I was hoping we would play Cincinnati, I would've loved the opportunity to guard Oscar Robertson."

"The fans down there really gave Oscar a tough time. I remember him saying he'd never come down there again to play. The hotels in Raleigh didn't accept blacks. So Michigan State and Cincinnati had to stay at this plantation-style house. We had food catered in and spent a lot of time with those guys."

The Spartans spent a lot more time celebrating victories that winter.

In the Big Ten opener against defending champ Indiana, they played without Green for the last 12:25 but won 79-77 on Walker's 6-footer.

Two games later, Green's dramatic tip of an Anderegg miss on the front end of a one-and-one situation gave MSU a 97-96 triumph at Illinois.

Before 16,181 fans at Minnesota's Williams Arena, the largest crowd to witness a Big Ten game in four years, Olson had 17 points in an 82-76 win.

And in the record-setting win over Michigan, Anderegg had 26 points and 11 rebounds, while holding the league's top scorer, M.C. Burton, to 11 points.

After clinching a tie for the title by outrebounding Purdue 71-49 in a 94-87 payback, the Spartans refused to share with an 86-82 win at Indiana.

"Indiana had jump shooters but not the greatest drivers," Anderson said. "We decided at halftime to hold our positions and rebound like crazy. I told John, 'When that ball goes up, you'd better get it!' And we only had one foul in the first 16 or 17 minutes in the second half.

"At one point, Branch McCracken, the wonderful coach at Indiana, ran down to yell at the referee and said, 'Do you realize that's just the second foul you've called on them this half?' He got all the way down to our bench, turned to me and said, 'Forddy, we're playing at our place!'"

MSU expected to earn a place in the Final Four but finally came up short.

They defeated Marquette and Jimmy McCoy, the younger brother of Julius, a 1956 Spartan All-American, 74-69 in a 23-team event.

But in the Mideast Region final in Evanston, Illinois, MSU was upset 88-81 by Louisville, a 10-time loser in the regular season.

That was despite a 29-point, 23-rebound game by Green and a 22-point effort by Anderegg, who shook off a deep thigh bruise.

"That was the year I thought we could go all the way," Anderson said. "Marquette had upset Kentucky, so we didn't have Kentucky to worry about.

"Louisville's center, Fred Sawyer, was a 7-footer. But he had a badly bruised heel. And they thought he wasn't even going to play (though he finished with 15 points and 14 rebounds).

"Instead, we came out and played one of the most miserable games we've ever played in our lives. To this day, I can't figure out what happened. Nothing went right. It was like the air coming out of a balloon."

Anderegg goes to his left and maneuvers past the Minnesota defense.

Green and Walker battle each other and Michigan's M.C. Burton for a rebound.

Should success be judged by an NCAA Tournament run, as in 1957, when a Final Four team finished 16-10—or by the regular season, as in 1959, when it was ranked No. 3 by the United Press and No. 7 by the Associated Press?

"The 1958–59 team had more talent," said Rand, nicknamed "Mr. Magoo" for his tendency to squint after giving up contact lenses. "We were the dominant team in the league, winning the Big Ten by four games."

"No question, the '59 team was better than the '57 team," Anderson said. "The '57 team had a special heart—a chemistry and character. But the '59 team had more ability. It was the best team I ever had at Michigan State."

And one of the best in Big Ten history.

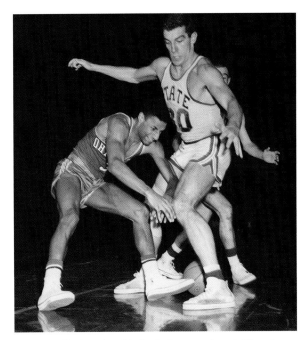

Olson says, "Don't go there," to the Buckeyes as a loose ball bounds between his legs.

The 1958-59 Spartans: Front—Larry Fanning, William Golis, Jim Stouffer, Bob Anderegg, head coach Forddy Anderson, Johnny Green, Tom Rand, Dave Richey and Dave Fahs. Back—Trainer Gayle Robinson, Tom Wilson, Harry Turak, Horace Walker, Lance Olson, Ted Wasson, Art Gowens, Bob Bechinski, John Young and manager Jack Ulmer.

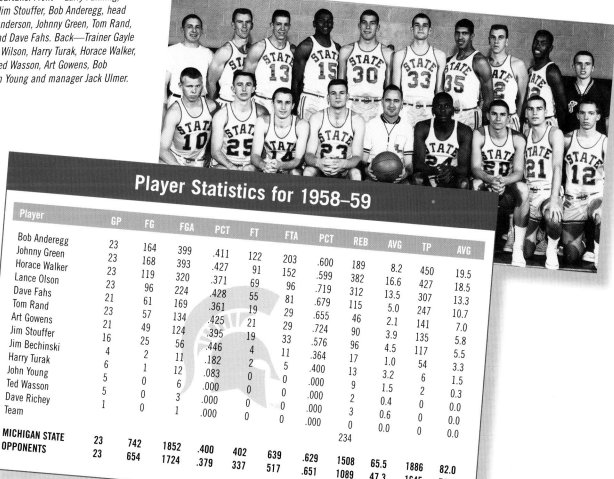

Player Statistics for 1958–59

Player	GP	FG	FGA	PCT	FT	FTA	PCT	REB	AVG	TP	AVG
Bob Anderegg	23	164	399	.411	122	203	.600	189	8.2	450	19.5
Johnny Green	23	168	393	.427	91	152	.599	382	16.6	427	18.5
Horace Walker	23	119	320	.371	69	96	.719	312	13.5	307	13.3
Lance Olson	21	96	224	.428	55	81	.679	115	5.0	247	10.7
Dave Fahs	23	61	169	.361	19	29	.655	46	2.1	141	7.0
Tom Rand	21	57	134	.425	21	29	.724	90	3.9	135	5.8
Art Gowens	16	49	124	.395	19	33	.576	96	4.5	117	5.5
Jim Stouffer	4	25	56	.446	4	11	.364	17	1.0	54	3.3
Jim Bechinski	6	2	11	.182	2	5	.400	13	3.2	6	1.5
Harry Turak	5	1	12	.083	0	0	.000	9	1.5	2	0.3
John Young	5	0	6	.000	0	0	.000	2	0.4	0	0.0
Ted Wasson	1	0	3	.000	0	0	.000	3	0.6	0	0.0
Dave Richey		0	1	.000	0	0	.000	0	0.0	0	0.0
Team								234			
MICHIGAN STATE	23	742	1852	.400	402	639	.629	1508	65.5	1886	82.0
OPPONENTS	23	654	1724	.379	337	517	.651	1089	47.3	1645	71.5

1966–67

Steve Rymal keeps control despite the pressure of three Hoosier defenders.

t wasn't the best Michigan State basketball team ever to take the floor—just the best never to make the NCAA Tournament.

The 1966–67 Spartans tied Indiana for the Big Ten title at 10-4 but had to stay home, since only one representative could advance to post-season play.

Since MSU's last NCAA appearance had been in 1959 and Indiana's was in 1958, the Hoosiers moved on while the Spartans, 16-7 overall, were left to wonder what might have been.

Ironically, that rule had worked the other way in 1957, sending Forddy Anderson's team to NCAA play and keeping the Hoosiers in Bloomington.

"As the years went by and people forgot we did win the title, the trivia was: 'Who did you share it with and why didn't you go to the NCAA Tournament?'" said Gus Ganakas, then a first-year aide to John Benington.

In two seasons, Benington had rebuilt the MSU program with 20 wins in 28 conference games and a 33-14 overall mark, after inheriting a 1-13, 5-18 team.

That respect was seen when eight of the Big Ten coaches picked the Spartans as the team to beat for the championship.

"They must not realize we lost Stan Washington and Bill Curtis," Benington said of his just-departed stars. "You can't lose two players like that and be rated that high in the nation."

Benington still had 6-foot-7 Matthew Aitch at center and a solid backcourt in John Bailey, who came to MSU on a golf scholarship, and Steve Rymal, who also played baseball.

But the key addition was 6-6 sophomore Lee Lafayette, an extremely gifted player who turned down UCLA and several other powers.

"Once in a scrimmage, Lee just went over somebody on a rebound, got the ball and jammed it down," Bailey said. "We all kind of stepped back

Matthew Aitch handles the ball in the open court.

and said, 'Whoa!' We remembered Stan as a great jumper. But Lee was explosive, too."

Juniors Art Baylor and Heywood Edwards and sophomore John Holms all contributed at forward.

"When Edwards came in, it was instant offense," Bailey said. "He was from New York. And he could really light it up."

With a lineup that was often interchangeable, Benington continued his emphasis on defense, as MSU went from worst to first in the conference, allowing 98.1 points in 1964–65 and 73.9 and 72.4 the next two years.

"To me, there was no question why we were good," Bailey said. "It was because we could play defense. We spent a lot of time on it and had a good concept of how it was supposed to be played."

"Guys took pride in playing their position and helping each other out," Aitch added. "If Rymal or Bailey ever got beat, I'd be there as the last line of defense. I'd feel bad if I didn't help them out."

After a 4-0 start, MSU slumped and dropped three out of four, falling out of the national rankings after it had reached the No. 5 position.

"We lost two games in the Quaker City Tournament in Philadelphia, came back and went through double sessions over the holiday break," Bailey said. "He just killed us. I never worked so hard.

"We'd practice in the morning. And when we hung up our jerseys, they'd be soaking wet. We'd leave, get something to eat, come back and the jerseys would still be drenched. We'd put them on and go back out for a couple more hours.

John Bailey prepares to play skin-tight, one-on-one defense.

"After the afternoon practice, the guys went back to their places and just collapsed. The next day, we'd do it all over again. It was torture."

"Benington's Boot Camp," as it came to be remembered, sparked MSU the rest of the season and showed the other side of a quick-witted coach.

In an 85-80 overtime win at Notre Dame, Benington left the court at the end of regulation in a parody of the college football titans' 10-10 tie in the "Game of the Century" less than three months earlier.

He also drew the ire of the Notre Dame faithful when he ordered the Spartans to stall in the last 90 seconds of regulation with the score tied.

"Play for the tie! . . . Play for the tie!" the Irish fans jeered, responding to the allegation Ara Parseghian had run out the final minute of the football game and didn't try to break the deadlock.

"John was joking around with Johnny Dee of Notre Dame before the game, saying that if it ended up deadlocked, they should both walk out and settle for a tie," Ganakas said. "John walked out so fans could get the point. He had that type of sense of humor."

Despite just one point from Lafayette and five from Aitch, the Spartans were rescued by Edwards' 22 points off the bench and Rymal's 22 points and a key steal in overtime.

"That was Rymal for you," Lafayette said. "His role could change from game to game. There were times when he'd do something and you'd think to yourself, 'Hey, I didn't know he had that in him!'"

The Spartans won four games by four points or less, including two in a week—79-77 at Purdue on Lafayette's putback with :02 showing and 67-66 over Minnesota, when no one was sure who hit the winning shot.

Down by one with :03 left, Rymal got the inbounds pass, took a couple of dribbles and launched a 40-footer that was short and to the right. But Lafayette leaped, grabbed the ball and stuffed it at the buzzer.

As some of the 9,128 fans carried Rymal and Lafayette off the floor, Minnesota coach John Kundla protested vehemently that Lafayette had jumped above the rim and was guilty of offensive goaltending.

Official scorer Larry Sierra and the game officials gave the basket to Rymal. But many observers in the press box, including MSU Sports Information Director Fred Stabley, picked Lafayette.

Kundla filed a protest with the Big Ten Conference. But two days later, when Benington brought the game film to his weekly press gathering, it was finally confirmed that Lafayette had scored the basket legally.

"I took the ball out of bounds," said Bailey, whose 17 points were undisputed. "We didn't have a specific play. And I was standing there for an eternity, trying to pass the ball to somebody. At four-and-a-half seconds in the five-second count, I threw the ball to Steve.

"There was a little mayhem after the game. Let's face it, you don't expect to win those types of games. Steve made a good shot just to get it close to the basket, while Lee had the poise to catch it and score."

Aitch's career high 31 points—many coming on jumpers over a Purdue zone—sparked a 75-71 win and gave MSU a share of the lead with two games left.

The Spartans and Indiana remained even after MSU's 67-59 win at Minnesota in a much-anticipated rematch.

But just before taking the floor in the final game against Northwestern, the Spartans learned Indiana had beaten Purdue to lock up a share of the title and the NCAA bid.

MSU answered by beating the Wildcats 79-66 for its 19th straight win at Jenison Field House and Benington's first title in 11 years of coaching.

"Sure, I'd like to go to the NCAA tourney," Benington said after the game. "But a share of the championship is better than none at all. I'm sure we would have been a good representative of the conference."

Steve Rymal makes a strong move to the basket.

"At the time, we thought, 'Why do they have this stupid rule?'" Lafayette said. "But we had to accept it. It was a big disappointment. You look back and think, 'If we'd won one more game or had a one-game playoff between the teams . . .'"

The teams split their regular-season series. And the Hoosiers thought it was only fair since the Spartans got to advance that way a decade earlier.

"We were glad to earn a share of the championship," said Aitch, a second-team All-Big Ten honoree. "At the same time, the win against Northwestern was a bit hollow. It gave us a piece of the title. But that was it. We felt we had a better team than Indiana and could have gone further."

In two seasons under Benington, they'd already come a long, long way.

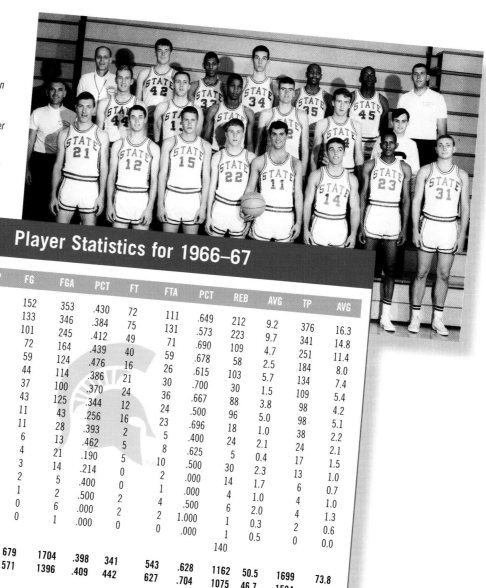

1966-67 Spartans: Front—James O'Brien, John Bailey, Steve Rymal, Richard Chappel, John Gorman, Richie Jordan, Vernon Johnson and Shannon Reading. Middle—Assistant Gus Ganakas, David Keeler, Ted Crary, Art Baylor, Jack Wynn, John Holms and manager John Warren. Back—Head coach John Benington, Gerald Geistler, Heywood Edwards, Tom Lick, Lee Lafayette, Matthew Aitch and assistant Bob Nordmann.

Player Statistics for 1966–67

Player	GP	FG	FGA	PCT	FT	FTA	PCT	REB	AVG	TP	AVG
Matthew Aitch	23	152	353	.430	72	111	.649	212	9.2	376	16.3
Lee Lafayette	23	133	346	.384	75	131	.573	223	9.7	341	14.8
Steve Rymal	23	101	245	.412	49	71	.690	109	4.7	251	11.4
John Bailey	18	59	164	.439	40	59	.678	58	2.5	184	8.0
Heywood Edwards	20	44	114	.476	16	26	.615	103	5.7	134	7.4
Shannon Reading	23	37	100	.386	21	30	.700	30	1.5	109	5.4
John Holms	19	43	125	.370	24	36	.667	88	3.8	98	4.2
Art Baylor	17	11	43	.344	12	24	.500	96	5.0	98	5.1
Richie Jordan	11	11	28	.256	16	23	.696	18	1.0	38	2.2
Ted Crary	11	6	13	.393	2	5	.400	24	2.1	24	2.1
Vern Johnson	13	4	21	.462	5	8	.625	5	0.4	17	1.5
Jerry Geistler	8	3	14	.190	5	10	.500	30	2.3	13	1.0
Tom Lick	4	2	5	.214	0	2	.000	14	1.7	6	0.7
John Gorman	3	1	2	.400	0	1	.000	4	1.0	4	1.0
Dave Keeler	3	0	6	.500	2	4	.500	6	2.0	4	1.3
Jim O'Brien	2	0	1	.000	2	2	1.000	1	0.3	2	0.6
Richard Chappel				.000		0	.000	1	0.5	0	0.0
Team								140			
MICHIGAN STATE	23	679	1704	.398	341	543	.628	1162	50.5	1699	73.8
OPPONENTS	23	571	1396	.409	442	627	.704	1075	46.7	1584	68.8

1985–86

The Spartans celebrate a win over Georgetown and a trip to the Sweet 16 in 1986.

t was five months of basketball madness—a season full of fun and fury.

The only title Michigan State was supposed to contend for in 1985–86 was a fourth straight crown in the Spartan Cutlass Classic.

Instead, Jud Heathcote's 10th MSU team was one of the most successful squads and arguably the most enjoyable to watch in school history.

The final numbers—a third-place finish at 12-6 in the Big Ten and a three-game run in the NCAA Tournament for a 23-8 overall mark—don't begin to tell the story.

There was controversy before the first exhibition game and after the final overtime buzzer. But sandwiched in between, amid the victories and the victims, was a steady stream of surprises and indelible memories.

With All-America guard Sam Vincent and center Ken Johnson gone from a 19-10 team in 1984–85, preseason optimism was as scarce as Heathcote's hair.

"None of us—not me, not my staff, not anybody—thought we could do what we've done," he said before a Sweet 16 matchup with second-ranked Kansas. "We might try to fool others. But we couldn't fool ourselves. We hoped we could squeeze out eight victories in the preseason and maybe six, seven, or eight in the Big Ten and get a bid to the NIT."

Even that so-so season wouldn't have happened without huge contributions from senior guard Scott Skiles, a player opposing fans loved to hate. And Skiles' status was in serious question after an impaired driving stop on November 7 in East Lansing that drives Heathcote daffy to this day.

Scott Skiles made the Hoyas dizzy with his drives and slick passes in Dayton.

Darryl Johnson rebounds and scores over Michigan's Gary Grant, as a befuddled Roy Tarpley looks on.

MSU fans weigh in with their vote for more than Player of the Year.

A five-day suspension meant Skiles would miss a tuneup against the Czech Nationals but face constant abuse on the road and mixed reactions at home. ESPN and ABC's Dick Vitale said Skiles shouldn't be allowed to play after a third arrest. But no one could stop him all season except Heathcote.

After six straight wins by from 20 to 43 points, the Spartans faced their first tough test and lost 82-80 at Iowa State, with Jeff Grayer and Jeff Hornacek, on a last-second layup in overtime.

Three more wins, including a 48-point blitz of Massachusetts, gave MSU a Lobo Classic championship in Albuquerque, New Mexico, and a 9-1 pre-conference mark.

After an 11-point loss at Ohio State, when cynics were already saying, "See what happens in the Big Ten?" the Spartans stunned Indiana 77-74 in Bloomington behind 21 points from starting center Carlton Valentine.

But after losing to Purdue and beating Illinois in Jenison Field House, MSU dipped to 2-4 in the league with losses at Iowa and Minnesota.

That game in Minneapolis featured arguably the best individual effort of the Spartans' first century. After receiving a shiner from Valentine in the morning shootaround, Skiles was 20-for-28 from the field and 5-for-5 at the line for 45 points in hostile Williams Arena. He would have had at least 56 and perhaps as many as 62, based on the official play-by-play, if there had been a 3-point shot in those days.

Seven nights later, an undersized team began a 9-1 stretch in the best way imaginable, with a 91-79 spanking of an arrogant Michigan team in Jenison.

Heathcote outcoached Bill Frieder, Skiles outplayed foul-prone shadow Gary Grant and junior guards Darryl Johnson and Vernon Carr took turns outrunning Antoine "The Pudge" Joubert.

"There's no question that was an All-America performance by Skiles," Frieder said of a 40-point statement. "I told people at my press conference we could take my walk-on and that kid and have the best guard combination in the country. Sooner or later, you people might figure it out, too!"

When Jim Spadafore of *The Detroit News* questioned the Wolverines' defense, they became much more defensive than when MSU hit 59.3 percent from the field.

"He's a great one!" Frieder said after Skiles was 15-for-20, plus 10-for-11 at the line. "I've said that all along. He was Player of the Week last week. And he came back with another great performance. . . . I'd like to have you guard him, Spadafore!"

"There's nothing you can do to stop him," Grant said. "All you can do is deny him the ball and hope he misses when he gets it. . . . He wasn't missing tonight."

Giving up nearly two inches and 25 pounds per starter, Heathcote tried to hide the 6-1 Skiles at forward on defense early and got Michigan center Roy Tarpley in foul trouble before the "Go Blue!" chants turned to "Go home!"

With Skiles an incredible 18-for-21 from the field, the Spartans beat Wisconsin next on the Big Ten MVP's 6-foot jumper with :07 showing.

"What can you do?" said Badger coach Steve Yoder. "Guard him at 20 feet

Larry Polec challenges the shot of Hoya center Ralph Dalton.

Skiles preaches togetherness to Barry Fordham, rear, and Vernon Carr, Larry Polec, and Darryl Johnson.

approach with little success, as Johnson scored 30 and Skiles 29.

"B.J. Armstrong came out and gave Scott a big Valentine's Day card," MSU assistant Herb Williams remembered about a February 13 date. "Everybody else had been aggravating him, talking about drunk driving. And one thing Scott could do was play angry. So they got this card and had everybody sign it."

After a payback of suspension-decimated Minnesota, it was time for the rematch with Michigan—another 15-point Spartan win, with Johnson scoring 26.

"That was a braggin' thing," he said. "Antoine was always billed as the best player in Michigan in high school. But I never shot as much. And when we beat them again. 'Toine kept bringing up the referees. . . . Shoot, we should've beat them by 30!"

Sweeps of Northwestern and Wisconsin set up a possible three-way tie for the title with Michigan and Indiana if MSU had beaten the Hoosiers instead of losing by 18 on a night when No. 4 had too little help.

"Scott's still the best player in the Big Ten," said Hoosier guard Steve Alford, after Skiles outscored him 33-31. "I don't think there's any doubt in anybody's mind. And there shouldn't be. He has had an unbelievable season."

Skiles had 43 in his final home game against OSU, then 31 to lead a fifth-seeded team past 12th-seeded Washington 72-70 in the first round of the Midwest Region in Dayton, Ohio. The Spartans rallied from 12 down in the second half to win on Skiles' two free throws with :02 to play, after he bowled over a CBS cameraman, traded shoves with the Huskies' Al Moscatel, and promised to score 50 against him.

"He just guts it out for 40 minutes," said Washington coach Andy Russo. "It's almost impossible to take your eyes off Skiles. He demands attention. He's arrogant, relentless, and driven."

In an 80-68 surge past fourth-seeded Georgetown, Skiles was at his pugnacious best, challenging 6-8, 240-pound Jonathon Edwards, then ripping a jumper from 30 feet and delivering the play of the Tournament, a 360-degree wraparound pass to senior forward Larry Polec for a fast-break lay-in.

"He came on the court with a combative glare and a defiant strut and left with blood dripping from his knees," wrote Karen Allen in *USA TODAY*. "In between, he encouraged and admonished his teammates, questioned officials, taunted opponents, and was always in the right place at the right time."

After an altercation with Hoya guard Michael Jackson on the way to the locker room, Skiles had 18 of his 24 points in the second half and told Georgetown giant John Thompson to get someone who could play better defense.

"I felt from the tipoff we had this game," Skiles said matter-of-factly. "I don't think there was a turning point. We were confident from the start."

and he moves out to 25 and scores. Guard him at 25 and he moves out to 30 and scores. Move out to 30 and he drives past you and scores."

After routing Northwestern, MSU rallied for an 84-80 triumph at Illinois, as Skiles and Johnson outscored guards Bruce Douglas and Glynn Blackwell 45-7.

"When we played in East Lansing, Skiles said he was All-World," Henson said. "What he has done the last three weeks just shows he recognized that fact before the rest of us. In 30 years of coaching, I've never seen a player make the shots that Skiles has."

Purdue stopped the Spartan Express 88-82, while chants of "Go to jail, Skiles! Go to jail!" filled Mackey Arena.

When Iowa came to East Lansing, George Raveling's team tried a different

His team was actually upset that Michigan had lost to Iowa State, preventing a chance to beat the Big Ten champs three times in one season.

Dreams of a Final Four berth in Dallas came to a crashing halt in a 96-86 overtime loss to second-ranked, top-seeded Kansas in Kansas City, Missouri, despite the surprise heroics of junior center Barry Fordham.

The nation's No. 1 shooters from the line missed three late tosses that would have sent them to a winnable Elite Eight game against North Carolina State, just after Verne Lunquist of CBS said, "If this comes down to a free-throw contest, Michigan State is excellent at 80 percent."

"The sad thing about the entire game was the malfunction of the clock," Heathcote said of a missing 15 seconds. "If even 10 seconds had gone off, the game would've been over."

Instead, the Spartans' season was. And as the NCAA looked at procedures to keep that timing travesty from happening again, it was time to appreciate 31 special happenings when the Skiles was the limit.

The 1985-86 Spartans: Front—Manager George Johnson, trainer Glen Porter, assistant Herb Williams, head coach Jud Heathcote, assistants Mike Deane and Tom Izzo and manager Tom McCall. Back—Mark Brown, Keith Hill, Todd Wolfe, Vernon Carr, Larry Polec, Ralph Walker, Jim Sarkine, Mario Izzo, George Papadakos, David Mueller, Scott Sekal, Barry Fordham, Carlton Valentine, Scott Skiles and Darryl Johnson.

Player Statistics for 1985–86

Player	GP/GS	FG	FGA	PCT	FT	FTA	PCT	REB	AVG	AST	TP	AVG
Scott Skiles	31/31	331	598	.554	188	209	.900	135	4.4	203	850	27.4
Darryl Johnson	29/29	216	371	.582	50	63	.794	96	3.3	116	482	16.6
Vernon Carr	31/31	168	300	.560	91	132	.689	167	5.4	95	427	13.8
Larry Polec	31/31	130	232	.560	70	82	.854	178	5.7	50	330	10.7
Carlton Valentine	31/3	80	123	.650	26	38	.684	98	3.2	7	186	6.0
Ralph Walker	31/4	33	60	.550	22	28	.786	87	2.8	12	88	2.8
Barry Fordham	31/25	37	73	.507	13	19	.684	113	3.7	11	87	2.8
Mark Brown	25/1	22	43	.512	13	16	.813	13	0.5	21	57	2.3
David Mueller	15/0	12	15	.800	8	12	.667	18	1.2	0	32	2.1
Scott Sekal	9/0	9	24	.375	0	0	.000	5	0.6	0	18	2.0
Mario Izzo	22/0	3	10	.300	4	8	.500	25	1.1	1	10	0.5
Todd Wolfe	1/0	2	3	.667	0	0	.000	1	1.0	0	4	4.0
Jim Sarkine	12/0	0	3	.000	3	4	.750	5	0.4	1	3	0.3
Keith Hill	1/0	0	3	.000	2	2	1.000	0	0.0	1	2	2.0
Andre Rison	6/0	0	2	.000	0	0	.000	1	0.2	4	0	0.0
MICHIGAN STATE	31/31	1043	1860	.561	490	613	.799	1016	32.8	522	2576	83.1
OPPONENTS	31/31	915	1972	.464	380	511	.744	946	30.5	494	2210	71.3

1991—92

Mark Montgomery takes charge and points to Kris Weshinskey, as Shawn Respert, Matt Steigenga, and Mike Peplowski look and listen.

Weshinskey fights for position against the Golden Gophers' Voshon Lenard.

The question in November 1991 was simple.

Would there be life after Steve Smith, a two-time All-American who left as Michigan State's top career scorer?

Though Jud Heathcote's 16th Spartan squad had other veterans back, there were serious concerns about its offensive punch and poise in critical moments.

The answers came early and often from many directions in a 22-8 campaign, the fifth-winningest effort in school history.

Junior center Mike Peplowski, a 6-foot-10, 270-pound presence, reached double figures in points and rebounds 12 times.

Senior point guard Mark Montgomery played excellent defense and had 190 assists, the most of any Big Ten player.

Redshirt-freshman guard Shawn Respert had nine games with 20 points or more and established himself as MSU's next great scorer.

And while senior forward Matt Steigenga delivered acrobatic dunks, junior forward Dwayne Stephens was dependable at both ends of the court.

"As a team, we really weren't overly worried about losing Steve," said sophomore guard Kris Weshinskey, a top reserve. "We knew we'd lost a great player. But we also knew we had good players back who knew how to win."

Part of the reason for that optimism stemmed from an eight-game exhi-

173

Dwayne Stephens plays defense against the Hoosiers' Alan Henderson.

bition tour of Australia in June—a trip that helped establish a closeness that led to later victories.

"The trip to Australia was a great experience," Weshinskey said. "We didn't have the greatest record. But we were able to see and do a lot together. During the season, you don't get that chance too often."

Sophomore center and key backup Anthony "Pig" Miller was photographed near a large pig statue. And Heathcote was seen trying to recruit a kangaroo.

He didn't need any more players in November, when the Spartans opened the season with a stunning championship effort in the Maui Invitational.

After beating Lamar and Rice, MSU spanked No. 2-ranked Arkansas 86-71, negating the vaunted Razorback press and handing Nolan Richardson's program its worst loss in 129 games.

Four Spartans scored in double-figures—soon to be a trademark of this team. And Arkansas' famed "40 Minutes of Hell" only applied to its 40 percent shooting from the field.

Respert, a virtual unknown to the Hogs, was the tournament MVP with 57 points and 10 assists the three days before Thanksgiving.

But it was the play of Montgomery, who had 11 of his 22 assists against Arkansas' star point guard Lee Mayberry, that made the biggest difference.

That championship set the stage for the program's first 10-0 start and lifted MSU to the No. 9 spot in the Associated Press poll.

Highlighting the streak was an incredible 90-89 win over Cincinnati on

December 21, when the Spartans overcame an 18-point deficit in the final 12:34.

The "Miracle on Kalamazoo Street" was complete when Weshinskey, who had missed the previous two games with mononucleosis, hit a 20-footer with 6.4 seconds left.

And in the most famous post-game speech in Breslin Center history, Bearcat coach Bob Huggins sounded more like "The Grinch Who Stole Christmas."

"I don't want any of this moral victory stuff," Huggins said. "We lost! And I don't want my players happy about it. I hope they have a miserable Christmas. I hope it bothers them as much as it bothers me."

MSU's fun ended with a 62-46 loss to seventh-ranked Ohio State, which was on its way to back-to-back Big Ten titles.

But the Spartans regrouped with another dramatic come-from-behind win, when they rallied from 11 down in the second half to beat Illinois in Breslin.

The 77-75 game was decided by a great coaching call and Weshinskey's 60-foot dash for an uncontested layup just before the buzzer.

After Montgomery drew a charge from Illinois' Rennie Clemmons with 3.6 seconds left, Heathcote ordered a long-distance give-and-go. And chief assistant Tom Izzo came up with the wrinkle to use Respert as a decoy.

Starting deep in his backcourt, Weshinskey hit Stephens, who had broken back to the ball. When Illinois forgot to cover the inbounds passer, a no-look flip over Stephens' right shoulder found a streaking Weshinskey, who could only be stopped by the clock.

"Looking back, I probably should've pulled up and shot a short jumper," Weshinskey said. "But I thought I could make the layup in time. And it just beat the buzzer."

MSU was 3-2 in the Big Ten and 13-2 overall when it met Michigan's "Fab Five"—freshmen Chris Webber, Juwan Howard, Jalen Rose, Jimmy King, and Ray Jackson—for the first time.

But the 15th-ranked Wolverines, 11-4, rallied from a 14-point second-half deficit and left Breslin with an 89-79 overtime win.

Before they headed home to Ann Arbor, the Fabs forever alienated themselves to Spartan fans with what can best be described as a series of crude gestures in response to more than two hours of insults.

Somehow, MSU's players put that devastating defeat behind them and won four of their next five games, with Peplowski collecting a career-high 16 rebounds at Wisconsin and leading his team in scoring in all four wins.

His 18 points paced the Spartans' 70-59 payback in Ann Arbor, when a frustrated Howard pushed Montgomery to the floor with :12 left.

"I remember Webber going in for a dunk by himself and laughing—kind of mocking us," Weshinskey said. "His feet got messed up. And he missed the shot. I thought that was funny. Most of those guys showboated too much.

"I never really liked Webber. I met him when he came in for his visit. He gave the impression, at least to me, that he thought he was big-time. And I didn't think we would ever be real good friends, even if he came here."

By that time, Peplowski, one of the most colorful and quotable players ever to wear an MSU jersey, had become almost a folk hero to the student section, which fed off his fist-pumping and arm-waving displays.

" 'Pep' played with a lot of energy and emotion—that's how he was," said Weshinskey, to this day, one of Peplowski's closest friends. "He went through a lot with his knees and all the surgeries. And he was able to fight through it all. I don't know if he ever got all the credit he deserved.

"He was seventh or eighth in the nation in field-goal percentage that year and was only averaging about nine shots per game. We probably should have tried to get more shots for him. But he was an outstanding player."

MSU closed out the Big Ten season with a pair of home victories, including a 64-53 decision over Iowa behind Steigenga's team-high 17 points.

After battling an ankle sprain and a stress fracture in his foot, it was a nice sendoff for one of the program's most enigmatic players.

"It was tough for Matt to get into a flow during the Big Ten season," Weshinskey said. "He was playing through pain and couldn't do all that he was capable of. But he never complained about it."

An 11-7 conference mark left the Spartans tied for third with Michigan. Seeded No. 5 in the Midwest Region in Dayton, Ohio, MSU topped No. 12 seed Southwest Missouri State 61-54 in first-round play.

That set up a rematch with none other than Cincinnati, as Huggins hoped his Easter would be happier than his Christmas.

It was, with the Bearcats eventually advancing to the Final Four.

Peplowski—who had sprained his ankle against Iowa, and a scoreless Steigenga were shadows of their usual selves in a 77-65 setback.

Fourth-seeded Cincinnati raced to a 17-point lead in the first half. And the Spartans shot just .385 from the field, despite Respert's 27 points.

It was a deflating finish for Montgomery and Steigenga, who left with 87 wins—more than any MSU seniors before or since.

They also left with a second 20-win season and proof the previous two seasons had been much more than a one-man show.

The 1991-92 Spartans: Front—Assistants Brian Gregory and Stan Joplin, Andy Penick, Kris Weshinskey, Mark Montgomery, head coach Jud Heathcote, Shawn Respert, Eric Snow, associate head coach Tom Izzo and assistant Jim Boylen. Back—Assistant strength coach Dave Ferguson, manager Scott Bernecker, Steve Nicodemus, Jon Zulauf, Dwayne Stephens, Mike Peplowski, Anthony Miller, Matt Steigenga, Daimon Beathea, manager Mike Stelmaszek and trainer Tom Mackowiak. Not pictured—Ron Haley.

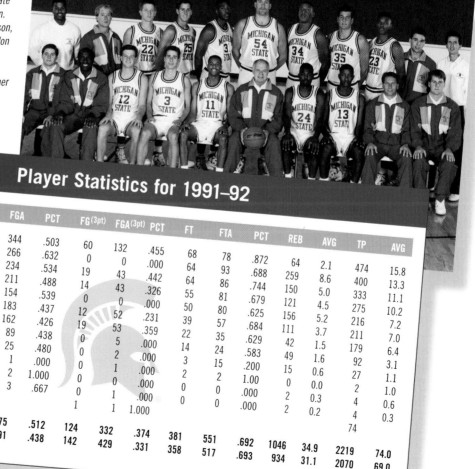

Player Statistics for 1991–92

Player	GP/GS	FG	FGA	PCT	FG(3pt)	FGA(3pt)	PCT	FT	FTA	PCT	REB	AVG	TP	AVG
Shawn Respert	30/30	173	344	.503	60	132	.455	68	78	.872	64	2.1	474	15.8
Mike Peplowski	30/29	168	266	.632	0	0	.000	64	93	.688	259	8.6	400	13.3
Dwayne Stephens	30/30	125	234	.534	19	43	.442	64	86	.744	150	5.0	333	11.1
Matt Steigenga	27/27	103	211	.488	14	43	.326	55	81	.679	121	4.5	275	10.2
Anthony Miller	30/3	83	154	.539	0	0	.000	50	80	.625	156	5.2	216	7.2
Mark Montgomery	30/30	80	183	.437	12	52	.231	39	57	.684	111	3.7	211	7.0
Kris Weshinskey	28/1	69	162	.426	19	53	.359	22	35	.629	42	1.5	179	6.4
Jon Zulauf	30/0	39	89	.438	0	5	.000	14	24	.583	49	1.6	92	3.1
Eric Snow	25/0	12	25	.480	0	2	.000	3	15	.200	15	0.6	27	1.1
Andy Penick	2/0	0	1	.000	0	1	.000	2	2	1.00	0	0.0	2	1.0
Mark Bluem	7/0	2	2	1.000	0	0	.000	0	0	.000	2	0.3	4	0.6
Ron Haley	13/0	2	3	.667	0	1	.000	0	0	.000	2	0.2	4	0.3
Team					1	1	1.000				74			
MICHIGAN STATE	30/30	857	1675	.512	124	332	.374	381	551	.692	1046	34.9	2219	74.0
OPPONENTS	30/30	785	1791	.438	142	429	.331	358	517	.693	934	31.1	2070	69.0

1994—95

In a battle of 24's, Shawn Respert whips past Michigan's Jimmy King.

t was the year of "Fire & Ice," a farewell tour and a serious run at the Big Ten title—a season that won't be duplicated in the next century of Spartan basketball.

Before that 22-6 ride began, Jud Heathcote asked for a theme to promote sharpshooting guard Shawn Respert, a National Player of the Year candidate, and backcourt mate Eric Snow, the league leader in assists and a top defender.

The choice was assistant coach Brian Gregory's brainstorm: "Fire" would describe Respert, since no one got hot any quicker. And "Ice" would represent Snow, who could freeze opponents' top shooters.

Much of the focus still centered on Heathcote, who would retire at the end of his 19th season in East Lansing and 24th as a collegiate head coach.

But first, there was time for one last curtain call—and for one more championship chase.

The Spartans were picked to contend, along with Indiana and Michigan, but wound up second in a season-long battle with Purdue, the same program MSU beat to win an outright crown in 1990.

Yet a perceived lack of respect was never far from anyone's mind, as Lindy's Basketball Annual ranked the Spartan backcourt and fans No. 8 in the conference and the coaching staff No. 10.

"When you look back at it now, they underestimated us," said sixth man Daimon Beathea. "Besides 'Fire & Ice,' we had every single area covered in our frontcourt. We had scoring with Quinton (Brooks), rebounding with Jamie (Feick) and a little bit of both with Jon (Garavaglia), while my game centered on defense. I really believe we outplayed every frontcourt in the Big Ten."

With the forwards and centers contributing, Respert and Snow led MSU to a 7-1 start, including an 85-71 blitz of Louisville in Breslin Center.

When the Cardinals were slow to get back on defense, the Spartans made them pay with a torrid transition game and .733 first-half shooting from the field in Heathcote's 400th career win.

Just before conference play began, Respert passed the 2,000-point mark in a bruising win over Long Beach State and said he didn't mind seeing wave after wave of attention from keying defenses.

"I'd love for every team to defend me that way," he said. "Soon, people are going to start to realize what I already know—that a lot of guys on this team can play."

They played well enough against 22nd-ranked Iowa in their Big Ten home opener, battling back from an eight-point deficit in the final 6:03. The Spartans won 69-68 on a 14-foot floater by Snow—a reversal of roles, with the assist coming from a triple-teamed Respert.

The following Saturday, it was Beathea who burned Oklahoma State and star center Bryant "Big Country" Reeves with :07.5 to play. His only 3-pointer all season gave the Spartans a 70-69 win on CBS.

"That had to be one of my biggest thrills as a player," Beathea said. "One of their starting guards played against me in high school. I see him all the time now. And I always remind him about it. I run to the corner, take a shot and ask him if he remembers."

Nicknamed "Fresh Prince" because of a likeness to actor and rapper Will Smith, Beathea was a jokester and a motivator whose contributions went beyond statistics.

"We used to call him a 'broke' Will Smith," Brooks said. "But when the coaches got on him, he'd turn it around and use it to pump up the rest of the team. Jud would say, 'Daimon! What are you doing?' And he'd say, 'OK, OK, I'll get it done!' Most of us would think, 'Why is he riding me like this?'

"He used to love to play video games. When we were both living in the dorms, he'd knock on my door at 3 or 4 a.m. and say, 'C'mon, man! Let's play some video games.' I'd say, 'Daimon, what are you doing?' But he'd want to play Sega football all the time."

MSU played just enough basketball for back-to-back wins over Michigan and Minnesota by a total of three points. Respert was a hobbling hero in Ann Arbor with 30 second-half points. And against the Golden Gophers, Garavaglia's 17-foot baseline jumper with :07 left was the difference.

The Spartans weren't just winning games. They were winning with flair and drama. With four wins by two points or less in three weeks, they seemed like a team of destiny.

"Winning all those close games was a payback for my freshman year, when we lost a lot of those," Brooks said of eight defeats by four points or less. "Shawn and Eric were so deadly, opponents automatically thought one of them was going to get the ball. Somehow, the ball would find its way into Daimon's or Jon's hands. And they'd step up and hit the shots."

With Heathcote's help, Brooks had a season-high 24 points in an 82-62 win at home over Penn State, as MSU tied its best record through 17 games at 15-2.

"He told me before the game I needed to play like 'The Worm,'" said Brooks, who didn't make the connection to all-out hustler Dennis Rodman. "I was a little confused. And everyone started laughing. I'm wondering what a worm slithering around on the ground has to do with the game."

Jamie Feick creates space against the Wolverines Makhtar Ndiaye.

Brooks was a gifted offensive player but was often overcome by nerves.

"Sometimes I'd get so nervous my palms would get sweaty," he said. "I'd get goosebumps and be out in the layup line shaking. It didn't matter how well I was playing. I could've had 130 points. It wouldn't have mattered."

Feick's contributions included 15 games with 10 or more rebounds and three with 15 or more. The 6-foot-9, 240-pounder was the Big Ten's No. 2 rebounder and provided quiet strength for the league's No. 1 rebounding team.

"I remember the two of us fighting for a rebound," Beathea said. "I always thought it was good when you had two guys hitting the boards. But going down the floor, Jamie snapped, 'Daimon! That's my rebound!' He was that possessed to grab every one. It was really no problem with me."

As part of Heathcote's final swing around the conference, Indiana coach Bob Knight gave his friend a beautiful, green-leather recliner. But the Hoosiers' parting gift was an 89-82 victory, despite 40 points by Respert—an Assembly Hall opponent record.

The gifts kept coming in every city. And Heathcote kept trying to put a humorous slant on his retirement so his players could stay focused.

"I tell people, 'Now that I'm retiring, I can finish my book,'" said Heathcote, who soon wrote *JUD: A Magical Journey*. "People would always say they didn't know I was writing a book. I'd tell them, 'I'm not . . . I'm reading one.'"

It wasn't as funny when MSU lost 78-69 to Purdue in Breslin—a game that would decide the Big Ten championship.

The Spartans bounced back with a 67-64 win over Michigan, completing their first sweep in that series since 1991, and a 67-61 payback against Indiana.

But Iowa knocked MSU out of first place with a 79-78 triumph on Andre Woolridge's last-chance basket, overshadowing Respert's 39 points.

The Spartans finished with a 97-72 trouncing of Wisconsin, when a tearful Snow left to a long ovation and Respert knelt and kissed the block "S."

After the game, a banner was raised in the north rafters: "JUD HEATHCOTE, HEAD COACH, 1976–95"—right between Earvin Johnson's No. 33 and Gregory Kelser's No. 32.

Entering the NCAA Tournament as the No. 3 seed in the Southeast Region,

On his farewell tour, Heathcote accepts a gift from Fighting Illini coach Lou Henson.

MSU met Weber State of the Big Sky Conference in Tallahassee, Florida, and led by nine at the half, thanks to .692 shooting from the field.

When a 14th-seeded opponent rallied with a 24-5 run, the Spartans found themselves down by 10. Though they got within two, they could never pull even.

"In the first half, we really jumped on them," Brooks said. "In the second half, it changed. That was the worst feeling I ever had in basketball—no Big Ten title and losing in the first round of the Tournament."

But they won with style that season more often than anyone ever imagined.

The 1994-95 Spartans: Front—Assistant Brian Gregory, David Hart, Ray Weathers, Steve Nicodemus, Shawn Respert, head coach Jud Heathcote, Eric Snow, Mark Prylow, Andy Penick, Thomas Kelley, associate head coach Tom Izzo. Back—Manager Matt Zimmerman, trainer Tom Mackowiak, assistant Stan Joplin, Daimon Beathea, Steve Polonowski, Jamie Feick, Jon Garavaglia, Quinton Brooks, manager Louis Johnson, equipment manger Dave Pruder and manager Jon-Paul Sweda.

Player Statistics for 1994–95

Player	GP/GS	FG	FGA	PCT	FG(3pt)	FGA(3pt)	PCT	FT	FTA	PCT	REB	AVG	TP	AVG
Shawn Respert	28/28	229	484	.473	119	251	.474	139	169	.869	111	4.0	716	25.6
Quinton Brooks	28/26	134	252	.532	1	10	.100	46	75	.613	145	5.2	315	11.3
Eric Snow	28/28	117	225	.520	7	24	.292	62	102	.608	92	3.3	303	10.8
Jamie Feick	28/28	111	180	.617	0	0	.000	54	93	.581	281	10.0	276	9.9
Jon Garavaglia	28/23	91	188	.484	10	31	.323	22	37	.595	143	5.1	214	7.6
Daimon Beathea	28/6	64	133	.481	1	5	.200	10	29	.345	99	3.5	139	5.0
Ray Weathers	27/0	36	87	.414	7	19	.368	15	24	.625	55	2.0	94	3.5
Steve Polonowski	27/1	22	46	.478	6	9	.222	14	20	.700	38	1.4	60	2.2
Andy Penick	14/0	7	17	.412	0	1	.000	2	2	1.000	3	0.2	22	1.6
Thomas Kelley	16/0	9	20	.450	0	0	.000	4	8	.500	8	0.5	22	1.4
Mike Respert	7/0	3	7	.429	3	8	.375	3	4	.750	1	0.1	9	1.3
Steve Nicodemus	11/0	4	10	.400	2	12	.167	2	2	1.000	5	0.5	13	1.2
Mark Prylow	12/0	2	13	.154	0	0	.000	3	4	.750	6	0.5	9	0.8
David Hart	4/0	0	2	.000				2	2	1.000	3	0.8	2	0.5
Team											84			
MICHIGAN STATE	28/28	829	1664	.498	158	387	.408	378	562	.673	1074	38.4	2194	78.4
OPPONENTS	28/28	720	1660	.434	177	520	.340	309	487	.635	887	31.7	1926	68.8

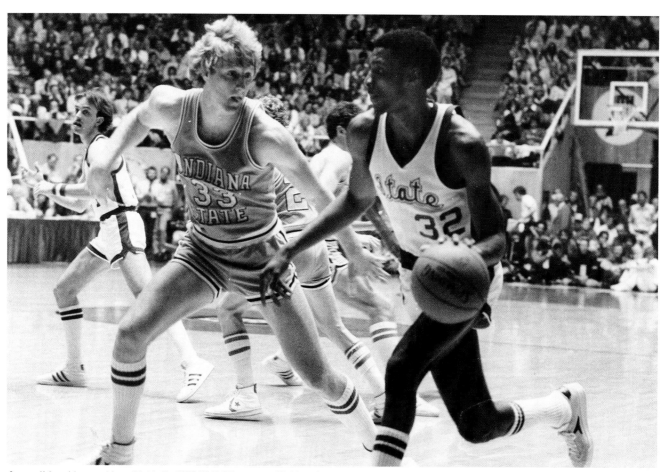

Gregory Kelser drives past Larry Bird in the 1979 NCAA title game, as Michigan State beats 33-0 Indiana State.

The Games
A Sweet (and Sour) 16

North Carolina, 1957

A halfcourt heave for an NCAA semifinal win was no good by a split-second.

But the game itself was better than good. It was the best in Michigan State history by a long shot.

After the Spartans had edged Notre Dame and spanked host Kentucky in the Midwest Region in 1957, it was on to Kansas City, Missouri, for a matchup with top-ranked North Carolina. *Sports Illustrated* previewed a still modest event with four pages and a strange sounding tag, "The Last Four."

Of the regional survivors in a 16-team field, second-ranked Kansas was the popular choice with 7-foot sophomore center Wilt Chamberlain. North Carolina and San Francisco were picked second and third.

MSU was given as much chance as the Washington Senators would have had in an American League pennant race against the all-powerful New York Yankees.

The Spartans had other ideas, as forward George Ferguson suggested after his team declawed the Wildcats and humbled legendary coach Adolph Rupp.

"Give us an hour with that scouting report, and we'll go out and beat them right now!" the captain said, speaking for several of his teammates.

First, however, there was the matter of winter term final exams once the post-Kentucky celebrations stopped. "Everybody has finals this week and these basketball finals are awfully big," said MSU coach Forddy Anderson, who gave his players Monday off while he attended the Big Ten schedule meeting in Chicago.

"We've arranged for the players to receive incompletes until after the trip. But some of the players have said they want to take at least half their exams before leaving again Thursday."

Anderson knew how to handle the pressure as well as anyone could, since his Bradley teams were NCAA runners-up in 1950 and 1954.

"We'll use the same stuff that brought us this far," he said after a Thursday workout in 10,000-seat Municipal Auditorium. "Balanced scoring, a strong bench, sound defense and a desire to win will have to carry us."

No one averaged more than guard Jack Quiggle's 15.5 points. But with forward Larry Hedden at 14.5, center John Green at 13.6 and Ferguson at 13.3, MSU was tough to defend.

And with the defense of guard Pat Wilson and the support of reserves Bob Anderegg, Chuck Bencie, and Dave Scott, the 16-8 Spartans were a surging team that had won 12 of its last 13.

"No one needs to tell us what a great team Frank McGuire has," Anderson said. "North Carolina's record speaks for itself. But we think we're just as good as the next team."

It was MSU vs. the 30-0 Tar Heels at 8:30 p.m. on Friday, March 22, in the first game of a doubleheader, with Kansas and San Francisco to follow.

But before the Jayhawks crushed the Dons 80-56, a capacity crowd enjoyed one of the greatest games in NCAA or NIT history.

To say North Carolina prevailed 74-70 in three overtimes doesn't begin to do the game justice. There were 26 lead changes and 11 ties in regulation.

And there's still some question whether justice was served with the outcome after the extra play.

The problems started in the opening minute when Quiggle sprained an ankle and played through pain in the second-longest NCAA Tournament game.

It was tied at 29 at the half, 58-all at the end of regulation, 64-64 after the first extra session and even at 66 after two OTs.

"It was one of the biggest heartbreaks a team could have," Anderson said. "We had it won so many times. With five minutes to go, we had a six-point lead and ran a perfect out-of-bounds play. But Quiggle blew the layup—something he never did. I didn't know about the ankle until later. Jack never told me about it."

He nearly made amends. After Green's free throws tied it at 58 with 1:57 left, the Spartans got the ball again. But Quiggle's swish from 40-feet was launched just as time expired.

MSU had another great opportunity at the end of the first overtime, leading 64-62 with 11 seconds left and Green at the line.

"We had a two-point lead when John was fouled," Anderson said. "All he had to do was make the first one, and we've got the game wrapped up. Of course, he missed it. And one of their players threw in a prayer to tie it."

That player was Tar Heel forward Pete Brennan. And his heroic shot was a short jumper from the side with three seconds showing.

Back in East Lansing, where the state high school tournament was being played in Jenison Field House, a young assistant sports information director could feel the drama from three states away.

"Someone in the press box had a radio," Nick Vista said. "We'd hear them say, 'Spartans by one! . . . They're down by two! . . . It's tied again!' But we all thought it was over in the first overtime."

Scott and Hedden missed free throws in the second overtime. But Green tied it at 66 with a tip-in. Finally, when Anderegg missed at the line and Quiggle committed two turnovers, North Carolina pulled away.

"I'm punch-drunk," McGuire said. "What was the final score? . . . We were lucky. Ordinarily, nine times out 10, we would've lost a game like this. But we've been playing like a team of destiny all year."

All-America forward Lenny Rosenbluth led the Tar Heels with 29 points but was just 11-for-42 from the field. Quiggle finished with 20 points. And Green had 18 rebounds and eight blocks against Rosenbluth.

"That was a very cocky Carolina team," Wilson said. "They had a little point guard, Tommy Kearns, who I'd still like to crunch today. But I think Quiggle's shot was good. I've never seen the tape and don't really want to."

The Tar Heels shot just 31.5 percent from the field. But MSU had even more difficulty with 28.8 percent accuracy.

"We didn't blow it," Anderson said. "We just lost to a better team. They say the boys should've made those free throws. I'd like to see some of the guys who criticized us step up and make them in that situation.

"We asked for and got 100-percent effort from every man on the team. Psychologically, you can't put toothpaste back in the tube. We drained

every bit of effort from every man we had."

The following night, with Quiggle sidelined the entire first half and Green out most of the second half with five fouls, San Francisco pulled away and won 67-60 in the consolation game.

A few moments later, North Carolina held the ball at every opportunity—as strategy against Chamberlain and to conserve energy—and beat the Jayhawks 54-53 for the title in three more overtimes.

But what if MSU had advanced to the final? Would there be two national championship banners in Breslin Center?

"There was no way I could've matched up with Wilt," Green said. "North Carolina played zone. And we didn't do that. I don't know if Wilt would've set any records. I know we would've had tremendous difficulty."

"Whether we could've won or not, we'll never know," Anderson said. "Each of those games was a monumental task. But I know we gave North Carolina as good a run as anyone could."

Twenty-five years later, Vista met McGuire at an NIT final and asked if he remembered the MSU game. "Do I remember?" McGuire roared. "Let me tell you how great they were. . . ."

MSU vs NORTH CAROLINA (March 22, 1957)

Michigan State

No.	Player	FG	FGA	FT	FTA	REB	F	TP
30	George Ferguson	4	8	2	3	1	5	10
33	Larry Hedden	4	20	6	7	15	5	14
24	Johnny Green	4	12	3	6	19	2	11
21	Jack Quiggle	6	21	8	10	10	1	20
35	Pat Wilson	0	3	2	2	5	1	2
23	Bob Anderegg	2	7	3	6	3	2	7
31	Charles Bencie	1	6	0	0	2	1	2
12	David Scott	2	3	0	2	3	1	4
	Team					7		
TOTALS		**23**	**80**	**24**	**36**	**65**	**18**	**70**

North Carolina

No.	Player	FG	FGA	FT	FTA	REB	F	TP
10	Lennie Rosenbluth	11	42	7	9	3	1	29
32	Bob Cunningham	9	18	3	5	12	5	21
35	Pete Brennan	6	16	2	4	17	5	14
40	Tommy Kearns	1	8	4	5	6	4	6
41	Joe Quigg	0	1	2	3	4	5	2
33	Danny Lotz	0	1	0	0	4	1	0
20	Bob Young	1	3	0	1	2	1	2
22	Ray Searcy	0	0	0	0	1	0	0
	Team					5		
TOTALS		**28**	**89**	**18**	**27**	**54**	**22**	**74**

SCORE BY PERIODS:	1st	2nd	OT	OT	OT	TOTAL
Michigan State	29	29	6	2	4	70
North Carolina	29	29	6	2	8	74

Officials: Ogden and Lightner
Attendance: 10,000

Ohio State, 1979

The deafening noise on February 1, 1979, did a great deal for the hearing aid industry.

But the events that week in Jenison Field House, with a meeting of troubled minds and three huge Michigan State basketball triumphs, did more for the eventual NCAA champions.

If you were anywhere in Ingham County that Thursday night, you could feel the vibrations as the Spartans stayed alive in the Big Ten race with an 84-79 overtime win against first-place Ohio State.

And if you were one of the 10,004 who jammed Jenison, as opposed to the 200,000 who have claimed they were there, your ears are still clearing.

Before Earvin Johnson hobbled from the training room to help save a sinking season, however, it was important for MSU to clear the air.

"Before we talk about the Ohio State game, we have to start at the beginning of the week," said co-captain Gregory Kelser. "We'd just lost by 18 points at Northwestern, a rock-bottom point for us. We were under-achieving like no team had ever underachieved."

At 4-4 in the conference and 11-5 overall, Jud Heathcote's club was still ranked 13th in the nation. But after a 15-3, 25-5 mark the year before, a .500 league record was hardly the road to the Final Four—everyone's pre-season expectation.

Things had to change before a visit from the seventh-ranked Buckeyes, 8-0 and 13-4, including a win over then-No. 1 Duke. And by tipoff, MSU had a new starting lineup, some old freedom and a totally different mindset.

"Jud gave us that Sunday off—the longest Sunday ever," Kelser said. "We had a players-only meeting on Monday, then a meeting when the coaches came in. It's funny how everyone's memory has gotten foggy over the years, but I remember it very, very well."

No one was happy. And in a session with equal parts heat and light, everyone had the chance to speak, though many chose to remain silent.

"My big complaint was that, as a sophomore, Jud had allowed me a great deal of freedom offensively," Kelser said. "I could shoot from outside and handle the ball. After Earvin came, a lot of that freedom was taken away. And that finally caught up with me. If I didn't have a jump shot, how was I going to get a guy to play up on me so I could drive around him?

"I was the first to speak up. Then, Earvin said we weren't running enough and that Jud was on our case too much. Jay Vincent said he couldn't play with all that screaming. And Ron Charles said the same thing. That's what really got Jud. He said, 'Bobo,' I can understand Earvin being unhappy. But I always thought you were like a rubber ball. We'd throw you against the wall. And you'd bounce right back.' We all called Ron 'Rubber Ball' after that."

Heathcote had his say, as he always did. But to this day, he insists the best analysis and most constructive comments came from a reserve guard and doctor-to-be, whose intelligence was respected by everyone.

"The guy who made the most sense was Mike Longaker," Heathcote said. "He could analyze just about anything. And Mike said, 'Hey, guys,

Jay Vincent establishes post position against Ohio State's Jim Ellinghausen.

we're not playing hard enough or well enough. We're not playing good enough on defense. . . . And maybe the coaches are on the players a little too much.'"

Whatever he said seemed to sink in, as the Spartans had their best practice of the season that Monday, from all recollections.

Another important change for the rest of the season was a shift in the starting lineup, though it didn't take place immediately.

"Jud wanted to start Gerald Busby in place of Terry Donnelly and Mike Brkovich instead of 'Bobo,'" Kelser said. "That day, Busby withdrew from school. Jud wanted to know if the players wanted him back. We all said we did. But he wouldn't come back. So 'Brk' and 'Bobo' started the next game."

MSU started to play the way everyone figured they would, with Donnelly soon returning as a starter. But first, it was time to jump-start a season.

Kelser hit a 14-footer for his team's first points and added two longer shots in a solid first half, as the Spartans shot 66.7 percent from the field.

But more than a 32-23 lead was in jeopardy when Johnson went down,

clutching his ankle and writhing in pain with 2:23 left until halftime.

"I told our medical staff, 'If there's any danger to Earvin, I don't want him to play, even if he wants to play,'" said Heathcote, who correctly thought his star had suffered a severe ankle sprain. "The doctors said, 'OK. . . . He won't be playing.'"

"We'd never had to play without him," Kelser said. "When you depend on a guy that much, you don't lose one-fifth of the team—more like a half."

MSU led 34-27 at the break but, with Kelser on the bench with four fouls, fell behind 39-38 with 14:13 to play. It wasn't exactly the news Johnson wanted to hear, listening to a radio with trainer Clint Thompson.

"If they'd beaten us, they'd have been 9-0, and we'd have been 4-5," Johnson said. "It would've been over. So I'm sitting there, crying like a baby. I said, 'That's it! . . . I'm going back!' He said, 'You can't.' And I said, 'Clint! Wrap me up!'"

Dr. David Hough had other ideas. But Johnson grabbed his shirt lapels.

"Doc had already made up his mind," Johnson said. "He said, 'No more tonight. You'll have to miss the next two games, too.' I said, 'Hey, Doc! The next two games (Northwestern Saturday and Kansas Sunday) won't mean a thing if we don't win this one! . . . I can play! . . . I can move!'"

Hough said, "See if you can jump. . . . Run down that corridor and back. . . . Turn your ankle in and out. . . . Okay? Go try it!"

When the door to the training room opened underneath the stands, enough fans could see Johnson to trigger an ovation unlike any ever seen or heard in Jenison or any other Big Ten facility.

"You couldn't hear anything," Johnson said. "It was like your eardrums had popped. It kept going and going and going. That place never let the sound out. And when an NBA arena would get a little loud, I'd tell guys, 'This place is nothing! You should've heard Jenison!'"

"It was the loudest I've ever heard an arena," Heathcote said. "It was one big wave—just absolutely deafening! . . . Gregory was at the table, waiting to come in. I think he thought they were applauding his return."

"Jud loves to tell that story," Kelser said. "It's funny. But it's not true. . . . I'm not crazy. I was looking toward the entrance as much as anybody. I'd seen Earvin at halftime. I knew he'd find a way to come back."

When he did, it was an easy coaching decision after a few assurances.

"Right away, I said to Clint, 'What's the scoop?'" Heathcote remembered. "He told me, 'The docs say he can play. There won't be any lasting damage.' And 'E' said, 'I can play! . . . I'm okay!'"

Heathcote waited roughly a third of a second and sent Johnson to check in. With everyone screaming and stomping, Vincent promptly scored on two putbacks. And by the time there was a stoppage of play, MSU led 48-43.

OSU scored the next six points, including two of guard Kelvin Ransey's game-high 25. That allowed Heathcote to joke to Johnson, "If we hadn't put you in, we'd have won in a breeze!"

It appeared victory was in hand again until a bizarre four-point play—a jumper by guard Todd Penn and two tosses by forward Jim Ellinghausen on a Johnson foul away from the ball—tied it at 64 with :28 showing.

But the overtime was all MSU. With Johnson scoring 15 of his 23 points in the final 4:27 of regulation and the five-minute extra session, Kelser adding 21 points on 9-for-13 shooting from the field and Vincent outscoring Buckeye center Herb Williams 19-18 and grabbing 12 rebounds, the race was on.

"Pure and simple, we had to have that," Kelser said. "As it was, we tied Iowa and Purdue. And Purdue had to settle for the NIT. But we beat Northwestern in the rematch. And when Ohio State lost at Michigan, we were only two games back. We couldn't have felt any better."

Johnson's ankle could have. But his team was healed, as pained opponents would soon discover.

OHIO STATE vs MSU (February 1, 1979)

Ohio State

No.	Player	FG	FGA	FT	FTA	REB	F	TP	A	BK	S	TO	MIN
15	Carter Scott, f	3	5	2	2	2	5	8	1	5	0	1	24
23	Jim Smith, f	3	4	0	0	5	5	6	0	0	0	0	24
32	Herb Williams, c	9	19	0	0	6	2	18	0	1	1	1	45
14	Kelvin Ransey, g	10	21	5	6	5	4	25	2	2	0	1	43
24	Todd Penn, g	2	4	0	0	1	1	4	4	1	0	0	36
45	Marquis Miller	2	3	0	0	2	2	4	2	0	0	0	13
41	Jim Ellinghausen	1	5	4	6	2	3	6	1	2	0	0	21
34	Mike Cline	4	5	0	0	1	2	8	2	2	0	0	17
22	Tony Hall	0	1	0	2	2	2	0	0	0	0	0	2
	Team					2							
	TOTALS	**34**	**67**	**11**	**16**	**28**	**26**	**79**	**14**	**15**	**1**	**3**	**225**

FG%: 1st Half: 13-29, .448. 2nd Half/OT: 21-38, .552. Game: 34-67, .507.
FT%: 1st Half: 1-2, .500. 2nd Half/OT: 10-14, .714. Game: 11-16, .688.

Michigan State

No.	Player	FG	FGA	FT	FTA	REB	F	TP	A	BK	S	TO	MIN
32	Gregory Kelser, f	9	13	3	5	7	4	21	0	3	1	3	29
15	Ron Charles, f	3	4	0	1	1	3	6	0	1	0	1	31
31	Jay Vincent, c	8	17	3	4	12	1	19	1	2	2	2	45
12	Mike Brkovich, g	2	5	6	7	1	3	10	1	4	0	0	40
33	Earvin Johnson, g	6	10	11	13	7	5	23	7	4	0	2	32
35	Rob Gonzalez	0	1	0	0	0	2	0	0	1	0	0	14
11	Terry Donnelly	2	6	1	2	1	0	5	2	1	0	0	34
	Team					2							
	TOTALS	**30**	**56**	**24**	**32**	**31**	**18**	**84**	**11**	**16**	**3**	**8**	**225**

FG%: 1st Half: 16-24, .667. 2nd Half/OT: 14-32, .438. Game: 30-56, .536.
FT%: 1st Half: 2-6, .333. 2nd Half/OT: 22-26, .846. Game: 24-32, .750.

SCORE BY PERIODS:	1st	2nd	OT	TOTAL
Ohio State	27	37	15	79
Michigan State	34	30	20	84

Officials: Richard Weiler, Phil Robinson, Ray Doran
Attendance: 10,004

Notre Dame, 1979

The scoreboard told the story when the nation's two best teams collided.

I f the 1979 NCAA Mideast Region Final wasn't the National Championship game, and many would argue it should have been, it was something better.

It was the most eagerly awaited Notre Dame–Michigan State matchup since a 10-10 football classic in Spartan Stadium 13 years earlier.

This time, the only ones disappointed were the Fighting Irish, after suffering an 80-68 whipping on NBC—then and now, the Notre Dame Broadcasting Company.

"They were a lot bigger than us and a very physical team, we thought," said MSU forward Gregory Kelser, who had six of his team's nine dunks on Sunday, March 18, in Indianapolis. "Bill Laimbeer (6-foot-11), Bruce Flowers, and Orlando Woolridge (both 6-9) were big. And (6-7) Bill Hanzlik was big for a guard.

"But at the press conference before the game, they called us the physical team and said they'd have to wear shoulder pads. I don't know if that

was gamesmanship or what. We'd never thought of ourselves as a physical team, even though we were from a physical conference."

Nor had MSU thought of itself as anything other than the best team in its region, if not in the country, which made a No. 2 seed and its consequences more distasteful.

"We wanted to wear our white uniforms," Kelser said. "We'd worn them the first two games of the Tournament in Murfreesboro, Tennessee. But they pulled rank as the No. 1 seed and made us wear green. That made us even madder."

The Spartans were as emotionally ready as any team could be and just as strategically sound, beginning with guard Mike Brkovich's opening slam.

"We had a plan to jump in front in the first few seconds and set the tone," Heathcote said. "Gregory used to hold guys with his other hand when he jumped center. He got almost every tip. So we put in a special play."

Normally, the 6-7 Kelser would soar as few others could and bat the ball

back to guard Terry Donnelly, positioned deep in the backcourt, when basketball still had a jump ball to open each half.

For this game, it was time to try something new—a designed play as devastating as any opening salvo in NCAA Tournament history.

The Spartans hadn't worked on the maneuver for more than a few minutes at one practice in Indy, though it looked as though they'd been perfecting and saving the "Go" play all season.

"Jud had noticed that Notre Dame didn't put anyone back on defense for the opening tap," said 6-8 point guard Earvin Johnson. "Greg jumped center and tapped the ball to me. Without looking, I batted it over my head to Brkovich, who was already streaking in for the dunk."

"Coach told me, 'As soon as the ball goes up, take off for the basket,'" Brkovich said. "He said, 'Don't worry, the ball will be there.'"

It was, and so was a bullet to the heart that paralyzed the Irish for much of the day in Market Square Arena.

"That's the genius of Jud Heathcote for you," Kelser said. "Maybe Notre Dame didn't need to put anyone back if they never lost the tap. I'd probably lost two all year. But Jud challenged me in practice. He said, 'Can you outjump this guy?' I said, 'Don't worry. I'll get it.' I had to be 90 percent on taps against everyone from Vladimir Tkachenko of the Soviet Union to Joe Barry Carroll of Purdue."

Before Kelser outjumped Woolridge, he reminded Brkovich the goal of the "Go" play wasn't a basket but a demoralizing first strike that would mean much more than two points.

"Before the game, I told him, 'Whatever you do, don't just lay the ball in. Go up and dunk it,'" Kelser said, showing senior leadership. "Then, Terry Donnelly stole their inbounds pass, and the tone was set."

At about that time, a wager was settled in the stands, with insider information resulting in an almost unfair payoff.

Two 16-year-olds who'd sneaked past security and eavesdropped on MSU's Saturday practice knew about the tip play and goaded Notre Dame fans into a $100 bet that Brkovich would dunk the ball in the first 10 seconds. It only took three for the young Spartans to collect and a few more for Phelps to find a new vocabulary.

"Years later, I talked to Danny Nee, an assistant at Notre Dame before he went to Nebraska," Heathcote said. "He said Digger never swore on the bench. But he knew their team was in trouble when Digger said, 'Oh, shit!' twice in the first 10 seconds."

Phelps remembered some of that sequence and can be excused for having selective recall about such a painful series of events.

"They scored off the opening tip, then stole the inbounds pass," Phelps said correctly. "It was 4-0 before we knew it."

Actually, it was only 2-0. MSU did steal the inbounds pass but turned the ball over before it could score. The Irish tied it at 2 and again at 6 before Brkovich, nicknamed "The Golden Arm," put his team ahead to stay with two long jumpers.

The rest of the day belonged to Kelser, an All-American and Academic All-American who delivered an All-World performance.

"Billy Hanzlik actually did a decent job on Magic," Phelps said. "We just couldn't guard Kelser. He had 20-some points."

Actually, he had 34 points and 13 rebounds—nearly half his team's production in both areas.

Meanwhile, Notre Dame's starting frontcourt of Laimbeer, Woolridge, and

Gregory Kelser rebounds over Notre Dame's Orlando Woolridge.

Tripucka managed a total of just 18 points and 11 rebounds.

Without 19 points apiece from Hanzlik and first sub Tracy Jackson, the Irish would have been beaten much worse.

" 'Special K' was absolutely brilliant that day," said Johnson, who chipped in with 19 points and 13 assists. "I'll never forget the sight of Greg going down the lane and dunking over three guys with his left hand."

Kelser actually missed his first six shots, then hit his last seven tries in a 34-23 first half and 15 of his last 19, including a personal-best six dunks.

He had 14 straight points for the Spartans midway through the first half, highlighted by a one-handed slam of an alley-oop feed from Johnson.

Terry Donnelly ties up Notre Dame's Kelly Tripucka as the Spartans thoroughly frustrate the Irish.

After Notre Dame drew to 48-41 with seven straight perimeter jumpers, MSU built a 80-63 lead before the Irish scored five meaningless points in the last 52 seconds.

"People have said that's the happiest they've ever seen me," Heathcote said. "And they're probably right. I shook my fists over my head. It was the realization that we'd made it to the Final Four, knowing how few teams had ever made it."

This one made history as the first MSU team in 22 years to advance that far.

"Everyone remembers Jud pumping his fists," Kelser said. "But in the locker room, he told us he was proud of us for playing the way we were capable of playing. And he said, 'Now, we're on to something even bigger.'"

They were on to the Special Events Center at the University of Utah for two games that weren't nearly as emotion-packed as this one.

MSU vs NOTRE DAME (March 18, 1979)

Michigan State

No. Player	FG	FGA	FT	FTA	REB	F	TP	A	TO	BK	S	MIN
12 Mike Brkovich, f	5	10	3	4	3	1	13	1	2	0	0	38.5
32 Gregory Kelser, f	15	25	4	8	13	4	34	1	3	2	1	39
15 Ron Charles, c	2	4	2	2	4	4	6	0	0	0	0	32.5
11 Terry Donnelly, g	1	1	2	2	2	3	4	0	1	1	1	36
33 Earvin Johnson, g	6	10	7	8	5	2	19	13	3	0	2	40
35 Rob Gonzalez	1	2	0	0	3	2	2	0	1	0	0	10.5
31 Jay Vincent	1	2	0	0	0	0	2	0	0	0	0	2.5
23 Mike Longaker	0	0	0	0	0	0	0	0	0	0	0	1
Team					3							
TOTALS	31	54	18	24	33	16	80	15	10	3	4	200

FG%: 1st Half: 14-27, .519. 2nd Half: 17-27, .630. Game: 31-54,.574.
FT%: 1st Half: 6-9, .667. 2nd Half: 12-15, .800. Game: 18-24, .750.

Notre Dame

No. Player	FG	FGA	FT	FTA	REB	F	TP	A	TO	BK	S	MIN
32 Orlando Woolridge, f	1	6	1	2	3	1	3	0	0	0	0	18
44 Kelly Tripucka, f	4	11	0	0	4	4	8	1	1	1	2	34
52 Bill Laimbeer, c	3	5	1	2	4	3	7	1	3	2	1	19.5
12 Rich Branning, g	4	14	0	0	3	4	8	4	2	0	1	33
42 Bill Hanzlik, g	7	12	5	5	5	5	19	4	0	0	1	30
30 Tracy Jackson	9	13	1	4	6	4	19	1	2	0	0	30.5
34 Bruce Flowers	0	1	0	0	6	3	0	1	4	1	2	16
24 Stan Wilcox	2	4	0	0	1	0	4	2	0	0	0	14.5
15 Mike Mitchell	0	0	0	0	0	0	0	0	0	0	0	4.5
Team					3							
TOTALS	30	66	8	13	35	24	68	14	12	4	7	200

FG%: 1st Half: 10-28, .357. 2nd Half: 20-38, .526. Game: 30-66, .455.
FT%: 1st Half: 3-6, .500. 2nd Half: 5-7, .714. Game: 8-13, .615.

SCORE BY PERIODS:	1st	2nd	TOTAL
Michigan State	34	46	80
Notre Dame	23	45	68

Officials: Frank Buckiewicz, Booker Turner, Bob Herrold
Attendance: 17,423

Indiana State, 1979

Earvin Johnson is in control in his first matchup against Larry Bird.

The spotlight shone on a pair of 33's. And when it finally dimmed oh so slightly, Indiana State, just the 10th unbeaten team in an NCAA Final Four, was 33-1.

Earvin Johnson, Gregory Kelser, and Terry Donnelly made sure of that, as Michigan State toppled Larry Bird and the Cinderella Sycamores 75-64 to win the 1979 national championship on Monday, March 26, in Salt Lake City.

But it was more than the biggest win in Spartan history—in any sport. It was the *Roots* of college basketball telecasts and the root of all growth in what was little more than a cult league, the NBA.

NBC's production, the first of many Johnson–Bird matchups, drew a 24.1 rating—still the collegiate record—and a 38 percent audience share.

Included in that audience was Michigan Governor James Blanchard, a loyal alumnus who slipped out of a dinner honoring Egypt's Anwar Sadat and Israel's Menachem Begin to watch the second half at the White House.

"That game took the NCAA Tournament to another level," said Al McGuire, who shared analyst duties with Bill Packer, while Dick Enberg handled the play-by-play. "That game was the launching pad."

In the second half of a Saturday afternoon doubleheader, No. 1-ranked ISU held off freshman Mark Aguirre and DePaul 76-74 at the 15,410-seat Special Events Center at the University of Utah.

That set up the contest—some would say battle—between two players who didn't care for each other much at the time but went on to become respected rivals, 1992 Olympic teammates, and friends.

"It's probably the biggest game I'll ever play in my life," said Bird, a 6-foot-9, 220-pound roving center. "I'm representing myself, my team, my school and the town of Terre Haute."

"Because of Larry, it was bigger than anything I ever experienced in college," said Johnson, a 6-8, 207-pound you-name-it, he'll-play-it. "He was a guy who played and thought the way I did. He'd do anything it took to win."

For the Spartans, it took a shrewd but controversial coaching decision by Jud Heathcote, who put Johnson on the scout team in practice to simulate Bird's amazing court vision—the only option he had.

"College basketball will never see two big men who are better passers in the same season—maybe not even in the same decade," Enberg said. "They had the incredible ability to anticipate, see the court, and get the feel of the game. I like to think I speak for every fan when I thank them for a year of incredible 'Oh, mys!'"

With Jud Heathcote's matchup zone-and-help defense, Bird can't find an open shot.

When "The Magic Man" and "The Hick from French Lick" squared off as a sophomore and a fifth-year senior, few knew they were watching a preview of the next decade. But they knew they were seeing something unique.

"It was a high-publicity, high-gloss team against country kids with one incredible athlete," said Len DeLuca, a college sports coordinator for CBS and ESPN. "The Final Four became a national event that year. And with both stars turning pro, it was as pivotal for the NBA as it was for the NCAA."

The television revenue from a 40-team NCAA Tournament that season was just over $5.1 million. By 1995, it had grown to a 64-team extravaganza worth $1.725 billion for seven years—enough to fund all NCAA operations and keep several strapped athletic departments afloat.

"It was a game I'll never forget for the hype, more than the game itself," said the voice of MSU, WKAR's Jim Adams. "With the telecast, I think my dad was the only one listening to me. But from the time we played Notre Dame on, all our broadcasts were carried around the world on Armed Forces Radio."

"It's still the highest-rated game of all time, which tells you something right there," Johnson said. "It turned a nice, little event into a spectacular. And to this day, I remember every detail—every joke and every shot. I just replay it over and over in my mind."

He could start with a warmup two days earlier, when the Mideast Region champs chewed the Pennsylvania Quakers into Quaker Oats. The Spartans walloped the surprise East Region survivors 101-67 in a game that wasn't that close.

Gregory Kelser plays keep-away from Bird.

"Special K" and "Magic" made Bird a sitting duck.

"Those two players took college roundball to another plane," McGuire said. "They put it on its afterburners and put passing—a beautiful art—back in the game."

The challenge for MSU was not to get mesmerized as so many Sycamore opponents had. That meant extra attention from Heathcote's patented matchup zone and double-teaming whenever Bird touched the ball, with the other defenders playing only the passing lanes.

That strategy worked about as well as anyone could have dreamed, with Bird just 7-for-21 from the field in a 19-point performance—eight below his average. And when the dream was over, he sat crying on the ISU bench, his head draped in a towel.

One of the many banners among the Spartan faithful read: "Bird may score, but Magic does more." And the first time it mattered, that's what happened.

An end-to-end dash and an off-balance, three-point play gave MSU its first lead at 5-4 and started Johnson on the way to a 24-point night and Final Four MVP honors.

But even before that, the winners were dunking, courtesy of Kelser. The winners' other All-American struck first as a passer, then stuffed a perfect alley oop feed from Johnson and deposited two long passes in the final minute.

Using his quickness against Bird, the 6-7 Kelser finished with 19 points, eight rebounds, and a surprising nine assists. But he also kept the game interesting by stumbling into Bird for a silly third foul just before halftime and picking up his fourth with 17:22 to play.

"The biggest story is the third team on the floor," said NBC sideline reporter Bryant Gumbel. "These officials are calling it very close."

"If we hadn't gotten in foul trouble, I think it might've been the biggest championship blowout in a long time," said Heathcote, whose team led 37-28 at the intermission and 44-28 when the game changed. "We were a great team with Gregory and Earvin in there and a very average team with either one on the bench."

With Johnson, who also had three fouls in the first half, instructed to play ball-control, the Spartans lost their momentum and 10 points of their lead.

But they were saved by the 6-2 Donnelly, who was 5-for-5 from the field and 5-for-6 at the line with the Sycamores ignoring him.

"I never really planned to shoot," Donnelly said, despite being told he would have open looks. "When Indiana State overshifted, they kept feeding me the ball. It was something different for me, that's for sure."

When ISU drew to 52-46, Kelser returned. And after a lunging, out-of-bounds save by forward Ron Charles, Kelser hit Johnson for a backdoor slam over Sycamore guard Bob Heaton. That basket and two free throws on an undercut made it 61-50 and ended the suspense.

"I don't believe in a breaking point," said first-year ISU coach Bill Hodges. "But that four-point play sure broke my heart. Michigan State is a great team. But if we'd hit our free throws, we'd have been right in it."

Johnson's dunk over Bob Heaton made the cover of Sports Illustrated.

Big Ten Commissioner Wayne Duke makes his presentation to Earvin Johnson.

The Sycamores were 10-for-22 at the line, while the Spartans were 23-for-33. That difference led to "The Hug"—a famous embrace between Johnson and Kelser in the closing seconds. But in the midst of all the partying and parade planning, there was time for one last Heathcote eruption.

"Afterward, some freelance writer from New York kept asking our players if they thought Bird had choked," Heathcote said. "I confronted him and told him I didn't like his line of questioning.

"I said, 'Let me tell you something! Larry Bird and Magic Johnson have two things you'll never appreciate—great hands and great vision. And Bird will be a great, great pro. Now, go write that!' Of course, he never did."

He should have. After MSU won the 41st NCAA crown, two of the greatest winners the sport has known renewed their rivalry in Boston and Los Angeles.

All they did was lead their teams to eight of the next nine NBA titles.

MSU vs INDIANA STATE (March 26, 1979)

Michigan State

No.	Player	FG	FGA	FT	FTA	REB	F	TP	A	TO	BK	S	MIN
12	Mike Brkovich, f	1	2	3	7	4	1	5	1	5	0	0	39.5
32	Gregory Kelser, f	7	13	5	6	8	4	19	9	1	2	2	32
15	Ron Charles, c	3	3	1	2	7	5	7	0	1	0	1	31
11	Terry Donnelly, g	5	5	5	6	4	2	15	0	2	0	1	39.5
33	Earvin Johnson, g	8	15	8	10	7	3	24	5	6	0	1	35.5
31	Jay Vincent	2	5	1	2	2	4	5	0	1	0	1	19
35	Rob Gonzalez	0	0	0	0	0	0	0	0	0	0	0	3
23	Mike Longaker	0	0	0	0	0	0	0	0	0	0	0	0.5
	Team					2							
	TOTALS	**26**	**43**	**23**	**33**	**34**	**19**	**75**	**15**	**16**	**2**	**6**	**200**

FG%: 1st Half: 14-27, .519. 2nd Half: 12-16, .750. Game: 26-43, .605.
FT%: 1st Half: 9-13, .692. 2nd Half: 14-20, .700. Game:23-33, .697.

Indiana State

No.	Player	FG	FGA	FT	FTA	REB	F	TP	A	TO	BK	S	MIN
40	Brad Miley, f	0	0	0	1	3	1	0	0	0	0	0	24.5
42	Alex Gilbert, f	2	3	0	4	4	4	4	0	1	1	0	20.5
33	Larry Bird, c	7	21	5	8	13	3	19	2	6	1	5	40
22	Carl Nicks, g	7	14	3	6	2	5	17	4	2	0	1	36.5
23	Steve Reed, g	4	9	0	0	0	4	8	9	0	0	0	36
30	Bob Heaton	4	14	2	2	6	2	10	2	2	0	1	22.5
44	Leroy Staley	2	2	0	1	3	2	4	0	0	0	0	17.5
20	Rick Nemeck	1	1	0	0	0	3	2	1	1	0	0	2.5
	Team					3							
	TOTALS	**27**	**64**	**10**	**22**	**34**	**24**	**64**	**18**	**10**	**2**	**6**	**200**

FG%: 1st Half: 11-29, .379. 2nd Half: 16-35, .457. Game: 27-64,.422.
FT%: 1st Half: 6-11, .545. 2nd Half: 4-11, .364. Game: 10-22, .455.

SCORE BY PERIODS:	1st	2nd	TOTAL
Michigan State	37	38	75
Indiana State	28	36	64

Officials: Henry Nichols, Gary Muncy, Leonard Wirtz
Attendance: 15,410

GAME PROFILE

Purdue, 1990

Purdue strongman Stephen Scheffler tries to gain possession in front of Mike Peplowski.

The best laid plans of mighty men sometimes go astray—and occasionally lead to Big Ten basketball championships.

That's what happened in the closing seconds on Sunday, March 11, 1990—the greatest game in Breslin Center history.

Michigan State's 72-70 triumph over Purdue would have been a classic if it hadn't been a title showdown at high noon.

But the way the Spartans won, with a spectacular comeback and one of the craziest plays you'll never see, was more than a crowd of 15,138 could bear.

"I knew it right from the start," said MSU center and emotional leader Mike Peplowski. "The atmosphere was just electric. It was such a big-time game. And every time we played Purdue, it was a frickin' war."

This time, it was a stunning matchup of teams picked for the second division. No one expected the Spartans and Boilermakers to combine for 28 conference wins—double their total from the year before.

Steve Grinczel of Booth News Service wrote, "ABC thought so little of this game before the season that it scheduled either Michigan–Iowa or Indiana–Illinois. It settled for the latter when it couldn't wrest control of MSU–Purdue from Raycom."

With the seventh-ranked Spartans one game ahead of the 10th-ranked Boilermakers, this one mattered—especially after MSU's 64-53 win in Mackey Arena five weeks earlier.

And with Jud Heathcote and Gene Keady matching wits and scowls as head coaches, the one team that couldn't win that day was the officiating crew—Jim Bain, Ed Hightower and Sid Rodeheffer.

"We didn't go in there thinking we were already at least co-champs," said MSU point guard Mark Montgomery. "It was like Jud said before before the game, 'We've already accomplished a lot. Now, it's time to get greedy!'"

Gordon Gekko, in the movie *Wall Street*, couldn't have said it better.

First, forward Ken Redfield, guard Kirk Manns, swingman Todd Wolfe, and center David Mueller were saluted for their contributions on Senior Day.

Then, the Spartans came out flying and grabbed a 10-0 lead, only to see Purdue score 13 in a row to go up 33-27 at halftime.

MSU went ahead 48-46 and led 59-56 with 6:29 to play. But the Boilermakers rallied for a 68-63 edge with 2:00 left.

All-America guard Steve Smith hit a pair of free throws. And Montgomery cut the deficit to one with an end-to-end layup, before Purdue guard Tony Jones made it 70-67 at the foul line.

Manns, who sat out the first half and three games before that with a fractured foot, hit a tough leaner from the left baseline with :32 left.

That's when the Spartans called timeout and came up with a plan to foul when the ball entered the forecourt, if not before.

"I just remember Coach Heathcote telling us to foul," said forward Dwayne Stephens. "The next thing I knew, the ball was loose."

On their third try to inbound the ball, Jones took a pass and switched hands on his dribble. Redfield's deflection squirted to Boilermaker center and league MVP Stephen Scheffler, who was tied up by Redfield and Stephens.

When the ball bounced away, Jones had a chance to gain possession but lost control again. For Stephens, it was the gift of a lifetime.

"When they got the ball in, we knocked it loose," Heathcote said. "They got it back. And we knocked it loose again. Suddenly, there's Stephens with the ball and Redfield running interference."

Stephens, a freshman, dribbled in from the left side and laid the ball softly

Steve Smith launches a jumper over the Boilermakers' Tony Jones.

over the rim for a layup louder than any slam could be.

"It was like everything was in slow motion," he said of a scramble sequence few could follow. "I hurt my wrist early in the year and was afraid to try to dunk. I didn't want to miss."

Trailing 71-70 with :20 showing, Purdue had plenty of time and got a great look at the basket on a 21-foot jumper by guard Woody Austin.

The ball sailed wide to Redfield, who flipped it to Smith with :03 to play. A quick foul and one of two free throws—Smith's game-high 22nd point—sealed the deal.

When the buzzer sounded, most Spartan players leaped over the scorer's table before hundreds of fans flooded the floor, with some students using the press row to practice their platform diving.

"We learned about that after beating Michigan," Montgomery said. "We knew the students would run on the court. And when they're all around you, you can't even breathe. We said, 'We're jumping over the table!'"

A few stragglers like forward Matt Steigenga didn't make it that far when a friend insisted on savoring the moment.

"I remember running out to midcourt to tackle Matt," Peplowski said.

MSU students swarm Sparty in a spontaneous Big Ten title celebration.

"When I got there, half the student body was on top on me."

"We all have a picture of the floor right after the game," Steigenga said. "I'm the only one you can't see. I'm standing right behind Mike."

Heathcote got caught in the crowd for almost a minute. When he finally emerged, his few remaining hairs were standing on end like Don King's.

A few moments later, the players returned to snip the nets. And it was easy to tell the winners from the whiners.

"It's unbelievable," Jones said. "I don't think this game will ever go away. . . . It hurts. We should have a piece of that championship."

"We deserved to win!" said Keady, who thought he saw a mugging, not just a personal foul. "It's a shame things turn out the way they do. It's an injustice. And it's sickening."

From MSU's perspective, it was brilliant defense—much like the "perfect pass coverage" by Spartan cornerback Eddie Brown that fall when Michigan receiver Desmond Howard would drop a deciding two-point conversion pass.

"Geno should know that Big Ten refs won't decide a game at the end," Peplowski said. "They had a great chance to win. They just didn't do it."

"It was one of those situations where you say, 'Was it a foul or wasn't it?'" Montgomery said. "When the ball came loose, Dwayne was right there. Bang-bang, he scored. There was probably a little foul . . . but not much."

"That sounds like something Mark would say," Stephens said with a laugh. "I know if I'd missed that shot, I wouldn't be allowed in East Lansing to this day. But I think Gene is still pissed off about that. I saw him at Jud's last Final Four party. And he said it was still a foul!"

Heathcote was no more sympathetic to the Boilermakers' travel and practice problems, with fog causing a charter diversion to Detroit and an arrival

by bus just 12 hours before tipoff.

"I feel bad Purdue didn't get to practice here," said Heathcote, who counts Keady among his closest coaching friends. "That's probably why they only shot 58 percent from the field, when everyone else who comes in here shoots about 38."

MSU assistant Tom Izzo's first job that day was to keep his boss from knocking himself sillier with a series of self-inflicted blows to the skull. But that was also the day of his first date with wife-to-be Lupe Marinez. . . . Talk about an auspicious beginning.

"We knew it would be a physical game," he said of the win, not the date. "We got off to such a great start. They battled back. And we were destined to win in as unbelievable a finish as I've ever seen."

With a 15-3, 26-6 mark, the Spartans received a No. 1 seed in the NCAA Tournament's Southeast Region, where they lost a controversial overtime game to Georgia Tech in the Sweet 16.

"I wanted to win that sonuvabitch in the worst way," Peplowski said of the Purdue game. "When it was over, I didn't know whether I should run, sit, walk, jump or cry. It was the way I felt when I asked my wife to marry me.

"I think a feeling like that is probably the reason some people do drugs. If you could bottle that high synthetically, everyone would want it. To try to describe it in one sentence is impossible. But once you taste it, you'll chase it for the rest of your life."

PURDUE vs MSU (March 11, 1990)

Purdue

No.	Player	FG	FGA	3 Pt. FG	3 Pt. FGA	FT	FTA	Reb. Off.	Reb. Def.	Reb. Tot.	F	TP	A	TO	BK	S	MIN
15	Ryan Berning, f	3	5	1	2	0	0	1	5	6	5	7	1	1	1	0	32
23	Chuckie White, f	3	7	0	0	1	3	1	0	1	2	7	0	3	0	1	24
55	Stephen Scheffler, c	7	10	0	0	4	4	1	2	3	3	18	2	3	0	0	35
10	Woody Austin, g	2	5	1	3	0	0	0	3	3	0	5	3	0	0	1	28
25	Tony Jones, g	6	11	2	2	7	8	2	0	2	4	21	4	2	0	1	33
21	Loren Clyburn	1	3	0	0	1	2	1	0	1	2	2	3	2	0	2	19
32	Jimmy Oliver	4	6	1	3	0	0	0	5	5	0	9	5	0	0	0	29
	Team							1	1	2							
	TOTALS	26	47	5	10	13	17	7	16	23	16	70	18	11	1	5	200

FG%: 1st Half: 11-21, .524. 2nd Half: 15-26, .577. Game: 26-47, .553.
3-Pt.%: 1st Half: 4-6, .667. 2nd Half: 1-4, .250. Game: 5-10, .500.
FT%: 1st Half: 7-10, .700. 2nd Half: 6-7, .857. Game: 13-17, .765.

Michigan State

No.	Player	FG	FGA	3 Pt. FG	3 Pt. FGA	FT	FTA	Reb. Off.	Reb. Def.	Reb. Tot.	F	TP	A	TO	BK	S	MIN
20	Ken Redfield, f	8	10	0	0	0	1	1	3	4	3	16	4	1	0	2	36
35	Matt Steigenga, f	3	6	0	0	2	2	1	1	2	3	8	3	2	1	1	32
54	Mike Peplowski, c	2	3	0	0	4	4	2	4	6	3	8	3	0	0	0	22
11	Mark Montgomery, g	3	7	1	2	0	0	0	2	2	3	7	1	1	0	1	29
21	Steve Smith, g	9	16	0	3	4	5	0	2	2	2	22	4	3	0	0	36
10	Kirk Manns	3	5	1	1	0	0	0	0	0	0	7	1	0	0	0	10
24	Todd Wolfe	0	1	0	1	0	0	0	0	0	0	0	0	0	0	0	5
31	Dwayne Stephens	2	4	0	0	0	0	0	0	0	2	4	1	0	0	0	21
42	Parish Hickman	0	0	0	0	0	0	0	2	2	1	0	1	1	0	1	9
	Team							1	0	1							
	TOTALS	30	52	2	7	10	12	5	14	19	17	72	18	8	1	5	200

FG%: 1st Half: 11-25, .440. 2nd Half: 19-27, .704. Game: 30-52, .577.
3-Pt.%: 1st Half: 0-4, .000. 2nd Half: 2-3, .667. Game: 2-7, .286.
FT%: 1st Half: 5-5, 1.000. 2nd Half: 5-7, .714. Game: 10-12, .833.

SCORE BY PERIODS:	1st	2nd	TOTAL
Purdue	33	37	70
Michigan State	27	45	72

Officials: Ed Hightower, Jim Bain, Sid Rodeheffer
Attendance: 15,138

Kentucky, 1948

MSC star and Kentucky transfer Bob Brannum proved a point to Adolph Rupp.

The largest crowd ever in Jenison Field House, a classic struggle for 40 minutes, and a near upset of mighty Kentucky are more than enough reasons to make this list. But the drama that led up to January 10, 1948, made the Wildcats' 47-45 escape from East Lansing a game for the ages.

To feel the emotion that Saturday evening, you have to know the history between "The Baron of the Bluegrass," Kentucky coach Adolph Rupp, and an All-American who left Lexington, Spartan center Bob Brannum.

After Brannum led the Wildcats to a 19-2 mark in 1943–44, he served two years in the Army at Fort Hood, Texas, where he met Robert Jones, a Lansing dentist and staunch Michigan State supporter.

When Brannum returned to Kentucky as a sophomore in 1946, he battled with Rupp and wound up playing behind center Alex Groza, who was two inches taller at 6-foot-7.

"One thing that kind of shook up Mr. Rupp was to have a married

The Spartan nucleus—from top, Bob Geahan, Hugh Dawson, Bill Rapchak, Don Waldron, and Bob Brannum —nearly stunned Kentucky.

Adolph Rupp and Ben Van Alstyne shake hands after a Wildcat escape.

ballplayer," Brannum said. "That was usually a 'have-to' in those days. But that wasn't the case with us.

"Let's just say we had our share of run-ins. He was pretty snotty about the whole thing. And by that time, I was no longer interested in Kentucky."

Only in beating the Wildcats senseless, which he nearly did after transferring with Jones' assistance.

Meanwhile, Rupp wanted to teach Brannum a lesson and to repay the Spartans for a huge upset three years earlier, after a rollerskater performed too long at halftime and drew complaints that Kentucky had become cold.

Thus, Rupp devised a plan to take advantage of Brannum's aggression and to foul him out by driving the lane or feeding Groza, a strategy that failed.

"You have to understand, Bob was a great, great competitor," teammate Bill Rapchak said of a player elected MSC's captain after just three games. "If I was in a street fight, I'd want him on my side. He led the NCAA in one statistic, averaging 4.9 fouls per game. I think he fouled out of every game except one."

He didn't foul out of the one that mattered most, playing 40 minutes and outscoring Groza 23-10 before 15,384—4,000 more than the previous high.

The biggest lead for either team was the Wildcats' five-point edge before halftime, when Rupp was so mad he took only his starters to the locker room.

The Spartans tied the game at 29, 32, 37, and 43 in the second half, the last time on two of Brannum's 10 baskets.

But Kentucky added a free throw by forward James Line and a basket and free throw by guard Ken Rollins, despite being held 25 points under its average.

Brannum couldn't hang onto a pass that would've meant a critical basket in the last 90 seconds. And another missed free throw didn't help against a team that would go on to win the NCAA title.

MSC was just 11-for-31 at the line and 4-for-16 in the second half, while the Wildcats were 15-for-24 and 11-for-13 after the break.

"We could've sent it into overtime," Brannum said, "From there, who knows? But it was one of the highlights of my career—of my life, really. I was glad to give such a big crowd a good show."

That summer, he gave up his final season of eligibility and signed a pro contract with the Sheboygan Redskins, in part to repay medical bills and to support his wife and 2-year-old daughter.

But even in defeat, "a personal victory for Spartan captain Bob Brannum," as the Associated Press called it, will never be forgotten.

KENTUCKY at MSU (January 10, 1948)

Kentucky

No.	Players	FG	FT	FTA	F	TP
22	Clifford Barker, f	1	0	3	3	2
27	Wallace Jones, f	0	2	4	2	2
15	Alex Groza, c	4	2	4	4	10
12	Ralph Beard, g	0	0	2	1	0
26	Ken Rollins, g	4	4	4	4	12
25	James Line	3	2	2	4	8
18	Dale Barnstable	1	5	5	3	7
3	Jack Parkinson	0	0	0	1	0
TOTALS		**16**	**15**	**24**	**22**	**47**

Michigan State

No.	Player	FG	FT	FTA	F	TP
6	Bill Rapchak, f	1	0	0	2	2
3	Bob Geahan, f	2	6	13	1	10
7	Bob Brannum, c	10	3	6	2	23
15	Don Waldron, g	2	1	3	5	5
16	Leon Hess, g	0	0	2	2	0
n/a	Stan Petela	1	0	2	1	2
9	Robert Robbins	0	0	2	4	0
5	Hugh Dawson	1	1	3	2	3
TOTALS		**17**	**11**	**31**	**19**	**45**

SCORE BY PERIODS:	1st	2nd	TOTAL
Kentucky	24	23	47
Michigan State	21	24	45

Attendance: 15,384

Ohio State, 1956

Julius McCoy drives by the Buckeyes' Robin Freeman in the greatest duel in Jenison history.

I t was the greatest duel in Michigan State basketball history. And if Spartan forward Julius McCoy didn't win that individual matchup, he left Jenison Field House with something sweeter—a 94-91 win over Ohio State and guard Robin Freeman.

Freeman finished with 46 points, one shy of the Big Ten record at the time, while McCoy answered with 40. But it was McCoy's steal and layup with 1:06 left that put his team ahead to stay on January 28, 1956, an icy Saturday night everywhere but inside Jenison.

"McCoy showed what a great all-around player he is," said MSU coach Forddy Anderson of his 6-foot-2 forward. "He gave us a great game on the boards, displayed the greatest variety of shots you could ask of a player and worked for every one of them.

"Then, all he did on defense was come up with the key steal of the game and draw a fifth foul on Frank Howard, Ohio's No. 2 man. If there's such a thing as an All-American, Julius was it."

So was Freeman, a 5-11 guard who fouled out for the only time in his career with 21 seconds left. He earned a standing ovation from a crowd of 12,154, then signed post-game autographs with McCoy for 10 minutes before leaving the court.

"I was just fortunate Forddy was coaching and not Pete Newell," said Freeman, who was 16-for-27 from the field and perfect on 14 free throws despite feeling sick. "Forddy's teams were nothing like Newell's on defense. They tried to press us the whole first half. That's how we scored 60 points."

Freeman had 28 points and McCoy 21 before halftime, when the

Buckeyes led by nine. But an 8-0 run, with two baskets by center Duane Peterson and a tip-in by guard Pat Wilson, put MSU ahead 80-79 with 5:59 left. It was the first of 13 consecutive lead changes.

"We actually considered letting Robin go by our man and guarding him from behind," Anderson said. "He released his jump shot so far behind his head, it was almost impossible to get to. And when he was hot, he was just unstoppable. We were fortunate to have a guy like Julius around."

"Robin was one of the greatest shooters ever to play the game," said McCoy, who was 15-for-26 from the field and 10-for-12 at the line. "Every time I played against him, my eyes lit up. I didn't think anyone could score better than I could."

McCoy was second in the Big Ten and fifth in the nation as a senior with 27.3 points per game, trailing Freeman, who was second in the country at 32.9.

"If Forddy said he thought I did a decent job on Robin, he must be getting senile," Wilson said. "I guess he could have scored 56. But they'd clear a side and let him take you off the dribble. This skinny, pale-faced kid had the finest touch I've ever seen.

"Forddy would holler, 'Get that S.O.B! Be more aggressive!' And I was a football player! Robin said, 'Relax, Wilson. It's just a game.' But each time I guarded him, it got worse. He loved to see me coming."

Anderson's strategy worked somewhat, as Freeman picked up four offensive fouls. But it took free throws by guard Jack Quiggle and Wilson to pad a one-point lead in the last 1:03.

OSU won the rematch 96-84 in Columbus, with Freeman outscoring McCoy 43-21. But a promising pro career ended when Freeman lost two fingers from his non-shooting hand in a wood-chopping accident.

"It wasn't the end of the world," said Freeman, an attorney in Springfield, Ohio. "The biggest salary in the NBA was $15,000. And if I'd made the St. Louis Hawks, they might have paid me $7,500. It wasn't like today. . . . If they'd paid me that kind of money, I'd have grown new fingers."

He couldn't have found a hotter hand.

OHIO STATE at MSU (January 28, 1956)

Ohio State

No.	Player	FG	FGA	FT	FTA	REB	F	TP
17	Jim Laughlin, f	5	16	4	4	6	2	14
11	Frank Howard, f	5	9	1	4	5	5	11
6	Don Kelley, c	3	9	4	6	11	5	10
4	Charlie Ellis, g	1	7	6	9	4	5	8
24	Robin Freeman, g	16	27	14	14	3	5	46
9	Mike Allen	0	0	0	1	3	0	0
3	Gene Millard	1	1	0	0	0	1	2
TOTALS		**31**	**69**	**29**	**38**	**32**	**23**	**91**

Michigan State

No.	Player	FG	FGA	FT	FTA	REB	F	TP
15	Julius McCoy, f	15	26	10	12	8	3	40
30	George Ferguson, f	3	5	6	6	6	4	12
34	Duane Peterson, c	6	16	0	3	14	1	12
35	Pat Wilson, g	5	9	1	3	7	4	11
21	Jack Quiggle, g	2	5	1	3	2	4	5
33	Larry Hedden	2	7	4	6	7	1	8
31	Charlie Bencie	0	3	0	0	2	1	0
32	Max Gonzenbach	0	0	0	0	0	0	0
23	Walt Godfrey	2	8	2	2	3	3	6
11	Harry Lux	0	0	0	0	0	0	0
TOTALS		**35**	**79**	**24**	**35**	**49**	**21**	**94**

SCORE BY PERIODS:	1st	2nd	TOTAL
Ohio State	60	31	91
Michigan State	51	43	94

Officials: Joe Conway, Lou Filippi
Attendance: 12,154

Kentucky, 1957

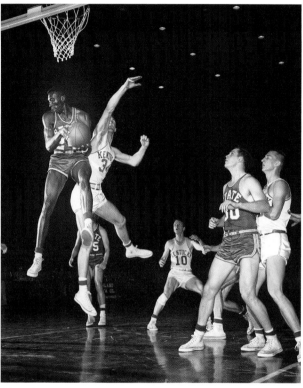

Johnny Green grabs one of his 18 rebounds over Kentucky's Ed Beck.

our trainer, Gayle Robinson," said Hall of Fame fill-in Jim Adams. "I flew to Lexington and did the game. And what a game it was! It was the biggest local audience I ever had."

With well-wishers and Kentucky fans congregating at the Hotel Phoenix, Forddy Anderson took his players to Harrington Lake, 30 miles south of Lexington, for an impromptu fishing trip.

"If you've ever been to an NCAA Tournament, the lobby of the hotel is a complete madhouse, just wall-to-wall people," Anderson said. "Everybody is trying to get tickets and calling players.

"Our idea was to just get out of there. It wasn't so much what we did. So we chartered a bus and got one of those little commercial fishing boats. John Green had never been fishing before. And he was the most excited guy around."

It wasn't as picturesque as you'd imagine, according to MSU guard Pat Wilson. But at least no one drowned.

"Forddy took us out on this little muddy pond," he said. "I can still picture Chuck Bencie and Johnny with these cane poles and their knees jammed up in the air. I can't remember a fish over three or four inches."

The big one didn't get away that evening, even when the Spartans trailed 47-35 at halftime and lost Green to fouls with the game tied at 58.

Bencie came off the bench with a heroic effort at center. Guard Jack Quiggle had 18 of his 22 in the second half, including a three-point play that blew the game open. And MSU scored 13 of the last 15 in an 80-68 stunner.

"Holding the vaunted Wildcats to 21 points in the second half, State shocked Rupp, his team, Governor 'Un-Happy' Chandler and the rest of a

I   t was the toughest challenge a team could have and the best second half in Michigan State history.

The Spartans' first NCAA Tournament featured a payback triumph over Notre Dame and a comeback for the ages against third-ranked Kentucky in the Midwest Region in Lexington on March 15 and 16, 1957.

After an airport pep rally, MSU arrived in "The Bluegrass State" as a surprise Big Ten co-champ at 10-4 and 14-8 overall.

Late Friday night, it was a time to be green, as the Spartans prevailed 85-83 over the Fighting Irish, who'd won 13 of their last 15.

Sophomore Johnny Green had 20 points and 27 rebounds, as MSU ruled the boards 66-40 and avenged a 10-point loss in South Bend two months earlier.

That meant a date with Adolph Rupp's Wildcats Saturday night in Memorial Coliseum, as hostile an environment as any tourney team has experienced.

The day began with a phone call to East Lansing. Play-by-play man Bob Shackleton, the eyes and ears of fans before tournaments were televised, lost his voice after Friday's game and needed help off the bench.

"I was covering a swim meet at about 10 a.m. when I got a call from

Forddy Anderson accepts the accolades.

MSU fans force an alternate landing at Capital City Airport after the shock of Kentucky.

partisan crowd with a 45-point binge that left Kentucky disorganized and completely whipped," wrote Jack Saylor of the *Detroit Times*.

"Fighting Green and White troops, marching from far in the ruck, rolled . . . with a comeback that should be remembered in these Kentucky hills as long as a boy bounces a ball," said George Alderton in the *State Journal*.

The celebration lasted two days for the players and their jubilant fans.

"I remember ending up in a chapel at a Catholic hospital," Wilson said. "The back row was filled with slightly hung-over basketball players. The first two rows were filled with nuns for the 4:30 a.m. mass."

"I remember the mob at the airport," Green said. "We had to land on a different runway. And 10,000 people came running toward us. It was kind of frightening. Then, back at Bryan Hall, the horns were blowing, and I wound up standing up in a convertible."

It was Anderson's birthday. And as the panty raids and parties continued, he smiled at the knowledge his team had done the impossible.

MSU vs KENTUCKY (March 16, 1957)

Michigan State

No.	Player	FG	FGA	FT	FTA	REB	F	TP
30	George Ferguson, f	5	15	5	6	12	3	15
33	Larry Hedden, f	4	16	2	6	7	2	10
24	Johnny Green, c	5	11	4	6	18	5	14
21	Jack Quiggle, g	9	22	4	4	4	4	22
35	Pat Wilson, g	3	10	0	0	3	0	6
23	Bob Anderegg	1	4	0	0	1	2	2
31	Chuck Bencie	2	5	1	2	5	1	5
12	David Scott	1	3	4	5	0	0	6
11	Harry Lux	0	1	0	0	0	0	0
34	Thomas Markovich	0	0	0	0	1	1	0
TOTALS		**30**	**87**	**20**	**29**	**51**	**18**	**80**

Kentucky

No.	Player	FG	FGA	FT	FTA	REB	F	TP
24	Johnny Cox	3	12	11	12	4	5	17
45	John Crigler	5	11	0	1	9	2	10
55	Ray Mills	0	2	2	4	4	2	2
25	L. Collinsworth	0	0	0	0	0	0	0
34	Ed Beck	2	10	0	2	16	2	4
10	Gerry Calvert	8	18	2	3	6	4	18
52	Vernon Hatton	6	13	3	5	7	1	15
50	Adrian Smith	0	1	2	3	1	0	2
70	John Brewer	0	1	0	0	0	0	0
40	Earl Adkins	0	0	0	0	0	2	0
TOTALS		**24**	**68**	**20**	**30**	**47**	**18**	**68**

SCORE BY PERIODS:	1st	2nd	TOTAL
Michigan State	35	45	80
Kentucky	47	21	68

Officials: Anderson and Mihalik
Attendance: 12,500

Michigan, 1966

Bill Curtis looks for an opening against the Wolverines' Cazzie Russell.

Defense didn't win the Big Ten basketball championship in 1966. That would have to wait a year.

But on Monday, March 7, 1966, it won a game that meant almost as much to Michigan State—an 86-77 triumph over National Player of the Year Cazzie Russell and three-time conference titleist Michigan.

Two days earlier, the season's lone Spartan-Wolverine matchup was supposed to be for the Big Ten crown and the league's one NCAA Tournament berth.

Instead, Michigan built a two-game edge as Russell scored 48 points in a win over Northwestern and MSU was stunned by 10 at last-place Indiana.

The hero for the Hoosiers with 25 points was guard Vernon Payne, who would later become a Spartan assistant coach and save the recruitment of Earvin Johnson. With that assist, he has long been forgiven.

Still, it's amazing to think how close MSU came to a worst-to-first turnaround in the first season under John Benington—from 1-13 in the Big Ten and 5-18 overall to 10-4 and 15-7, not counting wins over the Hawaiian Marines and Hawaiian Army in the Rainbow Classic.

The Wolverines ended the regular season at 11-3 and 17-7, then lost to

Kentucky in the Mideast Region final. But they arrived at Jenison Field House averaging a record 96.8 points in conference play.

The Spartans were allowing a league-low 73.6 per game—23.6 less than the previous year's yield under Forddy Anderson. And the hosts' way to play prevailed before a raucous sellout crowd of 12,283.

"The kids did a tremendous job," Benington said. "Any time you have that much enthusiasm, anything can happen. This was a tough game for Michigan. They were expected to win. They're expected to win every game they play."

The Wolverines had won five in a row over MSU, including all four games in Russell's career—a streak that was duly noted by Spartan senior forwards Bill Curtis and Stan Washington.

"We'd come so close the year before, when we were really undermanned," Curtis said. "All winter, I'd told people we were going to beat Michigan. I knew Cazzie would get his. But I also knew he'd give them up."

Russell finished with 34. But Curtis had 26 and Washington 23 that night.

"That was always the game I looked forward to playing," Washington said. "Oliver Darden of Michigan was from Detroit Western. And I was from Northwestern High. So there were serious bragging rights. To beat them for the first time was a great way to cap a college career."

That happened because of five heroes:

► Benington, who gambled and put 6-foot-7 center Matthew Aitch on Russell to restrict his passing.

► Aitch, a junior who "held Russell to 34 points" and answered with 12.

► Curtis, who had his finest game, with 26 points and 11 rebounds.

► Washington, who was 11-for-14 from the field in a 23-point farewell.

► And junior guard Steve Rymal, who added 15 points and solid defense against a team that was outshot 48.6 percent to 38.8.

"We didn't really play rotten," said Michigan coach Dave Strack. "But we certainly could've done better. You've got to give a lot of credit to Michigan State. They certainly played a fine game."

"The Indiana game may have helped us," Benington said. "We weren't tense. But we played with a lot of enthusiasm. I didn't do anything to build that enthusiasm. I just told the boys it was their game and to go play it."

The Spartans scored the first six points, including an 18-footer from Washington after just seven seconds.

Russell countered with 15 points in the first 9:45 as his team led 18-15.

That's when Aitch scored eight straight on a layup, a steal and stuff, a 10-footer, and a tip-in. After one Wolverine basket, Curtis and Washington scored the next seven to make it 30-20.

Michigan never got closer than five points again, trailing 45-36 at the half and 86-71 with 42 seconds left before fans flooded the court.

"I don't want to play pro ball," said Curtis, savoring the moment after an impromptu net-snipping party. "I just want to get back and study."

He's Dr. Curtis now. And a year later, MSU was rewarded for being patient.

Steve Rymal drives around John Clawson and challenges Craig Dill.

MICHIGAN at MSU (March 7, 1966)

Michigan

No.	Player	FG	FGA	FT	FTA	REB	F	TP
34	John Clawson, f	6	16	3	4	9	4	15
55	Oliver Darden, f	5	10	2	3	4	5	12
54	Jim Myers, c	4	14	0	1	11	3	8
33	Cazzie Russell, g	13	25	8	10	11	4	34
25	John Thompson, g	1	6	0	0	1	0	2
32	Dennis Bankey	1	2	0	0	0	0	2
24	James Pitts	0	2	0	0	1	0	0
40	Craig Dill	1	5	2	2	2	2	4
TOTALS		**31**	**80**	**15**	**20**	**39**	**18**	**77**

FG%: 1st Half: 15-39, .385. 2nd Half: 16-41, .390. Game: 31-80, .387.
FT%: 1st Half: 6-9, .667. 2nd Half: 9-11, .818. Game: 15-20 .750.

Michigan State

No.	Player	FG	FGA	FT	FTA	REB	F	TP
24	Stan Washington, f	11	14	1	4	9	4	23
25	Bill Curtis, f	10	21	6	7	11	3	26
45	Matt Aitch, c	6	13	0	1	9	5	12
12	John Bailey, g	1	5	3	4	2	0	5
15	Steve Rymal, g	5	12	5	7	5	2	15
42	Gerald Geistler	1	5	1	1	6	2	3
35	Bob Miller	1	1	0	0	0	1	2
43	Dick Holmes	0	1	0	0	0	0	0
23	Jim Kupper	0	0	0	0	0	0	0
TOTALS		**35**	**72**	**16**	**24**	**16**	**17**	**86**

FG%: 1st Half: 19-38, .500. 2nd Half: 16-34, .470. Game: 35-72 .490.
FT%: 1st Half: 7-10, .700. 2nd Half: 9-14, .642. Game: 16-24 .667.

SCORE BY PERIODS:	1st	2nd	TOTAL
Michigan	36	41	77
Michigan State	45	41	86

Officials: Kevin Donlan, Jerry Steiner
Attendance: 12,283

Notre Dame, 1974

Terry Furlow heats up with a jumper over Notre Dame's Gary Novak.

t should have been one of Michigan State's biggest basketball wins. Instead, it was merely a marvelous effort and a huge disappointment.

On Monday, February 4, 1974, the Spartans entertained more than third-ranked Notre Dame. They thrilled an overflow crowd of more than 12,500 in Jenison Field House and proved they could play with any team in the nation.

MSU shot a sensational 59.4 percent from the field and 76.5 percent at the foul line, while forcing the Fighting Irish into 23 turnovers.

Guard Mike Robinson and forward Terry Furlow combined for 53 points with 22-for-30 accuracy from the field and 9-for-9 work at the line. And with 50 points in the second half, the Spartans rallied from a nine-point deficit and led 89-85 with 2:27 to play.

But all anyone seems to remember is a rushed shot by Furlow with 11 seconds left and a prayer that was answered for Notre Dame's Billy Paterno.

The Irish arrived with a 15-6 mark, after ending UCLA's record 88-game win streak two days earlier. At 11-6, MSU was just as confident, thanks to a 76-74 win over Purdue that Saturday on Robinson's last-second 20 footer.

The Spartans were up 12-2 but trailed 43-39 at the half. Notre Dame led 76-67 with 7:56 left, when center Lindsay Hairston sparked a 14-2 MSU run. Things went sour again when Robinson was called for a charge and Irish center John Shumate hit a short turnaround to tie it at 89 with 1:12 left.

MSU coach Gus Ganakas ordered his team to run time off the clock before its final timeout at :22. Everyone figured the ball would go to Robinson, who could deliver another victory or, at worst, warm up for overtime.

"We wanted Mike to take the shot," Ganakas remembered. "We wanted to use a scramble-motion offense, as we did in the Purdue game, work the clock down and get an open shot for someone."

Furlow was open, all right. And after hitting 10 of 13 shots, he was bound and determined to get the next game-winner.

With Robinson alone on the left wing and 12-for-16 in a 31-point night, Furlow dribbled to the top of key, glanced at the clock and and launched an airball from 22 feet.

"That was Terry!" said guard Bob Chapman. "Certainly, it was an ill-advised shot. But Terry made a lot of those shots when games were on the line. He wanted the ball and made no bones about it."

"I think he'd just hit 10 of his last 11," said guard Benny White. "But he'd always been one who'd say, 'Let me be the hero or the goat.' The play was to get the ball to Mike. But Terry didn't care what anybody thought."

Most people thought, "What's he doing?" especially after Paterno nearly lost the ball, then launched an off-balance 20 footer that hit the rim twice and fell through with :02 to play—fitting for a team that shot 62.9 percent.

"If they'd made their shot, we'd have just thrown it in and hoped to get a shot with our I-formation offense," said Notre Dame coach Digger Phelps, referring to the schools' football rivalry. "Actually, I don't think Paterno even saw the rim on the last one. We were lucky to win."

Meanwhile, in the MSU locker room, Ganakas defended Furlow, who finished with 22 points, and told the team, "He's one of ours."

He was a sophomore who would go on to win games against Purdue and at Ohio State with buzzer-beaters the next two seasons. But no one knew that at the time—or cared about anything but a blown opportunity.

"It was really a tough one," Ganakas said. "We fought back and deserved the win. We dominated them in the second half. But we just had an unfortunate incident occur. And that was the game. Mistakes happen. They're part of basketball. And there's nothing you can do about them."

The victory cigar in his pocket had to wait a week—until an overtime win in Columbus, when the ball bounced the Spartans' way.

NOTRE DAME at MSU (February 4, 1974)

Notre Dame

No.	Player	FG	FGA	FT	FTA	REB	F	TP	A	TO
44	Adrian Dantley, f	5	13	5	8	9	4	15	1	2
35	Gary Novak, f	5	5	0	0	6	4	10	4	1
34	John Shumate, c	12	16	3	4	8	1	27	3	6
25	Gary Brokaw, g	9	15	3	5	3	3	21	6	6
15	Dwight Clay, g	6	10	0	0	1	2	12	4	4
55	Bill Paterno, f	2	3	2	3	5	0	6	0	0
21	Ray Martin, g	0	0	0	0	0	0	0	0	4
	Team					1				
	TOTALS	**39**	**62**	**13**	**20**	**33**	**14**	**91**	**14**	**23**

FG%: 1st Half: 19-31, .613. 2nd Half: 20-31, .645. Game: 39-62,.629.
FT%: 1st Half: 5-8, .625. 2nd Half: 8-12, .667. Game: 13-20, .650.

Michigan State

No.	Player	FG	FGA	FT	FTA	REB	F	TP	A	TO
25	Terry Furlow, f	10	14	2	2	4	2	22	0	4
42	Brian Breslin, f	1	3	0	0	2	3	2	1	0
45	Lindsay Hairston, c	8	16	0	0	9	2	16	0	1
12	Bill Glover, g	2	4	2	2	1	3	6	8	6
31	Mike Robinson, g	12	16	7	7	0	3	31	3	7
33	Edgar Wilson	1	1	2	4	0	3	4	1	0
41	Thomas McGill	1	4	0	0	4	1	2	0	2
32	Pete Davis	3	6	0	2	0	1	6	1	1
23	Benny White	0	0	0	0	0	0	0	0	1
	Team					1				
	TOTALS	**38**	**64**	**13**	**17**	**21**	**18**	**89**	**14**	**22**

FG%: 1st Half: 18-33, .545. 2nd Half: 20-31, .645. Game: 38-64,.594.
FT%: 1st Half: 3-5, .600. 2nd Half: 10-12, .833. Game: 13-17, .765.

SCORE BY PERIODS:	1st	2nd	TOTAL
Notre Dame	43	48	91
Michigan State	39	50	89

Officials: Dave Parry, Dick Furey
Attendance: 12,500

Indiana, 1975

Jeff Tropf works against the Hoosiers' Tom Abernethy.

"The setting was perfect for us," said Michigan State coach Gus Ganakas. "Indiana was ranked No. 1. And they were coming to our place. . . . It was such a great opportunity."

It was Saturday, January 4, 1975, an afternoon few Spartans will ever forget.

Many insist it was the worst day in MSU basketball history—and not just because of the final score: Hoosiers 107, Spartans 55.

With nearly a quarter-century of hindsight and healing, others say it was an embarrassing but essential moment for a resilient team and for important changes in the program that were eventually made.

The game itself was almost a footnote to the morning walkout and afternoon suspension of 10 players—four starters, six reserves, all African Americans.

But to this day, there's still a dispute about the cause of the protest.

Did frustration about a shrinking, second-class facility and third-rate treatment from the administration finally become too much to bear?

Were Ganakas' recent lineup switches and the logic behind them impossible to comprehend—if that understanding was even the players' concern?

Had the decision to start white freshman forward Jeff Tropf over senior Tom McGill sparked a racial incident over rights and grievous wrongs?

Or was it a combination of factors that led to a Friday night meeting of minority players at guard Bill Glover's apartment and a 10 a.m. line-in-the-sand confrontation between Ganakas and captain Lindsay Hairston?

"There has never been any racial problem with this team—not this year, not last year, and not the year before that," said soon-to-be Big Ten scoring champ Terry Furlow. "It just seems racial in such a white environment. . . . But if the same occasion arose, I'd walk out again."

"There were a lot of politics going on," said guard Benny White. "The administration wasn't concerned about winning. And when Gus had always preached seniority, then started a freshman, you had to be naive not to think it was racial. There had always been a white starter."

Forward Edgar Wilson suggested submitting a list of grievances, instead of considering a boycott. And guards Bob Chapman and Pete Davis, who had no idea he was slated to start for a 6-2 team, argued for a slower approach.

But when Ganakas announced the matchups, with Tropf on Indiana senior Steve Green, Hairston raised his hand and said, "Coach, Jeff can't guard Green." When a stunned Ganakas countered, "That's my decision to make," his players—and ultimately his job—went out the door.

"It was an unfortunate situation when the players got up and walked out on Gus," Chapman remembered. "I didn't think it was right at the time, even though I participated. A lot of things had built up. But it was portrayed as strictly a black–white issue with Jeff. That wasn't it at all."

When Ganakas realized the walkout was planned and possibly permanent, he told his assistants, Vernon Payne and Dick Versace, "We'll play without them. . . . Beaumont Tower is bigger than they are."

He chose to play a televised game with Tropf and as many junior-varsity players as his staff could locate near the end of a holiday break. After calling vice president Jack Breslin and gaining support, Ganakas learned the players were in the locker room. When he didn't receive an apology, he suspended all 10.

Hoosier coach Bob Knight—to this day, a friend and admirer of Ganakas—offered to have star guard Quinn Buckner talk to the returning players and was as helpful as an opposing coach could be.

A buzz, then torrents of boos from a construction-reduced capacity crowd of 6,500 in Jenison Field House greeted the public-address announcement, as the suspended players rose from the stands and left the building.

Spartan coaches Pat Miller, Gus Ganakas, Vernon Payne, Dick Versace, and Dominic Marino can only watch as Quinn Buckner and the Hoosiers roll.

When MSU took a 2-0 lead, injured varsity freshman Jim Dudley actually leaned to Ganakas and said, "Coach! If we hustle, we can beat them!"

The Spartans' last lead was 6-5. But Tropf was 8-for-10 from the field for a game-high 21 points, while Green had 12 and the reserves 60 for Indiana.

"I was very pleased to watch the team that Michigan State put out on the court," Knight said. "They really busted their tails and hustled. They did a helluva job out there. And I was impressed with the spirit of the MSU fans. They really supported their team and didn't get down on us."

The community came down hard on the rebelling players. But when Ganakas heard the words he wanted—a simple "We're sorry" from Hairston Sunday afternoon—they were reinstated for a game against Ohio State Monday.

The Spartans beat the Buckeyes without a practice, then hit a school-record 64.0 percent of their shots from the field in an emotion-packed win over Michigan the following Saturday. A payback at Notre Dame and a 17-9 record, the best since 1958–59, were nice but not enough to heal all wounds.

"The incident brought us together," Hairston said. "It let everyone come in and do what they had to do to help Michigan State win."

When the Spartans won titles three and four years later with Earvin Johnson and Gregory Kelser, Tropf had transferred—twice. And Ganakas had been replaced by a hard-line coach, Jud Heathcote.

No one ever questioned his lineups and lived to walk away.

INDIANA at MSU (January 4, 1975)

Indiana

No.	Player	FG	FGA	FT	FTA	REB	F	TP	A	TO	MIN
42	Steve May, f	5	11	0	0	5	1	10	4	0	24
34	Steve Green, f	5	6	2	2	3	1	12	0	1	17
54	Kent Benson, c	6	9	1	2	7	1	13	1	1	16
20	Bob Wilkerson, g	4	6	0	0	3	2	8	4	1	20
21	Quinn Buckner, g	1	5	2	2	0	2	4	3	4	14
31	John Laskowski	5	6	0	0	2	1	10	2	2	12
33	Tom Abernathy	1	4	0	0	2	0	2	2	0	15
45	Jim Crews	0	0	0	0	0	0	0	1	1	6
22	Wayne Radford	4	5	0	0	4	0	8	2	1	16
4	Steve Ahlfeld	2	5	0	0	0	1	4	0	2	11
40	Jim Wisman	4	5	0	0	1	3	8	5	2	11
32	Mark Haymore	6	12	0	0	8	2	12	3	2	15
43	Don Noort	5	10	2	2	8	1	12	0	1	8
25	Doug Allen	2	2	0	0	2	0	4	0	1	7
30	John Kamstra	0	0	0	0	3	0	0	1	1	8
TOTALS		**50**	**86**	**7**	**8**	**48**	**15**	**107**	**28**	**20**	**200**

FG%: 1st Half: 24-42, .571. 2nd Half: 26-44, .591. Game: 50-86, .581.
FT%: 1st Half: 5-6, .833. 2nd Half: 2-2, 1.000.Game: 7-8, .875.

Michigan State

No.	Player	FG	FGA	FT	FTA	REB	F	TP	A	TO	MIN
32	Gregory Lott, f	2	5	0	2	0	0	4	1	2	15
NA	James Bird, f	2	10	0	0	3	1	4	0	2	29
52	Jeff Tropf, c	8	10	5	7	7	2	21	1	1	37
44	Mark Talaga, g	3	8	2	2	0	2	8	4	7	32
NA	Jeff Lockett, g	2	7	0	1	1	1	4	5	8	19
12	Don Flowers	2	8	0	0	0	2	4	2	2	26
10	Gervus McCray	2	5	0	2	4	1	4	0	0	26
21	Kevin Vandenbussche	3	5	0	2	0	2	6	1	0	13
NA	James Antwine	0	0	0	0	0	0	0	0	1	2
25	Andrew Wolfe	0	1	0	0	0	0	0	0	0	1
TOTALS		**24**	**59**	**7**	**16**	**15**	**11**	**55**	**14**	**23**	**200**

FG%: 1st Half: 11-30, .367. 2nd Half: 13-29, .448. Game: 24-59, .407.
FT%: 1st Half: 0-4, .000. 2nd Half: 7-12, .583.Game: 7-16, .438.

SCORE BY PERIODS:	1st	2nd	TOTAL
Indiana	53	54	107
Michigan State	22	33	55

Officials: Dave Parry, Richard Weiler
Attendance: 6,500

Michigan, 1986

Scott Skiles fires a jumper over Michigan's Garde Thompson.

Yet, even before the first meeting with the Spartans, Frieder sounded an alarm: "People say we have the best guards in the country. Not only aren't they the best in the country, they're not the best in the league. That Skiles kid is absolutely phenomenal!"

Despite Skiles' 45-point effort at Minnesota the previous Saturday, *The Detroit News* focused on Grant with headlines like "Generally, great defense" and " 'General' Grant marshals forces to stop MSU's Skiles."

Grant may have held Georgia Tech's Mark Price to 2-for-13 shooting and Indiana's Steve Alford to six points in the first 30 minutes. But he'd given up 63 points in two games against the Spartans' Sam Vincent the year before.

And as Grant would soon discover, he had never faced a player with the shots and the swagger of No. 4, who was held—quite literally—to 40 points.

Skiles wound up 15-for-20 from the field, 10-for-11 at the line and had eight assists in a 91-79 shocker—a 17-point spread with five seconds left.

Tarpley, the reigning conference MVP, had just nine points and more fouls than rebounds, 5-4, in 16 minutes. Grant had eight points in 26 minutes before fouling out. And Joubert, better known as "The Judge," took a seat on the bench after fouling Skiles on a three-point play and flinging his wristbands into the crowd, drawing a technical foul that capped a delicious evening.

As he left the court, Joubert made the mistake of pointing a finger and hollering, "We'll get you in Ann Arbor!" to which Skiles answered, "Not unless you lose 20 pounds, Fat Boy!"

Johnson surveys the action against Michigan's Antoine Joubert.

I t was a night Michigan State basketball fans will talk about forever—and a game one mouthy Michigan player should never have mentioned.

When the sixth-ranked Wolverines invaded Jenison Field House on Saturday, January 25, 1986, they were 5-1 in a successful Big Ten title defense and 17-1 overall.

Unranked MSU was 2-4 and 11-5 and an undersized underdog everywhere but in Scott Skiles' mind.

With Roy Tarpley at center, Butch Wade, Richard Rellford, and Lansing's Robert Henderson at forward and Antoine Joubert, Gary Grant, and Garde Thompson at guard, Bill Frieder had a massive team in Ann Arbor that would finish 28-5.

With a Jordanesque tongue, Darryl Johnson wheels around Gary Grant.

Vernon Carr slices between Robert Henderson and Antoine Joubert.

"He likes to talk a little bit, and so do I," Skiles explained. "He's competitive. I'm competitive. But everything is left on the court in this league. Words were exhanged. And after the game, they didn't mean anything."

The outcome was all that mattered to Skiles' backcourt partner Darryl Johnson, who outscored Joubert, a rival from high school, 17-12.

"I remember that game like it was yesterday," Johnson said 12 years later. "Scott and Antoine didn't like each other—period. They were like cats and dogs. 'Toine said he wanted to score 50 against him."

In five games, he might have done that. And it didn't make Joubert any happier to read Frieder's comments after MSU shot 59.3 percent from the field.

"What happened? . . . They shot it in!" Frieder said. "Did you see the game? Did you watch Skiles hit nine in a row?. . . Then, why the hell did you ask a question like that? That's a stupid question! They shot it in from 30 feet. When they got ahead, they controlled the ball. They didn't turn it over. And if you fouled them, they went to the line and made it."

MSU coach Jud Heathcote spread the credit to third guard Vernon Carr and others, while admitting he was as surprised as anyone by the total domination.

"If you'd told me that before the game, I'd have thought you were crazy—as I usually do, Jack," Heathcote said. "I thought if we won the game, it would be on a shot from midcourt or something like that."

Joubert was still bitter more than three weeks later, when he said, "I could've gone where I could gun. . . . But then, I'd be like Scott Skiles—30 points a game and going nowhere."

He must have forgotten that he entered the first matchup as a career 36.1-percent shooter in Big Ten play, while Skiles was at 56.9 that year.

"If we played one-on-one to 21, I'd beat him," Joubert said in an ill-advised rant two days before the rematch in Crisler Arena. "I'll bet you $50—and I'll bet him $50, too! Go ahead and set it up."

On February 22, after Joubert had promised, "We're not going to lose this one—and you can quote that!" No. 19 MSU clobbered the No. 7 Wolverines, 74-59.

Skiles outscored Joubert 20-8. And Johnson was the best player on the floor with 26 points and eight assists.

The only downer for the Spartans was that Michigan was upset by Iowa State in the NCAA Tournament's Midwest Region before they could meet a third time.

MICHIGAN at MSU (January 25, 1986)

Michigan

No.	Player	FG	FGA	FT	FTA	REB	F	TP	A	TO	BK	S	MIN
40	Richard Rellford, f	6	10	8	9	8	3	20	0	1	1	3	25
53	Butch Wade, f	6	11	0	0	9	3	12	1	1	0	0	32
42	Roy Tarpley, c	4	7	1	2	4	5	9	0	3	3	0	16
25	Gary Grant, g	2	7	4	4	1	5	8	7	3	0	2	26
11	Antoine Joubert, g	6	8	0	0	0	3	12	6	3	0	0	37
41	Glen Rice	1	4	0	0	0	3	2	1	2	0	1	16
15	Robert Henderson	1	5	0	0	5	1	2	0	1	1	0	24
30	Garde Thompson	7	10	0	0	1	4	14	0	2	0	0	14
32	Billy Butts	0	0	0	0	0	0	0	1	2	0	0	1
	Team					0							
	TOTALS	**33**	**62**	**13**	**15**	**28**	**27**	**79**	**16**	**18**	**5**	**6**	**200**

FG%: 1st Half: 12-32, .375. 2nd Half: 21-30, .700. Game: 33-62, .532.
FT%: 1st Half: 7-8, .875. 2nd Half: 6-7, .857. Game: 13-15, .867.

Michigan State

No.	Player	FG	FGA	FT	FTA	REB	F	TP	A	TO	BK	S	MIN
23	Vernon Carr, f	5	10	6	10	3	3	16	0	2	0	0	37
35	Larry Polec, f	3	4	4	4	4	2	10	0	3	1	1	27
40	Barry Fordham, c	1	5	0	0	2	4	2	0	0	0	0	32
13	Darryl Johnson, g	6	11	5	6	4	1	17	2	1	0	3	36
4	Scott Skiles, g	15	20	10	11	4	1	40	8	4	0	3	39
45	Carlton Valentine	2	2	2	2	3	0	6	0	1	0	0	15
55	Mario Izzo	0	2	0	0	0	1	0	0	1	1	0	5
15	Ralph Walker	0	0	0	0	0	0	0	0	0	0	0	5
22	Andre Rison	0	0	0	0	0	0	0	0	0	0	0	1
34	David Mueller	0	0	0	0	0	0	0	0	0	0	0	1
30	Jim Sarkine	0	0	0	0	0	0	0	0	0	0	0	1
44	Scott Sekal	0	0	0	0	0	0	0	1	0	0	0	1
	Team					5							
	TOTALS	**32**	**54**	**27**	**33**	**25**	**12**	**91**	**10**	**14**	**2**	**7**	**200**

FG%: 1st Half: 16-30, .533. 2nd Half: 16-24, .667. Game: 32-54,.593.
FT%: 1st Half: 12-15, .800. 2nd Half: 15-18, .833. Game: 27-33, .818.

SCORE BY PERIODS:	1st	2nd	TOTAL
Michigan	31	48	79
Michigan State	44	47	91

Officials: Jim Bain, Ron Winter, Malcolm Hemphill
Attendance: 10,004

Kansas, 1986

I t was time for a classic upset in the NCAA Tournament's Midwest Region.

Suddenly, it was an overtime near-miss for one upset head coach.

It's true Jud Heathcote wanted to clean some clocks after Michigan State lost 96-86 to Kansas at Kemper Arena in Kansas City, Missouri.

But the dirty deed had already been done, leaving a sour aftertaste for a stunning Sweet 16 appearance.

When fifth-seeded MSU met the top-seeded, second-ranked Jayhawks on Friday, March 21, 1986, players, coaches, and fans asked if it was really Friday the 13th.

Kansas, coached by Larry Brown and paced by sophomore Danny Manning, was a heavy favorite on a floor where they were already 5-0 that year. At 33-3, and with overwhelming support from a capacity crowd of 16,800, they were supposed to overpower the Spartans, then finish off North Carolina State en route to Dallas and a Final Four semifinal against Duke.

Apparently, someone forgot to tell Scott Skiles and a 23-7 team that came in averaging 83.0 points and connecting as if its baskets were 3 feet wide. MSU was hitting 56.1 percent of its shots from the field and 80.5 percent at the line—No. 1 in the nation in both categories.

But against the 6-foot-10 Manning, 7-1 center Greg Dreiling, and 6-6 guard Calvin Thompson, the Spartans' lack of size figured to be a huge factor.

When it came to hearts, no one had bigger chambers than Skiles, who got entangled with the Jayhawks in the opening minutes and was booed unmercifully.

"We mentioned at the beginning of the broadcast that he's controversial," said CBS play-by-play man Verne Lundquist. "But to say Scott Skiles is controversial is to say the Philippine election might be tainted."

While Lundquist and analyst James Brown discussed whether Skiles should even be playing, considering his off-the-court problems, it was also mentioned that seven players had fouled out while trying to guard him.

Manning, who would lead Kansas to an NCAA title as National Player of the Year in 1988, drew his third foul with 8:00 left in the first half. But when MSU had a great chance to slice a lead that reached 46-37 at the break, Darryl Johnson was sidelined with three fouls 25 seconds later. And Skiles joined his backcourt partner with 6:51 showing—the first time either player had been slapped three times in the first half all season.

Heathcote had to slap himself when an unlikely source for scoring led the Spartans' second-half surge and put them ahead 62-61 with 10:07 left.

Barry Fordham, a 6-8 junior who averaged 2.4 points in the first 30 games, had 13 of his 15 points after the break and was 7-for-9 from the field.

"Barry had a tremendous ballgame," said MSU assistant Herb Williams. "It was the first time his mother had seen him play in college. When he'd shoot, Jud would say, 'What the hell is he . . . oh, okay!'"

Everything seemed OK when Manning fouled out with 2:21 left. MSU guard Vernon Carr hit one of two free throws to put his team up 76-72. But when the Jayhawks inbounded the ball, the clock either froze at 2:20 for

Jud Heathcote, about to erupt, notices the clock isn't moving.

15 seconds or was tragically mishandled by Kemper timekeeper Larry Bates.

"I noticed it first and screamed, 'The clock's not running! The clock's not running!'" Williams remembered. "It seemed like that went on forever."

With play in progress, Heathcote stormed to the scorer's table, screamed at Bates and pounded his fist. And when Kansas complained that Heathcote was out of the coaching box, Brown accidentally swatted an official's whistle with a rolled program—an automatic technical foul.

Scott Skiles penetrates and scores over Kansas' Cedric Hunter.

Darryl Johnson looks for room against Danny Manning's defense.

Skiles hit the two gift shots from the technical after a rare, critical miss on the front end of a one-and-one situation.

And when Fordham drained one final jumper, his team led 80-74 with just over a minute to play.

But Kansas scored on short jumpers by Cedric Hunter and Thompson and on a tip-in by reserve Archie Marshall with :10 left—10 ticks his team should never have had.

None of that would've mattered if the Spartans had hit just one more foul shot, with normally sure forward Larry Polec missing a one-and-one with :27 left and freshman guard Mark Brown long from the line with :19 to go.

"We missed some key free throws down the stretch," Heathcote admitted. "We led the nation in free throw shooting all year. Maybe it finally caught up with us."

When Brown was fouled deliberately, the clock kept running to :01 but was reset when referee Bobby Dibler decided to fix matters a few minutes too late.

With the score tied at 80, Skiles drove to the left of the lane and missed an off-balance heave to win it, then saw his team get outscored 14-2 in the last 3:29 of overtime.

"I like to have things in my control at the end of a game," said Skiles, who finished with 20 points. "I had 'em. And I didn't come through. I take responsibility for this loss. If I'd made a free throw, a freshman wouldn't have had to be there."

Kansas City immediately decided to spend $10,000 to replace the clock activator but couldn't sentence Bates to an afternoon alone with Heathcote.

"They blew it," said Ed Steitz, the official interpreter of NCAA rules. "It was the most blatant timing error I've seen in 30 years. It was a mistake that could've been rectified. A timing error or scoring error is always correctable. . . . I was appalled."

He wasn't alone.

MSU vs KANSAS (March 21, 1986)

Michigan State

No.	Player	FG	FGA	FT	FTA	REB	F	TP	A	TO	BK	S	MIN
23	Vernon Carr, f	7	13	3	6	4	3	17	3	2	0	0	42
35	Larry Polec, f	6	7	4	5	11	5	16	2	3	0	2	39
40	Barry Fordham, c	7	9	1	3	5	3	15	0	1	0	0	45
13	Darryl Johnson, g	4	11	2	2	4	4	10	9	2	0	1	37
4	Scott Skiles, g	6	14	8	10	2	3	20	7	4	0	1	38
15	Ralph Walker	0	1	2	2	3	1	2	0	0	0	0	11
24	Mark Brown	1	2	0	1	2	1	2	0	0	0	0	7
45	Carlton Valentine	2	4	0	0	1	0	4	0	0	0	0	6
	Team					5							
	TOTALS	**33**	**61**	**20**	**29**	**37**	**20**	**86**	**21**	**13**	**0**	**4**	**225**

FG%: 1st Half: 13-27, .481. 2nd Half: 17-25, .680. OT: 3-9, .333. Game:33-61, .541.
FT%: 1st Half: 11-14, .786. 2nd Half: 9-15, .600. OT: 0-0, .000. Game: 20-29, .690.

Kansas

No.	Player	FG	FGA	FT	FTA	REB	F	TP	A	TO	BK	S	MIN
25	Danny Manning, f	7	12	3	3	3	5	17	0	2	1	1	25
44	Ron Kellogg, f	7	12	0	0	5	5	14	2	1	0	0	24
30	Greg Dreiling, c	3	10	4	7	7	0	10	1	2	1	0	32
22	Cedric Hunter, g	4	9	3	4	4	3	11	10	0	0	3	43
35	Calvin Thompson, g	10	19	6	9	4	2	26	4	0	1	0	43
11	Mark Turgeon	0	1	0	0	0	2	0	1	1	0	1	7
23	Archie Marshall	7	12	2	2	13	2	16	1	1	0	0	31
24	Chris Piper	1	2	0	0	2	2	2	1	0	0	1	20
	Team					2							
	TOTALS	**39**	**77**	**18**	**25**	**40**	**21**	**96**	**20**	**7**	**3**	**6**	**225**

FG%: 1st Half: 17-30, .567. 2nd Half: 16-38, .421. OT: 6-9, .667. Game:39-77, .506.
FT%: 1st Half: 12-17, .706. 2nd Half: 2-3, .667. OT: 4-5, .800.Game: 18-25, .720.

SCORE BY PERIODS:	1st	2nd	OT	TOTAL
Michigan State	37	43	6	86
Kansas	46	34	16	96

Officials: Bob Dibler, Hank Armstrong, Pete Pavia
Attendance: 16,800

Georgia Tech, 1990

Mark Montgomery distributes the ball against Georgia Tech's Kenny Anderson.

Who said lightning never strikes twice in the same place? It zapped Michigan State for the second time in the 1990 NCAA Tournament's Sweet 16—another clock-marred defeat that should never have happened.

The site that Friday night was New Orleans, not Kansas City. And the lucky opponent was Georgia Tech, an 81-80 overtime winner in the Southeast Region.

"I don't like talking about that game," said a still-miffed Ken Redfield, then an MSU co-captain. "We got cheated, plain and simple."

Center Mike Peplowski added, "I never watched a tape of the game until I was asked to for this book. . . . And after watching it, I know why."

The fifth-seeded Yellow Jackets, 26-6 and winners of the Atlantic Coast Conference Tournament, featured "Lethal Weapon 3"—guards Kenny Anderson and Brian Oliver and forward Dennis Scott.

Anderson was the ACC Rookie of the Year, while Scott was the Player of the Year with a league-high 27.6 points per game.

Top-seeded MSU, 28-5, relied on junior guard Steve Smith, a better inside game than Tech, and the Big Ten's stingiest defense.

That didn't help Jud Heathcote's team in the first 1:34, when the Spartans had three turnovers in their first four possessions and trailed 8-0.

"When we called timeout, Jud said, 'What are we doing down here? Why don't we just pack up and leave right now? Now, go out there and PLAY!'" said point guard Mark Montgomery.

Smith had 16 of his game-high 32 points by the half. But Tech led 39-35.

MSU pulled even, then went ahead 71-67 with :53 left on a layup by backup center Parish Hickman, a huge factor with 13 points and 10 rebounds.

Anderson's driving layup and a no-call in knocking Hickman flat on his back cut the deficit to 73-71 with :25 showing.

On MSU's next possession, forward Dwayne Stephens dribbled to the basket but backed away and was fouled just before he could pass to Smith.

"I was so nervous," the freshman said. "When I stepped to the line, out of the corner of my eye, I saw the huge screens they had in the corners. I'm watching myself up there thinking, 'Oh, my God, what am I doing?' But I was able to make both shots."

Steve Smith steps to the line, where a win should have been sealed.

Anderson launches the game-tying jumper with no time remaining, as the CBS replay shows.

After a Tech timeout with :13 left, Anderson raced downcourt, breaking loose with a behind-the-back dribble to make it 75-73 with :06 to play.

"That's what broke our backs," Peplowski said. "We let Kenny go from one end to the other, unmolested, for a layup. If we had been able to turn him, another second or two would've come off the clock."

Redfield inbounded the ball to Smith, who was fouled by Oliver, as one second elapsed. And when Smith missed the front end of a one-and-one, Tech had another chance.

As Anderson dashed upcourt, Smith stuck a hand in and actually knocked the ball loose for an instant. But Anderson regained control, kept dribbling and launched a shot from just inside the 3-point line after time had expired.

Official John Clougherty first ruled it a 3-point shot, giving Tech an improbable one-point win.

But with Heathcote pleading to check with the fourth official and the timekeeper, umpire Charles Range overruled and said that Anderson's foot was on the line, sending the game into overtime.

"Our contention was the shot didn't beat the horn," Peplowski said correctly. "But Jud realized pretty quickly the refs were debating whether it was a 3-point shot. So he started to lobby that way."

In the extra session, MSU was up by one again with 23 seconds left. But Scott's strong drive to the basket put Tech up 81-80 with :07 left.

MSU's last shot, a rushed 40-footer by Redfield, hit the back of the rim.

And inexplicably, in viewing replays, the CBS crew of Quinn Buckner and Greg Gumble never noticed Anderson's tying shot came with :00 showing.

The NCAA wouldn't allow the officials to be questioned after the game. But reporters knew where to find Heathcote the next day.

"I'm madder now than I ever was after seeing all the replays," Heathcote fumed at the team's headquarters the following morning. "I have that sick feeling we got cheated again."

"A lot of people don't understand if the horns had been behind the backboards and above center court, the shot wouldn't have counted," Peplowski added. "But they weren't. The horn was in the middle of the Superdome. The officials are trained to hear the horn, not to watch the clock."

MSU had a hard time watching anything, knowing it would've played Minnesota two days later for a spot in the Final Four.

MSU vs GEORGIA TECH (March 23, 1990)

Michigan State

No.	Player	FG	FGA	3 Pt. FG	3 Pt. FGA	FT	FTA	Rebounds Off.	Def.	Tot.	F	TP	A	TO	BK	S	MIN
20	Ken Redfield, f	3	6	0	1	1	2	2	3	5	4	7	2	2	1	1	36
35	Matt Steigenga, f	2	9	0	0	0	0	1	3	4	4	4	3	3	0	1	35
54	Mike Peplowski, c	4	5	0	0	1	1	1	3	4	1	9	1	0	0	0	19
11	Steve Smith, g	13	22	3	5	3	4	1	4	5	0	32	6	4	0	2	44
21	Mark Montgomery, g	2	5	1	1	0	0	1	0	1	5	5	2	3	1	1	29
10	Kirk Manns	0	3	0	1	0	0	0	1	1	1	0	0	1	0	0	12
42	Parish Hickman	6	9	0	0	1	1	1	9	10	2	13	0	1	2	0	25
31	Dwayne Stephens	3	6	0	0	4	4	3	2	5	0	10	2	0	0	0	35
	Team							1	3	4							
TOTALS		**33**	**65**	**4**	**8**	**10**	**12**	**11**	**28**	**39**	**17**	**80**	**16**	**14**	**4**	**5**	**255**

FG%: 1st Half: 15-30, .500. 2nd Half: 18-35, .514. Game: 33-65, .508.
3-Pt.%:1st Half: 2-4, .667. 2nd Half: 2-5, .400. Game:4-8, .500.
FT%: 1st Half: 3-4, .750. 2nd Half: 7-8, .875. Game: 10-12, .833.

Georgia Tech

No.	Player	FG	FGA	3 Pt. FG	3 Pt. FGA	FT	FTA	Rebounds Off.	Def.	Tot.	F	TP	A	TO	BK	S	MIN
4	Dennis Scott, f	7	22	2	10	2	2	1	8	9	3	18	1	3	0	1	45
32	Malcolm Mackey, f	3	6	0	0	0	2	4	3	7	3	6	0	0	2	0	25
44	Johnny McNeil, c	4	6	0	0	4	4	1	5	6	5	12	0	1	0	0	37
12	Kenny Anderson, g	13	23	3	8	2	3	3	1	4	0	31	3	2	0	3	45
13	Brian Oliver, g	4	10	0	4	3	4	0	1	1	4	11	1	2	0	1	43
5	Karl Brown	1	2	1	1	0	0	1	0	1	3	3	1	1	0	2	29
15	Darryl Barnes	0	0	0	0	0	0	0	0	0	0	0	0	0	0	0	1
	Team							2	4	6							
TOTALS		**32**	**69**	**6**	**23**	**11**	**15**	**12**	**22**	**34**	**18**	**81**	**6**	**9**	**2**	**7**	**225**

FG%: 1st Half: 16-34, .471. 2nd Half: 16-35, .457. Game: 32-69, .464.
3-Pt.%: 1st Half: 4-12, .333. 2nd Half: 2-11, .261. Game: 6-23, .261.
FT%: 1st Half: 3-4, .750. 2nd Half: 8-11, .727.Game: 11-15, .733.

SCORE BY PERIODS:	**1st**	**2nd**	**OT**	**TOTAL**
Michigan State	35	40	5	80
Georgia Tech	39	36	6	81

Officials: John Clougherty, Mike Tanco, Charles Range
Attendance: 18,172

Purdue, 1997

Purdue's Brad Miller is smothered by Antonio Smith.

They did have Keady's undivided attention in a paint-peeling tirade at halftime that left just 10 seconds for warmups.

Long before that, the Spartans began to believe they could pull the upset in a 5 p.m. game that was moved up three hours so Boilermaker fans could watch their team win the Alamo Bowl.

A sweep that day wasn't to be.

"From Sunday on, all we talked about was winning," said MSU assistant Tom Crean. "There was a real air of confidence. We said, 'If we do this and this, we will win.' And I think that was the springboard for the whole year."

Four hours before tipoff, Izzo wasn't anywhere near as confident as he professed to be when he spoke to the Big Ten's youngest team.

"I think we'll have to score in the 70s to win," Izzo said from his hotel room, not knowing how good his defense would be. "And I think that'll be hard for us to do with some key offensive people hurt."

As long as the Spartans had point guard Mateen Cleaves to double the points of Purdue's starting backcourt, undersized center Antonio Smith to outrebound any two Boilermakers, and freshmen Andre Hutson and Charlie Bell to play like graduate students, nothing else mattered.

MSU held the hosts to 34.5 percent shooting from the field, had a 48-31 edge on the boards and shredded Purdue's attempt at a full-court press.

The Boilermakers' Jaraan Cornell is tied up by Mateen Cleaves.

No one could have seen it coming or known how much one win would mean.

But when Michigan State streamrolled Purdue 74-57 on Tuesday, December 30, 1997, it was the most important pre-New Year's Day triumph in Spartan history—and perhaps the biggest surprise.

With a 7-3 record after easing by Eastern Illinois three days earlier, MSU had no business thinking it could beat the fifth-ranked, 11-2 Boilermakers.

Yet, Tom Izzo's team did more than survive in West Lafayette, Indiana.

It dominated in every department, in the largest margin of victory for a Mackey Arena visitor in nearly 14 years.

"Michigan State played hard, with great effort, enthusiasm, and emotion," said a furious Purdue coach Gene Keady. "We had no emotion, no enthusiasm, no nothing."

"Mateen played like the guy we recruited," Izzo said of a soon-to-be Big Ten MVP. "Antonio was a foot over (massive Purdue center Brad) Miller on rebounds. And Hutson started to finish his shots."

From start to finish, there was little doubt, with Cleaves scoring the game's first six points and sparking a 13-2 run late in the first half.

When forward Jason Klein, Cleaves, and Bell hit 3-point shots during a Boilermaker drought, the lead grew to 12 and was never less than 10 in the last 23:07.

"I dreamed about it before the game," said Cleaves, after a 25-point, eight-assist effort. "I knew it was all on my shoulders."

No one's muscular shoulders were more important than Smith's. Despite giving up three inches, he outscored Miller 9-8 and outrebounded him 15-9.

When Hutson added 13 points and Bell had 11, the Spartans had a treasured victory they would need to earn a share of the conference crown with Illinois.

"If this was the real Michigan State, it might be wise to get in line for tickets right now," wrote Dave Matthews of the *Lansing State Journal*. "Especially if that was the real Purdue the Spartans converted into a confused, very ordinary looking basketball team."

MSU turned out to be every bit the team that silenced a student-less sellout crowd of 14,123. But Purdue would gain some revenge with a 99-96 overtime triumph on March 1 in East Lansing, forcing the Spartans to share a league title.

A little more than two months earlier, Izzo's team shared a sense of joy and accomplishment for an upset and a warning of more wins to come.

MSU at PURDUE (December 30, 1997)

Michigan State

No.	Player	FG	FGA	3 pt. FG	3 pt. FGA	FT	FTA	Off.	Def.	Tot.	F	TP	A	TO	BK	S	MIN
13	Antonio Smith, f	3	8	0	0	3	6	6	9	15	3	9	1	1	0	0	33
34	Andre Hutson, f	6	9	0	0	1	3	6	2	8	2	13	0	1	1	3	23
44	Jason Klein, f	3	9	3	8	0	0	2	4	6	3	9	2	1	1	0	29
12	Mateen Cleaves, g	9	18	1	3	6	9	0	2	2	1	25	8	5	1	1	36
14	Charlie Bell, g	4	10	1	3	2	2	3	2	1	1	11	3	1	1	2	32
11	David Thomas	0	4	0	0	0	0	1	2	3	0	0	1	2	0	2	9
30	Doug Davis	0	0	0	0	1	2	0	0	0	2	1	0	0	0	0	4
42	Morris Peterson	1	6	0	1	0	0	1	1	2	1	2	0	0	0	0	11
43	A.J. Granger	0	0	0	0	0	0	1	2	3	1	0	0	0	0	0	7
55	DuJuan Wiley	2	3	0	0	0	0	1	2	3	4	0	0	1	2	0	16
	Team							0	1	1							
	TOTALS	28	67	5	15	13	22	21	27	48	18	74	15	13	6	8	200

FG%: 1st Half: 16-38, .421. 2nd Half: 12-29, .414. Game: 28-67, .418.
3-Pt.%: 1st Half: 3-8, .375. 2nd Half: 2-7, .286. Game:5-15, .333.
FT%: 1st Half: 0-0, .000. 2nd Half: 13-22, .591. Game: 13-22, .591.

Purdue

No.	Player	FG	FGA	3 Pt. FG	3 Pt. FGA	FT	FTA	Off.	Def.	Tot.	F	TP	A	TO	BK	S	MIN
22	Jaraan Cornell, f	3	9	0	3	2	2	0	0	0	1	8	4	1	0	1	29
35	Brian Cardinal, f	7	14	1	2	3	4	1	4	5	5	18	1	0	1	0	25
52	Brad Miller, c	2	5	0	0	4	5	2	7	9	5	8	2	1	3	0	25
3	Chad Austin, g	2	14	1	8	4	4	1	3	4	2	9	0	2	0	0	36
15	Alan Eldridge, g	1	4	1	3	0	0	2	1	3	3	3	4	6	0	2	30
4	Mosi Barnes	0	1	0	0	0	0	0	0	0	0	0	0	0	0	0	1
5	Gary McQuay	4	6	0	0	3	4	2	2	4	1	11	0	2	0	1	26
20	Tony Mayfield	0	1	0	0	0	0	0	1	1	2	0	1	2	0	0	15
23	Mike Robinson	0	1	0	1	0	0	1	2	3	1	0	0	1	0	0	12
24	B.J. Carretta	0	0	0	0	0	0	0	0	0	0	0	0	0	0	0	0
	Team							1	1	2							
	TOTALS	19	55	3	17	16	19	10	21	31	20	57	12	15	4	4	200

FG%: 1st Half: 9-29, .310. 2nd Half: 10-26, .385. Game:19-55, .345.
3-Pt.%:1st Half: 1-9, .111. 2nd Half: 2-8, .250. Game:3-17, .176
FT%: 1st Half: 4-5, .800. 2nd Half: 12-14, .857. Game: 16-19, .842

SCORE BY PERIODS:	1st	2nd	TOTAL
Michigan State	35	39	74
Purdue	23	34	57

Officials: Ed Hightower, Ted Hillary, Phil Bova
Attendance: 14,123

Princeton, 1998

Some victories count more than one. This one validated an entire season.

A 63–56 win over Princeton in the 1998 NCAA Tournament sent Michigan State to the Sweet 16 and put a proud program back on the basketball map.

That triumph on Saturday, March 14, in the Hartford Civic Center also solidified Tom Izzo's claim to National Coach of the Year honors.

And it stamped sophomore point guard Mateen Cleaves as an All-American with an all-around game and all kinds of courage.

Antonio Smith helps the Spartans own the backboards.

After back-to-back losses to Purdue in the regular-season finale and to Minnesota in the opening round of the first Big Ten Tournament, the fourth-seeded Spartans were written off by *Sports Illustrated* and other publications.

"Upset loss to Minnesota and draw of slingshot-toting Eastern Michigan suggest an early exit," said *SI*'s East Region preview.

Instead, MSU moved to 21-7 late that Thursday with an 83-71 win over the 13th-seeded Eagles and the vaunted backcourt of Earl Boykins and Derrick Dial.

That wasn't enough to sway the experts, most of whom figured Izzo's team

Charlie Bell completes a great week by burning the Tigers.

would be backdoored and bombed from the perimeter by an Ivy League power.

"Princeton presents plenty of problems for teams that see them all the time," said North Carolina coach Bill Guthridge. "I can't imagine how hard it'll be for Michigan State with one day to prepare."

The eighth-ranked Tigers, 27-1, had just beaten UNLV 69-57 and were a popular choice to advance to Greensboro, North Carolina, where they could avenge their lone loss to the top-rated Tar Heels.

But a funny thing happened on the way to that rematch. Fifth-seeded Princeton was outplayed, outcoached, and out of the Tournament after the Spartans made a statement about themselves and the Big Ten.

With just 39 hours of preparation, Izzo and assistants Tom Crean, Stan Heath, and Mike Garland gave the players a brilliant-but-digestible game plan.

"Everyone wondered whether we'd take away the backdoor cut or the outside shot," Crean said. "We told our guys, 'We're going to play Michigan State defense and take it ALL away.' From that first meeting Friday morning, our guys were so inquisitive. They gave the coaches confidence."

Four 20-minute film sessions taught the Spartans all they needed to know.

And MSU was the only team to get up early that Saturday and make use of its morning shootaround—a critical decision for a team that would shoot 56.4 percent from the field, while the Tigers would miss five one-and-one free throw opportunities.

The Spartans, notorious slow starters, jumped out to a 10-0 lead.

With Antonio Smith directing traffic from the back line, MSU allowed just one backdoor layup all day and had a 39-15 rebound advantage.

And when Smith found freshman Charlie Bell on a similar move with :04 left in the half, the Spartans took a 33-31 lead to the locker room.

After building a nine-point lead, MSU failed to hit a field goal for a span of 6:07, while the Tigers gnawed away and finally drew even at 54.

But after a pair of free throws by forward Morris Peterson, Cleaves hit the day's key shot—a 23-footer with :34 left to make it 59-54.

"They backed off me, so I put it up," he said. "I guess God just carried it in. . . . It was meant for us to be in the Sweet 16."

Cleaves, his team's only double-figure scorer, led all players with 27 points, nine rebounds, five assists, and a few hundred smiles—not bad for someone who had just had a hideous wart removed from his forehead.

"He wanted it off before the game," said Sports Medicine Director Jeff Kovan. "I told him, 'If that thing gets infected, there's going to be one dead physician. . . . And wherever he is, Tom Izzo will be the No. 1 suspect.'

"Maybe that's why Mateen's shot stopped going to the left today. When we talked about wearing a bandage, he said he wanted to look like a warrior."

He played like one, too, as did a team that gave Princeton an education.

MSU vs PRINCETON (March 14, 1998)

Michigan State

No. Player	FG	FGA	3 pt. FG	FGA	FT	FTA	Off.	Def.	Tot.	F	TP	A	TO	BK	S	MIN
13 Antonio Smith, f	2	2	0	0	2	2	1	4	5	3	9	1	0	0	0	26
44 Jason Klein, f	2	3	0	1	0	0	2	3	5	1	13	0	2	0	1	30
34 Andre Hutson, f	4	5	0	0	0	0	1	3	4	3	9	1	3	0	0	24
12 Mateen Cleaves, g	9	13	3	5	6	9	0	9	9	2	27	5	7	0	2	37
14 Charlie Bell, g	2	7	1	1	1	2	1	2	3	2	6	1	3	0	0	28
11 David Thomas	0	1	0	0	0	0	2	1	3	2	0	0	0	0	0	10
30 Doug Davis	0	0	0	0	0	0	0	1	1	0	0	0	1	0	0	3
42 Morris Peterson	0	1	0	1	4	4	0	4	4	3	4	0	2	0	1	14
43 A.J. Granger	0	1	0	0	2	2	0	3	3	2	2	3	1	0	0	14
55 DuJuan Wiley	3	6	0	0	0	0	0	1	1	2	6	0	2	1	1	14
Team							0	1	1							
TOTALS	**22**	**39**	**4**	**8**	**15**	**19**	**8**	**31**	**39**	**20**	**63**	**11**	**22**	**1**	**5**	**200**

FG%: 1st Half: 14-25, .560. 2nd Half: 8-14, .571. Game:22-39, .564.
3-Pt.%:1st Half: 3-4, .750. 2nd Half: 1-4, .250. Game:4-8, .500.
FT%: 1st Half: 2-2, 1.000. 2nd Half: 13-17, .765. Game:15-19, .789

Princeton

No. Player	FG	FGA	3 Pt. FG	FGA	FT	FTA	Off.	Def.	Tot.	F	TP	A	TO	BK	S	MIN
15 Jim Mastaglio, f	2	8	0	6	0	1	1	5	6	4	4	3	0	0	3	39
32 Gabe Lewullis, f	4	12	1	6	4	8	2	1	3	4	13	0	1	0	4	39
30 Steve Goodrich, c	7	14	1	6	3	5	0	1	1	3	18	3	1	2	3	39
10 Brian Earl, g	5	13	5	10	0	0	1	1	2	4	15	2	2	0	3	40
21 Mitch Henderson, g	2	3	0	0	2	4	0	1	1	2	6	2	3	0	2	40
33 Nathan Walton	0	0	0	0	0	0	0	0	0	0	0	0	0	0	0	1
35 Phil Belin	0	0	0	0	0	0	0	0	0	0	0	0	0	0	0	1
45 Mason Rocca	0	0	0	0	0	0	0	0	0	0	0	0	0	0	0	1
Team							0	2	2							
TOTALS	**20**	**50**	**7**	**28**	**9**	**18**	**4**	**11**	**15**	**17**	**56**	**10**	**7**	**2**	**15**	**200**

FG%: 1st Half: 11-27, .407. 2nd Half: 9-23, .391. Game:20-50, .400.
3-Pt.%: 1st Half: 4-16, .250. 2nd Half: 3-12, .250. Game: 7-28, .250.
FT%: 1st Half: 5-7, .714. 2nd Half: 4-11, .364. Game: 9-18, .500.

SCORE BY PERIODS:	1st	2nd	TOTAL
Michigan State	33	30	63
Princeton	31	25	56

Officials: John Clougherty, Ted Valentine, Mark Reischling
Attendance: 16,105

In one of the last big wins under Ben Van Alstyne, the Spartans stop Marquette 57-54 in 1948 in Jenison Field House.

The Numbers

100 Years (and Counting)

All-Time Letterwinners
$=Information Unavailable

A

Aitch, Matthew A.; '66-67; C; 6-7; #45; St. Louis, Mo./Maplewood Richmond Heights
Anderegg, Robert H.; '57-58-59C; F; 6-3; #23; Monroe, Wis./Same
Anderson, Valda R.; '29; Mgr; SandCreek/Same
Archer, Lawrence C.; '18; G; #$; Derby/$
Armstrong, T. Robert; '53-54-55; C; 6-8; #12; Holland/Same
Armstrong, Mark; '97-98; Mgr.; Grand Rapids
Aubuchon, I. Chester; '39-40-42C; G; 5-9; #24; Gary, Ind./Horace Mann
Ayala Reginald (Rickey) P; '52-53-54; G; 5-6; #7;Brooklyn, N.Y./Tech

B

Bailey, John A.; '66-67-68; G; 6-0; # 12; Streator, Ill./Same
Balbach, Edward; 02-03-04C; G/C; $; no #; Grand Rapids/$
Barnard, John A; '32; F/G; $; no #; $/$
Barnes, Daron; '86; Mgr; $/$
Barnett, William D.; '10; $; $; no #; Pittsburgh, Pa./$
Barr, John H.; '21.; F; $; no #; Flint/$
Basich, Peter S.; '40-41; G; $; #4; Columbus, Ohio/$
Bates, Steven A.; '80-81-82; C; 6-10; #52; Fort Wayne, Ind./Wayne
Bauman, Paul J.; '45; G/F; 5-10; #8; Battle Creek/St. Phillip
Baylor, Arthur E.; '66-67; F; 6-6; #41; Washington, D.C/Mackin
Beathea, Daimon; '93-94-95-96; F; 6-7; #23; Elkhart, Ind./Memorial
Belknap, Leon V.; '09; $; $; no #; Whittemore/$
Bell, Charlie; '98; G; 6-3; #14; Flint/Southwestern Acad.
Bencie, Charles J.; '56-57-58; F/C; 6-6; #31; Gary, Ind./Froebel
Benington, John J. Jr.; '72; G; 6-1; #15; East Lansing/Lansing Gabriels
Benjamin, Sylvester (Rudy); 69-70-71; G; 6-3; #21; Dayton, Ohio/Roosevelt
Bennett, Byron D.; '32; Mgr.; $/$
Bernecker, Scott; '90-91-92-93; Mgr; East Grand Rapids/Same
Berry, William L.; '62-63-64; F; 6-2; #12; Winnemucca, Nev./Humboldt County
Beyer, G. Joseph; '45; G; 5-10; #3; Grosse Pointe/Same
Bibbens, Cleveland W.; '82; F; 6-6; #55; Pittsburgh, Pa./Brashear
Bilkey, Robert B.; '24; C; $; no #; Ishpeming/Same
Binge, Ronald E.; '70; F; 6-5; #44; East Detroit/Same
Bishop, Randy J.; '79-80; Mgr.; Grandville/Wyoming Lee
Blanchard, Charles M.; '01C-02; $; $; no #; Chesaning/ Same
Bluem, Mark; '92-93; F; 6-6; #20; Caro/Same
Boeskool, Randall D.; '31-32; C; $; no #;Grand Rapids/$
Bograkos, Timothy G.; '69-70; G; 6-1; #12; Flint/Central
Bostic Herbert H.; '80-81-82; F/G; 6-4; #44; Detroit/Royal Oak Shrine
Bouma, Robert D.; '68; Mgr; Grand Rapids/$
Bower, William R.; '50-51-52; F; 5-11; #4; Fort Wayne, Ind./South
Brannum, Robert W.; '48C; C; 6-5; #7; Winfield, Kan./Same
Braun, Norwin W.; '49; Mgr; Ann Arbor/$
Breslin, Brian S.; '71-72-74; F; 6-5; #42; East Lansing/Same
Brigham, G. Horbert; '18; F; $; 6-5; #13; Springfield, Pa./$
Brkovich, Donald; '79; F; 6-6; #21; Windsor, Ont./Lowe
Brkovich, Mike; '79-80-81CoC; G/F; 6-4; #12; Windsor, Ont./Lowe
Brookens, Harold A.; '61; G; 6-0; #14; Tulsa, Okla./Washington
Brooks, Quinton; '93-94-95-96CoC; F; 6-7; #40; Akron, Ohio/Firestone
Brown, Alfred; '77-78; F; 6-6; #25; Detroit/Haynesville (La.)
Brown, Arthur L.; '22; G; $; no #; Hastings/Same
Brown, Luke; '98; Mgr; Iron Mountain
Brown, Mark W.; '86; G; 6-0; #24; Hastings/Same
Burchill, Kenneth Q.; '51; Mgr.; Sault Ste. Marie/$
Burk, William R.; '41-42; G; $; #7; Whiting, Ind./$
Busch, Fred W.; '10-11C; F; $; no #; Detroit/$
Buysse, Maurice J.; '34-36; G; $; #8; $/$

C

Callahan, Leo A.; '37-38-39C; F; #5; Schenectady, NY/ Same
Campbell, Arthur L.; 09-10; Mgr.; Cheat Haven, PA/Same
Carey, Robert W.; '50-51-52; C; 6-5; #8; Charlevoix/Same
Carey, William R.; '51-52; F; 6-1; #13; Charlevoix/Same
Carlson, Leif F.;'51-52; F; 6-2; #17; East Lansing/Weehawken (NJ)
Carlson, Sherman; F.; '27; Mgr.; Howell/$
Carpenter, William E.; '37-38; G; $; #$; $/$
Carr, Vernon; '86-87; G/F; 6-6; #23; Detroit/Cody
Carrington, Matthew; '83; G; 6-1; #14; Flint/Central
Carruthers, Robert H.; '31; Mgr.; $/$
Casler, Jeff; '89-90-91; G; 6-0; #22; St. Johns/Same
Cawood, John F.; '43-47; F; 6-3; #16/21; Lansing/Eastern
Cawood, William E.; '80-81-82-83CoC; G/F; 6-7; #22; East Lansing/Same
Chamberlain, Ralph G.; '10-11-12C-13; C; $; no #; Grand Rapids/$
Chandler, Stanley L.; '62; C; 6-5; #31; Louisville, KY/Central
Chandnois, Lynn E.; '47; F; 6-2; #$; Flint/Central
Chapman, Robert; '75-76-77C-78CoC; G; 6-2; #44; Saginaw/Same
Charles, Ron A.; '77-78-79-80CoC; F; 6-8; #15; U.S. Virgin Islands/Central
Cherry, Steve; '98; F; 6-6; #20; Coldwater/Same
Christiansen, Paul C.; '70; Mgr.; Greenville/Same
Cleaves, Mateen; '97-98CoC; G; 6-2; #12; Flint/Northern
Cleveland, Andy; '95-96-97-98; Mgr.; Grand Rapids
Cohrs, William R.; '70-71-72; C; 6-6; #45; Vicksburg/Same
Cole, Clarence L.; '26; G; $; no #; Lowell/Same
Colvin, Carleton J.; '27-28; G; $; No #; East Lansing/$
Cooper, James A.; '02-C; $; $; no #; Owosso/$
Copeland, Bernrard Y.; '68-69; F; 6-6; #45; Inkster/Hillcrest (Brundidge, Ala.)
Corbitt, Donald R.; '54; G; 5-10; #9; Fort Wayne, Ind./Elmhurst
Coutre, James W.; '77-78; C; 6-9; #45; LaGrange, Ill./Benet Academy
Crary, Edward (Ted); '65-66-67; F; 6-5; #13; Springfield, PA/$
Curtis, William A.; '64-65-66C; F; 6-4; #25; Grand Rapids/South

D

Dalrymple, Max E.; '38-39-40C;G; $; #15; Port Huron/$
Dargush, Bennie J.; '37-38; C; $; #19; Amsterdam, N.Y./$
Davis, Charles E.; '39; Mgr; Rockford/$
Davis, Doug; '98; G; 6-3; #30; Columbus, OH/Westland
Davis, Peter A.; '73-74-75; G; 6-1; #32; Brooklyn, N.Y./Boys
Dawson, Hugh A.; '47-48-49; G; 6-0; #5; Hammond, Ind./Same
Dean, Paul W.; '69-70-71; G; 6-1; #23; Alma/Same
Dekker, James H.; '33-34; C; $; #21; $/$
DenHerder, Fred J.; '28-29-30; F/C; $; no #; $/$
Densley, Theodore B.; '69; Mgr; Detroit/$
Devenny, Robert H.; '53-54-55; G; 5-11; #3/10; Philadelphia, Pa./North Catholic
Dickeson, Verne C.; '27-28C-29; F; $; no #; $/$
Dickson, Robert M.; 06-07-08; $; $; no #; Lansing/$
Diehl, Roy H.; '42-43; F; 5-9; #8; Sturgis/Same
Divjak, Ronald; '62-63; F/C; 6-5; #22; East Chicago, Ind./Washington
Dodge, Glenn W.; '05; G; $; no #; Almont/$
Doerr, Maxwell; '30; Mgr; $/$
Donnelly, Terry R.; '77-78-79-80CoC; G; 6-2; #11; St. Louis, Mo./Parkway North
Douglas, Thomas H.; '63-64; G; 5-11; #20; Barrington, Ill./Same
Drew, Kenneth L.; '26-27C; G; $; no #; Tipton/$
Dryden, Marion; '98; Mgr.; Detroit
Dudley, James D.; '75; F; 6-5; #42; South Milwaukee, Wis./Racine Prairie
Duffield, Arnold W.; '32; F/G; $; no #; Lansing/$
Duthie, Herbert I.; '10-11; G; $; no #; Grand Rapids/$

E

Edwards, Heywood M.; '67-68; F/C; 6-6; #33;Broklyn, NY/ Boys
Eckstrom, William, R.; '51-52; F; 6-3; #12; Grant/Same
Eldred, Robert R.; '27; F; $; no #; Eaton Rapids/Same
Emery, Brian; '87-88; Mgr.; Perry/Same
Eva, Wesley L.; '23-24; C; $; no #; Vulcan/$
Evans, Monte; '97; G, #22; Detroit/Cass Tech

F

Fagan, Terrance, S.; '72; G; 5-11; #21; Flint/St. Michaels
Fahs, David L.; '59-60-61C; G; 5-9; #12; Monroe, Wis./Same
Falkowski, George; '38-39; F; $; #22; Flint/$
Fanning, Lawrence; '60; G; 6-0; #10; Gas City, Ind./Mississinewa
Feick, Jamie; '93-94-95-96 CoC; F; 6-8; #30; Lexington, Ohio/Same
Feldreich, Sten; '78; C; 7-0; #43; Bromma, Sweden/Same
Felt, Carl R.; '27-28-29C; C; $; no #; Muskegon/$
Ferguson, Christian S.; '61; G; 5-10; #10; Lansing/Sexton
Ferguson, George H.; '56-57C; F; 6-3; #30; Providence, R.I./North Providence
Ferrari, Albert R.; '53-54-55C; F; 6-3; #22; New York/Brooklyn Tech
Ferrell, Fred I.; '75-76; Mgr.; Detroit/$
Fessenden, Clarence W.; '21-22-23C; G; $; no #; Newaygo/$
Finn, John B.; '50; C; 6-4; #15; Escanaba/Same
Flowers, Donald; '78; G; 6-2; #21; Detroit/Hamtramck
Ford, Patrick; '83-84; G/F; 6-5; #44; Detroit/Cass Tech
Fordham, Barry; '84-85-86-87CoC; C; 6-8; #40/Buffalo, N.Y./Sweet Home
Fortino, M. Samuel; '45-46; F; 6-2; #6 Alma/Same
Fossum, Robert B.; '81; G; 5-9; #15; Okemos/Same
Foster, Walter J.; '19-20-21C-22; C; $; no #; East Lansing/$
Frankel, Charles M.; '45; C; 6-3; #4; Detroit/Northern
Franklin, Michael; '92-93-94-95; Mgr.; Grand Rapids
Fredericks, Charles C.; '25-26; G/C; $; no #;/Saginaw/$
Frimodig, Lyman L.; '14-15-16C-17; C/G; $; no #; Calumet/$
Frizzo, Leo V. '35; C; $; #9; $/$
Furlow, Terry L.; '73-74-75-76C; F; 6-5; #25; Flint/Northern
Furseth, Erik O.; '51-52-53C; F; 6-3; #5; Cleveland, Hts. Ohio/Same

G

Gale, Robert S.; '68-69-70; F; 6-5; #25; Trout Creek/Same
Ganakas, Gary E.; '71-72-73; G; 5-5; #11; East Lansing/Same
Garavaglia, Jon; '94-95-96-97; F; 6-9; #21; Allen Park/Aquinas
Garlock, Ronald B.; '35-36-37; G/F; #16; $/$
Garrett, George A.; '18-19-20C; G; $; no #; Elmhurst, N.Y./$
Gauthier, George E.; '11-12-13-14C; F; $; no #; Detroit/$
Geahan, Robert R.; '47-48-49C; F; 6-1; #3; Lansing/Sexton
Geistler, Gerald L.; '66-67-68; C; 6-9; #42; Detroit/Redford
Gent, George E. (Pete); '62-63-64; C/F; 6-5; #30; Bangor/Same
Gerard, Joseph E.; '40-41-42; F; $; #16; North Webster, Ind./$
Gibbons, James M.; '68-69-70CoC; C; 6-6; #41; Blissfield/Same
Gilkey, Edward A.; '20-21-22; F; $; no #; Lansing/$
Gilkie, Gerald; '79; F; 6-5; #43; Detroit/Kettering
Gill, William W.; '04; C; $; no #; $/$
Glover, William J.; '73-74-75; G; 6-2; #12; Pontiac/Central
Godfrey, Walter G.; '55-56C; G; 6-1; #23; Detroit/Cass Tech
Golis, William; '60; G; 6-0; #25; Bolivar, Pa./Laurel Valley
Gonzalez, Robert; '79-80; F; 6-7; #35; Detroit/Catholic Central
Gonzenbach, Max A.; '56-58; C; 6-8; #32/35; Milbank, S.D./Same
Gore, Timothy; '81-82-83-84; G; 6-4; #10; Erie, Pa/Cathedral Prep
Gorman, John E.; '66; G; 5-11; #11; Chicago, Ill./Fenwick
Goss, Robert W.; '11-12-13-14; G; $; no #; Fall River, Mass./$
Gowens, Arthur L.; '59; F; 6-2; #35; Lansing/Sexton
Graham, Ralph C.; '05-06; Mgr.; Owosso/$
Grams, Milton H.; '28; Mgr.; $/$
Granack, John M.; '46-49; F; 5-11; # 7; Hammond, Ind./Same
Granger, A.J.; '97-98; F; 6-9; #43; Findlay, Ohio/Liberty-Benton
Green, Harry A.; '43; Mgr.; Detroit/$
Green, John M.; '57-58-59C; C; 6-5; #24; Dayton, Ohio/Dunbar
Grove, Donald B.; '28-29-30; F; $ no #; $/$
Grove, Roger, R.; '29-30-31CoC; G/F; $; no #; Sturgis/$
Guess, Lorenzo; '98; G; 6-3; #5; Wayne/Memorial
Gutkowski, Ronald J.; '70-71-72CoC; F; 6-6; #24; Detroit/Catholic Central

H

Hackett, Paul M.; '25-26C; F; $; no #; Saginaw/$
Haftencamp, Joseph P.; '02-03-04; F; $; no #; Grand Rapids/$
Haga, Arthur J.; '29-30-31CoC; G; $; no #; Muskegon/$
Hairston, Lindsay; '73-74-75C; C; 6-7; #45; Detroit/Kettering
Haley, Ron,'91-92;F;6-6;#45;Saginaw/Nouvel

Hall, C.C.; '26; Mgr.; $/$
Hall, Jesse; '88-89-90; G; 6-3; #23; Venice, Ill./Same
Hall, Richard D.; '61; F/C; 6-4; #32; Manitowac, Wis./Lincoln
Hamilton, Geoffrey; '61-62-63; Mgr.; Three Rivers/$
Hammes, John H.; '18-20; G; $; no #; Newberry/$
Hannish, Claude C.; '06-07-08-09-10C-11; G; $; no #; Grand
Rapids/$
Harris, James P.; '55; F; 6-3; #25; Fort Wayne, Ind./Harlan
Hart, David; '93-94-95-96; G; 6-4; #4; Battle Creek/Central
Hartman L. Deneal; '52-53-54; F; 6-4; #13/19; Fort Wayne,
Ind./South
Hashu, Nickolas; '42-43-45C; G; 6-0; #9; Hammond, Ind./Same
Haun, Harold E.; '30; C; $; no #; $/$
Headen, John W.; '68; Mgr; Detroit/$
Heasley, Lloyd E.; '20-21-22C; F; $; no #; Zeeland/$
Hedden, Larry D.; '56-57-58; F; 6-5; #33; Gas City, Ind./Mississinewa
Henry, Charles A.; '38-39; G; $; #16; Huntinton, Ind./$
Herrick, Robert C.; '33-34-35C; F/G; $; #4; $/$
Hess, Leon; '48; G; 6-3; #16; Auburn, Ind./Same
Hickman, Parish; '89-90-91; F; 6-7; #42; Detroit/Bishop Borgess
Higbie, Charles C.; '18-20-21; C/F; $; no #; Napoleon/$
Hindman, O. Max; '39-40-41; C/F; $; #8; Gary, Ind./$
Hinkin, Paul E.; '54; F; 6-4; #13; Saginaw/Arthur Hill
Hoff, Guy F.; '11; F; $; no #; Buffalo, N.Y./$
Hoffman, Lee S.; '50; Mgr.; East Lansing/$
Hofkamp, Matt; '91; C; 6-10; #44; Ionia/Same
Holcomb, Monte S.; '31; F; $; no #; $/$
Hollis, Mark; '82-83-84-85; Mgr.; Port Huron/$
Holms, D. John; '67-68-69; F; 6-4; #24; Lansing/Sexton
Holmes, Richard; '64-65-66; F; 6-4; #33; Willard, Ohio/Same
Hood, Charles C.; '15-16; F; $; no #; Buffalo, N.Y./$
Hood, Oliver Z.; '26-27; F; $; no #; Ionia/$
Huck, Christopher D.; '72-73; Mgr.; Monroe/$
Huffman, Jaimie P.; '79; G; 6-3; #24; Lansing/Everett
Hultman, Vivian J.; '23; G; $; no #; Grand Rapids/$
Hutson, Andre; '98; F; 6-8; #34; Trotwood, OH/Trotwood-Madison
Hutt, Martin C.; '38-39-40C; F/C; $; #10;Schenectady, N.Y./$

I

Izzo, Mario F.; '86-87-88; C; 6-11; #55; Park Ridge, N.J./St.
Joseph Regional

J

James, Kurt M.; 80-82CoC; F; 6-7; #30; Pontiac/Northern
Johnson, Darryl D.; '84-85-86-87CoC; G; 6-2; #13; Flint/Central
Johnson, Derek; '92; Mgr.; $
Johnson, Earvin; '78-79CoC; G/F; 6-8; #33 (ret.); Lansing/Everett
Johnson, George; '83-84-85; Mgr.; Saginaw/$
Johnson, Ken F.; '84-85; F; 6-8; #00; La Jolla, Calif./LaJolla
Johnson, Louis, Jr.; '92-93-94-95; Mgr.; Muskegon Heights
Johnson, Robert B.; '53; F; 6-1; #6; Muskegon Heights/Same
Johnson, Vernon L.; '67-68; G; 5-11; #23; Saginaw/Same
Johnston, Rae J.; '50; Mgr.; River Rouge/$
Jones, Dudley P.; '41-42-46; G/F; 6-1; #5; Hammond,
Ind./Whiting
Jordan, Richard D.; '67; G; 5-7; #14; Fennville/Same
Joyce, Donn; '49; G; 6-0; #19; Greenfield, Ind./Same

K

Kathrein, John A.; '52; Mgr.; Chicago, Ill./$
Kaye, Richard P.; '79-80-81; F; 6-6; #42; Livonia/Detroit Catholic
Central
Keast, Roger; '32; F/G; $; no #; $/$
Keeler, David J.; '67; F; 6-6; #44; Moline, Ill./$
Keir, Gerald J.; '64; Mgr.; Snyder, N.Y./$
Kelley, Thomas; '95-96-97; G; 6-2; #3; Grand Rapids/Union
Kelser, Gregory; 76-77-78CoC-79CoC; F; 6-7; #32 (ret.);
Detroit/Henry Ford
Kemler, John; '66; Mgr.; Rochester/$
Kemp, Edward K.; '35; Mgr.; $/$
Kern, Sidney A.; '45; Mgr; Detroit/$
Kidman, James L.; '24; G; $; no #; Clyde, Ohio /$
Kilbride, Duane R.; '61; F/G; 6-2; #21; Kankakee, Ill./St. Patrick
Central
Kilgore, William; '71-72-73C; C; 6-7; #22; River Rouge/Same
Kircher, Alton S.; '32-33C; $; no #; Gladstone/$
Kirkpatrick, Steven; '70; G; 6-2; #32; Lafayette, Ind./ Jefferson
Kitto, Clyde A.; '24; C; $; no #; Gladstone/$

Klein, Jason; '96-97-98; F-G; 6-7; #11/44; Grosse Ile/Same
Kowalk, Clayton J.; '43; G/F; 5-11; #25; Eaton Rapids/Same
Kraft, Howard A.; '36-37-38C; F/G; $; #18; Niles/$
Krakora, Joseph G.; '45; G; 6-1; #12; Berwyn, Ill./Morton
Krall, William R.; '45-46; C; 6-8; #22; Detroit/Redford
Krehl, Edward C.; '05-06C-07C-08; $; no #; Buffalo, N.Y./$
Kucab, Jeff; '96-97-98; Mgr.; Grosse Ile
Kupper, James N.; '64-65-66; G; 6-0; #23; Louisville, Ky./St. Xavier

Kurtz, Lawrence D.; '18-19C-20; G; $; no #; Flint/$

L

Lafayette, Lee A.; '67-68-69C; F/C; 6-6; #35; Grand Rapids/South
Lalley, Patrick; '98; Mgr.; Holland
Lamers, John G. (Jack); '61-62-63C; G/F; 6-2; #15; Kimberly,
Wis./Same

MSU big men Kevin Willis and Ken Johnson battle for a rebound in a dramatic win over Iowa in 1984.

Larson, Edward L.; '34; Mgr.; Montague/$
Levin, Harvey A.; '65; Mgr.; Kankakee, Ill./$
Lewis, Tyrone L.; '72; F/G; #34; Ferndale/Same
Lick, Thomas W.; '67-68-69; C; 6-10; #34; Gaylord/Same
Lieberman, Albert G.; '49; Mgr.; Owosso/$
Lieberman, James K.; '72; Mgr; Owosso/Same
Lloyd, Gregory L.; '79; 6-1; G; #10; Lansing/Eastern
Longaker, Michael; '78-79-80; G; 6-1; #23; Warren/Same
Lumsden, David H.; '47; C; 6-5 #$; Lexinton, N.C./Same
Lux, Harry J.; '56-57; G; 5-10; #11; Chicago, Ill./Leo

M

MacDaugal, Everett R.; '40; Mgr.; Detroit/$
MacDonald, Timothy; '85-86-87-88-89; Mgr; Scio, N.Y./$
MacMasters, Hugh D.; '52; C; 6-6; #15; Hazel Park/Same
Mahaney, Robert C.; '51; Mgr.; Owosso/$
Maisner, Michael J.; '80-81-82; Mgr.; Marshall/$
Manns, Kirk; '87-88-89-90; G; 6-1; #10; North Judson, Ind./Same
Martin, John E.; '33; Mgr.; $/$
Marx, Harry B.; '25; G; $; no #; Monroe/$
Mason, Ellwood W.; '25; C; $; no #; Burton/$
Mathieson, Roderick R.; '12; F; $; no #; Detroit/$
Matson, Edward I.; '21-22; G; $; no # ; Dollar Bay/$
Matthews, Wallace B.; '25; Mgr.; $/$
May, Floyd E.; '43; F; 6-0; # 11; Schenectady, N.Y./Mt. Pleasant
Mazza, Matthew A.; '46-47; C; 6-2; #29; Niagara Falls, N.Y./Trott
McAuliffe, Thomas W.; '51; G; 6-0; #7; Chicago, Ill./ Leo
McCall, Tom; '84-85-86-87; Mgr; Detroit/$
McCaslin, Garold E.; '31-32-33C; C/F; $; #16; $/$
McClelland, Albert L.; '15-16-17C; G; $; no #; Holland/$
McCoy, Julius; '54-55-56; F; 6-2; #18/15; Farrell, Pa./Same
McGill, Thomas; '73-74-75; F; 6-4; #41; Flint/Northern
McGillicuddy, Robert J.; '28; G; $; no #; Lansing/$
McKerma, Parnell G.; '06-07-08-09C-10; $; no #; $/$
McMillan, Roy A.; '23-25; F; $; no #; $/$
Means, Clarence T. (Sonny); '50-51-52C; G; 5-11; #3; Saginaw/Same
Mekules, Frank A.; '41; C; $; #22; Detroit/$
Merz, Elmer H.; '08-09; $; no #; Detroit/$
Millar, Wilson F.; '03-04; Mgr.; Ray Center/$
Miller, Anthony; '92-93-94; F; 6-9; #34; Benton Harbor/ Same
Miller, Carl F.; '16; G; $; no #; Saginaw/$
Miller, Costa N. '61; Mgr.; $/$
Miller, Hiram H.; '13-14; F; $; no #; Tonawanda, N.Y./$
Miller, Ken; '98; C; 6-10; #54; St. Clair Shores/Lakeshore
Miller, Oscar R.; '14-15C; G; $; no #; Saginaw/$
Miller, Patrick F.; '70-71-72CoC; F/G; 6-2; #35; Menominee/Same
Miller, Robert E.; '65-66; F; 6-5; #35; Fort Wayne, Ind./Elmhurst
Miller W. Blake; '13-15; F; $; no #; Tonawanda, N.Y./$
Mills Herbert W.; '07-08-09; $; $; no #; Adrian/$
Milton Cedric L.; '73-74-75-76; C; 6-9; #24; Denver, Colo./Manual
Montgomery, Mark; 89-90-91-92 CoC; G; 6-2; #11; Inkster/Southgate Aquinas
Moore, John L.; '50; C; 6-7; #15; Ionia/Same
Morris, Robert M.; '39-40-41; F; $; #12; Grand Rapids/$
Morrison Randy M.; '81; G; 6-2; #23; Olivet/Same
Mudd, Richard D.; '82-83-84-85CoC; C; 6-9; #24; Washington, D.C./McKinley Tech
Mull, Anthony; '96-97; G; #10; 6-4; Flint/Southwestern
Mueller, David P.; '86-88-89-90; C; 6-9; #34; Racine, Wis./St. Catherine's
Murray, Byron M.; '17-18C; F; $; no #; Marquette/$
Muth, Charles K.; '33; G; $; #3; $/$

N

Nagel, Robert F.; '50; G; 6-2; #16; Lansing/Eastern
Nash, Ricky; '76; F; 6-4; #34; Saginaw/Same
Newman, Harold C.; '24; Mgr; East Lansing/$
Nicodemus, Steve; '93-94-95-96; G; 6-4; #22; S. Whitley, Ind./Whitko
Noack, William H.; '64; C; 6-8; #35; Lansing/Eastern
Nuttila, Matt E.; '23-24-25C; F; $; no #; Negaunee/$

O

O'Leary, Robert J.; '45; F; 6-0; #10; Portsmouth, N.H./ Same
Olson, Duane E.; '57; F/C; 6-5; #21; Detroit/Cass Tech
Olson, Lance E.; '58-59-60C; F; 6-4; #30; Green Bay, Wis./West
Osterink, Leonard J.; '37; F; $; #21; Grand Rapids/$

P

Pacynski, Stan L.; ' 22; F; $; no #; Bay City/$
Palm, Wayne V. '19-20-21; F; $; no #; East Lansing/$
Papadakos, George; '87-88TriC; C; 7-0; #41; Don Mills, Ont./St. Michael's
Patchett, Wendall T.; '32-33-34C; F; $; #9; East Lansing/$
Pattison, Benjamin P.; '11; G; $; no #; Caro/$

Paulson, Donald H.; '49; Mgr; $/$
Payton, Darwin R.; '77-78-79; Mrg; River Rouge/Same
Pedro, Gregory; '84-85; G; 6-4; #21; Staten Island, N.Y./St. Peter's
Penick, Andy; '91-95; G; 6-2; #12; Louisville, KY/Pleasure Ridge Park
Peplowski, Mike; '90-91-92-93CoC; C; 6-10; #54; Detroit/Warren De LaSalle
Peppard, David L.; '17; C; $; no #; East Lansing/$

With help from a ladder, 6-foot guard Mark Brown and 7-foot center George Papadakos are almost the same height—but not the same shoe size.

Superfan Duane Vernon in his basement—Party Central and a Spartan shrine.

All-Time Coaching Records

Coach	Years	Games	Won	Lost	Pct.
No Established Coach	1899	2	0	2	.000
Charles O. Bemies	1900-1901	7	5	2	.714
George E. Denman	1902-1903	11	11	0	1.000
Chester L. Brewer	1904-1910	95	70	25	.736
John F. Macklin	1911-1916	86	48	38	.558
George M. Gauthier	1917-1920	73	38	35	.520
Lyman L. Frimodig	1921-1922	45	24	21	.533
Fred M. Walker	1923-1924	39	20	19	.513
John H. Kobs	1925-1926	37	11	26	.297
Benjamin F. VanAlstyne	1927-1949	395	232	163	.589
Alton S. Kircher	1949-1950	22	4	18	.182
Peter F. Newell	1950-1954	87	45	42	.517
Forrest A. Anderson	1954-1965	249	125	124	.502
John E. Benington	1965-1969	92	54	38	.587
Gus G. Ganakas	1969-1976	173	89	84	.514
George M. (Jud) Heathcote	1976-1995	560	340	220	.607
Thomas M. Izzo	1995-	91	55	36	.604
ALL-TIME	**1899-1998**	**2,064**	**1,171**	**893**	**.567**

MSU center Kevin Willis towers over forward Ben Tower, who almost appears to have been hatched.

Season by Season Breakdown

YEAR	G	W	L	PCT.	COACH	CAPTAINS
1898-99	2	0	2	.000	No Established Coach	No Captains Selected
1899-00	4	2	2	.500	Charles O. Bemies	No Captains Selected
1900-01	3	3	0	1.000	Charles O. Bemies	Charles Blanchard
1901-02	5	5	0	1.000	George E. Denman	James Cooper
1902-03	6	6	0	1.000	George E. Denman	Joseph Haftencamp
1903-04	8	5	3	.625	Chester L. Brewer	Edward Balbach
1904-05	8	5	3	.625	Chester L. Brewer	Foley Tuttle
1905-06	13	11	2	.846	Chester L. Brewer	No Captains Selected
1906-07	16	14	2	.875	Chester L. Brewer	Edward Krehl
1907-08	20	15	5	.750	Chester L. Brewer	Roy Vondette
1908-09	15	10	5	.667	Chester L. Brewer	Parnell McKerma
1909-10	15	10	5	.667	Chester L. Brewer	Claude Hannish
1910-11	14	5	9	.357	John F. Macklin	Fred Busch
1911-12	15	12	3	.800	John F. Macklin	Ralph Chamberlain
1912-13	13	8	5	.615	John F. Macklin	Robert Goss
1913-14	12	8	4	.667	John F. Macklin	George Gauthier
1914-15	16	7	9	.438	John F. Macklin	Oscar Miller
1915-16	16	8	8	.500	John F. Macklin	Lyman Frimodig
1916-17	16	11	5	.688	George E. Gauthier	Albert McClelland
1917-18	16	6	10	.375	George E. Gauthier	Byron Murray
1918-19	18	9	9	.500	George E. Gauthier	Lawrence Kurtz
1919-20	23	12	11	.522	George E. Gauthier	George Garrett
1920-21	21	13	8	.619	Lyman L. Frimodig	Walter Foster
1921-22	24	11	13	.458	Lyman L. Frimodig	Lloyd Heasley
1922-23	19	10	9	.526	Fred H. Walker	Clarence Fessenden
1923-24	20	10	10	.500	Fred H. Walker	Wesley Eva
1924-25	19	6	13	.316	John H. Kobs	Matt Nuttila
1925-26	18	5	13	.278	John H. Kobs	Paul Hackett
1926-27	18	7	11	.389	Benjamin F. VanAlstyne	Kenneth Drew
1927-28	15	11	4	.733	Benjamin F. VanAlstyne	Verne Dickeson
1928-29	16	11	5	.688	Benjamin F. VanAlstyne	Carl Felt
1929-30	16	12	4	.750	Benjamin F. VanAlstyne	James VanZylen
1930-31	17	16	1	.941	Benjamin F. VanAlstyne	Art Haga, Roger Grove, Edward Scott
1931-32	17	12	5	.706	Benjamin F. VanAlstyne	Dee Pineo
1932-33	17	10	7	.588	Benjamin F. VanAlstyne	Garold McCaslin, Alton Kircher
1933-34	17	12	5	.705	Benjamin F. VanAlstyne	Wendall Patchett
1934-35	18	14	4	.778	Benjamin F. VanAlstyne	Robert Herrick, Milo Rouse, Arnold VanFaasen
1935-36	17	8	9	.471	Benjamin F. VanAlstyne	Daniel Reck
1936-37	17	5	12	.294	Benjamin F. VanAlstyne	Ron Garlock
1937-38	17	9	8	.529	Benjamin F. VanAlstyne	Howard Kraft
1938-39	17	9	8	.529	Benjamin F. VanAlstyne	Leo Callahan
1939-40	20	14	6	.700	Benjamin F. VanAlstyne	Max Dalrymple, Martin Hutt
1940-41	17	11	6	.647	Benjamin F. VanAlstyne	Robert Phillips
1941-42	21	15	6	.714	Benjamin F. VanAlstyne	Chester Aubuchon
1942-43	16	2	14	.125	Benjamin F. VanAlstyne	Carl Petroski
1943-44 No Schedule — World War II						
1944-45	16	9	7	.588	Benjamin F. VanAlstyne	Nickolas Hashu
1945-46	21	12	9	.571	Benjamin F. VanAlstyne	Oliver White
1946-47	21	11	10	.524	Benjamin F. VanAlstyne	Robin Roberts
1947-48	22	12	10	.545	Benjamin F. VanAlstyne	Robert Brannum
1948-49	21	9	12	.429	Benjamin F. VanAlstyne	Robert Geahan, Jack Wulf

YEAR	G	W	L	PCT.	COACH	CAPTAINS
1949-50	22	4	18	.182	Alton S. Kircher	Robert Robbins
1950-51	21	10	11	.476	Peter F. Newell	James Snodgrass
1951-52	22	13	9	.591	Peter F. Newell	Clarence (Sonny) Means
1952-53	22	13	9	.591	Peter F. Newell	Erik Furseth
1953-54	22	9	13	.409	Peter F. Newell	Keith Stackhouse
1954-55	22	13	9	.591	Forrest A. Anderson	Albert Ferrari
1955-56	22	13	9	.591	Forrest A. Anderson	Walter Godfrey
1956-57	26	16	10	.615	Forrest A. Anderson	George Ferguson
1957-58	22	16	6	.727	Forrest A. Anderson	Jack Quiggle
1958-59	23	19	4	.826	Forrest A. Anderson	Robert Anderegg, John Green
1959-60	21	10	11	.476	Forrest A. Anderson	Lance Olson, Horace Walker
1960-61	24	7	17	.292	Forrest A. Anderson	David Fahs
1961-62	22	8	14	.381	Forrest A. Anderson	Arthur Schwarm
1962-63	20	4	16	.200	Forrest A. Anderson	John Lamers
1963-64	24	14	10	.583	Forrest A. Anderson	George (Pete) Gent
1964-65	23	5	18	.217	Forrest A. Anderson	Marcus Sanders
1965-66	22	15	7	.682	John E. Benington	William Curtis
1966-67	23	16	7	.696	John E. Benington	Matthew Aitch
1967-68	24	12	12	.500	John E. Benington	John Bailey
1968-69	23	11	12	.478	John E. Benington	Lee Lafayette
1969-70	24	9	15	.375	Gus G. Ganakas	James Gibbons, Lloyd Ward
1970-71	24	10	14	.417	Gus G. Ganakas	Rudy Benjamin
1971-72	24	13	11	.542	Gus G. Ganakas	Ronald Gutkowski, Pat Miller
1972-73	24	13	11	.542	Gus G. Ganakas	William Kilgore
1973-74	24	13	11	.542	Gus G. Ganakas	Michael Robinson
1974-75	26	17	9	.654	Gus G. Ganakas	Lindsay Hairston
1975-76	27	14	13	.518	Gus G. Ganakas	Terry Furlow
1976-77	27	12	15	.444	George M. "Jud" Heathcote	Robert Chapman
1977-78	30	25	5	.833	George M. "Jud" Heathcote	Robert Chapman, Greg Kelser
1978-79	32	26	6	.813	George M. "Jud" Heathcote	Earvin Johnson, Greg Kelser
1979-80	27	12	15	.444	George M. "Jud" Heathcote	Ron Charles, Terry Donnelly
1980-81	27	13	14	.481	George M. "Jud" Heathcote	Mike Brkovich, Jay Vincent
1981-82	28	12	16	.429	George M. "Jud" Heathcote	Kurt James, Kevin Smith
1982-83	30	17	13	.566	George M. "Jud" Heathcote	Bill Cawood, Derek Perry
1983-84	28	16	12	.571	George M. "Jud" Heathcote	Ben Tower, Kevin Willis
1984-85	29	19	10	.655	George M. "Jud" Heathcote	Sam Vincent, Richard Mudd
1985-86	31	23	8	.742	George M. "Jud" Heathcote	Scott Skiles, Larry Polec
1986-87	28	11	17	.393	George M. "Jud" Heathcote	Darryl Johnson, Barry Fordham
1987-88	28	10	18	.357	George M. "Jud" Heathcote	Ed Wright, Carlton Valentine, George Papadakos
1988-89	33	18	15	.545	George M. "Jud" Heathcote	Ken Redfield, Todd Wolfe
1989-90	34	28	6	.824	George M. "Jud" Heathcote	Steve Smith, Ken Redfield
1990-91	30	19	11	.633	George M. "Jud" Heathcote	Steve Smith, Matt Steigenga
1991-92	30	22	8	.733	George M. "Jud" Heathcote	Mark Montgomery, Matt Steigenga
1992-93	28	15	13	.536	George M. "Jud" Heathcote	Dwayne Stephens, Mike Peplowski
1993-94	32	20	12	.625	George M. "Jud" Heathcote	Kris Weshinskey, Shawn Respert
1994-95	28	22	6	.785	George M. "Jud" Heathcote	Eric Snow, Shawn Respert
1995-96	32	16	16	.500	Thomas M. Izzo	Quinton Brooks, Jamie Feick
1996-97	29	17	12	.586	Thomas M. Izzo	Antonio Smith, Steve Polonowski
1997-98	30	22	8	.733	Thomas M. Izzo	Antonio Smith, Mateen Cleaves
Totals	**2,064**	**1,171**	**893**	**.567**		

Big Names in Spartan History

ALL-AMERICA
Chester Aubuchon, G, 1940
Julius McCoy, F, 1956
Jack Quiggle, G, 1957
John Green, C, 1959
Horace Walker, C, 1960
Ralph Simpson, F, 1970
Michael Robinson, G, 1974
Terry Furlow, F, 1976
Earvin Jonnson, F, 1978
Earvin Johnson, G, 1979
Gregory Kelser, F, 1979
Sam Vincent, G, 1985
Scott Skiles, G, 1986
Steve Smith, G, 1990
Steve Smith, G, 1991
Shawn Respert, G, 1994
Shawn Respert, G, 1995
Mateen Cleaves, G, 1998

CHICAGO TRIBUNE SILVER BASKETBALL
John Green, C, 1959
Earvin Johnson, G, 1979
Scott Skiles, G, 1986
Steve Smith, G, 1990
Shawn Respert, G, 1995

BIG TEN PLAYER OF THE YEAR
(MEDIA or COACHES)*
Jay Vincent, C, 1981
Scott Skiles, G, 1986
Shawn Respert, G, 1995
Mateen Cleaves, G, 1998
*Player of the year selected under auspicies of
Associated Press and United Press from '86 to '89.

ALL-BIG TEN SELECTIONS
First Team
Julius McCoy, F, 1956
Jack Quiggle, G, 1957
John Green, C, 1957-58-59
Horace Walker, C, 1960
Stanley Washington, F, 1966
Lee Lafayette, C, 1969
Ralph Simpson, F, 1970
Michael Robinson, G, 1972-73-74
Lindsay Hairston, C, 1974-75
Terry Furlow, F, 1975-76
Earvin Johnson, F/G, 1978-79
Gregory Kelser, F, 1979
Jay Vincent, F, 1980-81
Kevin Smith, G, 1981-82
Sam Vincent, G, 1984-85
Scott Skiles, G, 1986
Steve Smith, G, 1990-91
Mike Peplowski, C, 1992
Shawn Respert, G, 1994-95
Mateen Cleaves, G, 1998

Second Team
Albert Ferrari, G, 1953-55

Julius McCoy, F, 1954
Robert Anderegg, F, 1958-59
Jack Quiggle, G, 1958
Lance Olson, F, 1960
George (Pete) Gent, F, 1964
Stanley Washington, F, 1965
William Curtis, C, 1966
Matthew Aitch, C, 1967
Lee Lafayette, C, 1967-68
Gregory Kelser, F, 1977-78
Kevin Smith, G, 1981
Sam Vincent, G, 1983
Scott Skiles, G, 1985
Darryl Johnson, G, 1986-87
Kirk Manns, G, 1990
Shawn Respert, G, 1993
Eric Snow, G, 1995
Quinton Brooks, F, 1996

Third Team
George (Pete) Gent, F, 1962-63
Stanley Washington, F, 1964
Kevin Smith, G, 1982
Kevin Willis, C, 1983
Sam Vincent, G, 1984
Darryl Johnson, G, 1986
Steve Smith, G, 1989
Shawn Respert, G, 1992
Mark Montgomery, G, 1992
Mike Peplowski, C, 1993
Jamie Feick, C, 1995
Antonio Smith, F, 1997-98

BIG TEN DEFENSIVE PLAYER OF THE YEAR
Ken Redfield, F, 1990
Eric Snow, G, 1995

MOST VALUABLE PLAYER AWARD
(By vote of team to receive Chicago Tribune Award)
1951—James Snodgrass
1952—William Bower
1953—Albert Ferrari
1954—Albert Ferrari
1955—Albert Ferrari
1956—Julius McCoy
1957—George Ferguson
1958—John Green
1959—John Green
1960—Horace Walker
1961—Arthur Schwarm
1962—George (Pete) Gent
1963—Edward (Ted) Williams
1964—Frederick Thomann
1965—Stanley Washington
1966—Stanley Washington
1967—Matthew Aitch
1968—Lee Lafayette
1969—Lee Lafayette
1970—Ralph Simpson
1971—William Kilgore
1972—William Kilgore

1973—William Kilgore
1974—Michael Robinson
1975—Lindsay Hairston
1976—Terry Furlow
1977—Robert Chapman
1978—Gregory Kelser
1979—Earvin Johnson
1980—Jay Vincent
1981—Jay Vincent
1982—Kevin Smith
1983—Sam Vincent
1984—Sam Vincent
1985—Sam Vincent
1986—Scott Skiles
1987—Darryl Johnson
1988—Carlton Valentine
1989—Steve Smith
1990—Steve Smith
1991—Steve Smith
1992—Dwayne Stephens
1993—Mike Peplowski
1994—Shawn Respert
1995—Shawn Respert
1996—Quinton Brooks
1997—Ray Weathers
1998 —Mateen Cleaves

BEST DEFENSIVE PLAYER AWARD
1977—James Coutre
1978—Robert Chapman
1979—Earvin Johnson
1980—Terry Donnelly
1981—Rick Kaye
1982—Ben Tower
1983—Ben Tower
1984—Ben Tower
1985—Richard Mudd
1986—Barry Fordham
1987—Vernon Carr
1988—Ed Wright
1989—Ken Redfield
1990—Ken Redfield
1991—Dwayne Stephens
1992—Mark Montgomery
1993—Dwayne Stephens
1994—Eric Snow
1995—Eric Snow
1996—Daimon Beathea
1997—Ray Weathers
1998—Charlie Bell
　　　Mateen Cleaves
　　　Antonio Smith

MOST VALUABLE PLAVER AWARD
(By vote of press, radio, and television representatives to receive Charles S. Phillips Award)
1951 —Ray Steffen
1952—William Bower
1953—Albert Ferrari
1954—Albert Ferrari
1955—Albert Ferrari

1956—Julius McCoy
1957—Jack Quiggle
1958—John Green
1959—John Green
1960—Horace Walker
1961—Arthur Schwarm
1962—George (Pete) Gent
1963—Edward (Ted) Williams
1964—George (Pete) Gent
1965—William Curtis
1966—Stanley Washington
1967—Matthew Aitch
1968—Lee Lafayette
1969—Lee Lafayette
1970—Ralph Simpson
1971—William Kilgore
1972—Michael Robinson
1973—Michael Robinson
1974—Michael Robinson
1975—Lindsay Hairston
1976—Terry Furlow
1977—Gregory Kelser
1978—Earvin Johnson
1979—Earvin Johnson,
　　　Gregory Kelser
1980—Jay Vincent
1981—Jay Vincent
1982—Kevin Smith
1983—Scott Skiles
1984—Sam Vincent
1985—Sam Vincent
1986—Scott Skiles
1987—Darryl Johnson
1988—Ken Redfield
1989—Steve Smith
1990—Steve Smith
1991—Steve Smith
1992—Mike Peplowski
1993—Shawn Respert
1994—Shawn Respert
1995—Shawn Respert
　　　Eric Snow
1996—Quinton Brooks
1997—Ray Weathers
1998—Mateen Cleaves

MOST IMPROVED PLAYER AWARD
1963—William Berry
1964—Stanley Washington
1965—Edward (Ted) Crary
1966—Matthew Aitch
1967—Heywood Edwards
1968—James Gibbons
1969—Tom Lick
1970—Rudy Benjamin
1971—Paul Dean
1972—Gary Ganakas
1973—Benny White
1974—Lindsay Hairston
1975—William Glover
1976—Dan Riewald

1977—Ronald Charles
1978—Michael Brkovich
1979—Terry Donnelly
1980—Ronald Charles
1981—Ben Tower
1982—Kevin Willis
1983—Kevin Willis
1984—Larry Polec
1985—Sam Vincent
1986—Darryl Johnson
1987—Carlton Valentine
1988—George Papadakos
1989—Kirk Manns
1990—Kirk Manns
1991—Mark Montgomery
1992—Dwayne Stephens
1993—Eric Snow
1994—Anthony Miller
1995—Jamie Feick
1996—Ray Weathers
1997—Antonio Smith
      Mateen Cleaves
1998—Morris Peterson
      Jason Klein

INSPIRATION AWARD

1963—William Schwarz
1964—Marcus Sanders
1965—John Shick
1966—Edward (Ted) Crary
1967—Edward (Ted) Crary
1968—Gerald Geistler

1969—John Holms
1970—Steve Kirkpatrick
1971—Ronald Gutkowski
1972—Ronald Gutkowski
1973—Gary Ganakas
1974—Robert (Joe) Shackleton
1975—Lovelle Rivers
1976—Benny White
1977—Edgar Wilson
1978—Dan Riewald,
      Alfred Brown
1979—Mike Longaker
1980—Mike Longaker
1981—Mike Brkovich
1982—Derek Perry
1983—Derek Perry
1984—Ben Tower
1985—Scott Skiles
1986—Larry Polec
1987—Barry Fordham
1988—Todd Wolfe
1989—Todd Wolfe
1990—Todd Wolfe
1991—Mike Peplowski
1992—Matt Steigenga
1993—Mike Peplowski
1994—Kris Weshinskey
*1995—Eric Snow
*1996—David Hart
*1997—Steve Polonowski
*1998—DuJuan Wiley
* Was the Sportsmanship Award up to 1995

CAPTAIN'S AWARD

(Presented by team to outgoing captain)
1978—Gregory Kelser
      Robert Chapman
1979—Earvin Johnson
      Gregory Kelser
1980—Ronald Charles
      Terry Donnelly
1981—Jay Vincent
      Mike Brkovich
1982—Kurt James
      Kevin Smith
1983—Derek Perry
      Bill Cawood
1984—Ben Tower
      Kevin Willis
1985—Richard Mudd
      Sam Vincent
1986—Scott Skiles
      Larry Polec
      Barry Fordham
1987—Darryl Johnson
      Barry Fordham
1988—George Papadakos
      Carlton Valentine
      Ed Wright
1989—Todd Wolfe
      Ken Redfield
1990— Ken Redfield
      Steve Smith
1991—Steve Smith
      Matt Steigenga

1992—Matt Steigenga
      Mark Montgomery
1993—Mike Peplowski
      Dwayne Stephens
1994—Kris Weshinskey
      Shawn Respert
1995—Shawn Respert
      Eric Snow
1996—Jamie Feick
      Quinton Brooks
1997—Steve Polonowski
1998—No Award Given

UNSUNG PLAYER AWARD

1989—Jim Sarkine
1990—Dave Mueller
1991—Jeff Casler
1992—Ron Haley
1993—Jon Zulauf
1994—Erik Qualman
1995—Mark Prylow
1996—Antonio Smith
1997— Morris Peterson
1998—Andre Hutson
      Jason Klein

The Spartan Spirits show the same enthusiasm we've seen in "Jud's Jungle" and "The Izzone."

Spartan Leaders at a Glance

SCORING
Based on total points (Since 1926-27)

Year	Name, Pos.	GP	TP	Avg.
1926-27	V. Dickeson, f	na	162	—
	Carl Felt, c	na	87	—
	Oliver Hood, g	na	67	—
1927-28	V. Dickeson, f	na	100	—
	Carl Felt, c	na	80	—
	Fred DenHerder, f	na	73	—
1928-29	Arthur Haga, g	na	99	—
	James Van Zylen, f	na	97	—
	Fred DenHerder, c/f	na	68	—
1929-30	Roger Grove, f	na	91	—
	Don Grove, f	na	86	—
	Edward Scott, g	na	72	—
1930-31	Roger Grove, f	na	135	—
	Arthur Haga, g	na	120	—
	Dee Pinneo, f	na	102	—
1931-32	Randy Boeskool, c	na	80	—
	Dee Pinneo, f	na	77	—
	William Vondette, g	na	73	—
1932-33	Gerald McCaslin, f	na	92	—
	Arnold Van Faasen, c	na	77	—
	Alton Kircher, g	na	63	—
1933-34	Maurice Buysse, c	na	126	—
	Robert Herrick, g	na	95	—
	Arnold Van Faasen, f	na	86	—
1934-35	Arnold Van Faasen, c	na	133	—
	Robert Herrck g	na	108	—
	Milo Rouse, g	na	108	—
1935-36	Ron Garlock, g	na	109	—
	Howard Kraft f	na	100	—
	Maurice Buysse, c	na	71	—
1936-37	Leonard Oesterink, f	na	112	—
	Ron Garlock, g/f	na	109	—
	Howard Kraft, f/g	na	91	—
1937-38	George Falkowski, f	na	173	—
	Martin Hutt, f	na	164	—
	Leo Callahan, g	na	96	—
1938-39	George Falkowski, f	na	119	—
	Leo Calahan, g	na	98	—
	Martin Hutt, f	na	90	—
	Chet Aubuchon, g	na	90	—
1939-40	Chet Aubuchon, g	na	169	—
	Martin Hutt, f	na	150	—
	Max Hindman, c	na	122	—
1940-41	Max Hindman, f	na	144	—
	Joe Gerard, f	na	100	—
	Bob Phillips, g	na	90	—
1941-42	Joe Gerard, f	na	239	—
	Chet Aubuchon, g/f	na	129	—
	Dudley Jones, f	na	118	—
1942-43	John Cawood, f	na	118	—
	Oliver White, f	na	89	—
	Dan Pjesky, g	na	89	—
1943-44	No team due to WW II			
1944-45	Sam Fortino, f	17	203	11.9
	Bill Rapchak, c	15	176	11.8
	Robin Roberts, f	13	138	10.6
1945-46	Sam Fortino, f	21	251	12.0
	Robin Roberts, f	21	206	9.8
	Oliver White, g	21	173	8.2
1946-47	Bob Geahan, f	21	235	11.2
	Robin Roberts, f	21	188	9.0
	Oliver White, g	21	176	8.4
1947-48	Bob Brannum, c	22	344	15.6
	Bob Geahan, f	22	164	7.5
	Bill Rapchak, f	22	140	6.4
1948-49	Bill Rapchak, f	20	211	10.6
	Jim Snodgrass, g	20	145	7.3
	John Granack, f	18	121	6.7
1949-50	Dan Smith, f	22	207	9.4
	Jim Snodgrass, g	22	204	9.3
	Bob Carey, c	20	175	8.8
1950-51	Ray Steffen, c	21	186	8.9
	Bob Carey, f/c	21	174	8.3
	Bill Bower, f	20	139	7.0
1951-52	Keith Stackhouse, f	20	236	11.8
	Gordon Stauffer, g	22	210	9.6
	Bill Bower, f	22	207	9.4
1952-53	Al Ferrari, f	22	351	16.0
	Keith Stackhouse, f	22	272	12.4
	Bob Armstrong, c	22	229	10.4
1953-54	Julius McCoy, f	22	409	18.6
	Al Ferrari, f/g	22	316	14.4
	Bob Armstrong, c	22	201	9.1
1954-55	Al Ferrari, f	22	442	20.1
	Julius McCoy, f	22	368	16.7
	Duane Peterson, c	22	287	13.1
1955-56	Julius McCoy, f	22	600	27.2
	Duane Peterson, c	22	216	9.8
	Walt Godfrey, g	19	176	9.2
1956-57	Jack Quiggle, g	25	384	15.3
	Larry Hedden, f	26	372	14.3
	George Ferguson, f	26	343	13.1
1957-58	John Green, c	22	397	18.0
	Larry Hedden, f	22	355	16.1
	Bob Anderegg, f	22	319	14.5
1958-59	Bob Anderegg, f	23	450	19.5
	John Green, c	23	427	18.5
	Horace Walker, f/c	23	307	13.3
1959-60	Horace Walker, f/c	21	473	22.6
	Lance Olson, f	21	390	18.5
	Dave Fahs, g	21	252	12.0
1960-61	Dick Hall, f/c	24	390	16.2
	Art Schwarm, g	23	348	15.1
	Dave Fahs, g	23	318	13.8
1961-62	Pete Gent, f	22	311	14.1
	Art Schwarm, g	22	273	12.4
	Lonnie Sanders, f	20	219	10.9
1962-63	Pete Gent, f	20	329	16.4
	Marcus Sanders, f	20	295	14.7
	Ted Williams, c	13	212	18.0
1963-64	Pete Gent, f	24	506	21.0
	Fred Thomann, c	23	359	15.5
	Stan Washington, f	24	355	14.8
1964-65	Stan Washington, f	23	490	21.3
	Bill Curtis, f	23	447	19.4
	Marcus Sanders, f	23	427	18.5
1965-66	Stan Washington, f	22	397	18.0
	Bill Curtis, f	22	361	16.4
	Matthew Aitch, c	22	303	13.8
1966-67	Matthew Aitch, c	23	376	16.3
	Lee Lafayette, c/f	23	341	14.8
	Steve Rymal, g	23	251	11.4
1967-68	Lee Lafayette, c/f	24	405	16.8
	Heywood Edwards, f/c	24	235	9.7
	John Bailey, g	22	224	10.1
1968-69	Lee Lafayette, c/f	23	430	18.7
	Jim Gibbons, f	23	246	10.7
	Bernie Copeland, f	23	236	10.2
1969-70	Ralph Simpson, g	23	667	29.0
	Rudy Benjamin, g	24	302	12.5
	Jim Gibbons, f	24	246	10.2
1970-71	Rudy Benjamin, g	24	520	21.2
	Bill Kilgore, c	24	341	14.2
	Pat Miller, f/g	24	273	11.3
1971-72	Mike Robinson, g	24	594	24.7
	Bill Kilgore, c	24	357	14.8
	Pat Miller, f/g	24	221	9.2
1972-73	Mike Robinson, g	24	608	25.3
	Bill Kilgore, c	24	401	16.7
	Allen Smith, f	24	282	11.7
1973-74	Mike Robinson, g	23	515	22.4
	Lindsay Hairston, c	24	396	16.5
	Terry Furlow, f	24	339	14.1
1974-75	Terry Furlow, f	25	509	20.4
	Lindsay Hairston, c	25	482	19.3
	Bill Glover, g	25	301	12.0
1975-76	Terry Furlow, f	27	793	29.4
	Bob Chapman, g	27	395	14.6
	Gregory Kelser, f	27	316	11.7
1976-77	Gregory Kelser, f	26	565	21.7
	Bob Chapman, g	27	529	19.6
	Edgar Wilson, f	27	248	9.2
1977-78	Gregory Kelser, f	30	531	17.7
	Earvin Johnson, g/f	30	511	17.0
	Bob Chapman, g	30	369	12.3
1978-79	Gregory Kelser, f	32	602	18.8
	Earvin Johnson, g/f	32	548	17.1
	Jay Vincent, c/f	31	394	12.7
1979-80	Jay Vincent, c/f	27	582	21.6
	Ron Charles, f	27	392	14.5
	Mike Brkovich, g/f	27	238	8.8
	Terry Donnelly, g	27	238	8.8
1980-81	Jay Vincent, c/f	27	609	22.6
	Kevin Smith, g	27	364	13.5
	Mike Brkovich, g/f	25	206	8.2
1981-82	Kevin Smith, g	28	436	15.6
	Sam Vincent, g	28	328	11.7
	Derek Perry, f	28	241	8.6
1982-83	Sam Vincent, g	30	498	16.6
	Scott Skiles, g	30	376	12.5
	Kevin Willis, c	27	360	13.3
1983-84	Scott Skiles, g	28	405	14.5
	Sam Vincent, g	23	359	15.6
	Kevin Willis, c	25	275	11.0
1984-85	Sam Vincent, g	29	666	23.0
	Scott Skiles, g	29	514	17.7
	Ken Johnson, c	28	301	10.8
1985-86	Scott Skiles, g	31	850	27.4
	Darryl Johnson, g	29	482	16.6
	Vernon Carr, f/g	31	427	13.8

Year	Name, Pos.	GP	TP	Avg.
1986-87	Darryl Johnson, g	28	618	22.1
	Vernon Carr, g/f	28	386	13.8
	Carlton Valentine, f	28	311	11.1
1987-88	Carlton Valentine, f	28	371	13.3
	Ken Redfield, f	28	327	11.7
	Steve Smith, g	28	299	10.7
1988-89	Steve Smith, g	33	585	17.7
	Ken Redfield, f	33	458	13.9
	Kirk Manns, g	33	394	11.9
1989-90	Steve Smith, g	31	627	20.2
	Kirk Manns, g	31	475	15.3
	Ken Redfield, f	34	394	11.6
1990-91	Steve Smith, g	30	752	25.1
	Matt Steigenga, f	30	379	12.6
	Mike Peplowski, c	30	232	7.7
1991-92	Shawn Respert, g	30	474	15.8
	Mike Peplowski, c	30	400	13.3
	Dwayne Stephens, f	30	333	11.1
1992-93	Shawn Respert, g	28	563	20.1
	Mike Peplowski, c	28	406	14.5
	Kris Weshinskey, g	27	281	10.4
1993-94	Shawn Respert, g	32	778	24.3
	Anthony Miller, c	32	402	12.6
	Quinton Brooks, f	32	363	11.3
1994-95	Shawn Respert, g	28	716	25.6
	Quinton Brooks, f	28	315	11.3
	Eric Snow, g	28	303	10.8
1995-96	Quinton Brooks, f	31	505	16.3
	Jamie Feick, c	32	323	10.1
	Ray Weathers, g	31	302	9.7
1996-97	Ray Weathers, g	29	395	13.6
	Jon Garavaglia, f	29	303	10.5
	Mateen Cleaves, g	29	297	10.2
1997-98	Mateen Cleaves, g	30	484	16.1
	Jason Klein, f	30	337	11.2
	Charlie Bell, g	30	276	9.2

REBOUNDING
Based on Total Rebounds (Since 1955-56)

Year	Name, Pos.	GP	TP	Avg.
1955-56	Julius McCoy, f	22	219	10.0
	Duane Peterson, c	22	201	9.1
	George Ferguson, g/f	22	190	8.6
1956-57	John Green, c	18	262	14.6
	Larry Hedden, f	26	202	7.8
	George Ferguson, f	26	152	5.8
1957-58	John Green, c	22	392	17.8
	Larry Hedden, f	22	175	8.0
	Bob Anderegg, f	22	138	6.3
1958-59	John Green, c	23	382	16.6
	Horace Walker, f/c	23	312	13.5
	Bob Anderegg, f	23	189	8.2
1959-60	Horace Walker, f/c	21	373	17.7
	Lance Olson, f	21	246	11.7
	Art Gowens, f/c	8	93	11.6
1960-61	Ted Williams, c	24	288	12.0
	Dick Hall, f/c	24	218	9.0
	Jack Lamers, f/g	22	124	5.6
1961-62	Pete Gent, f	22	206	9.3
	Lonnie Sanders, f	20	115	5.7
	Ted Williams, c	21	105	5.0
1962-63	Bill Berry, f	20	184	9.2
	Pete Gent, f	20	152	7.6
	Ted Williams, c	13	136	10.4
1963-64	Stan Washington, f	24	245	10.2
	Fred Thomann, c	23	216	9.4
	Pete Gent, f	24	193	9.0

Year	Name, Pos.	GP	TP	Avg.
1964-65	Stan Washington, f	23	248	10.7
	Bill Curtis, f	23	232	10.0
	Marcus Sanders, f	23	141	6.1
1965-66	Stan Washington, f	22	234	10.6
	Bill Curtis, f	22	204	9.3
	Matthew Aitch, c	22	193	8.8
1966-67	Lee Lafayette, c/f	23	223	9.7
	Matthew Aitch, c	23	212	9.2
	Steve Rymal, g	23	109	4.7
1967-68	Lee Lafayette, c/f	24	253	10.5
	Bernie Copeland, f	23	159	6.9
	Heywood Edwards, g	24	150	6.2
1968-69	Lee Lafayette, c/f	23	237	10.3
	Bernie Copeland, f	23	159	6.9
	Jim Gibbons, f	23	132	5.7
1969-70	Ralph Simpson, g	23	239	10.3
	Jim Gibbons, f	24	174	7.2
	Ron Gutkowski, f	24	138	5.7
1970-71	Bill Kilgore, c/f	24	309	12.8
	Pat Miller, g/f	24	124	5.1
	Rudy Benjamin, g	24	95	3.9
	Brian Breslin, f	24	95	3.9
1971-72	Bill Kilgore, c/f	24	266	11.1
	Allen Smith, f	24	135	5.6
	Pat Miller, g/f	24	130	5.4
1972-73	Bill Kilgore, c/f	24	239	9.9
	Lindsay Hairston, c	24	190	7.9
	Allen Smith, f	24	154	6.4
1973-74	Lindsay Hairston, c	24	326	13.6
	Terry Furlow, f	24	171	7.1
1974-75	Lindsay Hairston, c	25	287	11.5
	Terry Furlow, f	25	171	6.8
	Jeff Tropf, f	25	135	5.4
1975-76	Gregory Kelser, f	27	260	9.5
	Terry Furlow, f	27	207	7.7
	Edgar Wilson, f	25	134	5.4
1976-77	Gregory Kelser, f	26	280	10.8
	Jim Coutre, c/f	27	147	5.4
	Edgar Wilson, f	27	127	4.7
1977-78	Gregory Kelser, f	30	274	9.1
	Earvin Johnson, g/f	30	237	7.9
	Ron Charles, f/c	30	120	4.0
1978-79	Gregory Kelser, f	32	278	8.7
	Earvin Johnson, g/f	32	234	7.3
	Ron Charles, f/c	32	162	5.1
1979-80	Ron Charles, f/c	27	241	8.9
	Jay Vincent, f/c	27	209	7.7
	Mike Brkovich, g/f	27	74	2.7
1980-81	Jay Vincent, c/f	27	229	8.5
	Derek Perry, f	27	104	3.9
	Ben Tower, f	27	103	3.8
1981-82	Derek Perry, f	28	151	5.4
	Ben Tower, f	28	129	4.6
	Kevin Willis, c	27	113	4.2
1982-83	Kevin Willis, c	27	258	9.6
	Ben Tower, f	30	141	4.7
	Derek Perry, f	30	116	3.9
1983-84	Kevin Willis, c	25	192	7.7
	Ken Jonnson, f	19	132	6.9
	Ben Tower, f	27	123	4.5
1984-85	Ken Johnson, c	28	285	10.2
	Richard Mudd, f	27	147	5.5
	Larry Polec, f	29	126	4.4
1985-86	Larry Polec, f	31	178	5.7
	Vernon Carr, f/g	31	167	5.4
	Scott Skiles, g	31	135	4.4
1986-87	Carlton Valentine, f	28	157	5.6
	Barry Fordham, f	28	135	4.8
	Vernon Carr, f/g	28	125	4.5

Year	Name, Pos.	GP	TP	Avg.
1987-88	George Papadakos, c	25	142	5.7
	Carlton Valentine, f	28	157	5.6
	Ken Redfield, f	28	143	5.1
1988-89	Steve Smith, g	33	229	6.9
	Ken Redfield, f	33	225	6.8
	Matt Steigenga, f	33	149	4.5
1989-90	Steve Smith, g	31	216	7.0
	Ken Redfield, f	34	232	6.8
	Mike Peplowski, c	28	162	5.8
1990-91	Mike Peplowski, c	30	206	6.9
	Steve Smith, g	30	183	6.1
	Matt Steigenga, f	30	148	4.9
1991-92	Mike Peplowski, c	30	259	8.6
	Anthony Miller, c	30	156	5.2
	Dwayne Stephens, f	30	150	5.0
1992-93	Mike Peplowski, c	28	279	10.0
	Dwayne Stephens, f	28	156	5.6
	Anthony Miller, f	27	139	5.2
1993-94	Anthony Miller, c	32	287	9.0
	Quinton Brooks, f	32	142	4.4
	Shawn Respert, g	32	127	4.0
1994-95	Jamie Feick, c	28	281	10.1
	Quinton Brooks, f	28	145	5.2
	Jon Garavaglia, f	28	143	5.1
1995-96	Jamie Feick, c	32	303	9.5
	Quinton Brooks, f	31	175	5.7
	Jon Garavaglia, f	31	140	4.5
1996-97	Antonio Smith, f	29	306	10.6
	Jon Garavaglia, f	29	170	5.9
	Morris Peterson, f	29	97	3.4
1997-98	Antonio Smith, f	30	262	8.7
	Andre Hutson, f	30	156	5.2
	Charlie Bell, g	30	133	4.4

FIELD GOAL PERCENTAGE—
Minimum 100 attempts (Since 1946-47)

Year	Name, Pos.	GP	TP	Avg.
1946-47	Robin Roberts, f	81	208	.389
	John Cawood, f	43	113	.381
	Bob Geahan, f	87	247	.352
1947-48	Bob Brannum, c	124	319	.389
	Bill Rapchak, g	59	193	.306
	Bob Robbins, g	48	174	.276
1948-49	John Granack, f	42	116	.362
	Bill Rapchak, g	89	240	.357
	Jack Wulf, c	42	121	.347
1949-50	Bob Carey, c	65	145	.448
	Jim Snodgrass, g	77	240	.321
	Bill Rapchak, f	64	221	.290
1950-51	Sonny Means, g	39	103	.378
	Bill Bower, f	48	143	.336
	Ray Steffen, c	74	231	.321
1951-52	Gordon Stauffer, g	77	211	.365
	Sonny Means, g	41	116	.352
	Keith Stackhouse, f	84	244	.345
1952-53	Bob Armstrong, c	96	253	.379
	Al Ferrari, f	114	328	.348
	Keith Stackhouse, f	96	276	.348
1953-54	Bob Devenny, g	53	141	.376
	Julius McCoy, c	136	379	.359
	Bob Armstrong, c	76	228	.333
1954-55	Duane Peterson, c	107	229	.467
	Bob Devenny, g	80	195	.410
	Bob Armstrong, c	53	132	.402
1955-56	Julius McCoy, f	228	538	.423
	Jack Quiggle, g/f	59	149	.396
	Walt Godfrey, g	70	179	.391

1956-57	George Ferguson, f	137	320	.428
	Jack Quiggle, g	142	355	.400
	John Green, c	96	247	.389
1957-58	John Green, c	164	320	.512
	Bob Anderegg, f	123	304	.404
	Larry Hedden, f	154	407	.378
1958-59	Lance Olson, f	96	224	.428
	John Green, c	168	393	.427
	Tom Rand, g	57	134	.425
1959-60	Dave Fahs, g	108	250	.432
	Horace Walker, f/c 177	413	.428	
	Lance Olson, f	150	365	.410
1960-61	Jack Lamers, f/g	84	190	.422
	Dick Hall, f/c	143	339	.421
	Art Schwarm, g	135	376	.359
1961-62	Bill Schwarz, g	71	171	.415
	Pete Gent, f	124	314	.395
	Lonnie Sanders, f	95	246	.386
1962-63	Bill Schwarz, g	67	160	.419
	Pete Gent, f	128	313	.408
	Fred Thomann, c	50	123	.407
1963-64	Fred Thomann, c	145	302	.480
	Stan Washington, f	144	310	.464
	Bill Berry, f	71	155	.458
1964-65	Stan Washington, f	185	390	.474
	Bill Curtis, f	175	378	.462
	Ted Crary, f	83	189	.439
1965-66	Bill Curtis, f	149	306	.487
	Stan Washington, f	153	323	.474
	Matthew Aitch, c	128	285	.449
1966-67	Heywood Edwards, g	59	124	.476
	John Bailey, g	72	164	.439
	Matthew Aitch, c	152	353	.430
1967-68	John Bailey, g	86	186	.462
	Heywood Edwards, g	99	225	.440
	Lee Lafayette, c/f	149	339	.439
1968-69	Lee Lafayette, c/f	155	335	.436
	Jim Gibbons, f	88	202	.435
	Bernie Copeland, f	99	241	.411
1969-70	Pat Miller, g/f	83	158	.525
	Jim Gibbons, f	96	208	.461
	Rudy Benjamin, g	118	262	.450
1970-71	Bill Kilgore, f/c	134	256	.523
	Pat Miller, g/f	122	247	.493
	Brian Breslin, f	72	153	.471
1971-72	Bill Kilgore, f/c	142	244	.581
	Allen Smith, f	94	195	.482
	Pat Miller, g/f	91	198	.459
1972-73	Bill Kilgore, f/c	163	284	.574
	Mike Robinson, g	259	536	.483
	Allen Smith, f	128	265	.483
1973-74	Bill Glover, g	69	119	.580
	Lindsay Hairston, c	167	323	.517
	Terry Furlow, f	150	297	.505
1974-75	Bill Glover, g	124	227	.546
	Lindsay Hairston, c	200	373	.536
	Terry Furlow, f	205	391	.524
1975-76	Gregory Kelser, f	136	264	.517
	Edgar Wilson, f	67	131	.511
	Bob Chapman, g	166	349	.476
1976-77	Terry Donnelly, g	87	163	.534
	Bob Chapman, g	220	413	.533
	Jim Coutre, f/c	62	122	.508
1977-78	Gregory Kelser, f	221	362	.610
	Ron Charles, f/c	71	122	.582
	Jay Vincent, f/c	137	239	.573
1978-79	Ron Charles, f/c	115	173	.665
	Gregory Kelser, f	246	451	.545
	Terry Donnelly, g	83	155	.535
1979-80	Ron Charles, f/c	169	250	.676
	Jay Vincent, f/c	233	451	.517
	Terry Donnelly, g	89	186	.478
1980-81	Derek Perry, f	83	138	.601
	Ben Tower, f	61	104	.587
	Kevin Smith, g	145	266	.545
1981-82	Derek Perry, f	99	200	.495
	Kevin Willis, c	73	154	.474
	Sam Vincent, g	130	282	.461
1982-83	Kevin Willis, c	162	272	.596
	Patrick Ford, g/f	55	108	.509
	Ben Tower, f	74	149	.497
1983-84	Ben Tower, f	63	110	.573
	Larry Polec, f	64	122	.525
	Sam Vincent, g	130	261	.498
1984-85	Ken Johnson, c	128	212	.604
	Larry Polec, f	103	180	.572
	Sam Vincent, g	245	450	.544
1985-86	Carlton Valentine, f	80	123	.650
	Darryl Johnson, g	216	371	.582
	Vernon Carr, f/g	168	300	.560
	Larry Polec, f	130	232	.560
1986-87	Carlton Valentine, f	135	217	.622
	Darryl Johnson, g	247	467	.529
	Vernon Carr, f/g	144	285	.505
1987-88	George Papadakos, c	102	157	.650
	Carlton Valentine, f	155	272	.570
	Ken Redfield, f	136	265	.513
1988-89	Matt Steigenga, f	115	206	.558
	Kirk Manns, g	139	260	.535
	Parish Hickman, f	68	134	.508
1989-90	Matt Steigenga, f	138	235	.587
	Mike Peplowski, c	60	110	.546
	Parish Hickman, f	85	156	.545
1990-91	Mike Peplowski, c	99	158	.627
	Matt Steigenga, f	148	282	.525
	Dwayne Stephens, f	61	123	.496
1991-92	Mike Peplowski, c	168	266	.632
	Anthony Miller, c	83	154	.539
	Dwayne Stephens, f	125	234	.534
1992-93	Mike Peplowski, c	161	252	.639
	Anthony Miller, f	76	124	.613
	Shawn Respert, g	192	399	.481
1993-94	Anthony Miller, c	162	249	.651
	Quinton Brooks, f	153	287	.533
	Eric Snow, g	91	177	.514
1994-95	Jamie Feick, c	111	180	.617
	Quinton Brooks, f	134	252	.532
	Eric Snow, g	117	225	.520
1995-96	Quinton Brooks, f	195	346	.564
	Antonio Smith, f	56	120	.467
	Jamie Feick, c	116	268	.433
1996-97	Antonio Smith, f	92	163	.564
	Thomas Kelley, g	80	165	.485
	Ray Weathers, g	139	305	.456
1997-98	DuJuan Wiley, c	78	125	.624
	Andre Hutson, f	87	142	.613
	David Thomas, g	38	81	.469

FREE THROW PERCENTAGE—

Minimum 50 Attempts (Since 1946-47)

Year	Name,Pos.	GP	TP	Avg.
1946-47	Bob Geahan, f	61	93	.656
	Oliver White, g	44	75	.587
	John Cawood, f	29	54	.537
1947-48	Bob Brannum, c	96	156	.615
	Bob Geahan, f	38	70	.543
	Bob Robbins, g	27	53	.509
1948-49	John Granack, f	37	60	.617
	Bob Robbins, g	31	55	.564
	Jack Wulf, c	36	64	.563
1949-50	Jim Snodgrass, g	50	72	.694
	Bill Rapchak, f	35	55	.636
	Dan Smith, f	37	61	.607
1950-51	Bob Carey, f/c	54	79	.683
	Gordon Stauffer, g	35	53	.661
	Bill Bower, f	43	67	.641
1951-52	Gordon Stauffer, g	56	69	.810
	Bill Bower, f	53	74	.717
	Bob Carey, c	46	74	.621
1952-53	Al Ferrari, f	123	178	.691
	Keith Stackhouse, f	78	125	.624
	Bob Armstrong, c	37	64	.587
1953-54	Bob Armstrong, c	49	65	.754
	Julius McCoy, f	137	187	.733
	Keith Stackhouse, g	46	66	.697
1954-55	Al Ferrari, f	152	192	.792
	Duane Peterson, c	73	109	.670
	Bob Armstrong, c	62	93	.667
1955-56	George Ferguson f/g	65	93	.699
	Julius McCoy, f	144	214	.673
	Larry Hedden, f/c	54	83	.651
1956-57	Jack Quiggle, g	100	140	.714
	George Ferguson, f	69	97	.711
	Larry Hedden, f	78	122	,639
1957-58	Jack Quiggle, g	75	104	.721
	Bob Anderegg, f	73	118	.619
	Larry Hedden, f	47	77	.610
1958-59	Horace Walker, f/c	69	96	.719
	Lance Olson, f	55	81	.679
	Bob Anderegg, f	122	203	.600
1959-60	Horace Walker, f/c	119	149	.798
	Lance Olson, f	90	132	.681
	Art Gowens, f	51	75	.680
1960-61	Dick Hall, f/c	104	130	.800
	Art Schwarm, g	78	101	.772
	Dave Fahs, g	76	102	.745
1961-62	Jack Lamers, f/c	51	67	.761
	Pete Gent, f	63	83	.759
	Art Schwarm, g	57	82	.695
1962-63	Jack Lamers, f/g	47	61	.770
	Ted Williams, c	70	92	.761
	Marcus Sanders, f	73	97	.753
1963-64	Bill Schwarz, g	40	51	.784
	Stan Washington, f	67	86	.779
	Marcus Sanders, f	78	108	.722
1964-65	Stan Washington, f	120	141	.851
	Bill Curtis, f	97	124	.782
	Marcus Sanders, f	105	138	.761
1965-66	Stan Washington, f	91	114	.798
	Bill Curtis, f	63	83	.759
	Steve Rymal, g	44	60	.733
1966-67	Steve Rymal, g	49	71	.690
	John Bailey, g	40	59	.678
	Matthew Aitch, c	72	111	.649
1967-68	Harrison Stepter, g	44	54	.815
	John Bailey, g	52	71	.732
	Lee Lafayette, f/c	107	161	.664
1968-69	Jim Gibbons, f	79	98	.714
	Lloyd Ward, g	37	54	.685
	Harrison Stepter, g	45	68	.662
1969-70	Ralph Simpson, g	139	169	.822
	Lloyd Ward, g	50	62	.806
	Jim Gibbons, f	54	73	.740
1970-71	Rudy Benjamin, g	116	160	.725
	Ron Gutkowski, f	37	54	.685
	Bill Kilgore, f/c	73	111	.658

Year	Name, Pos.			
1971-72	Mike Robinson, g	104	147	.707
	Pat Miller, g/f	39	56	.696
	Gary Ganakas, g	41	63	.651
1972-73	Mike Robinson, g	90	113	.796
	Lindsay Hairston t/c	35	54	.648
	Bill Kilgore, f/c	75	117	.641
1973-74	Mike Robinson, g	99	128	.773
	Terry Furlow, f	39	59	.661
	Lindsay Hairston, c	62	96	.646
1974-75	Terry Furlow, f	99	120	.825
	Bill Glover, g	53	65	.815
	Benny White, g	57	71	.803
1975-76	Terry Furlow, f	177	202	.876
	Bob Chapman, g	63	77	.818
	Edgar Wilson, f	59	76	.776
1976-77	Terry Donnelly, g	40	52	.769
	Edgar Wilson, f	46	63	.730
	Bob Chapman, g	89	124	.717
1977-78	Bob Chapman, g	65	81	.802
	Terry Donnelly, g	41	52	.788
	Earvin Johnson, g/f	161	205	.785
1978-79	Earvin Johnson, g/f	202	240	.842
	Mike Brkovich, g/f	53	66	.803
	Terry Donnelly, g	46	61	.754
1979-80	Terry Donnelly, g	60	68	.882
	Mike Brkovich, g/f	50	67	.746
	Kevin Smith, g	50	69	.725
1980-81	Mike Brkovich, g/f	56	65	.862
	Kevin Smith, g	74	101	.733
	Derek Perry, f	36	50	.720
1981-82	Sam Vincent, g	68	91	.747
	Kevin Smith, g	76	106	.717
	Derek Perry, f	43	60	.716
1982-83	Scott Skiles, g	69	83	.831
	Sam Vincent, g	133	172	.773
	Derek Perry, f	60	81	.741
1983-84	Scott Skiles, g	99	119	.832
	Sam Vincent, g	99	122	.811
	Larry Polec, f	40	51	.784
1984-85	Sam Vincent, g	176	208	.846
	Larry Polec, f	46	56	.821
	Scott Skiles, g	90	114	.790
1985-86	Scott Skiles, g	188	209	.900
	Larry Polec, f	70	82	.854
	Darryl Johnson, g	50	63	.794
1986-87	Darryl Johnson, g	111	122	.910
	Barry Fordham, f	53	67	.791
	Vernon Carr, f/g	87	113	.770
1987-88	Steve Smith, g	69	91	.758
	George Papadakos, c	49	68	.721
	Carlton Valentine, f	61	89	.685
1988-89	Kirk Manns, g	47	56	.839
	Steve Smith, g	129	169	.763
	Matt Steigenga, f	57	77	.740
1989-90	Kirk Manns, g	70	81	.864
	Matt Steigenga, f	74	95	.779
	Steve Smith, g	116	167	.695
1990-91	Steve Smith, g	150	187	.802
	Matt Steigenga, f	70	100	.700
	Mike Peplowski, c	34	50	.680
1991-92	Shawn Respert, g	68	78	.872
	Dwayne Stephens, f	64	86	.744
	Mike Peplowski, c	64	93	.688
1992-93	Shawn Respert, g	119	139	.856
	Mike Peplowski, c	84	126	.667
	Dwayne Stephens, f	39	59	.661
1993-94	Shawn Respert, g	142	169	.840
	Quinton Brooks, f	54	70	.771
	Anthony Miller, c	78	136	.574
1994-95	Shawn Respert, g	139	160	.869
	Quinton Brooks, f	46	75	.613
	Eric Snow, g	62	102	.608
1995-96	Thomas Kell]ey, g	45	57	.790
	Quinton Brooks, f	114	152	.750
	Ray Weathers, g	59	86	.686
1996-97	Mateen Cleaves, g	57	79	.722
	Thomas Kelley, g	62	86	.721
	Morris Peterson, f	36	51	.706
1997-98	Charlie Bell, g	69	87	.793
	Andre Hutson, f	52	69	.754
	Mateen Cleaves, g	111	158	.703

ASSISTS
Based on total assists (Since 1975-76)

Year	Name, Pos.	GP	TP	Avg.
1975-76	Benny White, g	27	106	3.9
	Terry Furlow, f	27	87	3.2
	Bob Chapman, g	27	55	2.0
1976-77	Edgar Wilson, f/g	27	93	3.4
	Terry Donnelly, g	27	93	3.4
	Gregory Kelser, f	26	67	2.6
1977-78	Earvin Jonnson, g/f	30	222	7.4
	Terry Donnelly, g	30	72	2.4
	Bob Chapman, g	30	61	2.0
1978-79	Earvin Johnson, g/f	32	269	8.4
	Terry Donnelly, g	32	63	2.0
	Gregory Kelser, f	32	56	1.8
1979-80	Mike Brkovich, g/f	27	96	3.6
	Terry Donnelly, g	27	93	3.4
	Kevin Smith, g	27	93	3.4
1980-81	Kevin Smith, g	27	130	4.8
	Mike Brkovich, g/f	25	60	2.4
	Jay Vincent, f/c	27	50	1.9
1981-82	Kevin Smith, g	28	126	4.5
	Sam Vincent, g	28	55	2.0
	Derek Perry, f	28	38	1.4
1982-83	Scott Skiles, g	30	146	4.2
	Sam Vincent, g	30	66	2.2
	Ben Tower, f	30	51	1.7
1983-84	Scott Skiles, g	28	128	4.6
	Sam Vincent, g	23	68	2.9
	Ben Tower, f	27	38	1.4
1984-85	Scott Skiles, g	29	168	5.8
	Sam Vincent, g	29	117	4.0
	Larry Polec, f	29	28	1.0
	Darryl Johnson, g	22	28	1.3
1985-86	Scott Skiles, g	31	203	6.5
	Darryl Johnson, g	29	116	4.0
	Vernon Carr, f/g	31	95	3.1
1986-87	Darryl Johnson, g	28	112	4.0
	Vernon Carr, f/g	28	94	3.4
	Ed Wright, g/f	28	61	2.2
1987-88	Ed Wright, g	28	91	3.3
	Steve Smith, g	28	82	2.9
	Ken Redfield, f	28	64	2.3
1988-89	Ken Redfield, f	33	131	4.0
	Steve Smith, g	33	112	3.4
	Mark Montgomery, g	33	105	3.2
1989-90	Steve Smith, g	31	150	4.8
	Ken Redfield, f	34	106	3.1
	Mark Montgomery, g	34	97	2.9
1990-91	Mark Montgomery, g	29	169	5.8
	Steve Smith, g	30	109	3.6
	Matt Steigenga, f	30	63	2.1
1991-92	Mark Montgomery, g	30	190	6.3
	Dwayne Stephens, f	30	85	2.8
	Shawn Respert, g	30	62	2.1

Year	Name, Pos.	GP	TP	Avg.
1992-93	Eric Snow, g	28	145	5.2
	Dwayne Stephens, f	28	97	3.5
	Shawn Respert, g	28	73	2.6
1993-94	Eric Snow, g	32	213	6.7
	Shawn Respert, g	32	81	2.5
	Kris Weshinskey, g	32	73	2.3
1994-95	Eric Snow, g	28	217	7.8
	Shawn Respert, g	28	85	3.0
1995-96	Thomas Kelley, g	32	114	3.6
	Ray Weathers, g	31	70	2.3
	Jamie Feick, c	32	75	2.3
1996-97	Mateen Cleaves, g	29	146	5.0
	Thomas Kelley, g	29	62	2.1
	Ray Weathers, g	29	59	2.0
1997-98	Mateen Cleaves, g	30	217	7.2
	Charlie Bell, g	30	40	1.3
	Jason Klein, f	30	38	1.2

STEALS
Based on total steals (Since 1977-78)

Year	Name, Pos.	GP	TP	Avg.
1977-78	Earvin Johnson, g	30	71	2.3
	Greg Kelser, f	30	47	1.6
	Bob Chapman	30	45	1.5
1978-79	Earvin Johnson, g	32	75	2.3
	Greg Kelser, f	32	53	1.6
1979-80	Kevin Smith, g	27	46	1.7
	Ron Charles, f/c	27	30	1.1
	Mike Brkovich, g/f	27	29	1.1
1980-81	Kevin Smith, g	27	38	1.4
	Jay Vincent, f/c	27	26	1.0
1981-82	Sam Vincent, g	28	41	1.5
	Kevin Smith, g	28	39	1.4
	Ben Tower, f	28	14	0.5
1982-83	Sam Vincent, g	30	44	1.5
	Scott Skiles, g	30	33	1.1
	Kevin Willis, c	27	27	1.0
1983-84	Scott Skiles, g	28	40	1.4
	Sam Vincent, g	23	32	1.4
	Darryl Johnson, g	28	25	0.9
1984-85	Scott Skiles, g	29	48	1.7
	Sam Vincent, g	29	42	1.4
	Larry Polec, f	29	21	0.7
1985-86	Scott Skiles, g	31	54	1.7
	Darryl Johnson, g	29	42	1.4
	Larry Polec, f	31	21	0.7
1986-87	Darryl Johnson, g	28	60	2.1
	Ed Wright, g/f	28	22	0.8
	Barry Fordham, f	28	15	0.5
1987-88	Ken Redfield, f	28	50	1.8
	Ed Wright, g	28	34	1.2
	Steve Smith, g	28	27	1.0
1988-89	Ken Redfield, f	33	46	1.4
	Steve Smith, g	33	43	1.3
	Mark Montgomery, g	33	43	1.3
1989-90	Ken Redfield, f	34	44	1.3
	Steve Smith, g	31	25	0.8
	Mark Montgomery, g	34	25	0.7
1990-91	Mark Montgomery, g	29	52	1.8
	Dwayne Stephens, f	30	22	0.7
	Steve Smith, g	30	16	0.5
1991-92	Mark Montgomery, g	30	48	1.6
	Shawn Respert, g	30	34	1.1
	Dwayne Stephens, f	30	30	1.0
1992-93	Eric Snow, g	28	27	1.0
	Shawn Respert, g	28	24	0.9
	Dwayne Stephens, f	28	20	0.7

Year	Name,Pos.	GP	TP	Avg.
1993-94	Eric Snow, g	32	57	1.8
	Shawn Respert, g	32	43	1.3
	Quinton Brooks, f	32	28	0.9
1994-95	Eric Snow, g	28	52	1.9
	Shawn Respert, g	28	38	1.4
	Jamie Feick, c	28	26	0.9
1995-96	Quinton Brooks, f	31	30	1.0
	Jamie Feick, c	32	24	0.8
1996-97	Antonio Smith, f	29	29	1.0
	Morris Peterson, f	29	19	0.7
1997-98	Mateen Cleaves, g	30	73	2.4
	Antonio Smith, f	30	27	0.9

BLOCKED SHOTS—
Based on total blocked shots (Since 1979-80)

Year	Name,Pos.	GP	TP	Avg.
1979-80	Ron Charles, f/c	27	51	1.9
	Jay Vincent, f/c	27	7	0.3
1980-81	Ben Tower, f	27	16	0.6
	Jay Vincent, f/c	27	11	0.4
1981-82	Richard Mudd, f/c	26	15	0.6
	Kevin Willis, c	27	12	0.4
	Derek Perry, f	28	10	0.4
1982-83	Kevin Willis, c	27	35	1.3
	Richard Mudd, f/c	29	10	0.3
	Ben Tower, f	30	10	0.3
1983-84	Ken Johnson, f	19	24	1.3
	Kevin Willis, c	25	24	0.9
	Larry Polec, f	28	11	0.4
1984-85	Ken Johnson, c	28	72	2.6
	Richard Mudd, f	27	17	0.6
	Larry Polec, f	29	7	0.2
1985-86	Barry Fordham, c	31	20	0.6
	Ralph Walker, f	31	10	0.3
	Larry Polec, f	31	9	0.3

Year	Name,Pos.	GP	TP	Avg.
1986-87	George Papadakos, c	27	12	0.4
	Darryl Johnson, g	28	10	0.4
	Vernon Carr, f/g	28	10	0.4
	Carlton Valentine, f	28	10	0.4
1987-88	George Papadakos, c	25	35	1.4
	Ed Wright, g	28	5	0.2
1988-89	Steve Smith, g	33	12	0.4
	Matt Steigenga, f	33	12	0.4
1989-90	Matt Steigenga, f	34	30	0.9
	Steve Smith, g	31	17	0.5
1990-91	Matt Steigenga, f	30	32	1.1
	Mike Peplowski, c	30	17	0.6
1991-92	Matt Steigenga, f	27	23	0.9
	Mike Peplowski, c	30	17	0.6
	Anthony Miller, c	30	12	0.4
1992-93	Mike Peplowski, c	28	24	0.9
	Anthony Miller, f	27	20	0.7
	Quinton Brooks, f	22	9	0.4
1993-94	Anthony Miller, c	32	29	0.9
	Quinton Brooks, f	32	26	0.8
1994-95	Quinton Brooks, f	28	16	0.6
	Jamie Feick, c	28	12	0.4
1995-96	Quinton Brooks, f	31	18	0.6
	Jamie Feick, c	32	14	0.4
1996-97	DuJuan Wiley, c	24	19	0.8
	Ray Weathers, g	29	8	0.3
1997-98	DuJuan Wiley, c	30	50	1.7
	Andre Hutson, f	30	24	0.8

THREE-POINT FIELD GOALS
Based on total three-point goals (since 1982-83)

Year	Name,Pos.	GP	TP	Avg.
1982-83*	Scott Skiles, g	20	24	1.2
	Sam Vincent, g	20	5	0.2

Year	Name,Pos.	GP	TP	Avg.
1986-87	Kirk Manns, g	28	35	1.2
	Darryl Johnson, g	28	13	0.4
	Vernon Carr, g	28	11	0.3
1987-88	Kirk Manns, g	28	27	0.9
	Steve Smith, g	28	14	0.5
1988-89	Kirk Manns, g	33	69	2.1
	Todd Wolfe, g	29	26	0.9
	Steve Smith, g	33	22	0.7
1989-90	Kirk Manns, g	31	81	2.6
	Steve Smith, g	31	45	1.4
	Mark Montgomery, g	34	12	0.3
1990-91	Steve Smith, g	30	66	2.2
	Mark Montgomery, g	29	22	0.7
	Andy Penick, g	27	21	0.8
1991-92	Shawn Respert, g	30	60	2.0
	Dwayne Stephens, f	30	19	0.6
	Kris Weshinskey, g	28	19	0.7
1992-93	Shawn Respert, g	28	60	2.1
	Kris Weshinskey, g	27	37	1.3
	Dwayne Stephens, f	28	16	0.6
1993-94	Shawn Respert, g	32	92	2.9
	Kris Weshinskey, g	32	37	1.2
	Eric Snow, g	32	13	0.4
1994-95	Shawn Respert, g	28	119	4.3
	Jon Garavaglia, f	28	10	0.4
	Ray Weathers, g	27	7	0.3
1995-96	Ray Weathers, g	31	39	1.3
	Jamie Feick, c	32	20	0.6
	Jason Klein, g	28	13	0.5
1996-97	Ray Weathers, g	29	53	1.8
	Jason Klein, g	29	24	0.8
1997-98	Jason Klein, f	30	69	2.3
	Mateen Cleaves, g	30	51	1.7
	Morris Peterson, f	27	23	0.9

* Three-point shot used in Big Ten and NIT Games Only

Keith Stackhouse wrestles the ball away from a Buckeye and causes a scream heard halfway to Columbus.

Spartan Team Records

SEASON

Points—2,592; 34 games; 1989-90
Average—92.1; 24 games; 1963-64
Field Goals—1,043; 31 games; 1985-86
Field Goal Attempts—2,093; 23 games; 1964-65
Field Goal Percentage—.561; 31 games; 1985-86
Free Throws—559; 32 games; 1978-79
Free Throw Attempts—775; 32 games; 1978-79
Free Throw Percentage—.799; 31 games; 1985-86
Three Point Field Goals—176; 30 games; 1997-98
Three-Point Field Goal Attempts—493; 30 games; 1997-98
Three-Point Field Goal Percentage—.431; 34 games; 1989-90
Rebounds—1,508; 23 games; 1958-59
Rebound Average—65.5; 23 games; 1958-59
Assists—576; 34 games; 1989-90
Victories—28; 34 games; 1989-90

GAME

Points—121, vs. Morehead State, 12/1/92 at East Lansing (MS 121-53)
Field Goals—50, vs. Oklahoma, 12/21/63 at Tempe, AZ (MS 118-100); vs. Morehead State, 12/1/92 at East Lansing (MS 121-53)
Field Goal Attempts—101, vs. Brigham Young, 12/23/63 at Provo, Utah (BY 95-90); vs. Indiana, 3/5/60 at East Lansing (IU 86-80)
Field Goal Percentage—.738, vs. Minnesota (31-42), 2/28/87 at Minneapolis, MN (MS 77-67)
Free Throws—44, vs. Illinois-Chicago (53 attempts), 12/3/83 at East Lansing (MS 99-82)
Free Throw Attempts—53, vs. Illinois-Chicago (44 made), 12/3/83 at East Lansing (MS 99-82)
Free Throw Percentage—1.000, vs. Illinois (18 for 18) 1/12/86 at East Lansing (MS 58-51)
Three -Point Field Goals—12, vs. Purdue, 1/25/89 at East Lansing (MS 106-83); vs. Iowa, 1/13/90, at East Lansing (MS 87-80)
Three-Point Field Goal Attempts— 26, vs. Michigan (10 made), 1/10/98 at Ann Arbor (UM 79-69); vs. Wisconsin (7 made), 1/17/96 at Madison (UW 61-48)
Rebounds—84, vs. Ohio State, 1/19/59 at East Lansing (MS 92-77); vs. Iowa, 2/15/64 at East Lansing (MS 107-82)
Assists—32, vs. Morehead State, 12/1/92 at East Lansing (MS 121-53)
Fouls—41, vs. Northwestern, 2/2/52 at Evanston (N 86-76)
Victory Margin—99, vs. Alma, 2/1/02 at East Lansing (MS 102-3)
Defeat Margin—52, vs. Indiana, 1/4/75, at East Lansing (IU 107-55)
Combined Score—218, vs. Oklahoma, 12/21/63 at Tempe, AZ (MS 118-100)

BIG TEN GAME

Points—110, vs. Purdue 3/1/65 at East Lansing (MS 110-92)
Field Goals—46, vs. Wisconsin, 1/6/64 at East Lansing (MS 106-90); vs. Wisconsin, 1/25/75 at East Lansing (MS 105-87)
Field Goal Attempts—101, vs. Indiana, 3/5/60 at East Lansing (IU 86-80)
Field Goal Percentage—.738, vs. Minnesota (31-42), 2/28/87 at Minneapolis, MN (MS 77-67)
Free Throws—40, vs. Ohio State (45 attempts), 2/24/83 at East Lansing (MS 101-94)
Free Throw Attempts—49, vs. Wisconsin (36 made), 1/8/55 at East Lansing (MS 94-77)
Free Throw Percentage—1.000, vs. Illinois (18 for 18), 1/12/86 at East Lansing (MS 58-51)
Three-Point Field Goals—12, vs. Purdue, 1/25/89 at East Lansing (MS 106-83); vs. Iowa, 1/13/90 at East Lansing (MS 87-80)
Three-Point Field Goal Attempts— 26, vs. Michigan (10 made), 1/10/98 at Ann Arbor (UM 79-69); vs. Wisconsin (7 made), 1/17/96 at Madison (UW 61-48)
Rebounds—84, vs. Ohio State, 1/19/59 at East Lansing (MS 92-77); vs. Iowa, 2/15/64 at East Lansing (MS 107-82)
Assists—26, vs. Purdue, 1/25/89 at East Lansing (MS 106-83)
Fouls—41, vs Northwestern, 2/2/52 at Evanston (N 86-76)
Victory Margin— 37, vs. Northwestern, 1/18/95 at East Lansing (MS 93-56); 34, vs. Wisconsin, 2/22/58 at East Lansing (MS 93-59); vs. Northwestern, 2/27/86 at Evanston (MS 82-48)
Defeat Margin—52, vs. Indiana, 1/4/75 at East Lansing (I 107-55)
Combined Score—210, vs. Indiana, 1/11/64 at East Lansing (MS 107-103); vs. Illinois, 3/9/65 at Champaign (IL 121-89)

MSU TOP POINT TOTALS

1. 121, vs. Morehead State, 12/1/92 at East Lansing (MS 121-53)
2. 118, vs. Oklahoma, 12/21/63 at Tempe, AZ (MS 118-100)
3. 117, vs. Ball State, 12/29/94 at East Lansing (MS 117-95)
4. 111, vs. Cleveland State, 12/12/94 at E. Lansing (MSU 111-68)
5. 110, vs. Purdue, 3/1/65 at East Lansing (MS 110-92)
6. 109, vs. Northern Michigan, 11/30/63 at East Lansing (MS 109-86)
— 109, vs. Western Michigan, 12/13/78 at Kalamazoo (MS 109-69)
8. 107, vs. Iowa, 2/15/64 at East Lansing (MS 107-82)
— 107, vs. Indiana, 1/11/64 at East Lansing (MS 107-103)
— 107, vs. Iowa, 2/22/64 at Iowa City (MS 107-89)
— 107, vs. Northwestern, 2/29/64 at East Lansing (MS 107-97)
— 107, vs. E. Tennessee St., 12/9/93, at E. Lansing (MS 107-81)
13. 106, vs. Wisconsin, 1/6/64 at East Lansing (MS 106-90)
— 106, vs. Purdue, 1/25/89 at East Lansing (MS 106-83)
15. 105, vs. Wisconsin, 1/25/75 at East Lansing (MS 105-87)
— 105, vs. Iowa, 1/5/76 at East Lansing (MS 105-88)

Breslin was better late than never—and better than almost all the rest.

Breslin and Beyond

t was Jack Breslin's idea in 1965.

And it has carried his name at Michigan State University since 1989.

So if the Jack Breslin Student Events Center was a bit slow in coming, what matters is it was well worth the wait.

In its first nine seasons, 1,945,268 fans have watched the Spartan men play basketball—an average crowd of 14,303 for 136 games.

They've seen MSU win 109 times for an .801 success rate.

But there's more to the story than wins and losses—and commencements, concerts, circuses, and trade shows.

There's the career of "Mr. MSU," who was instrumental in developing funding for 65 campus buildings and was even better at building relationships.

There's the fulfillment of a dream, with a facility that was nearly constructed two decades earlier.

And there's the effect of Breslin Center on the Spartan program, with 10 straight seasons of post-season play after just eight prior appearances.

Let's start with Breslin himself, the captain and most valuable player of the school's 1945 football team and the 1946 senior class president.

From the day John Hannah brought him back to campus in 1950, Breslin served his alma mater for 38 years, mostly at the vice presidential level, before dying of cancer on August 2, 1988.

Hannah and Breslin made quite a team—a five-star general and one of history's best lieutenants.

But Breslin's dream of an all-events building was rejected in a student referendum in 1969, a rotten time to get anything approved with the turbulence on campus.

It took another 15 years before President Cecil Mackey pushed through a package of athletic facilities, including an indoor football facility, an indoor tennis building, and an East Campus home for intramurals.

The plan has been financed through a fee increase of $2 per credit hour.

And at the groundbreaking in July 1986, Breslin was thrilled to have "Student" linked with his name on a true all-events site.

"You're looking at the proudest person in the whole world," he said. "Sometimes, I wonder if it's all a dream. It's hard to imagine a building bearing my name."

Breslin could watch construction from his office in the Hannah Administration Building but died 15 months before the new facility opened.

The collapse of a crane and the plunge of a 160-ton ceiling truss in February 1988 caused a lengthy delay.

A $35 million, double-deck structure that was supposed to open that fall cost $43 million and was dedicated on November 9, 1989.

"It took us a long time to build an arena," said Athletic Director Doug Weaver. "But when we did, we did it right."

Weaver and many others, including Earvin Johnson, loved Jenison and hated to see its era end.

But most people figured a place like Breslin, with 15,138 seats, was long overdue.

And no one was happier to move than Jud Heathcote, who coached 13 of his 19 seasons in Jenison.

"It almost makes me cry that it took so long," said Forddy Anderson, MSU's coach from 1954–65. "We should've had a new facility when we were on top in the late '50s. I wanted to spread Jenison out and make it a 15,000-seat arena. I said, 'If we don't build it, the people down the road will. They'll take all the momentum away from us.' And that's just what happened."

When Breslin was built, the Michigan High School Athletic Association Boys Basketball Finals returned to East Lansing.

So did consistently good Spartan teams.

"One of the keys to the turnaround was a new facility," said point guard Mark Montgomery. "Four years in Jenison would've been tough on anyone. But in Breslin, our student body was right on top of you. I remember other teams talking about how hard it was to play there."

It certainly could be. Michigan's Rumeal Robinson was lured into a running conversation with the crowd in a Spartan win over the defending NCAA champs in 1990—the night Breslin became a home.

Ten days later, a wild win over Purdue wrapped up an undisputed Big Ten title and left little doubt of the noise potential.

"When our crowd really gets into it, we can play with anyone," said forward Morris Peterson of a building with a new, center-hung video board for 1998. "We've seen that kind of excitement before. Maybe we just have to win more games before it's that way all the time."

That's a great goal for the Spartans' second century of "MAGIC MOMENTS."

Breslin Center

Breslin's best individual performances

1. 43—Shawn Respert, MSU vs. Minnesota, 2-23-94 (MSU, 85-68)
2. 41—Alan Henderson, Indiana, 3-9-94 (MSU, 94-78)
3. 40—Shawn Respert, MSU vs. Indiana, 3-9-94 (MSU, 94-78)
4. 38—Steve Smith, MSU vs. Central Michigan, 12-20-90 (MSU, 74-61)
5. 36—Steve Smith, MSU vs. Michigan, 3-1-90 (MSU, 78-70)
6. 35—Steve Smith, MSU vs. Evansville, 12-18-90 (MSU, 81-76)
7. 35—Shawn Respert, MSU vs. Illinois, 2-15-95 (MSU, 68-58)
8. 33—Kirk Manns, MSU vs. Iowa, 1-13-90 (MSU, 87-80)
9. 33—Steve Smith, MSU vs. Minnesota, 1-19-91 (MSU, 73-64)
10. 33—Shawn Respert, MSU vs. Ball State, 12-29-94 (MSU, 117-95)

Jack Breslin and Jud Heathcote loved MSU and shared in its victories.

Photo Credits

The photographs in this book have been provided by Michigan State University Sports Information Services and the Lansing State Journal, with the following additional credits:

Associated Press, 144 (left)
Eileen Blass, 230
Brian Burd, 65, 132, 184, 192 (right)
Greg DeRuiter, back flap, 8 (left), 11, 12, 28, 68, 69, 113, 168, 169 (right), 170, 216, 229, 233
Detroit Pistons, 54
Kevin W. Fowler, 29, 126, 127, 128, 152, 153 (left), 153 (right), 154
Margie Garrison, 35, 92, 176, 177, back cover
Matthew Goebel, 148 (right)
Phil Greer/Champaign-Urbana Courier, 89 (left)
Matt Grimaldi, 58
Chris Holmes, 196
Jahn & Ollier, 116, 117 (left)
Magic Johnson/Los Angeles Times, 7, 8 (right)
Lexington Herald-Leader, front flap, 202 (left), 202 (right)

Life Magazine, 49
Lou McClellan, 61
Michigan State University Archives & Historical Collections, 14, 115, 140 (right)
Michigan State University Public Relations Department, 226
NCAA Photos, cover
Nickelodeon/Terry deRoy Gruber, 13 (top left)
David Olds, 4, 172
Steve Parker/Deseret News, 123, 124
Brian Quinn, 212
Ray's Picture Service, 2
Rod Sanford, 6, 91 (left), 93 (right), 94, 194
Susan Tusa, 100
Adam C. Williams, 36
Chuck Wing, 211, 237